Non

Will Be Left

How the Church Has Been Misled on the
Second Coming and the Rapture.

===========================

Philip Jackson

The Second Coming of Christ is a key doctrine. Many believers
have been taught views which are not Biblical. Others ignore it
entirely, since the subject is difficult to grasp. This book clarifies
the return of Christ as taught by the apostles, understood by the
Church Fathers, and sets aside contemporary illusions and false
teaching. Included are hundreds of theological and scripture
references. Jesus will return one way--His way. His return and
the rapture are clearly defined by the author.

Cornerstone Books   Santa Ana, California

ISBN   978-1-7354708-0-1

First Edition

CONTENTS

"We believe, and therefore speak. We speak in love, but not in soft words and trimming sentences. We shall not court controversy, but we shall not shun it when the cause of God demands it."

Charles H. Spurgeon, 1834 - 1892

Introduction

According to many of our most popular prophecy experts, the rapture of the church should have occurred by now. We have moved into the 21st century without a hint of this remarkable event which, according to them, must precede the final seven years of this age. The rapture is the sudden removal of the church and its transport to heaven for seven years. During this time, they claim, the world will experience the judgment of God. Hal Lindsey brought this concept to the attention of the general public with startling reality when he wrote *The Late Great Planet Earth* in 1970. This book, along with a number of similar works by him, popularized dispensational[1] thinking and made the term "rapture" a household word. When writing about premillennialism,[2] Craig A. Blaising refers to Lindsey's efforts as "dispensational apocalypticism."[3] Lindsey took the graphic images of the Book of Daniel and John's Apocalypse and made them flow in a popular vein alongside of current events which were developing in Israel and elsewhere. He made the sensational digestible. The scenario Lindsey advanced generically presented an event to occur in 1981. The calculations were based on Israel being established as a nation in 1948 and then counting forward one generation: forty years. This placed the Second Coming at 1988. Subtracting seven years for the 70th week of Daniel, which is the tribulation period associated with Daniel 9:27, the rapture was to have occurred by 1981.[4] Along the way, Lindsey became nervous about his calculation and tended toward the thought of a postponement. In a 1977 *Christianity Today* article, he stated he "didn't know how long a biblical

---

[1] A particular view which divides the ages into periods according to the manner of God's dealing with men. See Glossary for Dispensationalism and other related terms.
[2] See Glossary
[3] Blaising, Craig A.; Kenneth L. Gentry; Robert B. Strimple; Darrell L. Bock. *Three View on the Millennium and Beyond.* Grand Rapids, MI: Zondervan, 2002. Blaising on "Premillennialism." p. 192
[4] Smith, Chuck. *End Times.* Costa Mesa, CA: Maranatha House Pub., 1978. p. 35. Smith spelled out the formula and stated the Lord could come back for His church "anytime before 1981." Is this not date setting?

generation is. Perhaps somewhere between sixty and eighty years."[5] This kind of vacillation is unhealthy, indeed, since it shows the original interpretation was unfounded.

As the church knows, it remains on the earth to the present moment. Because this event did not take place as predicted, a number of other notable prophecy experts who espoused Lindsey's view altered the length of a generation from the forty year period, extending it to sixty years and more.[6] Some have modified their view entirely.[7] But even these adjusted calculations are questionable, since using the same model, a sixty year generation would have placed the rapture in the year 2001. All of the faulty generation/year calculations only add an element of confusion where it should not be. Also, if the "experts" really are experts, then there should be no need for the revision of terms or definitions as time progresses. The Bible itself should be sufficient as a guide without misleading, unwarranted adjustments. And, of course, reality speaks loudly--we are still here.[8]

In raising this as a question, it is for the purpose of examining the doctrine of the Second Coming of Christ more carefully. Our hope is to increase mutual understanding, and to provide a rational, reasoned alternative to those who are hearing dispensational teaching and do not investigate further. This is not the "scoffing" and "mocking" which the Apostle Peter refers to.[9] The question

---

[5] Quoted by Dewey Beegle from *Christianity Today*. April 15, 1977, p. 40. See: Beegle, Dewey M. *Prophecy and Prediction*. Ann Arbor, MI: Pryor Pettingill Pub., 1978. p. 214

[6] Fruchtenbaum, Arnold. *The Footsteps of the Messiah. A Study of the Sequence of PropheticEvents*. Tustin, CA: Ariel Press, 1984. p. 445. Chuck Smith indicated on an October 3, 2005, radio broadcast that a generation could be seventy years. He admitted to changing his earlier view ["Pastors Perspective," KWVE, 109.7 FM, Oct. 3, 2005]. Is this not date accommodation?

[7] Smith, Chuck. *The Word For Today Bible. New Testament*. Nashville, TN: Thomas Nelson Pub., 2005. p. 49 [Sidebar]. It is ironic that the whole context was shifted from a rapture-friendly, 1948, forty-year formula into a "national or ethnic group." It seems since 1988 is long past, Smith's former "proof" is worthless.

[8] See chapter on "Some Little Words" for additional treatment of "Generation."

[9] 2 Pt 3:3-4

raised here is not one of speaking *against* a rapture of the Church. Our intent is to focus more clearly on this critical area of teaching, so all in the Body of Christ will know for certain what Jesus meant when He said, "...he will send forth his angels with a loud trumpet call and they will gather his elect from the four winds, from one end of the heavens to the other."[10] This is the Second Coming which will initiate the age to come, and yes, the rapture will occur right on time.

The idea of a "generation" is a pivotal detail gleaned from the Olivet discourse where Jesus explains that this "generation will certainly not pass away until all these things have happened."[11] It is unfortunate that confusion has arisen and continues over the definition of a "generation." We must note here that the generation Jesus spoke of was the one who would see all the things He detailed and not some group of people locked into a "forty year" shackle of misinterpretation. As we examine more closely the Biblical passages that affect this teaching, we will find that other texts clarify the setting in which Jesus spoke and help us with concerns we may have about this subject today. Also, we must understand why the Apostle Paul wrote as he did to the Corinthian church and to the Thessalonian church who heard him teach personally. Why did they need help in grasping these important components of eschatology[12]? We hold Paul in high esteem for his immense contribution to the establishment of the Church. We easily accept that. Why, then, do we have difficulty with his end-times teaching? The Apostle Peter warned us that Paul's "letters contain some things that are hard to understand, which ignorant and unstable people distort...."[13]   We must be sure that no distortion has crept into our understanding of what is yet to come--yes, the rapture.

In recent years, Tim LaHaye spread the popularity of the idea of the pre-tribulational[14] rapture, even beyond the efforts of Hal Lindsey. Dr. LaHaye's

---

[10] Mt 24:31

[11] Mt 24:34

[12] The last things. [See Glossary].

[13] 2 Pt 3:16

[14] Note: "pre-tribulational" will be referred to as "pre-trib" in the following portions of this book.

series of *Left Behind* books written with Jerry B. Jenkins attracted a whole new audience since these works were written as fiction. The major success of the LaHaye books encouraged publishers to expand the fiction market, and now many other authors are producing fictional works regarding end-times events along with other areas of Biblical interest. This raises another important question: how are they using Scripture for the truth they claim is interwoven in these books? And, how do we know that any of this is reasonable, other than *just fiction*, when the event they graphically portray for us was a 1981 washout? Has all this evolved into just a story--fiction based on a myth? May this not be the case! We must have the courage to look even more closely at the Biblical texts involved, so we can re-evaluate our beliefs and come forth with a clear, sound, correct view which will parallel Scripture and not grieve the Spirit of God.

Our safest standard will be Scripture itself, and the Bible must be used so as to stand on its own. Peter warned us that "you must understand that no prophecy of Scripture came about by the prophet's own interpretation."[15] The prophecies we read in the Bible are by inspiration, the origin being "the Holy Spirit"[16]--not men. We have been warned by the Lord Jesus to be on our guard against men.[17] He also noted that if we have come to a misunderstanding of doctrine we "are in error because [we] do not know the Scriptures or the power of God."[18] With this in mind, we must proceed with caution when considering these important doctrinal areas--"we must pay more careful attention, therefore, to what we have heard."[19] Even if all others err and neglect Scripture in context, we must stand with the truth and discard immediately those things which contradict the plain teaching of the Word of God. The chapters that follow are dedicated to that end, whereby Scripture will take priority over popular views, and common sense will underwrite a clearer understanding of the Second Coming of Christ.

Faber's Rule is worth consideration regarding the importance of holding to

---

[15] 2 Pt 1:20
[16] 2 Pt 1:21; 2 Tim 3:16-17
[17] Mt 10:17; Mk 13:9, 23, 33
[18] Mt 22:29
[19] Heb 2:1

Scripture:

> If a doctrine totally unknown to the primitive Church, which received her theology immediately from the hands of the Apostles, and which continued long to receive it from the hands of the disciples of the Apostles, springs up in a subsequent age, let that age be the fifth century, or let it be the tenth century, or let it be the sixteenth century, such doctrine stands on its very front impressed with the brand of mere human invention.[20]

The tragedy involved with much of the popular teaching about the rapture of the church is that it is a repetition of an "ism" rather than Biblical orthodoxy. Far too many teachers and preachers merely repeat the pre-trib ideas and conclusions of others who have gone before them. Much of the evangelical church hears about a system of interpretation without being informed that it is only one of the theological views regarding the end of the age. The result is that a great number of people in the church believe something they never examined personally. This has caused many to bypass Biblical truth. British preacher, G. Campbell Morgan, superb Bible expositor of a generation past, approached Scripture with the highest regard. When he prepared to teach a book of the Bible, he would first read it fifty times, and *then* begin his study-- before teaching.[21] When he was looking into the possibility of teaching through the Book of Revelation, he found his understanding of the early removal of the church in conflict with what he read. As a result, he discarded the pre-trib view as error. Since he had already written on the subject and was not pleased with his former position being in print, he went to his publisher, acquired the original plates, and destroyed them.[22] Toronto's great missionary preacher,

---

[20] Quoted in: Silver, Jesse Forest. *The Lord' Return. Seen in History and In Scripture As Pre-Millennial and Imminent.* Chicago, IL: Fleming H. Revell, 1914. p. 63. Quote is by George Stanley Faber. Further to this, see the chapter on "History."

[21] Morgan, G. Campbell. *The Study and Teaching of the English Bible.* London: James Clarke, n.d. p. 37

[22] Morgan, G. Campbell. From a question posed to him in 1943, two years before his death. [See Appendix].

Oswald J. Smith, experienced the same revelation once he came face to face with the truth about the Second Coming. He was won over by a careful reading of Matthew chapter twenty-four. He discovered that the Lord Jesus returns once, and only once, after the tribulation of those days.[23] Today we need more honest men taking an honest look at the full message of truth.[24] We must be absolutely sure the truth stands on its own, and we with it.

Samuel Tregelles offered a sound reminder about the importance of Scripture:

> When a point has been established by full proof from Holy
> Scripture, it is often impossible, and in general needless, to meet
> each objection or difficulty which may be raised. It is often
> impossible, because all the modes in which different objectors will
> find difficulties may be unknown to those who rest on the simple
> warrants of the Word of God.[25]

Tregelles was referring specifically to the challenge of convincing hardcore pre-trib advocates of the truth, even from God's word. Herein, you will find simple, basic Biblical evidence of a single second advent. The scriptural references all point to the Lord Jesus returning one time only at the end this age.

As we get closer and closer to this glorious event, there has never been a more critical time than now to fully understand end-times teaching, especially with regard to the rapture of the Church.

---

[23] Smith, Oswald J. From his personal testimony on this doctrine. [See Appendix].

[24] This has been the case with many Bible teachers and pastors, *i.e.*, A.W. Pink, Robert Gundry, Robert van Kampen, and many others. See Appendix for the testimony of Corrie ten Boom, Robert Cameron, Robert Chapman, G. Campbell Morgan, Charles Spurgeon, T. T. Shields, and others.

[25] Quoted in: Fraser, Alexander. *The Return of Christ in Glory*. Scottsdale, PA: The Evangelical Fellowship, 1953. p. 70

NONE WILL BE LEFT

Bible prophecy is a very popular topic within evangelical circles. Once genuine interest is stirred, a believer may discover there are different schools of thought in conflict with each other. This can be noted in basic ideas and in a number of the details. It may not be apparent at the first hearing, but it will emerge if someone pursues the subject in earnest. The one clear exception is that all Christendom believes that Christ will physically return again to the earth. This is the doctrine of the Second Coming. Our present examination of these matters is directed towards the difficulties between the historic pre-millennial view and the more recent, popular theory which portends a rapture of the church prior to the last seven year period. This is pre-tribulationalism or simply "pre-trib." When a simple presentation is given of the pre-trib view, which by definition places the translation (rapture) of the Body of Christ prior to the tribulation period,[1] much of it sounds reasonable. This sustains interest, because it promotes a sense of relief that a believer will not have to face the horrors of the man of sin[2] or wrath of the worst kind.[3] Once this teaching has been embraced, a believer can seemingly examine more of the Bible without trepidation. The overall, critical point which has been ignored or simply misinterpreted is that of *judgment*. The basic doctrinal view held by the Church has always been that the Lord will return in power to judge the world. In haste to teach and reinforce pre-tribulationalism, the issue of judgment has been given a lesser place within the framework of pre-trib understanding. However, we must remember Biblically that the Lord Himself will descend again to earth primarily to judge the wicked and establish His Kingdom. The event is thoroughly described by the prophets in the Old Testament and expounded amply by the apostles in their writings in the New Testament. What must be perceived without any confusion is the fact that when the Lord does return, He will come as the Lion,

---

[1] The final seven years. [See Glossary].

[2] Dan 9:27; Mt 24:15; 2 Thess 2:3; Rev 13:1ff. This is the Antichrist.
See Glossary.

[3] 1 Thess 5:9 is often used broadly to reinforce the idea that the church is not to face wrath.

8

not the Lamb, and will not just hold unrighteous men to account, but destroy them. This will occur when He comes at the end of the age as heaven is opened, and He is riding upon the white horse as described by the Apostle John in the Book of Revelation. This will be judgment. He will be accompanied by the armies of heaven, and He will "strike the nations."[4] The unbelieving wicked will be dealt with at this time. None will escape. None will survive. None will be left![5]

The core of church belief is founded upon this truth, yet many Bible teachers ignore the historic creeds, the church fathers, the early definition of this as described in the *Didache*,[6] and the writers of the Bible themselves. All the prophets looked forward to this reality of judgment and framed it entirely within the context of their warnings to Israel. Some Bible readers and teachers have lost sight of this or have adjusted it to fit into their system of theology which minimizes judgment and overly amplifies the pre-trib rapture theory. Other expositors redefine the future events as having already taken place at the time of Jerusalem's destruction by the Roman legions in 70 A.D.[7] Both of these competing views promote a sense of escape and minimally take into consideration the real purpose behind what is coming which is the Lord's retribution upon all His foes and those who have been the destroyers of His people.[8] Again, when He comes He will thoroughly eliminate His foes and ours, and we will stand with Him in glory to inherit His Kingdom. Jesus draws our attention to this in the Olivet Discourse.[9] He describes this future event

---

[4] Rev 19:11-21

[5] Ps 21:9-10

[6] *The Didache* or *The Teaching of the Twelve Apostles* specifies that "all created mankind shall come to the fire of testing, and many shall be offended and perish." The ones to survive will be "they that endure in their faith." They will be saved by Christ Himself. This indicates that none will survive except Christ's own when He comes at the end of the Tribulation. Lightfoot, J.B. & J.R. Harmer. *The Apostolic Fathers*. Grand Rapids, MI: Baker Book House, 1987. p. 235. See Appendix for the 1884 English translation of chapter 16 by Hitchcock and Brown. [See Glossary]. See chapter: "History."

[7] This teaching is known as *preterism* which claims all or part of the Book of Revelation was fulfilled in 70 A.D.

[8] Psalm 2 offers a simple overview of this. See Rev 18:21-24 for a brief summary of the judgment of Babylon.

broadly with an illustration of sheep and goats. Those on His right will inherit--inherit "the kingdom prepared for you since the creation of the world."[10] Likewise, His enemies--illustrated as "goats"--will be destroyed. They will be judged. They will be commanded by the Lord to depart--they are "cursed" and are to go "into the eternal fire prepared for the devil and his angels."[11] While this is a graphic description,[12] and none of us are really sheep or goats, the point is well made by the Lord Jesus that the wicked will face eternal judgment--none of them will survive. Some Bible expositors attempt to redefine this as another in a number of judgments. However, it is used by the Lord as a word picture to warn in advance about the nature and finality of His omnipotent act of retribution upon unrepentant mankind. It is an erroneous proposition to shape this into another event, when the Lord's own explanation is sufficient.

Many pre-trib teachers and writers amplify a fearful picture of seals, trumpets, vials, and bowls with which they embellish and color to increase the fear factor for their audience. Often it produces the feeling of great anxiety, so the hearers or readers will quickly embrace the rapture idea. On other occasions, we are told of great suffering and persecution for those left behind and, in particular, Israel. The general tenor of this plays on a person's emotions and increases their sense of not wanting to be left in harm's way. In the process, the retributive elements of a righteous God are passed over, especially with regard to His power to protect His own.[13] Due to this imbalanced approach, the actual return of the Son of Man coming to judge the quick and the dead is distorted. However, we find in David's writings that God's throne was plainly established for judgment.[14] This He will do at the end of the age on "the Day."[15] He will then "judge the world," and rule, reign, and govern His people.[16] Yes,

---

[9] See Glossary.
[10] Mt 25:34
[11] Mt 25:41
[12] Jesus often employed metaphors as He spoke and taught.
[13] Jn 17:11-12, 15; Jn 10:27-28; Is 31:5; Job 5:21; Ps 12:7; 32:7; Prov 2:8; 2 Thess 3:3
[14] Ps 9:7
[15] Is 24:1-3
[16] Ps 9:8

the judgment itself will be overwhelming, but when complete, the wicked will be no more. Scripture states they will be destroyed.[17] You will not see them. They will disappear.[18] They will be swept away.[19] We will see the arrogant no more.[20] Once again, none will be left. The fact that the Lord does this *when He comes* places the entire concept of a pre-trib rapture at extreme risk. Solomon states simply: "When the storm has swept by, the wicked are gone, but the righteous stand firm forever."[21] This is not an unreliable meteorological prediction. Neither is it allegory or a metaphor. It is wisdom speaking about the fate of the wicked--none of them will survive. This kind of scripture should cause us to reconsider the entire pre-trib idea. Judgment itself precludes any possibility of two phases of Christ's return with survivors. Only those who belong to Him will be fully redeemed at that time. Yes, He is coming for His own, but the wicked will be judged. Those who delight in wickedness will be condemned and taken for judgment.[22]

The Apostle Paul writing to the Corinthian church made the distinction between the two kinds of people--righteous and wicked. His rhetorical question about who is eligible to enter the kingdom has only one answer: "the wicked do not inherit the kingdom of God."[23] This is the same apostle who wrote extensively in chapter fifteen of the same letter about the Second Coming and judgment. He also laid out further detail in his epistles to the church at Thessalonica. In context, he made the clear contrast between those who know God and qualify as sanctified, regenerated believers, as opposed to the wicked who will be judged and removed. This, of course, will be the case when Jesus returns. In the same context, Jesus described the separation of the sheep and goats, previously mentioned. This distinction between the righteous and the wicked is neutered by those with a pre-trib understanding, since they believe that some people will come to Christ during the Tribulation period and enter

---

[17] Ps 21:9-10; Ps 145:20
[18] Is 29:20; Ps 37:10, 20, 34, 38; Mal 4:1
[19] Ps 58:9-11
[20] Is 33:18-19
[21] Prov 10:25
[22] Mt 13:41-43; 2 Thess 2:9-12
[23] 1 Cor 6:9

the kingdom in their natural bodies.[24] According to Paul, this can never happen. He clearly denoted them as the ones storing up wrath for the day and who will be removed when the Lord appears.[25] This was the Lord's own teaching as He described the end of the age in Matthew thirteen. The parable of the wheat and tares is stated and then explained. We are told in the simplest of terms that this is how it will be at the end of the age. Note that it is the Lord's explanation that clears this up: the angels come and separate the wicked, and they are burned.[26] This should make the issue lucid: the wicked will be taken away. Only the righteous remain and enter His kingdom. The Apostle Peter affirmed this stating that it is believers only who "will receive a rich welcome into the eternal kingdom of our Lord and Savior Jesus Christ."[27]

If we consider David's words in Psalm five, we see not only his understanding, but also that which the Apostle Paul would have held to since the verses' meaning is so obvious. Note: God "cannot dwell" with the wicked. The arrogant "cannot stand" in His presence. All liars are destroyed, along with the bloodthirsty and the deceivers.[28] David also asserted that he will come into the Lord's house--not the wicked. Why? They have been judged--taken away. None of them will survive what is coming on the earth. Peter writing later described the elements melting in fervent heat.[29] No man will survive this in a body of flesh. Hence, Paul made the case for the believers' way to "survive" the destruction of the heavens and earth through an instantaneous change. He stated this will take place in a flash. We will put on immortality and receive new, imperishable, immortal bodies.[30] Pre-trib advocates commonly attempt to use this part of Corinthians to support the rapture and then place these verses some seven years before the event Paul refers to. We know Paul intended this to happen at the end of the age, because he briefly directed us to the Second

---

[24] Pentecost, J. Dwight. *Things To Come. A Study in Biblical Eschatology*. Grand Rapids, MI: Zondervan, 1972. p. 546
[25] Rm 2:5; 2 Thess 1:6-10
[26] Mt 13:37-43; also affirmed in Mt 13:49-50
[27] 2 Pt 2:11
[28] Ps 5:4-6. Compare to Rev 21:7-8. Also, Paul, 1 Cor 6:9
[29] 2 Pt 3:10
[30] 1 Cor 15:50-57

Coming in previous verses in the same chapter.[31] The purpose of the fifteenth chapter is not just to restate the Gospel, but to reinforce the reality of the resurrection--ours--because Christ died and rose on the third day. He also is coming again, when we will be resurrected--at the same time He judges the wicked. When the entire chapter is read, the balance begins to emerge, and we can see this as one event, when the Lord delivers judgment and salvation at the same time.[32] Paul's own interpretation of the writings of the Old Testament prophets[33] would have affirmed for him that there would be a set day for judgment and not a series of events or phases where some of the church was to be removed, others left behind, and then further confusion about the number of resurrections. Paul mentioned only one resurrection, only one day, and expanded on this in other epistles. Otherwise, we face the impossible dilemma of the righteous and the wicked entering the kingdom of God when the millennial period begins. This violates Scripture. The particular verses refuting this theory are noted above. At this point we are faced with the truth: no unbelieving soul will join the elect believers and enter the Lord's kingdom when He returns. In like manner, no unregenerate person can enter heaven now, so none of the wicked will join the Body of Christ once judgment occurs. The verdict is final. Otherwise Christ is lying about how to come to the Father and inherit eternal life.[34] We also know that a person must do this while living, and that there is no secondary option after death. This would be heresy.[35] There is no provision within orthodox Christian teaching for a believer to become changed into some altered state of existence. This would force New Age teaching or eastern mysticism into the proposition, which also would be heretical. This oversight brought about by dispensational teaching and incorporated into pre-trib theories places a delusional interference where it

---

[31] 1 Cor 15:22-24

[32] Heb 9:27-28

[33] Especially Isaiah and Zechariah

[34] Jn 14:6

[35] This is a heretical teaching known as "the doctrine of a second chance" [See Glossary]; also known as "future reprobation." Orr, James. *The Christian View of God and the World*. 1902. rpt. New York, NY: Charles Scribner's Sons, n.d. p. 343. Note: Ecc 9:10; Is 38:18; Ps 115:17-18; 88:10-12; Jn 3:18. Also, this would open the option for universalism in some form which is heresy [See Glossary].

should never be. Yes, someone can receive Jesus Christ for salvation during the tribulation, but it will be no different than today. We know this, since Jesus Himself will not appear until the end "after the distress of those days" to gather the church.[36] Paul underscored all of this throughout 1 Corinthians chapter fifteen, so we will have assurance about our place with the Lord and know that the wicked will not be among us. In other words, once "the Day" is upon us, we will be rescued, and the rest of reprobate mankind will perish. None will be left.

Isaiah the prophet pointed ahead to aspects of the first coming of Christ as well as the second. He referred to "the day of the Lord" with specific description, so we can anticipate some of the terrifying events at the end of the present age. In Isaiah 13:9 and following there is a brief, ample description regarding the day as one of cruelty, anger, and desolation. The Lord will make the land desolate and "destroy the sinners within it."[37] This is what takes place at the end of the age as confirmed elsewhere by Isaiah, the prophet Joel, and the Lord in the Olivet Discourse. Since, all sinners will be There destroyed at this time, it would be incredible to conceive of them passing through this catastrophe and living in the Kingdom age. Isaiah stated that this day "will come like destruction,"[38] and that the sun, moon, stars will be darkened.[39] There will be a major cosmic disturbance affecting the entire earth. This is validated by Joel[40] and then affirmed by Peter when he preached in Acts two.[41] The Lord Jesus in responding to apostolic inquiry quoted Isaiah and emphasized this reality: the sun will be darkened; the moon will not give its light; the heavenly bodies, shaken.[42] He said plainly that this cosmic upheaval will occur after "the distress of those days," meaning after the tribulation. The conclusion, then, is simple: first, earthly distress caused by wicked men, then a heavenly response-- judgment--when the cosmos unravels, and finally full wrath when all of the

---

[36] Mt 24:29-30
[37] Is 13:9
[38] Is 13:6
[39] Is 13:10; Is 24:23; Is 34:4; Is 64:1
[40] Joel 2:30-31
[41] Acts 2:19-20
[42] Mt 24:29.

wicked are judged and removed. They will vanish.[43] Isaiah repeated and emphasized the full nature of this stating the Lord will "lay waste to the earth" and "devastate it." He said it will be the same for everyone no matter their station in life, their title, their wealth, or their location--"it will be the same." The Lord will "lay waste" to the earth and plunder it "totally."[44] Confirming the other prophets, the Psalms,[45] and Peter, Isaiah wrote, the "earth's inhabitants are burned up."[46] When these scriptures are laid out and compared, there is no possibility men in their natural state will survive and be able to enter the millennial reign of Christ.

It may seem unnecessary to spend time reviewing the future fate of the wicked as opposed to the righteous. However, within popular pre-trib circles, a good number of their spokesmen make a case for two classes of people who will enter the thousand year reign. Based on a faulty interpretation of Revelation 3:10 ("them that dwell upon the earth," KJV) and a biased reading of Isaiah 65:17-25 (the "new heavens and new earth"), a number of pre-trib teachers have reshaped these texts into an additional class of mankind who survive seven years of horrific tribulation—and God's wrath—and are then able to continue life without an immortal body. They are referred to as "earth dwellers." The concept of identifying them as a distinct group has been in circulation for some time. It was mentioned by some of the earlier dispensational prophecy writers including F. C. Jennings,[47] L. Sale-Harrison,[48] and Harry Ironside.[49] These men employed the phrase as part of their comments on the church of Philadelphia in the third chapter of the Book of Revelation. More recently, popular pre-trib authorities, Tim LaHaye and Thomas Ice developed this into a key portion of the defense of their theory that the wicked and righteous will be together.[50] However, in the process they

---

[43] Is 16:4

[44] Is 24:1-3

[45] Ps 96:10-13; Ps 97:3-5

[46] Is 24:6

[47] Jennings, F.C. *The Seven Letters.* London: Pickering & Inglis, n.d. p. 181

[48] Sale-Harrison, L. *The Wonders of the Great Unveiling.* London: Pickering & Inglis, n.d. p. 61

[49] Ironside, H. A. *Lectures on the Book of Revelation.* Neptune, NJ: Loizeaux Bros., 1973. p. 72

conflict with each other which generously adds to the confusion with the entire theory. Dr. LaHaye claimed that the unregenerate will exist alongside of believers after the Second Coming and judgment.[51] He attempted to justify the existence of those in their natural bodies by claiming they will be the result of the "preaching of the 144,000 Jews and the two witnesses" during the Tribulation period.[52] Dr. LaHaye insisted they "will enter Christ's 1000-year millennial kingdom in their natural bodies."[53] His theory is impossible, since when Christ does come, He will judge all the wicked by fire. All unbelievers in their natural bodies will be consumed. Dr. LaHaye made this claim solely to support his rejection of the post-tribulational rapture. His claim runs counter to Scripture, even though he affirmed in the same article that "…Matthew 25:41 indicates that all unbelievers will be sent into 'the eternal fire,'" thus leaving no one with a natural body to enter the millennial kingdom."[54] Within one short column, he contradicted himself and increased confusion where there should be clarity. His priority at all cost--against common sense--is to remove the church before the Tribulation.

Dr. Ice produced an article on this matter in 2003, attempting to make a case for the legitimacy of "earth dwellers." He wrote that not one of them repents, and all end up in the Lake of Fire. He stated that they are tested during the tribulation and are those who "receive the mark of the beast."[55] Unwittingly, he directly contradicted Dr. LaHaye, since the Second Coming of Christ ends the lives of all the wicked. No "earth dweller" can survive judgment by fire. Hence, Dr. Ice offered unwarranted embellishment of the Revelation 3:10

---

[50] They must do this to support their claim that the church is removed before the Tribulation and *knowing* that many Bible verses clearly show believers *in and going through* the last seven years. *e.g.*, Dn 7:25; 8:12; 11:33-35; Mt 24:15; 2 Thess 1:6-10; 2 Pt 3:10-16. Note: Is 43:2. Continue reading this chapter for their comments.

[51] LaHaye, Tim. "Pre-Trib Perspectives." Vol. 8. Num. 9. January, 2004. p. 3, He places two groups together: "Christians *and* the people in their natural bodies." [emphasis added].

[52] LaHaye, Tim, and Ed Hindson. *The Popular Encyclopedia of Bible Prophecy*. Eugene, OR: Harvest House, 2004. p. 351.

[53] *Ibid.*

[54] *Ibid.*

[55] Article accessible online at: www.pre-trib.org/article-view.php?id=347

passage he commented on. Since these two men were the editors and principals of the Pre-Trib Research Center, responsible for the information coming from their "think tank,"[56] it must be concluded that somebody was not thinking.

Another contemporary, popular pre-trib exponent, Mark Hitchcock, bluntly proposed and expounded on the two millennial groups as if it were possible. He wrote there will be those who "have survived the tribulation" and "will enter the kingdom in their natural bodies." He designated them to be "believers."[57] However, this is not possible, since no one can enter the Kingdom age in a natural state. Hitchcock openly contradicted the words of Paul in Corinthians, where the apostle says "we *all* will be changed."[58] Either we are changed, or we are among those who have been taken away to judgment.[59] Other options do not exist. However, this group which Hitchcock described, according to him, will dwell as they do today still possessing "the sinful nature."[60] Here, he contradicts himself, since "believers" have been regenerated and possess a new, Godly nature through the indwelling Holy Spirit. The "sinful nature" is gone. He, also, presented an open contradiction to the Scripture, where we read that "*all* sinners will be destroyed."[61] Either they have repented and are now true believers eligible for kingdom entry, or they face death and eternal separation.[62] Hitchcock attempted to answer the question of what life will be like during the millennium, however his answer is unsound due to an invalid interpretation of Isaiah 65. His claims that life will be normal are wishful thinking brought about by pre-trib assumptions repeated again and again. The people he portrays will not enter into marriage, have children, work, and "possibly die,"[63] since the weight of Biblical truth says that there will be no

---

[56] From the masthead of "Pre-Trib Perspectives," any issue, last page.

[57] Hitchcock, Mark. *101 Answers to the Most Asked Questions About the End Times.* Sisters, OR: Multnomah Pub., 2002. p. 217. Note this conflicts directly with Dr. LaHaye's statement above that "no one with a natural body" will enter the "the millennial kingdom." These contradictions do nothing to validate pre-trib teaching.

[58] 1 Cor 15:51 [emphasis added].

[59] Mt 13:40-43

[60] Hitchcock. *Ibid.* p. 217

[61] Ps 37:38 [emphasis added]; Is 13:9

[62] Rm 6:23

[63] Hitchcock. *Ibld.* p. 217

more death![64] This reality regarding death sets aside his other false assumptions as well, and we are left with the fact that no flesh will survive to enter the millennium, and neither will those who do enter be anything other than the redeemed in glorified bodies. While Hitchcock seems to understand the general principle that "the righteous will enter the millennial kingdom and the lost will be cast into eternal fire,"[65] he ends up contradicting himself and leaving his readers with major confusion about those who will be in the millennium. His conjecture is not a helpful response to those reading his *101 Answers*. He also is in conflict with Dr. Ice, as noted above.

The confusion in this area is rampant and borders on the chaotic. Thomas Ice, editor of Pre-Trib Perspectives, writing again in 2007, confounded his declaration from four years before.[66] He bluntly wrote with regard to the millennium: "it will be a time of *both mortals and immortals living together* in the kingdom."[67] All of a sudden, he is in conformity with Dr. LaHaye and Mark Hitchcock. It should be obvious at this point that the conclusions these men have offered have minimal value. They are almost like the witnesses brought in to testify against Christ who could not agree among themselves.[68] Dr. Ice further complicated this issue when he wrote in 2009 that "...Jewish and Gentile *mortals* who enter the millennium will *start off as* 100 per cent *believers*."[69] Surely this represents a major contradiction within the same statement. No mortal enters the kingdom age. It also contradicts the Apostle Paul regarding the mortal putting on immortality and the change which occurs to believers when the Lord comes.[70] Further, there will be no half-way believers in the age to come. All will be "in Christ," or they will have been previously judged. Only one group of people will be there--God's faithful.[71]

---

[64] Rev 21:4; 1 Cor 15:54-57. With regard to marriage, note the Lord 's words in Mt 22:30! Note: 1 Cor 15:26

[65] Hitchcock. *Ibid*. p. 185

[66] As noted previously in this chapter.

[67] Ice, Thomas. "Pre-Trib Perspectives." Vol. 8. Num. 51. November/December, 2007. p. 8 [emphasis added].

[68] Mk 14:56

[69] Ice, Thomas. "Pre-Trib Perspectives.'" Vol. 8, Num. 68. August, 2009. p. 7 [emphasis added].

[70] See 1 Cor 15:42-57. Dr. Ice is at odds with Paul and the Scripture.

Paul specified the make-up of this in his letter to the Ephesians. He reminded them that as believers we all share in the one and same promise. All who have come by faith will inherit the kingdom. Believing Gentiles and Israel will share in the future promise.[72]

Mark Cambron, in compiling his doctrinal reference work, *Bible Doctrines*, bluntly claimed that in the millennium there will be sin. He reinforced this error by saying: "Human nature has never changed from one dispensation to another." Of course, with this he bypassed the purpose of the Cross for dealing with sin once and for all. He assured readers that those who sin "will be born of saved parents who come out of the tribulation alive."[73] Here, he ignores Jesus' plain statement that there will be no marriage in heaven, and we will be like the angels--no spouses, no physical union, no born children.[74] He conveniently forgot the overwhelming judgment by fire which leaves no one alive who has not repented. Cambron also stated there will be death but only for the unbeliever. So, we see another broad assertion of conditions that cannot be. This occurs when the scripture is left out of the dynamic and in its place is inserted a teaching which cannot be supported at all. Jesus came to earth to render sin finished permanently and to provide for His own a new age to come in the future without sin, death, or the presence of the unregenerate.[75]

Wim Malgo, founder of The Midnight Call, also a staunch defender of the pre-trib theory, exceeded many of his dispensational sympathizers with his assumptions. He stated that "...in the millennium *the enemies* of God will be tolerated."[76] While he qualified this saying they must "submit to His sovereign rule,"[77] this contradicts Scripture and violates the very reason for God to judge the wicked. If Malgo and others who share this idea are right, then there was

---

[71] Is 35:8-10

[72] Eph 3:6. Note, also, Heb 11:39-40

[73] Cambron, Mark G. *Bible Doctrines. Beliefs That Matter.* Grand Rapids, MI: Zondervan, 1981. p. 281

[74] Lk 20:34-36

[75] Heb 7:25, 27; 10:12-14, etc.; Jn 19:30; Rev 21:4

[76] Malgo, Wim. *1000 Years Peace.* West Columbia, SC: The Midnight Call, Inc., 1984. p. 70 [emphasis added].

[77] Malgo. *Ibid.*

never any reason for God to judge sin in Israel through the Mosaic Law, or to permit His Son to be put to death on Calvary, or to judge the wicked world by fire in the Second Coming. Why do all that if someone can merely "submit" during the millennium?[78] This is a gross distortion of the sovereign plan and purpose of God for redemption. In addition, consider that leaving mortals in place after the Second Coming offers no improvement over the current covenant. According to Scripture, there is to be no lowering of the requirement to be righteous. The idea of a mixed multitude during this time conflicts openly with the Lord's concern about the wicked and their potential to corrupt Israel while His people were surrounded by evil nations.[79] It also conflicts with Paul's concern about the church having divisions due to corrupting influences. His concern was for the church to be presented to the Lord "blameless" on the Day. Any dual standard in the coming kingdom would violate and contradict all previous requirements for God's people to be holy and righteous.[80] Jesus made it clear that the wheat and the tares would grow together until the end of the age--and then, *no more*. The tares are to be removed. None will be left.

Arnold Fruchtenbaum has also embraced the idea of unregenerate mortals entering the Millennium who will later die: "The meaning of Isaiah 65:20 is that only unbelievers will die at the age of one hundred in the Millennium."[81] He then compounded his error by proffering the extreme suggestion that believers "will receive their glorified bodies at the end of the Millennium."[82] This is in direct contradiction of the Lord's words when He assured us that the resurrection will occur when He returns[83] and Paul's words describing the event in detail when mortality puts on immortality.[84] Fruchtenbaum then insisted that Revelation 20:4-6 is for only tribulation saints and "completes the first resurrection," which in his mind accounts for the first resurrection in

---

[78] This is another vague reference to the idea of a "second chance" or "universalism." See Glossary.

[79] 2 Kings 17:15; Dt 12:1-7. Note Paul, 1 Cor 15:33

[80] Note Paul: 2 Cor 6:14-7:1; Phil 2:14-16; 1 Thess 3:12-13

[81] Fruchtenbaum, Arnold. "Ariel Ministries News Letter." Tustin, CA: Winter, 2003. p. 4

[82] Fruchtenbaum. *Ibid.*

[83] Mt 24:30-31; Jn 5:24-29

[84] 1 Cor 15:53-54

Revelation 20--and the resurrection when the pre-trib rapture occurs. Yet, his fanciful idea merely creates two first resurrections which opposes scripture. In actuality, the Bible states all the dead who belong to God are raised when Jesus returns and not in stages. Paul made this clear as he wrote to the Thessalonians reminding them that the dead in Christ rise first, then, we who are still alive-- both when Christ returns.[85] Paul nowhere suggests there is another resurrection for the children of God. No Bible writer teaches a tri-part resurrection. Arnold Fruchtenbaum, like many other pre-trib advocates, merely brings confusion which helps no one understand the Second Coming and the Millennium. Dave Hunt attempted to accommodate the dilemma of who will live in the Millennium, by creating two classes of people. In response to a question on the transformation of those alive at the end of the tribulation, he stated with regard to those who come to believe during the tribulation that "most of them" will be martyred and will be resurrected at the Second coming. His model, following the pre-trib theory, already removed the church at "the Rapture." He then said those who came to faith during the seven years will continue to live on the earth just as they were. By this, he then established a second group of believers, Jews and Gentiles, "who become believers during the Tribulation" and will "continue on earth during the Millennium in their same earth bodies." He claimed that for them, "no transformation is needed."[86] He also intimated that some of them may live "the entire 1,000 years," falsely assuming there will be death. This totally rejects scripture which states there is only one time for the resurrection which is when Jesus returns at the Second Coming, and there will be no more death.[87]

A scarce book by Arthur H. Lewis dealing with millennial difficulties helps to capture the nature of the problem of evil in the millennium.[88] He approached this subject as an amillennialist, yet in short order he exposed the serious problem concerning who will be there--saints and sinners, as claimed by the pre-tribulational camp. He referenced many of the most notable dispensational

---

[85] 1 Thess 4:16-17
[86] Hunt, Dave. "The Berean Call." Vol. XXIII, No. 3, March 2008. "Q & A," p. 5
[87] 1 Cor 15:22-23; Rev 20:5; Rev 21:4. Note 1 Cor 15:26; Is 25:7-8
[88] Lewis, Arthur H. *The Dark Side of the Millennium*. Grand Rapids, MI: Baker Book House, 1980.

authorities as he laid out the inconsistency of a perfect kingdom infected with evil. He leveled his guns on "the premillennialists," yet is plainly contending with the dispensationalist who opens the door for sinful, wicked people whom the pre-trib experts think will inhabit the messianic age. While we do not agree with his amillennial view, we can certainly concur with his exposure of the fallacy within the pre-trib camp. One particular outcome he noted is the possibility of an expanding population during this time.[89] He described the potential of the unregenerate progeny of the saints then outnumbering them given one thousand years as a birthing time frame.[90] This being the case, Lewis warned that using the dispensational model, evil will actually increase at this time. He quoted John Walvoord, J. Dwight Pentecost, Rene Pache, Charles Ryrie, Hal Lindsey, and others who are all major voices holding to or in some way supporting this aberrant view. John Walvoord appears to be the primary exponent causing further confusion with this Biblically invalid idea. He agrees in general that the wicked will be "put to death at the second coming" but continued to state that children born during this time will "merely profess to follow the King" and then later "revolt" at the end of the millennium.[91] He goes on to say that some of the progeny "will not actually be born again,"[92] opening wide the door for two classes of people in the thousand year reign of Christ. Walvoord's oversight is caused by his unsound interpretation of Isaiah 65, 1 Corinthians 15, and Revelation 20.[93] He proposed this idea in 1959.[94] However, his postulation in 1964 reflects his frustration in not being able to account for "natural bodies" in the millennium, except for the pre-trib view. He clearly said

---

[89] This violates Jesus' response to the Sadducees: "at the Resurrection," no marriage [Mt 22:30]. Marriage ends when He comes. It continues "up to the day" [Lk 17:27]. Then, it is no longer possible, since we "will be like the angels in heaven" Mark states that when the dead rise, "they will neither marry or be given in marriage" [Mk 12:25]. In the age to come, redeemed believers will have imperishable bodies with no need to replenish the earth.

[90] *Ibid.* p. 12

[91] Walvoord, John F. *The Millennial Kingdom.* Grand Rapids, MI: Zondervan, 1979. p. 302.

[92] *Ibid.* p. 317

[93] Isaiah 65 is conditional; 1 Cor 15 is unconditional; Rev 20 is definitive. These are treated elsewhere in this work.

[94] *Ibid.* The original publication of *The Millennial Kingdom* was 1959.

"all unbelievers are purged out" at the Second Coming, yet claimed the rapture solves this problem just by moving the event seven years ahead, placing it at the beginning of the tribulation. He admitted this is a serious difficulty, even calling it an "insuperable problem."[95] The problem lies within his own confusion, since he insists on an early removal of the church. In his commentary on Matthew, he stated that the believing survivors of the tribulation are saints and when judged, "they are not given new bodies, but enter the millennium in their natural bodies, in keeping with the millennial predictions of Scripture which describes the saints as bearing children, building houses, and otherwise having a natural life."[96] Again, we see the unfounded contention of a Bible teacher who adjusts the texts to match his own bias. No one in the millennium will be in a natural body living a natural life. The change to immortality as described by Paul in First Corinthians supersedes any latter-day theory. In the final analysis, all that Dr. Walvoord has done is confuse the matter and further distort what Paul wrote in his epistles. There cannot be natural bodies in the millennium, the very conclusion that Arthur H. Lewis helps us see. The Apostle Paul was clear when he said flesh and blood cannot inherit. Likewise, Jesus defined life after He returns to be without marriage, meaning no children will be born. It is unfortunate that the pre-trib idea with its unique reinterpretations has supplanted clear scripture. The distinctive here is that many pre-trib advocates, along with Mark Hitchcock and the others noted above, assume some form of natural life to continue when the Second Coming occurs. This is not Biblically valid, yet held as a teaching by them, since it seemingly supports their pre-trib position at large. Once again, the major flaw in all of this is the fact that no flesh will survive the fire of judgment. It should be basic to our doctrinal understanding that "flesh and blood cannot inherit the kingdom of God, nor does the perishable inherit the imperishable."[97] We also must consider carefully that the only "offspring" in the coming kingdom will be those raised up just as David will be raised and restored to reign.[98] This will

---

[95] Walvoord, John F. *The Church in Prophecy*. Grand Rapids, MI: Zondervan, 1964. p. 106

[96] Walvoord, John F. *Matthew. Thy Kingdom Come. A Commentary on the First Gospel*. Grand Rapids, MI: Kregel Pub., 2002. p. 203

[97] 1 Cor 15:50

[98] Zech 12:10-13; 2 Sam 12:23; Heb 11:39-40

23

be the family setting at that time which will be accomplished through the resurrection at the last day.[99] David, his family, and his clans will be present.[100] All other families of the faithful will be raised also. This is what resurrection is all about. This is why the true nature of the Second Coming is so important. And, we must surely know that the wicked--all of them--will be taken to judgment.

This consideration is brought to light in the Gospel of Luke. In chapter seventeen we find the Lord Jesus dealing with a challenge from the Pharisees who are inquiring about the kingdom. On the surface, this seems to be a reasonable inquiry, except these men, like the Sadducees, hold Jesus in low regard and had continually challenged His words and authority. These men wanted to know when the kingdom of God was to come. Their query was likely initiated by Jesus' frequent mention of the kingdom. He responded by saying that it was not visible. Then he turned to His disciples with a fuller explanation, so they would understand more clearly about the kingdom to come.[101] It is interesting to note that on this occasion these disciples heard Jesus describe His coming--the Second Coming--*before* they heard His teaching of the Olivet Discourse. Notice that to the Pharisees, He said the kingdom was not visible. These experts in the Law did not recognize the fact that the King, their Messiah, was standing before them. But the disciples knew and admitted who Jesus was.[102] Hence, His explanation to them was more clear and full.[103] Notice that to His disciples He said His coming--the Son of Man-- would be *visible* and like the "lightning" seen in the heavens from one end to the other. It is this section of the response that must be understood by the church today. Jesus warned about other voices claiming to know where He was when these things were in the offing. Yet he said, "Do not go running after them."[104] He must first suffer (death and then resurrection). Later, on the Day,

---

[99] Jn 6:44; Ps 16:9-10; Ps 61:5
[100] Ps 16:9-11
[101] It would be helpful here to refer to the text in Luke 17:20 through Luke 18:8
[102] *e.g.,* Jn 1:49; Jn 6:69
[103] Consider Jesus' words in Mt 13:11-12
[104] Lk 17:23. See, also, the Appendix for the early church's position as stated in chapter 16 of *The Teaching of the Apostles.*

the sky would reveal His coming--like lightning. Meanwhile, the generation He spoke with--"this generation"--must reject Him. At this point, Jesus began to illustrate the reality about His appearance on the Day. He compared it to the time of Noah and, also, the time of Lot. In each case, people were involved with routine activities "up to the day," and then suddenly judgment fell. The text in Luke is clear: in *both* cases, the wicked were "destroyed." A number of our popular prophecy interpreters claim this is an example of or a type for the rapture. Yet, Jesus is clear. He said it "will be just like this on the day the Son of Man is revealed."[105] In other words, there will not be an event some seven years prior--no early removal of believers. We must remember that He already told them not to heed any voices claiming they "knew" where Jesus was--*prior to the "lightning" which will light up the sky "from one end to the other."* As a result of this, these disciples now knew that Jesus was to return accompanied by heavenly signs, and that the wicked will be *taken away* for judgment. Jesus said--"destroyed them all." This illustrates plainly that when He returns, the wicked will be removed, just as He explained this event to the disciples in the parable of the wheat and the tares[106]--taken and burned. None will be left. Thinking along these lines, we find that the disciples heard about the Second Coming of Christ on at least six occasions prior to the Lord delivering the Olivet Discourse.[107] He explained the event both with parables and in clear terms. It is our contemporary experts that seem to have difficulty with this. We must hold to the Lord's own teaching: He will return once at the end of the age. His own who long for His appearing[108] will be rescued, and the rest are to face judgment.

Notice, too, that the Lord's teaching about this continues into chapter eighteen. He spoke about a persistent widow who was continuing to bother a judge. Her persistence paid off, and often expositors make this the lesson, however Jesus was still teaching about His return. He noted that His "chosen ones" who are patient and persistent will get justice (the wicked are to be judged—taken away). Yet, He is concerned about His faithful followers holding on to the end.

---

[105] Lk 17:30
[106] Mt 13:36-43, 49-50
[107] Found in Mt 13. Lk 17, Mt 16, Mt 19, Lk 20, Lk 22, and note, also, Jn 14.
[108] 2 Tim 4:8

And, because of the severity of the last days, at the close of this section in Luke, the Lord asked a penetrating question: "However, when the Son of Man comes, will he find faith on the earth?"[109] This question is valid, because the Body of Christ will remain on the earth until the end and face severe trial and persecution. There will be betrayal, rebellion, and all the forces of evil will be unleashed. Who will stand? Who will survive? The truly faithful, since the body of Christ will be tested and purified.[110] This explanation by the Lord about the coming kingdom--whether it is to be visible or invisible--carries much important weight in assisting us with our understanding of what is yet to come. However, it should be clear by reading this that no wicked rebel will survive.

A brief reminder of the Lord's ability to completely destroy those who oppose him or His purposes is worth considering. Early in the history of Israel, they entered Egypt, few in number. Eventually this turned from a safe refuge from famine into bondage. Under the Lord's direction, Moses stood against Pharaoh and led the people, now over a million in number, out of Egypt. When Pharaoh pursued them with his army, the Red Sea was a formidable barrier, and it seemed that there was no escape. Yet, the Lord parted the sea, had Moses lead the people to safety, and at the same time He destroyed Pharaoh and his army. "Not one of them survived."[111] The Lord preserved His own and destroyed the wicked all at once. This is true for the last judgment as well. When Jesus comes, no person who is not one of God's people will survive. It is worthwhile to think back before this to Noah. He and his family survived. All the rest of mankind, the wicked were destroyed--"Every living thing that moved on the earth perished."[112] Noah was preserved through it. Not one unrighteous person survived. At the time of Lot, there was grievous sin occurring in Sodom and the surrounding cities on the plain. Lot and his family were living in the city, and the Lord was going to judge all the wicked there. Two angels removed Lot and his family, and then the Lord "overthrew those cities and the entire plain, including all those living in the cities."[113] None of the wicked survived. Only

---

[109] Lk 18:8
[110] Mt 24:12-13
[111] Ex 14:21-28
[112] Gen 7:21

26

those the Lord saw as worthy were removed. Both acts occurred at the same time. In Proverbs we find a terse warning about those who are evil: "Do not fret because of evil men or be envious of the wicked, for the evil man has no future hope, and the lamp of the wicked will be snuffed out."[114] This short extract from this book of wisdom portrays the same foreboding destiny for the wicked at the end of the age. They will be snuffed out. None of them will be left.

Solomon surely understood the fate of those who rejected God's counsel, preferring their own "wisdom." He openly branded this as folly.[115] It is clear that much of what is considered to be sound theologically today is lacking in substance and fails Solomon's tests. He clearly said, "When the storm has swept by, the wicked are gone, but the righteous stand firm forever."[116] This leaves no room for those who prefer earthly interpretations of Scripture to find favor with God and be welcomed into His kingdom. If they do not hold to His truth and have resisted His Spirit, they will be in grave danger. Their only option is to be swept away. This is why the gospel will be preached during the tribulation, so those who have embraced error can still turn to God for salvation. They, too, now redeemed, will be among those waiting to welcome the Lord at His return. Those who reject God's final offer of grace will not be left alive. They will be judged. None of them will survive His fiery wrath.[117] None will be left.

Those who hold to a pre-trib position are by definition also premillennial in their thinking. Hence, as premillennialists they must hold to the statement that Jesus returns to commence the millennial age: His 1,000 year reign. This occurs at the time the Lord renovates the earth after the destruction brought on by judgment. While some Bible teachers claim this restoration takes place later, there is no way that the redeemed can inhabit the remains of a fiery judgment, a heap of ashes, after the armies of heaven bring fire on the earth.[118] The earth is

---

[113] Gen 19:25
[114] Prov 24:19-20
[115] Prov 5:23; 13:20; 15:21
[116] Prov 10:25; Ps 24:19-20; Ps 104:33-35; Ps 145:20; Ps 34:16; Ps 97:3
[117] 2 Thess 2:9-12; Mt 13:40-43

renewed at that time in order to fulfill the Lord's promise to restore creation for His own people.[119] In his excellent work on Daniel, Robert Culver, provides a brief, clear description of the timing of the great "cosmic disturbances," the nature of the destruction, and what is to follow. Culver noted that the intent of Isaiah and the other prophets was to establish that "the coming Messianic Kingdom shall occupy from the first 'the new heavens and [a] new earth.'"[120] His work stressed the prophet Daniel's understanding which overall includes the judgment of the wicked once and for all. That will be the final blow to evil on the earth. All reprobates, unrepentant sinners, and enemies of the Lord will be consumed in the fire to come on the earth. None of them will be left. We must take a sober look at every facet of the Second Coming and the Lord's judgment. We, too, are accountable.

---

[118] Mal 3:5; Rev 19:15
[119] Is 35:1-10; 65:17ff; 32:15-20; 4:2-6; 2:2-5; 55:12-13; Rev 21:1-4
[120] Culver, Robert. *Daniel and the Latter Days*. Westwood, NJ: Fleming H. Revell, 1954. p. 177-179ff

THE ERROR OF IMMINENCE

One of the most important points taught by those who hold to the idea of a pre-tribulation rapture of the church is the claim that this event is imminent. Periodically we hear from some of the well-known prophecy teachers that this event could occur momentarily, even before their message is finished. Pastor Chuck Smith of Calvary Chapel, Costa Mesa, California, wrote pointedly in 1981: "The Rapture can happen at *any moment*--and it's exciting to realize that as a Christian you may never finish reading this article."[1] Major claims are made that no prophetic event needs to take place which would prevent the rapture from happening--at this very moment. Popular Bible teacher Dr. David Jeremiah stated, "It could happen at any time, even before the next beat of your heart."[2] Even the great British writer, C. S. Lewis, was caught up into this distraction. He noted that the "curtain may be rung down at any moment: say, before you have finished reading this paragraph."[3] Late Radio Bible Class teacher, M. R. DeHaan, underscored this by saying: "There is a secret coming of Christ mentioned frequently in the Scriptures," which he claimed would occur "secretly like a thief" to "take place before the tribulation days."[4] Dr. Walter Martin[5] used to refer to this mindset as "any-moment-itus."

For years we have been told that the church could be removed in a flash on any day at any time. We have heard that the removal of the church is a sign-less,[6]

---

[1] Smith, Chuck. "Last Times." Fall/1981. Costa Mesa, CA: Calvary Chapel of Costa Mesa. p. 8

[2] Jeremiah, David. *Jesus' Final Warning*. Nashville, TN: Word Pub., 1999. p. 69

[3] Lewis, C. S. *The World's Last Birthday and Other Essays*. "The World's Last Night." New York, NY: Harcourt Brace Jovanovich, 1973. p. 105

[4] DeHaan, M. R. *35 Simple Studies on the Book of Revelation*. Grand Rapids, MI: Zondervan, 1988. p. 70. Dr. DeHaan also states we must "distinguish between the two events, the *secret* rapture before the Tribulation and the *public* appearance at the close of the Tribulation." p. 240-241 [Emphasis in the original]. DeHaan exemplifies the secret, imminent teaching of the dispensational theory.

[5] Dr. Martin was the founder of the Christian Research Institute and author of the *Kingdom of the Cults*.

church-only event[7] which will cause the world to go into upheaval.[8] Explanations for this, courtesy of the ungodly that remain, range from the church's abduction by space aliens to our judgment.[9] We have been told that this event will open the door for the Antichrist who will assume power when the church is gone, and then the tribulation period will begin. Dr. David Breese stated: "Our disappearance is the event that will end the church age and trigger the beginning of the Tribulation."[10] We have been informed that the world will be pleased that the restraining presence of the church has been taken away. Now all men can do as they like. Some prophecy teachers tell us that after our departure, God will begin to judge the world--His wrath being unleashed.[11] This facet of the rapture is often supported through the use of Paul's statement to the Thessalonians that "...God did not appoint us to suffer wrath but to receive salvation through our Lord Jesus Christ."[12] Our most notable pre-trib authorities assure us that we are not to face wrath, and we have been exempted

---

[6] Smith, Chuck. *The Final Act*. Costa Mesa, CA: The Word For Today, 2007. p. 107. Smith states "There are *no unfulfilled signs* or prophecies. All the necessary prophecies have already been fulfilled. This means the rapture could take place *at any time*." [emphasis added]. Lindsey, Hal. *Planet Earth: The Final Chapter*. Beverly Hills, CA: Western Front, Ltd., 1998. p. 125

[7] Missler, Chuck. *Prophecy 20/20*. Nashville, TN: Thomas Nelson, 2006. p. 96. He refers to an event which applies only to "believers who are translated in secret." This is a not- so- subtle reference for a *secret rapture*.

[8] Smith, Chuck. *Dateline Earth*. Old Tappan, NJ: Fleming H. Revell, 1989. p. 42. Smith says, "watch out, because the restraining power of the Holy Spirit will be removed, and all hell will break loose." LaHaye, Tim F. *Christ and the Tribulation. Revelation. Volume II*. La Mesa, CA: Post, Inc., 1966. p 67. LaHaye states: "It is evident that the first 21 months of the Tribulation Period consists of horrific events."

[9] Missler, Chuck, & Mark Eastman. *Alien Encounters*. Coeur d'Alene, ID: Koinonia House, 1997. p. 199; also, Hindson, Ed. *Is the Antichrist Alive and Well?* Eugene, OR: Harvest House, 1998. p. 33; Hunt, Dave. *Global Peace*. Eugene, OR: Harvest House, 1990. p. 208

[10] Breese, Dave. *What to Do If You Miss the Rapture*. Colton, CA: World Prophetic Ministry, Inc., 1995. p. 5

[11] Smith. *Dateline Earth*. p. 42

[12] 1Thess 5:9

from what is to follow during the seven years of tribulation. They emphatically state this is Jacob's time of trouble [Jer 30:7], that Israel will face this, and the church has no part in it. Is this what Paul meant--no signs, no warning, no witness or testimony by the church at the end? To understand what this apostle intended, the context must be examined carefully, along with the actual purpose for him to address this issue with the Thessalonians in his two earliest epistles.

In 2006, the Pre-Trib Research Center included an article in their newsletter which dealt with the topic of Israel. The author, Dr. Thomas Ice, made a number of excellent points in his piece, a defense of "Modern Israel's Right To The Land."[13] He offered the following statement: "In other words the seven-year tribulation period will begin with the signing of a covenant between the Antichrist and the leaders of Israel." We have heard this assertion many times from numerous other teachers. He went on to say: "The tribulation *cannot begin* until the seven-year covenant is made" [emphasis added]. Dr. Ice related the fact of Israel's re-gathering to be a "modern miracle" and connected it directly to Antichrist's coming "peace pact with Israel." This may appear sound, however, in the conclusion to this article, he stated that the "ancient and scattered people have returned to their ancestral homeland after almost two millennia, making the peace covenant of Daniel 9:24-27 *possible for the first time since A.D. 70*" [emphasis added]. A simple reading of this last statement reveals how the bias of this interpretation undermines the entire concept of imminence--the very core of what Dr. Ice and the Pre-Trib Research Center were committed to. This blatant contradiction shows the irony of attempting to use Scripture to support a view which cannot be accounted for by Scriptural means. This is why the Apostle Paul told us: "'Do not go beyond what is written'."[14] Most erroneous pre-trib conclusions are like this--distortions which can be easily remedied if the Scripture is held up in context and used to test the tentative proposition. It was Paul who also reminded the church at Thessalonica and us to "Test everything. Hold on to the good."[15] We must

---

[13] Ice, Thomas. "Pre-Trib Perspectives," Vol. 8, Num. 39, October 2006. p. 7
[14] 1 Cor 4:6
[15] 1 Thess 5:21

conclude, then, that Dr. Ice did not test everything, and that his admission that this peace covenant--"possible for the *first time*"--simply and plainly disembowels the idea of a doctrine of imminence and renders it a fallacy. He reinforced his position in a later issue of "Pre-Trib Perspectives" in response to a similar question: "When Israel became a nation in 1948, was it a fulfillment of Bible Prophecy?" Dr. Ice answered affirmatively and proceeded to say that the reestablishment means that Israel "is *now poised* in just the setting *required* for the revealing of the Antichrist and the start of the tribulation...."[16] Again, we see a continuance of the same blindness. There cannot be a redundant, open-ended imminency. The pre-trib rapture is either going to happen *now*, or it is not imminent at all. Dr. Ice obliterated two thousand years of imminency with his use of Israel's return in 1948. The Lord's return must be honestly portrayed as something set to happen only when all of the Biblical pieces are in place. False "early warnings" set into a doctrinal framework easily mislead the unwary Christian.

Dr. John Walvoord, highly respected Dallas Theological Seminary exponent of imminence, fell into the same error when attempting to support his pre-trib proposition. He stated that "probably the most obvious feature of our day in the light of prophecy is the United Nations. *For the first time* there has been a workable union in which the great nations of the world have participated actively."[17] His assertion "for the first time" excludes the possibility of imminence prior to the UN's founding in 1945. What is seen in this kind of "proof" is a forced deliberation to make the supposition palatable at the expense of reality. This means that the Scripture texts are fully at risk for adjustment at the whim of the interpreter. This problem permeates this area of theology in particular. Sound hermeneutical principles are ignored. In the same book Dr. Walvoord continued this line of distended thinking when he attempted to prove imminence in a chapter entitled "The Imminent Translation of the Church." He produced not a single Bible verse to support his question:

---

[16] Ice, Thomas. "Pre-Trib Perspectives." Vol. 8, Num. 56. June, 2008. p. 8 [emphasis added].

[17] Walvoord, John F. *The Return of the Lord.* Findlay, OH: Dunham Pub., 1955. p. 14 [emphasis added].

"Do the Scriptures present the fulfillment of the hope of His return as an imminent event, i.e., as possible of fulfillment at any moment?"[18] What followed his inquiry was a litany of claims to support the rapture prior to the tribulation upon which he attempted to implant an imminent event. He did not include *any* Scripture as proof. Again, he failed to underline the claim with the Bible and left us with mere conjecture.

Dr. Tim LaHaye also followed suit with his assertion that "...unfulfilled prophecies have to do with the future, many of which are being fulfilled in our lifetime."[19] Continuing this logic, it would lead us to conclude that, since there are many unfulfilled prophecies relating to the return of Christ, the rapture could not have yet occurred, since many Biblical statements are *yet* future. Because the pre-trib view has artificially placed the rapture just prior to or at the commencement of the last seven years, those who teach this idea are forced to juggle events as they happen in order to maintain the idea of imminency. This does not work! Dr. LaHaye closed the door on logic when he wrote "our generation has *more reason* to believe Christ could return for His second coming than *any generation before us*."[20] He is, of course, insisting by this that the rapture would precede the Second Coming, and he inadvertently errs by inferring that previous generations had *less or no reason* to assume an imminent pre-trib rapture would occur in *their* lifetime. It is interesting to note that some thirty-five years prior to these remarks, Dr. LaHaye rarely mentioned imminence. It appears he used the word just one time in a work he published in 1972. Instead, he listed multiple *signs* which must be fulfilled prior to Christ's return. The primary sign he employed was World War I, using the date 1914, as the event which "ushered in the beginning of the end."[21] Several of his chapters dealt with a multitude of signs--not imminency. At the same time, he

---

[18] Walvoord. *The Return.* p. 49

[19] LaHaye, Tim. "Pre-Trib Perspectives." Vol. 8, Num. 54. March/April, 2008. p. 3

[20] LaHaye. *Ibid.* He also makes the same claim in: LaHaye/Jenkins. *Are We Living in the End Times?* Wheaton, IL: Tyndale House Pub. Inc., 1999. p. 61 [emphasis added].

[21] LaHaye, Tim. *The Beginning of the End.* Wheaton, IL: Tyndale House, Pub., 1972. p. 39

specifically highlighted Israel's founding in 1948 as a sign.[22] Continuing this pattern, Dr. LaHaye reinforced his premise that The Great War (1914) is the "monumental event,"[23] basing his entire book on a *number of signs*--and "the first great sign, World War I."[24] This is a clear case of speculation. The Bible does not point to a specific conflict by name. The Great War in 1914 is not the scriptural signal to bring in the end. This is not what Jesus described in Matthew 24 when He outlined the end of the age in the Olivet Discourse. Other prophecy teachers have also followed this error. David L. Cooper was keen on this. Likewise, Messianic prophecy teacher, Arnold Fruchtenbaum, supports this view.[25] The obvious fallacy with Dr. LaHaye's 1972 position is the continued use of *signs* to support the idea of imminence for a supposedly sign-less event. Dr. LaHaye employed a modified view of this in 2001 when he wrote "war" is "not part of the sign," and "wars are not *the* sign that the end is near."[26] This is not a correction of his previous blunder. He was employing a subtle form of double-speak, since he brought up World War I just two pages later. He wrote it "alone does not constitute *the* sign" and must include "unprecedented famines."[27] He then combined "a world war, famines, pestilences, and simultaneous earthquakes"[28] in order to maintain his theory that 1914 was critical to support all his claims. All he has done is add to the confusion. Well-respected Bible expositor, Donald Grey Barnhouse stood against this error of using a world war as a pretext. He wrote at the time of World War Two [1940]: "Now we are quite ready to believe that the war that is being found today is the greatest war so far in history, but it is not the war

---

[22] *Ibid.* p. 43ff. LaHaye's chapter is entitled "The Infallible Sign."

[23] *Ibid.* p. 93

[24] *Ibid.* p. 161

[25] Arnold Fruchtenbaum replicates this error in *The Footsteps of the Messiah*. p. 437. In light of this, consider [Dan 9:26] "The end will come like a flood: war will continue to the end, and desolations have been decreed." War will be ever-present until the end of the age, and, therefore cannot be *the* sign.

[26] LaHaye, Tim, and Jerry B. Jenkins. *Perhaps Today. Living Every Day in the Light of Christ's Return*. Wheaton, IL: Tyndale House, 2001. p. 73 [emphasis in the original].

[27] LaHaye/Jenkins, *Ibid.* p. 75-76 [emphasis in the original].

[28] *Ibid.* p. 76

spoken of by Christ."[29] An objective review of this train of thought, hopefully, will lead to a rethinking of the whole concept of imminency. The prophet Daniel reminded us: "War will continue to the end."[30]

A more cautious approach with the teaching about the return of Christ and the rapture is needed--one that encompasses the event as stated in Scripture, avoiding pre-suppositions of any kind which would by nature yield a questionable interpretation. Human reason will not suffice. Peter the apostle warned us regarding private interpretation.[31] Tim LaHaye and Thomas Ice have introduced tension into the imminency question by employing conflicting terms. Dr. LaHaye continued to insist on multiple "signs" prior to the rapture,[32] while Dr. Ice shifted the nomenclature noting them to be "stage setting" events. He attempted to deflect controversy about signs for a sign-less event stating: "Stage-setting is not the 'fulfillment' of Bible prophecy. So while prophecy is not being fulfilled in our day, it does not follow that we cannot track 'general trends' in current preparation for the tribulation."[33] His claims are even worsened by his insistence in the same article that the "rapture is a signless event," "imminent," and could "take place at any moment."[34] Noticeably, the Pre-Trib Research Institute adjusted its terminology and applied less controversial terms. In place of the term "imminent sign," the words "general trends" and "stage setting" have been used.[35] The alteration in language still does not help either clarify the theory or validate it more reasonably. It just makes the view worse, since no adjustment in language can justify outright error. We must carefully read scripture when it is used to support ideas related

---

[29] Barnhouse, Donald Grey. *The Invisible War*. Grand Rapids, MI: Zondervan, 1965. p. 264

[30] Dan 9:26

[31] 2 Pt 1:20 (KJV)

[32] LaHaye, Tim. "Pre-Trib Perspectives." *The Generation That Will "See" the Return of Christ.* Volume 8, No. 32. March 2006. p. 1-3

[33] Ice, Thomas. "Pre-Trib Perspectives." *The Situation in the Middle East.* Volume 8, No. 38. September 2006. p. 4. This is fanciful double-speak.

[34] *Ibid.* p. 1

[35] LaHaye, Tim. "Pre-Trib Perspectives." *Sharia Law Invades the Gridiron in My Home Town.* Thomas Ice. *Consistent Biblical Futurism – Part V.* Volume 8. No. 81. October 2010. p. 1, 6

to pre-trib teaching, especially imminence. We must seek the Holy Spirit's guidance and avoid human preferences regardless of the brilliant personality associated with it.

Bible teacher, M. R. DeHaan, who was for many years a popular expositor on the radio, taught often about the Second Coming and the pre-trib removal of the church. His views were dispensational and accepted by many who listened to his broadcasts. His books, also, reprinted many times influenced others who never heard him speak. He was emphatic about a two-stage return of Christ. We have noted above his thoughts on the secret rapture. He also fell into the imminency trap and unknowingly contradicted the idea in his commentary on Daniel. He concluded: "And surely there has never been an age in history when more light has been shed upon the truth, when there has been more understanding on the part of those who really want to know God's will concerning the truth of the Second Coming of the Lord Jesus Christ. The very interest you yourself are showing in the truth of the *imminent* return of the Lord Jesus is the evidence of the inspiration of this Word."[36] Note how he contradicted himself regarding imminency. He stated that *never before* has there been a time when we have had more light and, then, emphasized the imminent return. His use of the former ages not having as much light would indicate a time when imminency was not probable or possible. He, then, applied subjective thinking when he pointed to the "interest you yourself have," as if this is the driving factor in the Second Coming and the rapture of the church. The return of Jesus Christ does not depend on our feelings, our understanding of it, or our acceptance of it. He is coming to judge the quick and the dead and will be right on time, no matter what we believe. Luke recorded the words of Paul pointing to the time of the Second Coming and rapture: "For he has set a day when he will judge the world with justice by the man he has appointed. He has given proof of this to all men by raising him from the dead."[37] Paul the Apostle who wrote much on the return of Christ surely sets this straight here: the day of the return is on God's calendar--in the

---

[36] DeHaan, M. R. *Daniel the Prophet. 35 Simple Studies in the Book of Daniel.* Grand Rapids, MI: Zondervan, 1975. p. 314 [emphasis added].

[37] Acts 17:31

future--even though it is not on ours. This is why Jesus taught us to take into account the signs he spoke of in the Olivet Discourse and elsewhere. It is one thing to hold to a view. It is quite another to freely apply scripture verses to make the text speak where it does not.

An earlier example of this kind of liberty regarding imminence was stated by Kenneth Wuest who was associated with Moody Bible Institute for many years. In his work, *Great Truths to Live By*, he wrote in detail about the soon return in the chapter, "Jesus of Nazareth--His Coming For His Church." Wuest stated emphatically, "There are no prophecies unfulfilled which would withhold His coming."[38] This is the standard approach to imminence which was unknowingly refuted by Dr. Ice and Dr. LaHaye. Wuest continued with the dispensational presentation and expanded his thoughts:

> To teach that the church will go through the tribulation period, is to *nullify* the biblical teaching of the imminent return of the Lord Jesus for the Church. Events on earth are not yet in readiness for the Great Tribulation. Indeed, at this writing (1951), that period *cannot come for years yet*. But the Lord may return for His Church at any moment. Paul (Phil 4:5), Peter (I Pet. 1:13-15), and John (I John 3:2, 3) all make the imminent coming of our Lord a ground for appeal for holy living and diligent service.[39]

Dr. Wuest's zeal for encouraging holiness, sanctification, and committed service is commendable, yet he created new problems. He might wish us to overlook the idea that the removal of the Church is the event to commence the Tribulation period (as stated by Dr. Breese above) or just blindly accept the idea of imminence which he already presented as a presupposition. If what Dr. Wuest says actually is a "Great Truth" to live by, then it deserves more than snappy statements which far too many Bible believers never check for themselves. Please note that he wrote this in 1951 (published 1952), and the generation he subscribed to has passed us by. He even stated that world events

[38] Wuest, Kenneth S. *Great Truths To Live By*. Grand Rapids, MI: 1952, rpt. Eerdmans, 1977. p. 135
[39] *Ibid.* p. 140 [emphasis added].

"are not yet in readiness," expecting readers to ignore the calendar completely. We are now in the 21ˢᵗ century, and Dr. Wuest's claims are in a state of suspension, which does not help the idea of a soon return of Christ.

Further, consider the implications of imminency through the ages. If the Lord came ("at any moment") in the third century, what church would be present in the succeeding years? What would be in its place in the 1500s, and who would reform what? This is a flagrant contradiction conceptually and, like Dr. Ice's effort, fails to pass muster. It also chaffs against the idea of dispensations,[40] especially as applied by many pre-trib teachers when they proceed through the dispensational explanation of the church ages as described in the second and third chapters of the book of Revelation. This comparison is the antithesis of the idea of the dispensations themselves. The "any moment" trigger itself refutes the concept of the church ages. If it could occur at any moment, then it is not possible to stretch this dispensational interpretation over several divisions of the church age, since with "imminence" the church is supposed to be gone. Dr. John R. Rice, an avowed pre-trib advocate, noted this problem in a message he delivered, "Jesus May Come Today." He said that the "Bible has nothing to say about being types representing church history," noting this to be merely "a matter of human fancy." He was commenting on notes in the Scofield Reference Bible which he found offensive regarding church ages and was disturbed about claims of the church now being "in the Laodicean age."[41] In the body of his message, Dr. Rice repudiated this whole concept and noted that those who hold to this "surely do not realize how presumptuous their position is."[42] He went on to say "if any one of the seven classifications beside the first one be accurate, then Jesus could not have come until after 316 A.D. Paul, then, was a fanatic, religious nut, to be looking for Jesus to come in his lifetime."[43] Quite surprisingly, he named John Nelson Darby, C.I. Scofield, and

---

[40] See Glossary
[41] Rice, John R., "Jesus May Come Today," reprinted in *Great Preaching on the Second Coming.* Curtis Hutson, compiler. Murfreesboro, TN: Sword of the Lord, 1989. p. 235
[42] *Ibid.* p. 236
[43] *Ibid.* p. 236

Harry Ironside as proponents making "a grievous assumption," each of them "on a flimsy basis, without any direct scriptural statement."[44] He blasted them directly for their arrogance to "go beyond Scripture with a man-made doctrine which is heresy."[45] Considering the title of Dr. Rice's message, this honest, hard-hitting rebuke is stunning, indeed!

Another important consideration regarding the pre-trib authorities mentioned above: If an imminent coming is taught by Paul, Peter, and John (see above quote from Wuest) as the basis of this doctrine, then what *really* does initiate the Tribulation? Is it the "signing of the covenant," which Dr. Ice claims is the event which brings it about--it "*cannot begin* until the seven year covenant is signed" (see above quote)? Or is it the rapture itself, per Dr. Breese? If we consider this as they have presented it, then we cannot have these two events separated, since how could we have a raptured church, say, in the 4th century and then a covenant with the antichrist in the 21st century or later? What then is the Church's purpose? And if the Church is raptured hundreds of years before the covenant with the man of sin, why would the Lord delay in judging the earth, since all would be in full corruption with no restraining Church present? Pastor Chuck Smith opened up the discord with this contradiction and unknowingly set aside imminence when he wrote:

> As we *approach the day* the Lord takes His church out of this world, it would only be fitting that He make us more aware of the promise to the church of being caught up before the great tribulation. Why would the Lord reveal it to Martin Luther, John Calvin, or any Reformation church leaders? *They weren't living in the age when the church was to be taken out.*[46]

This admission only confounds the ability for those sincerely attempting to understand the Second Coming. Chuck Smith's statement is one of many

---

[44] *Ibid.* p. 236-237

[45] *Ibid.* p. 237

[46] Smith, Chuck. *The Final Act.* Costa Mesa, CA: The Word For Today, 2007. p. 192 [emphasis added].

examples which litter the landscape courtesy of so-called prophecy experts. Imminence in its original form always included the return of Christ to judge and at the same time bring relief to those who were anticipating His coming. This is why Jesus offered caution, admonition, and signs in the Olivet Discourse. He spoke about this event at other times, also. The fullness of His statements must be taken into account to prevent distortion, intentional or otherwise.[47] When the Lord's words are read carefully, the dispensational perspective, which Chuck Smith held to vigorously, would be clarified by scripture itself. We would then see the Lord coming as He said at the end of the age with His angels in power, glory, and to settle all accounts, plus establish His Kingdom visibly.[48]

At the very least, the concept of imminence and the anytime removal of God's people raises more questions than it resolves. It has all the marks of a device to merely support a non-doctrine. The idea is based on extra-Biblical concepts. It would be of greater benefit to carefully reconsider the rapture in its Scriptural context. On that basis, we must object to the idea that this teaching is sound doctrine. Dispensational teachers who employ handy in-house references have for some time attempted to add credence to this teaching by calling it "The Doctrine of Imminence."[49] Unfortunately, this idea is merely a unique feature of their creation to support the pre-trib theory. J. Dwight Pentecost in an attempt to deflect criticism of this idea away from J. N. Darby as the originator inserted a reference from Henry C. Thiessen, also a staunch believer in imminence.[50] He included a quote where Thiessen states the early church and the Fathers held to the Lord's coming "as imminent," and that they were "not interested in the possibility of a Tribulation period in the future."[51] However, this contradicts the fathers' own writing and, also, the view of John Walvoord whom we have referenced elsewhere in this chapter on this issue. Pentecost did

---

[47] See Mt 24, Mk 13, Lk 17, Lk 21, etc.

[48] Mt 13:36-43, 47-50; Mt 24:29-31; 1 Cor 15:22-24

[49] Notably, Gerald Stanton; also, commonly, Chuck Missler. *Prophecy 20/20.* p. 98

[50] Pentecost, J. Dwight. *Things To Come. A Study in Biblical Eschatology.* Grand Rapids, MI: Zondervan, 1977. p. 203

[51] *Ibid.*

say that "the early church may not be clear on all points,"[52] but the purpose underlying his reference is markedly leveraged toward "the doctrine of imminence." So, he revealed his bias openly. Also, those who read *Things To Come* are not told to check out the Church Fathers to verify the facts regarding Dr. Pentecost's claims or Thiessen's.[53] The idea of imminence will be explored more thoroughly in the chapters ahead beside the Biblical texts that affect the nature of this very important teaching.

In that light, we will let the Apostle Paul speak to this key point: "Don't let anyone deceive you in any way, for that day *will not come* until the rebellion occurs and the man of lawlessness is revealed, the man doomed to destruction"[54]. His words resonate clearly with the very concern we address here. Paul speaks distinctly of *two things first*. This is in the exact context of "...the coming of our Lord Jesus and our being *gathered* to him."[55] There should be no confusion with this statement in the Thessalonian epistle, yet those who support imminence and the pre-trib rapture distort this teaching by Paul to mean an event some seven years earlier than what the Apostle had in mind. Again, with this kind of thinking more problems are created, since then you end up with multiple resurrections and a variety of raptures.[56] Pastor Chuck Smith claimed there would be "a second rapture" for martyrs during the tribulation as he

---

[52] *Ibid.*

[53] See Chapter: "History."

[54] 2 Thess 2:3 [emphasis added].

[55] 2 Thess 2:1 [emphasis added].

[56] Smith, Chuck. *The Final Act.* p. 181. Smith claims "The first resurrection covers a *period of time* and encompasses *many different events*." This opens the door for a multitude of raptures. Note, too: Arnold Froese who has incorporated two raptures, one vertical for the church to heaven and a second for the Jews "raptured horizontally from the four corners of the earth to Israel." Froese also embraces "His third coming" which contradicts clear scripture. Froese, Arnold. *The Great Mystery of the Rapture.* Columbia, SC: The Olive Press, 1999. p. 28-29, 193. Also, note: Charles Capps advocates a separate rapture for the 144,000. Capps, Charles. *End Times Events—Journey to the End of the Age.* Tulsa, OK: Harrison House, Inc., 1997. p. 145. Creating multiple events out of thin air is radical, un-Biblical, and heretical.

discussed this issue on a "World News Briefing" broadcast.[57] The idea of a *multiplicity* of raptures is nowhere supported in scripture and certainly not present in Paul's Thessalonian letters.[58] If the current view of imminence is invalid, then the Word itself will show us where popular teaching is wrong. And as Wuest indicated, it will be nullified! Notably, Dr. Walvoord agreed with Dr. Wuest, stating if another view is correct, "we must give up the doctrine of the imminent coming of the Lord...."[59] With this he admits to a major weakness in his position. Elsewhere, it is interesting to note that Dr. Walvoord exposes himself and proffers a sound interpretation of this passage when he stated this rebellion (apostasy) "means a falling away or a departure in a doctrinal sense."[60] He also wrote that this "departure" is not the rapture "as some have understood this."[61] This contradicts his assertion in his book, *The Rapture Question*, where he alluded to this being the rapture, even to mention another supporter of this idea, E. Schuyler English.[62] In his 1979 revision of this work, Dr. Walvoord once again cited English, stating it to be "another evidence" of the church's departure.[63] Through this we see that Dr. Walvoord is clever in his construct and possibly hoped his readers would not see the conflict. But, Paul's position is clear: before we are gathered there will be *the* apostasy (rebellion) and *the* man of sin will be revealed.[64] The Greek text contains the definite article next to "apostasy." It will be *the* apostasy--*the* rebellion of unimaginable consequences. Paul was very concerned that believers not be led astray about the order of events at the time Jesus is returning. It is best to adhere to Paul and his teaching and not be persuaded by

---

[57] Smith, Chuck. "World News Briefing." August 23, 2012. Rebroadcast 08-24- 2012. KWVE. 107.9 FM.

[58] See Chapter: "The Danger of Complacency."

[59] Walvoord. *The Return*. p. 49

[60] Walvoord, John F. *The Thessalonian Epistles*. Grand Rapids, MI: Zondervan, 1991. p. 74

[61] *Ibid*, p. 74

[62] Walvoord, John F. *The Rapture Question*. Findlay, OH: Dunham Pub. Co., 1957. p. 71- 72

[63] Walvoord, John F. *The Rapture Question. Revised and Enlarged Edition*. Grand Rapids, MI: Zondervan Pub. Co., 1979. p. 67-68

[64] 2 Thess 2:3-4

someone or something which is in conflict with scripture.

In his comments on Paul's second epistle to the Thessalonians, Frederic Godet noted the intent of Paul's words: "In chapter ii, Paul reminds the Thessalonians of what he had already taught them when amongst them, namely, that the glorious return of Christ must be preceded by a manifestation of a directly opposite nature, that of the *Man of Sin*."[65] Godet also wrote that the appearance of the Man of Sin (Antichrist) "presupposes two facts which have not yet been realized: *first*, the great falling away of humanity from God," and "*secondly*, the overthrowing of a power which St. Paul mysteriously designates by the expression "*that which restraineth*" (neuter), and "*he that restraineth*" (masculine)."[66] This sequence disallows any sense of an imminent, any-moment return, since Paul placed critical events prior to the Second Coming. With this detail provided by this Apostle, no believer then or now should expect the Lord to arrive secretly some seven years prior to another Second Coming. In the preceding chapter of his epistle, Paul also reminded the Thessalonians that the Lord was to come in glory and not before.[67]

There has been an overt attempt in recent years to prove that the church always held to imminence, meaning a pre-trib, any-moment rapture. This point has come to the forefront of the debate through the rebuttals of those defending pre-trib views against those who hold the post-trib position. They are at times called "opponents" of pre-trib teaching.[68] They are a nemesis for pre-trib teachers, since they claim that pre-trib teaching is of a recent origin, something not notably endorsed prior to 1830. The dispensational response has been to quote a variety of church authorities[69] and then present edited extracts from the

---

[65] Godet, Frederic L. *Studies in Paul's Epistles*. 1889. rpt. Grand Rapids, MI: Kregel Pub., 1984. p. 28

[66] Godet. *Ibid.* p. 28-29 [emphasis in the original].

[67] 2 Thess 1:6-10

[68] Also opposing imminence are those in the a-millennial and post-millennial camps (especially preterists).

[69] Note: Most of the quotes are from those favorable to the teaching of J. N. Darby in the 19th and 20th centuries; many references have been taken out of context or misquoted.

early Church Fathers. The problem with this is that the authorities and Fathers faced a variety of challenges--a secret rapture not among them. The great sway of the church, from Augustine forward, was the challenge from much corruption and conflict. It was rife with competition among the hierarchy, establishment of liturgy and ritual, and political infighting. It was concerned about the Second Coming, but other doctrinal issues were more pressing.[70] George Eldon Ladd presents a fair treatment of the fathers, as does Robert Gundry.[71] In his attempt to refute some of the post-trib authorities and their use of the church fathers (men preceding Augustine), Dr. Walvoord candidly admitted the "preponderance of evidence seems to support the concept that the early church did not clearly hold to a rapture preceding the end time tribulation period."[72] This admission does not help him make a strong pre-trib claim at all. He compounded this dilemma and revealed his own confusion saying: "Most of the early church fathers who wrote on the subject at all considered themselves already in the great tribulation."[73] Either Dr. Walvoord did not understand the Fathers, or he did and purposely ignored their clear statements. Also, we say "confusion" with regard to Dr. Walvoord's statement, because he obviously confused "tribulation" here with "the great tribulation." Further, if the Fathers were thinking that they were already in the tribulation, they would have been looking forward to the Second Coming in glory, including Christ coming to judge.[74] In their minds, *that* would have been a realistic anticipation and would have meant "imminent" to them at that time. For them, this would have included the translation[75] of the saints as described by Paul.[76] Note,

---

[70] See: Schaff, Sheldon, Kurtz, Cairns, Eusebius, Bruce, Cadoux, Ramsay, Robertson, Latourette, Shelley, etc. See chapter herein: "History" for the views of the Church Fathers.

[71] See: Ladd, George Eldon. *The Blessed Hope*; Gundry, Robert. *The Tribulation and the Blessed Hope*. Also, note Gundry carefully with regard to Ephraem the Syrian in *First the Antichrist*.

[72] Walvoord, John F. *The Blessed Hope and the Tribulation*. Grand Rapids, MI: Zondervan, 1980. p. 24

[73] *Ibid*.

[74] Acts 17:31

[75] Rapture [See Glossary].

[76] 1 Cor 15:51-51; 1 Thess 4:16-17

inadvertently, Dr. Walvoord confessed to a reality: if the Fathers *really* believed in dispensational imminence, they would not have anticipated *more* tribulation, especially, as they did, since they were in actuality looking forward to the Antichrist.[77] Instead, they would have been asking "why are we still here?" They did not. In their trials they were looking first for the "man of sin," then for Christ to appear. This is exactly what the apostles believed and plainly what Paul wrote to the church at Thessalonica. The Fathers were much clearer in their thinking than Dr. Walvoord who seems to have a talent for confusing facts. Hence, we must go back to the scripture. Any dispute in this area can be settled by reading the Fathers themselves.

Since dispensational teaching regarding the imminent return of Christ and the rapture is closely associated with the fundamentalist movement, it would seem that it would hold a prominent place in their most important literature. This is not so. In 1909, Lyman Stewart saw the need to strengthen the Christian faith since Modernism was taking its toll on mainline denominations. He and his brother, Milton, worked with A. C. Dixon to produce a series of volumes defending conservative doctrine. In 1917, these works were published in four volumes which are still available.[78] In the chapter on "The Hope of the Church" by John McNicol and the chapter by Charles R. Erdman on "The Coming of Christ" the rapture is not even mentioned. Dr. Erdman presented a sound premillennial position which amply defends the orthodoxy of the New Testament writers. In dealing with imminency, he wrote that it "does *not* mean '*immediate*,' noting: "'Imminence' as related to our Lord's return indicates *uncertainty* as to time, but *possibility* of nearness."[79] He wrote this from the understanding of Paul's writings and Peter's who anticipated the "fiery judgments."[80] Though other works at this time were heavily in favor of the church being removed, it was not present in the major effort by the Stewarts to present a strong, authoritative reference for the conservative side of the church.

---

[77] Mt 24:15, the Antichrist is revealed at the mid-point of the last seven years. See Dan 9:26-27.

[78] Dixon, A. C.; Louis Meyer, R. A. Torrey, eds. *The Fundamentals*. 4 Volumes. Los Angeles, CA: The Bible Institute of Los Angeles, 1917.

[79] *The Fundamnentals*. Volume 4. p. 310 [emphasis in the original].

[80] *Ibid.* p. 311

This is a serious problem, since Lyman and Milton Stewart were fully supportive of dispensational teaching.

Norman Cohn from the University of Durham, England, in his historical survey of the millennium faced the issue of imminency and explained the context well. The imminence that was understood in the minds of believers from the earliest time was that of facing the Antichrist. This was accepted and drawn together with Jewish apocalyptic ideas and their interpretation of Daniel. Also taken into account were other prophetical writings and the Apocalypse by the Apostle John. It was John who warned that "the antichrist is coming."[81] This concept continued through the writing of Tertullian, the Montanists, and, later, Justin Martyr, Iraeneus, Lactantius, and Commodianus in the fifth century.[82] Lactantius wrote clearly expecting to see "that madman (antichrist)" coming against the righteous, and that after this "the heavens shall be opened in a tempest, and Christ shall descend with great power...."[83] Surely this is plain: first antichrist, then Christ. At this time, when Christ comes, the "godless" will be judged. The "signs" people watched for were those associated with the rise of antichrist.[84] Then, they knew Christ would soon arrive. When Dr. Thomas Ice attempted to define some of the thinking of the "Apostolic Fathers" in an article for the Pre-Trib Research Center, he admitted they were "postribulational."[85] Then, he attempted to superimpose on them "the pretribulational feature of imminence,"[86] as if they really believed and taught dispensational pre-tribulational imminence. They did not. Dr. Ice, like Dr. Walvoord, either does not understand their thinking at all, or he does, and is deliberately making an attempt to mislead us. Norman Cohn's statements are right on the mark. Lutheran scholar, Bengt Hagglund, offers a plain summary of this: "The eschatology of the Apostolic Fathers included the idea that *the*

---

[81] 1 Jn 2:18

[82] Cohn, Norman. *The Pursuit of the Millennium.* New York, NY: Harper & Bros., 1961. p. 8-13

[83] *Ibid.* p. 12

[84] *Ibid.* p. 21

[85] Ice, Thomas. "A Brief History of The Rapture." Pre-Trib Research Center, 2003. p. 1

[86] *Ibid.*

end of time was imminent, and some of them (Papias, Barnabas) also upheld the doctrine of an earthly millennium."[87] They were simply expecting Christ to return to judge the wicked, rescue the righteous, and establish His kingdom. Unfortunately, our popular prophecy experts have reconstructed these events and have left those who seek truth in a perilous state--without Biblical understanding.

Now, consider carefully that the very things that the Apostle Paul warned the Thessalonians about which were to occur before Christ's return were happening in their province. They were facing hatred, violence, extreme persecution, forced confessions, brothers being put to death, and the humiliation of denying Christ thanks to the governing authorities in Thessalonica. Read through his first Thessalonian letter and the first chapter of 2 Thessalonians. Then it will become evident that Paul's summary statements are there to provide them with consolation and hope as they face this.[88] He already warned them in person. With regard to the Antichrist, Paul asserted that his destruction will occur when the Lord comes in glory. This is the context of the second letter he sent to the church at Thessalonica. Paul soundly made this point as he described the return of the Lord in chapter one. We must never distort Paul's teaching in the letter in which he says is the same as being there in person--"when I was with you."[89] The reason Paul wrote these brief statements in this epistle is due to the fact he already taught them personally about the Second Coming, and they now required a reminder. Then, as now, deception is harmful and prevalent.[90] Again, Paul said, "Do not let anyone deceive you in any way," echoing the Lord's own words, "Watch out that no one deceives you."[91] At the present hour, an honest reconsideration of

---

[87] Hagglund, Bengt. *History of Theology*. St. Louis, MO: Concordia Pub. House, 1968. p. 23 [emphasis added].

[88] Read 2 Thessalonians 1:6-10 and the promised relief from horror and threat which they faced from Rome will become apparent. Paul describes the Second Coming in condensed form as he previously taught them. They were very concerned, since their persecution was real and daily. Note: 1 Thess 1:6; 2:14; 3:4; 2 Thess 1:4-5; 2:5.

[89] 2 Thess 2:5

[90] 2 Thess 2:2

[91] Mt 24:4

47

imminence is necessary, since the dispensational definition is misleading and offers a false sense of security with regard to the end of the age when evil will increase. Believers must not yield to recent ideas which parallel a softening of orthodoxy reminiscent of the fight against modernism two generations ago. In that light, Louis Berkhof reminds us that we may be looking at "a concoction of ancient errors, dressed up according to the latest fashion."[92] Some of the devil's schemes are ancient, yet they work well today, since he is a polished craftsman. Paul knew this and wrote plainly, so we would know what to look for at the end of the age. Clearly, the Apostle's efforts are to encourage us to use much discernment and hold to what he wrote and nothing less.[93] A. T. Robertson understood Paul's intention when he wrote: "The struggle with the Man of Sin was *first* to come."[94] This truth puts the idea of imminence on very shaky ground. We, too, should be able to discern Paul's intent and be on guard against deception.

Gottlieb Lunemann, writing in H. A. W. Meyer's Commentary on the New Testament, offered insight into the reasons for Paul's second epistle to the church in Thessalonica. He noted that in the first epistle the believers' anxiety about their friends' deaths had been assuaged, but now there was apprehension that the advent of the Lord was immediately at hand. Lunemann described the attitude of the Thessalonians to be based on "divine revelations," forged epistles, and false testimony alleged to be from an apostle.[95] He expressed "the state of matters which gave *occasion* for the composition of the second Epistle. Its *design* is threefold. *First*, The apostle wished--and this is the chief point--to oppose the disturbing and exciting error, as if the advent of Christ was even at the door, by further instructions. *Secondly*, He wished strongly and emphatically to dissuade from that unsettled, disorderly, and idle disposition into which the church had fallen. *Thirdly*, He wished by a laudatory recognition

---

[92] Berkhof, L. *Aspects of Liberalism*. Grand Rapids, MI: Wm. B. Eerdmans, 1951. p. 114

[93] 2 Thess 2:3; 2:15; 3:14

[94] Robertson, A.T. *Paul the Interpreter of Christ*. NY: George H. Doran, 1921. p. 118 [emphasis added].

[95] Quoted in: Goodwin, Frank J *A Harmony of the Life of St. Paul*. rpt. Grand Rapids, MI: Baker Book House, 1977. p. 206

of their progressive goodness to encourage them to steadfast perseverance."[96] As seen in Lunemann's comments, Paul was admonishing this church that the return of Christ was not imminent, that they must settle their minds on the order of events he taught them in person which he highlighted in the first chapter of this epistle,[97] and that they must remain firm in their faith not being moved by strange and conflicting reports. Simply, they must persevere until the time the Lord returns in glory--even to face the man of sin and the great rebellion.[98] Meyer's commentary was completed in 1859. Hence, Lunemann's interpretation is contemporary with that of Darby and the Plymouth Brethren. It also represents the intent of Paul and leads us to orthodoxy and the reality of a single return of the Lord without an imminent, secret rapture.

In the Old Testament, the prophet Habakkuk notably framed the issue of imminence by recording the Lord's concern about things to come. The future lies ahead, and the Lord reminds us: "For the revelation awaits an appointed time; it speaks of the end and will not prove false. Though it linger, wait for it; it will certainly come and will not delay."[99] The events at the end of this age are surely to happen--at the end and not before. At that time, there will be no delay. It can only be imminent at that time. The prophet Isaiah affirmed this, noting the time the Lord comes in glory to judge.[100] He provided assurance of the outcome and the timing: "The least of you will become a thousand, the smallest a mighty nation, I am the Lord; in its time I will do this swiftly."[101] When the Lord comes the second time, all the events will come about "swiftly." The church will see this unfold. It will be a heightened time of anticipation. We must wait until then. Urgent expectancy does not denote the type of imminence promoted today. The key is to understand the magnitude of what is yet to come. As Robert Chapman, friend and co-laborer with J. N. Darby, noted regarding the idea of an imminent secret rapture: "...I am ready, but it is not in the Bible."[102]

---

[96] Goodwin. *Ibid.* p. 207 [emphasis in the original].
[97] 2 Thess 1:6-10
[98] 2 Thess 2:3-4
[99] Hab 2:2-3
[100] Is 59:16-20
[101] Is 60:22

J. B. Lightfoot noted the attitude of the Apostles with regard to the return of the Lord as he expounded on Paul's first letter to the church in Thessalonica. Bishop Lightfoot was looking at the broad picture of their ministry which included their obligation to hold to the truth of the salvation message and to offer hope to those who understood the Lord's promise to return. While imminency is major component today in dispensational circles, it was not neglected in the first century. Rather, it was the apostolic rationale to properly balance it in context with the Scripture. Lightfoot wrote:

> The tone and temper exhibited by the Apostles in relation to this great event is intended as an example to the Church in all ages. She is to be ever watchful for the Advent of her Lord, yet ever to pursue the daily avocations of life in calmness and sobriety.[103]

Bishop Lightfoot expressed this reminder in the context of the Second Coming which he noted to be at the time of "the Resurrection and the Judgment" and not at some previous secret, any-moment return.[104] It is the central thought of judgment which disturbs people. Christians have a unique perspective of God's judicial plans offered to them through the Bible, yet it remains an ominous threat. This is why a rapture prior to tribulation is appealing. But, it is not a sound view. It remains an unsupportable theory. Knowledge of the scriptures without suppositional influence is the answer. The query posed by D. Martyn Lloyd-Jones is valid: "So I ask you again, are you prepared to, in your ignorance, to risk and jeopardize your eternal destiny on a theory or supposition?"[105] This question is useful as a filter for a host of other doctrines as well. Here, though, we must be willing to x-ray every facet of what has been claimed to be true as issued from the dispensational camp.

---

[102] Peterson, Robert L. *Robert Chapman. A Biography*. Neptune, NJ: Loizeaux Bros., 1995. p. 171. See Appendix for full reference. Also quoted in: Lang, G. H. *AnthonyNorris Groves. Saint & Pioneer*. 1949. rpt. Miami Springs, FL: Schoettle Pub. Co., 1988. p. 293

[103] Lightfoot, J. B. *Notes on the Epistles of St. Paul*. Peabody, MA. Hendrickson Pub., 1999. p. 67

[104] *Ibid.* p. 66

[105] Lloyd-Jones, D Martyn. *The Heart of the Gospel*. Wheaton, IL: Crossway Books, 1991. p. 105

Robert Cameron, who dealt extensively with the "any-moment" problem, raised an important point from a practical observation. He related the many times that the Lord kept His people in place during extremely trying times. On many occasions in history, believers have been present on the earth and have faced harsh struggles of the worst kind. The church through generations has faced severe persecution and violence. Dr. Cameron remarked: "The Tribulation will be at the time when the Antichrist and the powers of darkness are making their final effort to overthrow the government of God and to crush His faithful servants out of existence; and will the Church thus be deprived of the honour of showing her devotion and supreme loyalty at that crucial moment?"[106] The idea of imminence would be contrary to the call for believers to stand firm to the end--even at the risk of life. The Apostle John, who faced the terror of Rome, noted the Lord laying His life down for us. He then wrote: "And we ought to lay down our lives for our brothers."[107] All believers must take stock of the Biblical warnings for the future and be prepared to offer fully all that God has endowed them with--even their very life. The battle is the Lord's, yet we are His foot soldiers who are commissioned to do our utmost on the frontlines. To share in the victory, we must stand and defend the Faith in the day of evil.

Imminence? What better way to distract God's people and put them at ease when we have all been called to be on guard against the enemy's schemes[108] and hold to sound doctrine.[109] The devil's last bastion of hope is to corrupt God's people still on earth. He can do nothing against Christ. The Lord disarmed him at the Cross of Calvary. But Satan can do great harm by convoluting doctrine regarding events which have not yet come to pass and muddying the waters for the Body of Christ. What fertile ground for confusion.

---

[106] Cameron, Robert. *Scriptural Truth About The Lord's Return*. Chicago, IL: Fleming H. Revell, 1922. p. 95-96
[107] 1 Jn 3:16
[108] 2 Cor 2:11
[109] Titus 1:9

THE DANGER OF COMPLACENCY

There are many people who hear of the Second Coming of Christ, especially as it relates to the last seven year period, the Tribulation, and then do not give this topic a second thought. The response often heard is that the Lord will work all this out, and we should not concern ourselves. We are told that there are more important issues to deal with, *e.g.*, social justice, salvation, or the Great Commission. If a Bible teacher, a ministry, a tape, or a book comes along offering insight into the rapture, the seventieth week of Daniel, judgment, Christ's appearing in glory, or any other future event which requires serious consideration, complacent believers tell us it will all pan out. Sometimes, they are referred to as "pan-millennialists."[1] This is just synonymous term for those who are too dull to the truth to examine the Scriptures like the Bereans to see if these things are so.[2] Consequently, by default they have fallen into an attitude of complacency. At some future date, though, the Lord will move some of those holding the "pan" into the fire. For many, their comfort zone will change abruptly. It is dangerous for any believer to treat this doctrine regarding the Lord's return lightly. Jesus on more than one occasion told those who were with Him to "keep watch" and "be ready."[3] Well respected British preacher and Bible expositor, J. C. Ryle, noted that true Christians should observe events in their day. He defined it as "a duty," and "a sin to neglect it." He made the case from the Lord's own rebuke on the Jews for not "'discerning the signs of the times' (Matt 26:3)." Bishop Ryle clearly warned about "falling into their error."[4]

If we show concern here for those with an attitude of neutrality toward the return of the Lord, it must not be confused with a general disinterest in the propagation of the Gospel. The mission field historically has been filled for

---

[1] A colloquial term for those who assume God will take care of this--it will all pan out.
[2] Acts 17:11
[3] Matthew 24:35, 44; Luke 12:35. See chapter: "The Second Coming."
[4] Ryle, John Charles. *Ryle's Expository Thoughts on the Gospels. Mark.* rpt. Grand Rapids, MI: Zondervan Pub. House, n.d. p. 288

generations by men and women of all denominational persuasions with various eschatological beliefs. Their motive has been to take the Gospel message to those unreached peoples around the globe. This has been a major undertaking by various mission groups, especially since the 1800s when the debate about millennialism became a centerpiece of discussion. Premillennialists were in the forefront of this missionary endeavor regardless of their doctrinal stance on Christ's return being either before or after the tribulation. As George Marsden noted: "Premillennialists were enthusiastic about mission efforts because one of the signs of the end was that the Gospel would have been preached to all nations."[5] Mission conferences brought to light the challenges of accomplishing this vast task under the Great Commission. However, dispensational teaching about a rapture embedded a false hope in those reached, and when trouble came, as with the Communist takeover in China, thousands of Christians perished. Many thought the Lord would rescue them. He did not. Their false sense of security was sustained by the pre-trib theory which led many to think they would never face the horror of extreme persecution and mass executions. Their antichrist was Mao Zedong.[6] In the early 1950s, China Inland Mission was forced to withdraw its workers. The reality of facing Christian persecution is on the rise today. Open Doors, a ministry for the persecuted church, reported that the number of martyrs doubled from 2012 to 2013.[7] It has increased since then, and other agencies report numbers in the thousands. Today, with cold blooded executions by Islamic groups in the Middle East, no western Christian should think they are immune. Europe is fully at risk. Britain, France, Germany, and Sweden are prime targets, openly welcoming Islamic immigrants. The grand design of Islam is to kill all those who refuse to submit. This conflict is ongoing and is much akin to what the early believers faced from Rome. No Christian should minimize this danger, especially with the baseless, popular view of a rapture before trouble starts. The early church was warned about facing extreme evil. It

---

[5] Marsden, George M. *Fundamentalism and American Culture. The Shaping of Twentieth-Century Evangelicalism: 1870-1925.* New York, NY: Oxford University Press, 1982. p. 68

[6] See: Appendix for comments from Corrie ten Boom regarding persecution in China.

[7] www.reuters.com/article/2014/01/08/us-christianty-persecution-report-idBREA070PB20140108

is a genuine, longstanding warning for us. We must not be complacent about current or approaching events.

Late Bible teacher, Chuck Missler, a staunch promoter of a pre-trib rapture, published an article by John Loeffler which cautioned against a faulty understanding of the rapture. Loeffler's premise called attention to what he described as the "Rapture Myth." This would be a false assumption that the church would not see any "trial, suffering, conflict," or "do spiritual battle," because "we aren't going to endure God's wrath in the time of tribulation." He, then, stated "we may well endure the *world's* wrath before Christ returns."[8] Within this portion of the article Loeffler freely made a concession that the Body of Christ will be on earth to face wrath from men--and that there are those who teach full exemption from all trouble. Missler and Loeffler knew that there are sufficient scripture passages that point to the church facing peril at the end and that much of the church globally suffers now. Also known by them is the effect of the popular teaching that believers will not face the antichrist. Loeffler branded this false assumption of exemption from wrath as "comfort." It is a type of escape which undermines all facets of the teaching of the return of Christ. Consequently, we learn from Loeffler's article that someone with a pre-trib view knows trouble precedes the Second Coming, the Church is not exempt, and due to the popular rapture model, there is an attitude of complacency that has settled into the minds of many believers.

Writing in *Things To Come*, J. Dwight Pentecost from Dallas Theological Seminary highlighted his misunderstanding of the peril the body of Christ will face. He was building on the claims of C. I. Scofield who boldly stated there is "no syllable of Scripture which affirms that the church will enter the great tribulation."[9] In his attempt to promote the idea that the epistles were silent on the harsh tribulation in the seventieth week, Pentecost went on to say:

---

[8] Missler, Chuck. *Personal Update. The News Journal of Koinonia House.* Loeffler, John. "The Rapture Myth." Vol. 12. No. 3, March 2000. P. 6-7 [emphasis in the original].

[9] Pentecost, J. Dwight. *Things To Come. A Study in Biblical Eschatology.* Grand Rapids, MI: Zondervan Pub. House, 1971. p. 211

Inasmuch as the persecutions of this age [when Paul wrote] and the wrath of the seventieth week vary in kind and character, not just in intensity, it is not sufficient to say that if one is prepared for the lesser he will also be prepared for the greater. The silence in the Epistles which would leave the church unprepared for the tribulation argues for her absence from that period altogether.[10]

Please note that Pentecost had listed various verses in the same section which in context are in direct opposition to his extreme claim. Paul warned the church in 2 Thessalonians of those points he had taught them previously in person. They thought they were soon to face the Antichrist and worse.[11] What Scofield and Pentecost have done is neutralize the extreme persecution the early church faced in their attempt to remove the church before any trouble would arise. However, the Thessalonians and others were being executed for their belief in Christ and were rightfully concerned about the hour they were in. Pentecost blindly created a claim from "silence" with his own assertion when Paul laid out the reality. With this reconstruction of Paul's intent, Pentecost engendered support for a sense of complacency which is detrimental to understanding the nature and scope of the dangers Paul and these believers faced.

This neglectful disconnect regarding the danger of full persecution was also propagated in earlier days by J. N. Darby and William Kelly who edited Darby's writings and wrote extensively on his own. Kelly provided the seed bed of distortion when he described the Thessalonians as being "ignorant as to the details of the Lord's coming" and "not acquainted with the details of prophecy."[12] He claimed this in spite of Paul's own statement that he had told them "these things."[13] This allowed Kelly to insert his ideas which in context totally ignored how and why the Thessalonians were being put to death. Kelly asserted "they were so full of the expectation of a returning Saviour, that they

---

[10] Pentecost. *Ibid.* p. 211
[11] 2 Thess 1:6-10; 2:3-4
[12] Kelly, W. *Lectures on the Second Coming and the Kingdom of the Lord and Saviour Jesus Christ.* London: W. H. Broom, 1876. p. 145-146. He implied that experts in his day (the 1800s) knew what Paul really meant.
[13] 2 Thess 2:5

never so much as contemplated the thought of any from among them dying. They were just then startled by the fact that some brethren did fall asleep"[14] This is a very glaring oversight, since it makes the church where Paul taught to be a church at rest except for a few untimely deaths. With representatives of the Empire demanding a life or death oath for allegiance to Caesar, Kelly's claims are without merit.

The early Church was concerned about the Lord's return. There is no question about this. But, believers then were not centered on the issue of imminence in the way our popular teachers today describe their beliefs. First century Christians had a genuine personal concern due to more immediate difficulties, since they were already undergoing persecution in different forms courtesy of the Roman Empire and, for some, their own countrymen.[15] History attests to the harsh persecution in many of the provinces in the Roman Empire. Imperial Rome was held up for allegiance, and Caesar worship had increased, especially in the western regions of the empire. In the provinces, the deified Caesars, the *Divi Imperatores*, were "the gods of the state and, along with the *Genius* of the reigning emperor, were the divinities which were everywhere worshipped."[16] This automatically caused polarity between those who looked to God the Creator and those who looked to Caesar. An example of this can be seen during the trial of Jesus when He was before Pilate. One of the devices the Jews employed to coerce the Roman governor to rule in favor of Christ's death was the threat of disloyalty to Caesar. Pilate was attempting to free Jesus, but the Jews continued to shout, "If you let this man go, you are no friend of Caesar. Anyone who claims to be a king opposes Caesar."[17] Pilate relented. He knew that the hint of neglect to his senatorial appointment as Roman procurator or a mention of dishonor to Caesar on his part would be akin to treason.[18] Consequently, Jesus was handed over to be crucified. Dr. Thomas M. Lindsay

---

[14] Kelly. *Lectures on the Second Coming....* p. 147

[15] 1 Thess 2:14; 2 Cor 11:26

[16] Lindsay, Thomas M. *The Church and the Ministry in the Early Centuries.* London: Hodder & Stoughton, 1907. p. 346. See also: Deissmann, Adolf. *Light from the Ancient East.* 1927. rpt. Grand Rapids, MI: Baker Book House, 1980. p. 342ff

[17] John 19:12

[18] Lindsay. *The Church.* p. 348

offered a succinct picture describing the plight of believers who had to face the Roman Empire:

> Only Jews and Christians refused to bend before the new divinities. It was this imperial state religion which confronted Christian confessors everywhere; refusal to sacrifice to the emperor (either the living ruler in the East, or the *Divi* and the *Genius* in the West) was the supreme test to which Christians were subjected, and which produced martyrdoms....[19]

Christians were easy prey. They were known in the community and became exposed by their witness of Christ. The very name "Christian" was sufficient to bring criminal charges.[20] Tacitus noted that Christians were considered "enemies of the human race" holding to dangerous superstition.[21] Celsus referenced their "contempt of law and custom in secret associations."[22] History records that according to Seutonius' testimony, "...in Nero's police regulations Christians as such were classed with common criminals, and that implies that Christianity was *already* regarded as practically proof of crime."[23] This continued for many years. Peter mentioned this in his first epistle, as he reminded the church not to be surprised by their "painful trial" and "suffering." Believers faced this because of "the name of Christ." This was not difficulty, hardship, or distress caused by natural events. It was Rome. Peter said, "...if you suffer as a *Christian*, do not be ashamed, but praise God that you bear *that name.*"[24] E. G. Selwyn in his extensive examination of the Greek text in his commentary on Peter's first epistle described the realism of persecution early

---

[19] Lindsay. *The Church.* p. 348

[20] Tenney, Merrill C. *New Testament Times.* Grand Rapids, MI: Baker Books, 2004. p. 126-127. Tenney notes that the "very name 'Christian' became synonymous with subversion," and that they "came to be classed with criminals."

[21] Lietzmann, Hans. *A History of the Early Church.* London: Lutterworth Press, 1961. Vol. I. p. 155

[22] *Ibid.*

[23] Purves, George T. *Christianity in the Apostolic Age.* 1900. rpt. Grand Rapids, MI: Baker Book House, 1955. p. 279 [emphasis added].

[24] 1 Peter 4:12-19 [emphasis added]. Note also: Mt 5:11-12

in the history of the church. He pointed to the similarities between 1 Thessalonians and 1 Peter in this regard and noted "...that the inevitability of persecution was a regular part of the Apostolic teaching from the beginning."[25] He connected the record by Luke of persecution in the Book of Acts to that which is evident in Peter and Paul's letters. Selwyn stated that the persecution and suffering "have been experienced also in other parts of the Church" and was not a surprise or shock to believers. It was an expected "part of the Christian vocation."[26]

True believers disdained the imperial cult[27] and were bound by divine ownership[28] not to bend their knee but to Christ. They were marked by their stand against the "theocratic despotism"[29] of the day. The challenge they were forced to endure was a life or death proposition. A confession of Christ was the touchstone whereby believers could be quickly identified. It became a simple tool for criminal conviction by confessing "Caesar is Lord" or "Christ is Lord." This became a brief and final judicial process. The confession of Christ was a "mortal insult" considered "treason to the Emperor."[30] The Apostle Paul noted this reality when he wrote his first letter to the church in Corinth. He said that "...no one speaking by the Spirit of God says, 'Jesus be cursed,' and no one can say 'Jesus is Lord,' except by the Holy Spirit."[31] In that context, he mentions "dumb idols." These would be the local deities and those representing Caesar that cannot speak. Pagans swore allegiance to them, but no true Christian could. A Christian would rather face death, which Paul mentioned in his second epistle to the church in Corinth. When he was in Asia, Paul stated

---

[25] Selwyn, Edward Gordon. *The First Epistle of St. Peter. The Greek Text with Introduction, Notes and Essays*. New York, NY: Macmillan, 1969. p. 441-450

[26] *Ibid.* p. 450

[27] Angus, S. *The Environment of Early Christianity*. New York, NY: Charles Scribner's Sons, 1917. p. 85-89, describes the revival of Roman religion with emperor worship as a focal point; the cult of the emperors.

[28] 1 Corinthians 6:19-20

[29] Workman, Herbert B. *Persecution in the Early Church*. Cincinnati, OH: Jennings & Graham, 1906. p. 98

[30] Workman. *Persecution*. p. 101

[31] 1 Corinthians 12:3

that he and those with him "despaired even of life," and they "felt the sentence of death."[32] Since Paul noted this to be a "deadly peril," the incident was a close call with a charge from the authorities to confess either Caesar or Christ as Lord. He and his companions were delivered.[33] Frederic Godet hinted at the exclusive nature of the words as Paul employs them, especially regarding the Lord being addressed by name: Jesus. He noted the abbreviated language which would apply: "Jesus accursed!" or "Jesus Lord!" This was the confession formula once a Christian was apprehended and forced to bow to Caesar or confess Christ.[34]

Sir William M. Ramsay wrote of this[35] as it related to Paul's encounter with the Roman authorities in Philippi where the Apostle and Silas caused a major disturbance. When brought before the magistrates, they were charged with "advocating customs unlawful for us Romans to accept or practice."[36] Paul and Silas were "Jews" and were "throwing the city into an uproar."[37] In the process, they were severely beaten, thrown into prison, and guarded carefully.[38] Their release was secured by an earthquake, however when the magistrates learned they were Roman citizens, they were hastily encouraged to move on. If their citizenship was not Roman, they may have faced the ominous challenge of "Caesar" or "Christ." They, nonetheless, risked their lives. They were not complacent, nor were they thinking about an imminent return of Christ. Their focus was on continuing the proclamation of the Gospel.

Paul and Silas, then, arrived in Thessalonica. Here the opposition became hostile, and the conflict escalated due to charges that they had "caused trouble all over the world" and now were "defying Caesar's decrees, saying there is

---

[32] 2 Corinthians 1:5-11

[33] *Ibid.*

[34] Godet, Frederic Louis. *Commentary on First Corinthians.* 1889. rpt. Grand Rapids, MI: Kregel Pub., 1979. p. 612

[35] Ramsay, Sir William M. *The Church in the Roman Empire.* 1897. rpt. Grand Rapids, MI: Baker Book House, 1954. p. 250

[36] Acts 16:21

[37] Acts 16:20

[38] Acts 16:23

another king, one called Jesus."[39] Again, these servants of Christ were in the crosshairs of Rome.[40] The death threat was obvious. At night, however, the brothers at Thessalonica sent Paul and Silas on to Berea.[41] We emphasize this, because they left behind a church which would have to live or die holding to the new life they possessed in Christ which stood opposed to imperial Rome, its deities, and Caesar himself. It was no longer two men facing hostility, trials, suffering, and persecution--but an entire church with each believer at risk.

Once brought before the authorities, a Christian would face a three-part test. First, an oath of allegiance to the Roman gods was administered; then, an offering of frankincense and wine was made before images of the gods and the emperor; third, the believer was to curse Jesus Christ.[42] As noted above, Paul alluded to this when he later wrote the Corinthians. To them he warned: those who said "Jesus be cursed" were not speaking by the Holy Spirit. Likewise, those who confessed "Jesus is Lord" did so by the Holy Spirit.[43] He was highlighting the exact moment of the trial by the Roman authorities and the result. Under Roman justice, the death sentence was carried out immediately.[44] All this was a serious threat to Paul and Silas. Sir William Ramsay noted: "Moreover, Paul at Thessalonica had found the Roman administration the enemy of the Gospel. He was accused of treason to the Emperor and of setting up a rival Emperor, and was practically condemned in absence by the magistrates. Their action, covered by the name of loyalty to Caesar, made it impossible for him to return soon to Thessalonica, eager as he was to do so."[45]

---

[39] Acts 17:6-7

[40] Tenney. *New Testament Times*. p. 280. "The Jewish leaders knew how to play upon the prejudices of their Roman neighbors by suggesting that Paul and Silas were subversive persons who were advocating the rule of another king." This ploy escalated the threat of capital charges considerably.

[41] Acts 17:10

[42] Benko, Stephen. *Pagan Rome and the Early Christians*. Bloomington, IN: Indiana University Press, 1986. p. 10

[43] 1 Cor 12:3

[44] Benko. *Pagan Rome*. p. 1

[45] Ramsay, Sir William M. *The Cities of St. Paul. Their Influence on His Life and Thought*. 1908. rpt. James Family Christian Pub., n.d. p. 426

This is the environment to which Paul addressed his two epistles to the church at Thessalonica which the church today must reconsider in the light of this open hostility. Ramsay also noted: "The history of the Empire needs to be rewritten from this point of view: the relation of the government to the new universal religion determined the vicissitudes of its fate. The historians who write the story of the Empire devote an occasional footnote, or a paragraph, or a special chapter to what are called the 'Persecutions'. They miss entirely the deeper facts of the situation."[46]

Our failure to comprehend the overwhelming threat of death--martyrdom--to our early brethren in the church--dulls our present-day insight into their realities. This should alter the way we interpret Paul's letters to the Thessalonians where he often mentions the trials, suffering, and persecution to which we have assigned a much milder meaning. He wrote to people who were *daily* faced with death.[47] Today, the church should undertake another reading of 1Thessalonians 4:13, where the Apostle encourages those believers not to grieve like the rest of men "about those who fall asleep." These were most likely not natural deaths, but executions of those who refused to deny Christ and to honor Caesar and allegiance to Rome. Paul was writing to a group of potential martyrs. "The word 'martyr' comes from the Greek word *martus*, which means 'witness'."[48] This is not witnessing as we would incorporate today into an evangelism program, but it was testifying for Christ--at the risk of life. Early church *witness* meant death.[49] Our awareness of this should place the entire epistle into a much more critical position and cause us to reconsider the future implications of persecution for ourselves, since the actual events Paul warned of in both Thessalonian epistles are yet to come.

Dr. Donald Grey Barnhouse amplified this perilous threat in his commentary

---

[46] Ramsay. *The Cities of St. Paul.* p. 71
[47] Gives a clearer meaning to 1 Cor 15:31 and Rm 8:36
[48] Ruffin, C. Bernard. *The Days of the Martyrs.* Huntington, IN: Our Sunday Visitor, 1985. p. 1
[49] Vine/Unger/White in *Vine's Complete Expository Dictionary of Old & New Testament Words.* Nashville, TN: Thomas Nelson, 1996. p. 681: "'martyr,' one who bears witness by his death."

on Thessalonians:

> We know from Pliny the Elder that it was in Thessalonica that the first Gentiles were killed in the Roman Empire, because it was the local Roman Governor in that part of the country who said that every Christian had to bow before a statue of Augustus Caesar.[50]

Note the Apostle Paul mentioning the threat of this to those at Thessalonica, as he wrote encouraging them as they faced severe trials: "In fact, when we were with you, we kept telling you that you would be persecuted. And it turned out that way as you well know" [1 Thess 3:4].

Paul was thankful for them in their stand, since it showed that God's word was at work in them as believers.[51] His pastoral concern was clear as he strove to offer encouragement from afar. He wanted them to continue their stand and be strong in the face of opposition from the hostile acts of pagans, Jews, and the Roman authorities in this city: "For you, brothers, became imitators of God's churches in Judea, which are in Christ Jesus: You suffered from your own countrymen the same things those churches suffered from the Jews, who killed the Lord Jesus and the prophets and also drove us out" [1 Thess 2:14].

Following this, in 1 Thessalonians three, Paul resonated with his own sense of encouragement--even in the face of his own persecution--that the Thessalonians were standing firm in their faith.[52] He was clear that they "are standing firm in the Lord"[53] In other words, these believers were not complacent. They could not be, since their testimony was known to the church and noted by their enemies. Hence, they faced hostility, trials, and persecution. The Lord Jesus warned about this, so all believers would stand firm in the face of evil with Himself being the sovereign example: "I have told you these

---

[50] Barnhouse. Donald Grey. *Thessalonians. An Expositional Commentary.* Grand Rapids, MI: Zondervan, 1988. p. 89

[51] 1 Thess 2:13

[52] 1 Thess 3:7

[53] 1 Thess 3:8

things, so that in me you may have peace. In this world you will have trouble. But take heart! I have overcome the world."[54] Paul knew the Lord Jesus as his model[55] and passed this on to the Thessalonians. This apostle well knew hostility and persecution. He had no apprehension about this reality facing other churches and individuals as well. As soon as Paul was converted on his notable journey to Damascus, originally undertaken to further persecute the church, he was at risk of life and limb. Once regenerated by the Holy Spirit, he faced extreme hostility from the Jews there due to his preaching and "proving that Jesus is the Christ."[56] This resulted in a conspiracy by those in Damascus to murder the newly born apostle, and his firsthand experience with persecution was immediate.[57] This was also the case in Jerusalem. Before Paul departed for Damascus, when he was Saul of Tarsus under the authority of the chief priests to put the saints in prison and vote for their death,[58] he was welcome and accepted. But, as Paul the Apostle? No! He faced death *himself*, again, after "speaking boldly in the name of the Lord" and debating the Grecian Jews.[59] They attempted to kill him. Now, Paul was no longer welcome in Jerusalem. His life was at risk, and the brothers aided him sending him off to Tarsus.[60] These events, early in Paul's new life as a believer, show us without question his life was immediately at risk, and he faced persecution, because he was open, bold, and never complacent about his call or his obligation to speak out publicly about the Lord Jesus Christ. Like a shadow, persecution of all kinds followed him to the end. Paul was candid about this when he wrote to the Corinthians: "I face death every day--yes as surely as I boast about you in Christ Jesus our Lord."[61] He was not alone in this. He affirmed this when he wrote to the church in Rome: "For your sake we face death all day long; we are considered as sheep to be slaughtered."[62]

---

[54] John 16:33; also, Luke 21:12; Matthew 5:10-12

[55] 1 Cor 11:1

[56] Acts 9:22

[57] Acts 9:23

[58] Acts 26:9-11

[59] Acts 9:28-29

[60] Acts 9:30

[61] 1 Cor 15:31

When we see Paul traveling and teaching later, we observe the same sense of urgency and the same consistent devotion to the kind of warnings he offers the Thessalonians. He expressed this to the Corinthians: "...in danger from my own countrymen, in danger from Gentiles; in danger in the city, in danger in the country, in danger at sea; and in danger from false brothers."[63] Paul told them this, because he "was constantly on the move," and so the church at Corinth would know that this problem with persecution and the threats from various enemies was not in just one place. It was occurring in many locations in the Roman Empire. Just as Paul had been in Thessalonica, he also had been in Corinth and knew their circumstances relating to persecution. He mentioned "the present crisis" to them[64] as an encouraging note. His epistle to the church in Rome, likewise, noted the shared challenge of persecution. Paul pointed to "our present sufferings."[65] In other words, they too were at risk and could not afford to be indifferent. This is in part why Paul was permitted to suffer as he did, so the church of his day, and we at this hour, would know the danger which is coming and not to fall into a state of complacency.

Paul wrote his second epistle to the church in Thessalonica and commended them as they endured the trials which came against them. These threats also faced many other believers, like Paul, who became enemies of Rome. They were at risk from pagans, Gentiles, and their Jewish brethren. He made clear the divine purpose:

> All this is evidence that God's judgment is right, and as a result you will be counted worthy of the kingdom of God, for which you are suffering [2 Thess 1:5].

Paul expressed the sovereign purpose for their extreme suffering as "evidence" of the righteous nature of God in using their perseverance under trial as proof of His ability to judge aright--even with suffering. The apostle also noted that

---

[62] Rom 8:36
[63] 2 Cor 11:26
[64] 1 Cor 7:26
[65] Rom 8:18

God will "pay back" those who cause this--evidence of the ultimate retribution of God at the end of the age.[66] The persecution is temporary--judgment is *eternal*. Theologian, Theodor Zahn, commented on the conditions in Thessalonica at the time Paul was writing the two epistles. He wrote that conditions there were "growing worse from day to day."[67] The shift in treatment by Rome with increased hostility and persecution accounts for the tone of Paul's second letter in which he reminded them of his previous teaching regarding extreme suffering.

In addition to this, consideration should be given to Luke's account of the riot in Thessalonica in Acts seventeen. This is where Paul and Silas were threatened with judgment for "defying Caesar's decrees."[68] The entire context of Luke's narrative deals with the confrontation with the civil authorities--high treason. It is important to note that something never mentioned is illness. This record by Luke carefully provides the evidence that the apostles' lives were threatened by Rome and not disease or illness. Luke being a physician and a meticulous historian would likely make note of health issues if it were of importance. Rather, he details the life and death issue for the two apostles. No malady is mentioned. Hence, the actual threat of death for their defiance of Rome is accurately presented in the discourse [Acts 17:1-9]. This fact helps to provide a clearer meaning to Paul's later statement to the Thessalonians whom he does not want to "be ignorant about those who fall asleep."[69] A.T. Robertson noted the serious nature of this as he described this encounter between Paul and Caesar in Thessalonica. He wrote that Paul observed "the worship of the Roman Emperor" there, and some of his language may have reflected his indignation in the synagogue.[70] Robertson also pointed out that it was here in Thessalonica "the shadow of Rome was cast on the cross," and Paul began to face this reality.[71] This was a serious incident which Paul did not forget. He

---

[66] 2 Thess 1:6-10

[67] Zahn, Theodor. *Introduction to the New Testament*. 1909. rpt. Minneapolis, MN: Klock & Klock, 1977. Vol. 1, p. 222

[68] Acts 17:7

[69] 1 Thess 4:13

[70] Robertson, A.T. *Luke the Historian in the Light of Research*. NY: Charles Scribner's Son, 1936. p. 197

personally faced off with Roman authority here. His concern about this is reflected in many of his epistles. He knew that the power of Rome was now to be a formidable opponent of the church. Luke verifies the death threat in Acts seventeen. As Paul's companion and one of his caretakers, he knew that the reality of execution by Rome was a more serious danger than a medical problem. Luke was not worried that Paul would perish from ill health. On the contrary, it was more likely to be brought about by Caesar. As Paul's life played out, indeed he appealed to Caesar and to Rome he went, apparently in good health.[72] Yet, through Paul's many trials--"persecutions" among them--he said he delighted in them: "For when I am weak, then I am strong."[73]

Luke helps us to see the full color of this event in Thessalonica as it transpired, when the local rulers, "politarchs," in this "free city"[74] were quick to respond to this incident, since they were "thrown into turmoil."[75] This confrontation became the flashpoint for Paul's full recognition[76] of the conflict between the Lord Jesus and the Roman emperor.[77] He now knew there would be danger everywhere, and this hastened his departure from the city. This adds to his warning to the church in Ephesus, another free city, where he stated that we are in a struggle against the rulers, authorities, and the "powers of this dark world" and, also, those in the "heavenly realms."[78] Paul learned in Thessalonica the

---

[71] *Ibid.*

[72] Acts 25:11. Paul's illness, an eye problem, was not life threatening, Gal 4:13-15.

[73] 2 Cor 12:10

[74] Robertson, A.T. *Luke the Historian in the Light of Research.* NY: Charles Scribner's Son, 1936. p. 195ff. Free cities in the Empire were self-governed, yet answered to Rome, leaving much power with the magistrate himself.

[75] Acts 17:8

[76] Tenney. *New Testament Times.* p. 278. Tenney notes Paul's previous conflict in Philippi "may have been the first official contact with the Roman colonial system in the course of his ministry." The subsequent event in Thessalonica would have amplified Paul's understanding of the brutal "Roman pattern" of justice.

[77] "The Roman Emperor was worshipped here as elsewhere and Paul proclaimed Jesus as Lord, not Caesar (1 Cor 12:1-3)." See: Robertson, A.T. *Paul the Interpreter of Christ.* NY: George H. Doran, 1921. p. 121.

[78] Eph 6:12

meaning of this "struggle." Luke's faithful depiction of these events aids us to see the true spiritual conflict behind this hostility from the Roman authorities. We find this genuine reality amplified in the Thessalonian epistles which explain why Paul wrote to them early on, shortly after his visit in 52 A.D. They were facing much persecution, and the brothers were at risk for their lives from Rome. The shadow of death was cast by Rome and not illness. Again, when Paul writes, "Brothers, we do not want you to be ignorant about those who fall asleep...,"[79] his concern was death through execution--not natural causes, disease, or by some accidental circumstance. Since he wrote very soon after leaving them (52 A.D.), it would not allow enough time to elapse for a church to face large-scale attrition through natural deaths within its newly formed congregation. He ends the chapter writing: "Therefore, encourage each other with these words."[80] They needed hope in the face of Rome--not death alone. Surely, in the light of this, the thought of complacency was not a desirable Thessalonian attribute, another reason for the apostle reminding them not to be idle.[81]

In his comments on the church at Thessalonica, J. B. Lightfoot concisely summarized the concerns that Paul had as he ministered to them:

> His preaching seems to have turned mainly upon one point--the approaching judgment, the coming of Christ. They had been invited at their conversion to await the Son of God from heaven. They were warned that He would come, as a thief in the night. At the same time they were told that many things must happen first, that Antichrist must gather strength, that 'the Restrainer' must be removed. Around this one doctrine the Apostle's practical warnings and exhortations had clustered. He warned them that they must suffer tribulation, the tribulation which was to usher in the end of all things, the persecution from the power of Antichrist. He bade them abstain from impurity lest they

---

[79] 1 Thess 4:13

[80] 1 Thess 4:18

[81] 1 Thess 5:14

should find vengeance in the day of the Lord's coming. He had charged them to walk worthily of God who was calling them to His kingdom and glory.[82]

This effort by Paul to encourage and comfort believers is proof that he was always aware of the state of the church. He was burdened by the challenges they faced in every congregation. This is demonstrated when he bade farewell to the Ephesian elders at Miletus in Acts twenty; also, when he considered the individual believers serving elsewhere after he departed as noted in his letters. We see this as Paul prayed for them, concerned "for all the churches."[83] The Thessalonians were no different. Paul wrote of his concern for them and "could stand it no longer. I sent to find out about your faith."[84] This tells us without question that there was no apathy in the Apostle Paul's ministry. Likewise, he never passed on to others liberty with their work to become lax about those things which conformed to the Gospel and the essentials of sound doctrine. His warning to those who were idle was purposed to call each believer into action.[85] We also see this as he passed the torch along to Timothy: "Preach the Word: be prepared in season and out,"[86] and when he directed Titus: "You must teach what is in accord with sound doctrine."[87] This would include doctrine regarding the Second Coming, the rapture, and judgment. These are areas where no one is permitted to be complacent. Paul emphasized this thought when writing the church at Rome, bringing the Gospel together with the reality of judgment: "This will take place on the day when God judges men's secrets through Jesus Christ, as *my gospel* declares."[88] Paul's gospel included judgment--a sound reminder to the church in Rome and to us that each of us will be accountable on the day Christ returns. This leaves no room for any believer to take these

---

[82] Lightfoot, J. B. *Biblical Essays.* 1893. rpt. Grand Rapids, MI: Baker Book House, 1979. p. 260

[83] 2 Cor 11:28; Note, also, the many individuals named in Romans chapter 16.

[84] 1 Thess 2:5

[85] 1 Thess 5:14; 2 Thess 3:6

[86] 2 Tim 4:2

[87] Titus 2:1

[88] Rom 2:16 [emphasis added].

matters lightly.[89]

Notably, the scriptural record reflects the hostility which was a recurring danger for the young churches. With the demand for allegiance to the Empire before them, believers understood the reality of pledging their lives for the Lord's purposes or submitting to the dictates of Rome. The former would translate quickly into a capital offense and require their life. The latter would allow them to return home. The Apostle Paul knew that many chose the former. Consequently this heightens the tension when he writes to the young Thessalonian church about those who are alive and remain. He states this twice in his first letter to the Thessalonians: (1) "we who are still alive;" (2) "we who are still alive and are left."[90] The loss of life was courtesy of Caesar. It was Nero who was ruling at this time. During this period, persecution was on the increase, since the Roman court had ruled Christianity was a threat to the state--"tantamount to an attack on the Roman way of life, and thenceforward Christians could at *any time* be brought to trial on a capital charge."[91] This raises a present-day need to rethink these events, since, as Paul described them, they are to occur shortly before the return of the Lord, and this is a cataclysmic event set to unfold in the future, possibly in our day. The judicial challenge to our faith at that time will not be "Caesar" or "Christ." It will be "Christ" or "Antichrist."[92] Paul actually was writing for us. So we must not slip into a state of apathy and fail to be prepared. Paul's overall concern was to be sure that the church was alert and ready to face the antichrist. This is not the case today with the pre-trib view which has supplanted the warnings of scripture. In their place, we have false comfort and an attitude of immunity which is not Biblical. It is dangerous. The church today must discard any form of deception, no matter the source, and stand in the plain sense of scripture.

This excursion with Paul and his companions helps us to see the extent of the

---

[89] 2 Cor 5:10; Rm 14:12

[90] 1 Thess 4:15 and 4:17 respectively.

[91] Caird, G.B. *The Apostolic Age.* [Studies in Theology]. London: Gerald Duckworth Co., Ltd., 1955. p. 164. [emphasis added].

[92] Rev 11:2; 13:5-8; 13:11-17; Mt 24:15. This will be the final 42 months of severe suffering and rampant persecution.

danger he and the churches faced daily. This is an historical reference to use as a measurement for interpreting the warnings Paul and the other apostles gave us. They amplify the words of Jesus in His Olivet Discourse. Yet, further to all this, the Apostle John provided words for us in his Apocalypse. John was given a broad and graphic overview of things in the future which the church will face. His authority to write these things was from the Lord Himself. John was taken up for a heavenly perspective of the events which will culminate at the end of the age when the Lord comes to judge. The visions he was privileged to see included the persecution of the church. At that time, believers, denoted as "saints," will face major hostility from the "beast" who will "exercise his authority for forty-two months."[93] He will be empowered by Satan and wage war against the saints.[94] The saints referred to are believers--those who know Him and have their names written in the Lamb's book of life.[95] This is not just persecution of Israel. It will include all those alive at the time.[96] All who are Godly will be affected. A second beast will enforce this, also under the power of Satan. A mark will be given to those who worship and serve the beast, referred to elsewhere as the Antichrist[97] and the man of sin.[98] Others-- believers--will be imprisoned or put to death.[99] John's vision yields a true picture of this, as Christians face suffering, persecution, trial, and death, all at the hands of the evil, global system of the Antichrist. There is no evidence in scripture offering the church an exemption from this--unless someone has been brought under the deception that the church has already been removed. That thought is entirely set aside by Paul--and here, by John. The Lord, too, issued His warning to us that we would see the Antichrist.[100] These admonitions must not be ignored. They are a body of core truths to bring us to recognize the fact that the church will contend with the Antichrist. Can any believer ignore this and be complacent about personally examining these warnings?

---

[93] Rev 13:1-8
[94] Dan 7:21-22, 25
[95] Dan 12:1; Rev 13:8; 21:27
[96] Lk 21:35; Rev 13:7-8
[97] 1 Jn 2:18 2 Thess 2:3-4
[98] 2 Thess 2:3-4
[99] Rev 13:9-10
[100] Mt 24:15

Just as the prophet Amos warned the "complacent in Zion" of approaching danger, so the words of the New Testament must aid readers to be sober in looking at what is to come. He was concerned about those who had a false sense of security.[101] All believers today must be secure in the truth alone, not a theory. The Lord spoke through His prophet Zephaniah of the time when He will "search Jerusalem with lamps and punish those who are complacent."[102] They were apathetic and thought the Lord would "do nothing either good or bad." Their indifferent attitude ensured personal judgment. As the church has evolved today many ignore individual responsibility as believers. This is a dangerous position for the Lord's people to be in. When "the Day" comes, it "will be the same for priest as for people, for master as for servant."[103] We must examine the scriptures and recognize the truth of the words from the Lord's servants who have amply warned us.

---

[101] Amos 6:1
[102] Zeph 1:12
[103] Is 24:2

THE PITFALL OF EAGERNESS

Another component of the conflict surrounding the viability of the pre-trib view is the sense of urgent anticipation regarding the rapture. People like the idea of escaping the horrors of the Antichrist and not facing heavy-duty persecution, so they are eager to be removed by the rapture and not participate in the horrors of Revelation chapter thirteen. Obviously, no one wants to endure the kind of wrath described by the Apostle John in the Apocalypse. Likewise, no one wishes to face what we read in the prophets as they describe judgment in the Old Testament. We might think the Gospel references and the epistles' brief recounting of what is to come is easier to digest than what came from Patmos or the pen of an Old Covenant spokesman. Yet, the "popular view" taught today almost always leads to the idea that we can look forward to "the Day" as if there was no threat at all. Opponents of pre-trib teaching have even described it as escapism: "the great escape."[1] This is not for lack of support, since some pre-trib proponents have branded it as escape. Paul Crouch of Trinity Broadcasting Network wrote: "The Great Escape of believers from the time of trouble is based on biblical doctrine and not just on wishful thinking."[2] Evangelist Jack Van Impe has amplified this premise by entitling one of his books *The Great Escape* with the subtitle: *Preparing for the Rapture, the Next Event on God's Prophetic Clock.*[3]

The real problem here is exacerbated by the false hope of evading any kind of

---

[1] Hindson, Ed. *Is the Antichrist Alive and Well?* Eugene, OR: Harvest House, 1998. p. 193; Dixon, Michael. *Where Did the Pretribulation Rapture Go?* Cypress, CA: Sheva Foundation, 1981. p. 33. Some of the idea regarding "escape" may be drawn from Luke 21:36, erroneously used as a pre-trib proof text. Note the reference to the "Rapture Myth" in an earlier chapter as presented by John Loeffler for Chuck Missler in the context of the church facing tribulation. .

[2] Crouch, Paul. *The Shadow of the Apocalypse. When All Hell Breaks Loose.* New York, NY: G. Putnam's Sons, 2004. p. 70

[3] Van Impe, Jack. *The Great Escape: Preparing for the Rapture, the Next Event on God's Prophetic Clock.* Nashville, TN: Word Pub., 1998.

wrath to come at the end of the age. The basic premise established by pre-trib teaching is one of distortion, since the Body of Christ will visibly see the end, just as Jesus said in the Olivet Discourse: "Even so, when *you see all these things*, you know that it is near, right at the door."[4] In context, the clarity is sharp, since Jesus is warning those who read His words, that in the future they will definitely see and experience this grand event which leads to His glorious return. That future church will "see all these things"! Jesus emphasizes this in Matthew twenty-four: "So when you *see* standing in the holy place 'the abomination that causes desolation,' spoken of through the prophet Daniel...."[5] This is a definitive warning, and if we fail to grasp The implications, the Lord sends us back to the prophet Daniel.[6] Nothing yet unfinished which has been given to us by the prophets will be unfulfilled at the end. Jesus began His ministry warning the hearers then present that this would be the case: "Do not think that I have come to abolish the Law or the Prophets; I have not come to abolish them but to fulfill them. I tell you the truth, until heaven and earth disappear, not the smallest letter, not the least stroke of a pen, will by any means disappear from the Law until everything is accomplished."[7] Everything will be accomplished, just as it is written. We must weigh the prophets' warnings as we measure the implications of eschatology and not be trapped by any unwarranted eagerness.

If we look back to the Old Testament writings, the Day of the Lord is often mentioned. The prophet Amos clearly warned about misplaced anticipation: "Woe to you who long for the day of the Lord! Why do you long for the day of the Lord? That day will be darkness, not light."[8] This makes the notion of zealous anticipation something to be reconsidered. Prophets were commissioned for exactly this purpose--to bring God's people to their senses and face off to the truth. The blindness of Israel is much like our blindness today, especially when we are helped along with teaching measured by popular

---

[4] Mt 24:33 [emphasis added]. Also note Is 40:5
[5] Mt 24:15 [emphasis added].
[6] *Ibid.*
[7] Mt 5:17-18
[8] Amos 5:18

standards favorable to the hearer as opposed to the full counsel of God. Amos continued with examples. His graphic portrayal is purposed to shake us into rethinking the Day itself: "It will be as though a man fled from a lion only to meet a bear, as though he entered his house and rested his hand on the wall only to have a snake bite him. Will not the day of the Lord be darkness, not light--pitch-dark, without a ray of brightness?"[9] The very pitfall embraced by many in the church today is the core warning of this prophet--there will be no escape, and the darkness will be complete. The sense brought to us by Amos is not to look forward to this--*unless* we fully comprehend the complete event. The popular teaching of today does not aid us in fully understanding what is coming, because so much is glossed over[10] or reinterpreted. When we read the prophets, we find much was for their hour of need and much more was written for us. The wise Bible student will not ignore the writings of the prophets.[11] We must refrain from being hasty and thereby overlooking important points that affect doctrine. We must consider everything that is eschatological in nature, even if the verses are controversial.

The Apostle Peter emphasized the priority of considering the fullness of Scripture: "And we have the word of the prophets made more certain, and you will do well to pay attention to it, as a light shining in a dark place, until the day dawns and the morning star rises in your hearts."[12] His concern was with those whose zeal might lead them to follow "cleverly invented stories"[13] as opposed to the whole truth. He knew the danger of this and warned against the possibility of being "carried away by the error of lawless men."[14] They were present and active then as now. His remedy was to "grow in the grace and knowledge of our Lord and Savior Jesus Christ."[15] The alternative would be to

---

[9] Amos 5:19-20

[10] Smith, Chuck. *Calvary Chapel Distinctives.* Costa Mesa, CA. The Word for Today, 2000. p. 53, The admission is made that he glosses over "certain passages of Scripture," since they point to "controversial issues." His statement is general but, nonetheless, a candid admission to the exclusion of controversy.

[11] 1 Cor 10:11

[12] 2 Pt 1:19

[13] 2 Pt 1:16; Rm 10:2

[14] 2 Pt 3:17

fall victim to stories and myths. We must take note, since in context he is speaking of the Day of the Lord when Jesus returns like "a thief."[16] He also wrote that others, "ignorant and unstable people," were distorting Paul's teaching on this subject.[17] Peter well knew the difference between "things of men" and the Holy Spirit's "full message."[18] He once was brash and full of zeal but was tempered by God's Spirit.[19] He learned to wait for the "power from on high."[20]

All of this present-day emphasis on "any moment" removal and the idea we will not face any of the tribulation period is very misleading. It is like a thirsty man pursuing a mirage. It is a rush to remove the Body of Christ at the very time the voice of truth is needed the most. The writer of Hebrews calls for believers to rethink their responsibility as members of the body of Christ with regard to "things that accompany salvation." The expectation is for all to "show this same diligence to the *very end*."[21] This means believers are to stand courageously through the full tribulation period. This will require "faith and patience"--then, we will "inherit what has been promised."[22] The thought of being removed before the end is clearly not in the thoughts of the author of Hebrews. We are called to stand firm until the Lord arrives. The voice of truth will be needed throughout the tribulation period, just as many risk their lives today in the mission field. The penalty for conversion in many Muslim nations is death, yet the work goes on, and the Gospel is preached. Paul made the point with Timothy that the church is "the pillar and foundation of the truth."[23] He stated this for Timothy's edification and our benefit. The "conduct" that Paul reinforced is the need for the truth "once delivered"--deposited with the Body of Christ--to be held up, taught, broadcast, and defended by the leaders of the

---

[15] 2 Pt 3:18
[16] 2 Pt 3:10
[17] 2 Pt 3:16
[18] See Matthew 16:23 and Acts 5:20
[19] Pr 19:2; Rm 10:2
[20] See Luke 24:49 and Acts 1:8
[21] Heb 6:9, 11 [emphasis added].
[22] Heb 6:12
[23] 1 Tim 3:15

church.[24] This is in the light of his warning that "some will abandon the faith and follow deceiving spirits and things taught by demons."[25] Immature saints are the ones most at risk. So, Paul sounded the alert for the end of the age, and we see this critical responsibility being assigned to Timothy, Titus, and others, as they were to be the next generation of church leaders. "Watch your life and doctrine closely. Persevere in them, because if you do, you will save both yourself and your hearers."[26] This charge was sound instruction then and now. It balances anticipation of the Lord's return with full understanding. In the light of Jesus' words, the end of the age will be a time of distress--"great distress unequaled from the beginning of the world until now--and never to be equaled again"[27] We must soberly address this and balance our hope for His return with rational thinking. Our resolve must be firm--even in the face of evil. Sometimes we forget that the term "Christian" equates with our witness--and is synonymous with "martyr."[28] We must not forget Stephen, the first defender of the faith, who held the nation of Israel to account.[29] He then paid with his life and joined the Lord in glory. In the Book of Revelation, as John wrote the words from the Lord to the seven churches, all the promises were directly dependent on "he who overcomes."[30] This is the charge to stand to the end with no sense of a previous removal. It also affirms that the rewards for them and other believers will be given at the end and not before--just as the Lord said.[31] John wrote knowing there would be martyrs during the tribulation period. They are mentioned in chapter six.[32] At all times, believers are to be prepared to give their life for the one who gave His life for theirs.[33] It is within this context that

---

[24] See 1 Timothy 3:1-16 and Titus 1:5-2:1 for the fundamental leadership requirements--established earlier in the Book of Acts [Note Acts 6:3-4].

[25] 1 Tim 4:1

[26] 2 Tim 4:16

[27] Mt 24:21

[28] See Matthew 10:18; Mark 13:9; Luke 21:13; Acts 1:8; John 15:26-27 (All are in the face of opposition and danger). Also, 1 John 3:16

[29] Acts 6 and 7

[30] Note the warnings to the seven churches in Revelation 2 and 3.

[31] Rev 22:12; note Acts 17:30-31

[32] Rev 6:9-11

[33] 1 Jn 3:16

martyrdom takes on its true character and sets aside any false thought of believers exiting before the Lord's set time.[34] Master preacher, Charles Spurgeon, asked pointedly: "Would your modern gospel create the spirit of the martyrs?"[35]

We can see that Paul emphasized the Gospel truth as the imperative message for the church, even to be preached and broadcast to the end, as he addressed these concerns with the church at Thessalonica. In chapter two of his second letter, there is a notable picture of conditions at the end. He stated that there will be "all kinds of counterfeit miracles, signs, and wonders."[36] This will be the tactic of Satan to deceive "even the elect."[37] All manner of evil and deception will be unleashed, yet the truth will also be present--and rejected--by "those who are perishing."[38] So, we can see that those who reject the Gospel will face God's powerful delusion, since they prefer to believe the lie.[39] This clearly shows they have "delighted in wickedness," have not "believed the truth," and will be judged eternally for preferring the "lie" and not the "truth."[40] In other words, this Apostle is not expressing today's concept of zeal for the rapture at all, other than to be prepared for the unbridled display of "the work of Satan."[41] Paul wanted the saints in Thessalonica to be prepared to stand, holding to his teachings (and no other),[42] and to remember "the Lord is faithful, and will strengthen and protect you from the evil one."[43] Nowhere here is the idea formed or taught that believers are leaving--only that they must be prepared for what is to come. This truth conflicts heavily with the desire to escape tribulation found in popular teaching today.

---

[34] Consider Rev 2:10 and Job 14:5

[35] Spurgeon, C. H. *The Cross Our Glory*. From a sermon preached September 18, 1885.

[36] 2 Thess 2:9

[37] Mt 24:24

[38] 2 Thess 2:9

[39] 2 Thess 2:10

[40] 2 Thess 2:11-12

[41] 2 Thess 2:9

[42] 2 Thess 2:15

[43] 2 Thess 3:3

We must remember that the foremost obligation of the church as given by Jesus under the Great Commission is to bring the Gospel into the public arena through preaching and teaching [Mt 28:19-20]. This, of course, is to include everything He said and not contemporary likes and dislikes. Our selective exclusion of certain unpleasant portions of the end of the age brings forth a "different gospel" which we have also been warned about.[44] Jesus was distinct in His emphasis of the fact this was to be carried on "to the very end of the age."[45] This concurs with the statements in Hebrews, those by Peter, Paul, and the other New Testament writers in this regard--the truth will be present and available, and the Gospel will be preached, even to the end of the present age. Our zeal, then, must be about the commissioned work, prepared in advance for us to do,[46] and not for the distraction of contemporary ideas, even if they appear reasonable and we like them. We must anticipate only those things contained in the Word of God.

Peter learned the right view on anticipation. It is the one we must use to balance the complete picture of "the Day." Note what he wrote: "But the day of the Lord will come like a thief. The heavens will disappear with a roar; the elements will be destroyed by fire, and the earth and everything in it will be laid bare. Since everything will be destroyed in this way, what kind of people ought you to be? You ought to live holy and godly lives as *you look forward to the day* of God and speed its coming. That day will bring about the destruction of the heavens by fire, and the elements will melt in the heat. But in keeping with his promise we are looking forward to a new heaven and a new earth, the home of righteousness. So then, dear friends, since *you are looking forward to this*, make every effort to be found spotless, blameless and at peace with him."[47] Peter is clear. He pointed to the day of judgment with its destruction and not a rapture event. He stated this with ample description, knowing that Paul's teaching about the end was being distorted.[48] Certainly if Peter wished to

---

[44] 2 Cor 11:4

[45] Mt 28:20

[46] Eph 2:10

[47] 2 Pt 3:10-14 [emphasis added]. See: Culver, Daniel. *Daniel and the Latter Days.* p. 177-179

[48] 2 Pt 3:16. Consider Jer 23:16-33.

clarify a need for the church to be focused on an imminent rapture, he would have included it here. He did not. We must not think Peter overlooked something. In the light of this graphic chapter, in the context of the whole epistle, he reminds us we will *see* the full range of events regarding the day the Lord returns.

Notice Peter, also in context, shows us that "the day of God" and "the day the Lord" are synonymous with "the 'coming' he promised."[49] Peter is sure of this. He wants the church to be sure also. There is but one Day. It is our popular teaching which has rearranged the facts. Peter even warned about this in his effort to enlighten us about those who twisted Paul's teaching in this area: "He writes the same way in all his letters, speaking in them of these matters. His letters contain some things that are hard to understand, which ignorant and unstable people distort, as they do the other Scriptures, to their own destruction. Therefore, dear friends, since you already know this, be on your guard so that you may not be carried away by the error of lawless men and fall from your secure position."[50] This is where we have arrived today, thanks to overly fervent promotion of a pre-trib rapture. We read in Proverbs: "It is not good to have zeal without knowledge, nor to be hasty and miss the way."[51] Solomon's warning and Peter's have the same purpose. Further, we must not separate Peter and his eschatological teaching from that of Paul. They both are speaking of the same day and the same event. The early church heard Peter, they listened to Paul, and they were willing to face death as martyrs, be it the stoning of Stephen,[52] the execution of James with the sword,[53] or the wild beasts that Paul mentions.[54] In this light, the expectation was martyrdom with hope in the resurrection of the dead as promised by the Lord. The testimony of the first Christians was to expect persecution and death.[55] Tertullian emphasized this when he wrote his *Apology* chastising Rome and elevating

---

[49] 2 Pt 3:4
[50] 2 Pt 3:16-17
[51] Pr 19:2
[52] Acts 7:54-60
[53] Acts 12:1-2
[54] 1 Cor 15:32
[55] 1 Thess 3:4; Mt 5:11-12; Jn 15:20

martyrdom: "Nothing whatever is achieved by each more exquisite cruelty you invent; on the contrary, it wins men for our school."[56] Our priorities should match theirs without misguided haste to depart this world.

Some "Twos" To Consider

In the light of statements above, let us look at a few points, as questions may have arisen. We often hear eschatology presented uniformly with the pre-trib thought pattern, so clarification on a few things at this juncture will be helpful.

1. **Two Kinds of Wrath**. One of the points consistently employed with pre-trib teaching is the idea we will never face wrath. Verses are given [1 Thess 1:10; 5:9; Rom 5:9] which supposedly underwrite this hope.[57] However, there is a basic misunderstanding. Take Romans 5:9, for example: Paul stated specifically *"God's wrath."* This is the distinction omitted when the pre-trib view is presented. There are *two kinds of wrath*. We face the wrath of evil men who oppose God's work continuously. We also have been taught by the prophets, Jesus, and Apostles that God's wrath will be poured out on the wicked at the time of judgment which occurs at the end of the Tribulation. Paul noted the difference within his Thessalonians epistles. He purposely used the words "trial," "suffering," "persecution," and "death" to identify those realities that believers faced on a regular basis. He used the word "wrath" to indicate God's judgment. The difficulty occurs when we confuse both kinds of wrath without clearly defining them. Pre-trib teachers refrain from teaching distinctly here, since it would interfere with us gaining the full understanding of our true protection by the Lord before He comes to judge. We must plainly see *two kinds of wrath*. One is from men, and the other is God's wrath. They are not the same. When Paul admonished the believers in Colosse, he reminded them that

---

[56] Quoted in: Glover, T. R. *The Conflict of Religions in the Early Roman Empire*. p. 326

[57] Hitchcock, Mark. *The Complete Book of Bible Prophecy*. Wheaton, IL: Tyndale House Pub., 1999. p. 46. He claims "the entire Tribulation period is one of pounding judgment against the rebellious world," and this "continues all the way to the Second Coming." This is not possible until the midpoint when the Antichrist reveals himself, commences his global reign, and his assault on all believers [2 Thess 2:3-4; Rev 13:1ff].

they "used to walk in these ways." He was calling attention to their former "earthly nature: sexual immorality, impurity, lust, evil desires and greed, which is idolatry." He said: "Because of these, the wrath of God is coming."[58] Paul's simple words define the recipients of God's wrath--the ungodly--not believers. If the Colossians were in danger of God's wrath, Paul would have worded this in a different manner. As elsewhere, the wicked face God's wrath, not Christians. Frank White noted the difference in connection with believers not being appointed to wrath: "But tribulation on the way to glory is one thing, and "wrath"--penal judgment--quite another."[59] Truly, we are exempt from the judicial arm of the Lord bringing retribution on the wicked. As believers, we will *never* face God's wrath, and this is all Paul is saying.

2. **Two Days**. We are told that the Day of the Lord and the Day of Christ are two different days by pre-trib teachers. Heavy emphasis is placed on "the Day of Christ" being the day when Christ comes for His church and removes us. "The Day of the Lord," then, becomes the second phase of the Second Coming when Jesus comes back with the saints to judge the world.[60] However, note again how Peter employs these terms as one and the same.[61] He specified the time when Christ returns--and the church is still here. Peter already identified the event "when the Chief Shepherd *appears*"[62] as the same coming when all are present on earth. Nowhere does Peter hint the church will exit early. Consider, as an example, the person of Christ: is there any difference between "Jesus Christ," "Christ Jesus," or "Jesus of Nazareth"? Of course not. We are speaking of the *same* Jesus. The terms are synonymous and point to the same man: our Lord Jesus. Likewise, the Day of the Lord, the Day of Christ, and the Day of God are all the same day. While these terms in context may encompass other facets of the end of the age, in no way do they permit a separation into two comings by Christ seven years apart. This type of verbal reclassification is

---

[58] See Colossians 3:5-8

[59] White, Frank H. *The Saints' Rest and Rapture*. Chelmsford, Essex: The Sovereign Grace Advent Testimony, n.d. p. 17

[60] C. I. Scofield lists the two with their distinctions. See: *The Scofield Reference Bible*. p. 1271

[61] 2 Pt 3:10-16

[62] 1 Pt 5:4 [emphasis added].

harmful to those that genuinely seek to understand the events as written in scripture. Eminent New Testament theologian, Theodor Zahn, expressed Paul's argument that this day, "*The* Day of the Lord," could not have occurred previously, since Paul noted earlier that it "could not have come before '*the* falling away' and the revelation of '*the* man of lawlessness,' which Christ is to destroy at His second coming."[63] Affirming Paul's words, Zahn stated that "the church should expect the appearance of a single false Christ," hence the church would be present at that time leaving no possibility for a two-day, two-phase appearing.[64] As Dr. Walter Martin noted: "It should never be forgotten that the day of the Lord and the day of Christ are interchangeable in the New Testament Greek, and the deliverance for the Church from the tribulation is promised at the advent of Jesus Christ."[65]

3. **Two Phases**. Consistently pre-trib teachers say the Second Coming is made up of two parts. They justify this by saying the predicted advent of the Messiah (Jesus) was two events--the First Coming, then the Second Coming--not seen clearly by the prophets in their day. This allows them to separate the Second Coming into two parts with the Lord coming *for* His church at the beginning of the tribulation and then returning *with* the host of heaven at the end.[66] However, no verse anywhere in the Bible makes this distinction, and they know it.[67] Bible teacher Gerald Stanton admitted: "Of course, the Bible does not come out clearly and say, 'The rapture of the Church will occur before the Tribulation.'"[68] In spite of their admissions, what we really see in Scripture is a number of different details describing the same event. None of the pre-trib

[63] Zahn, Theodor. *Introduction to the New Testament*. 1909. rpt. Minneapolis, MN: Klock & Klock, 1977. Vol. 1, p. 226. Zahn's exposition clearly demonstrates a single return with the church present to the end. [emphasis in the original].

[64] Zahn. *Ibid.* p. 228

[65] Martin, Walter. *Essential Christianity. A Handbook of Basic Christian Doctrines*. Ventura, CA: Vision House, 1990. p. 99

[66] Chafer, Lewis Sperry. *Major Bible Doctrines. 52 Vital Doctrines of Scripture Simplified and Explained*. Revised by John F. Walvoord. Grand Rapids, MI: Zondervan Pub., 1980. p. 331

[67] Walvoord, John F. *The Rapture Question*. Findley, OH: Dunham Pub., 1957. p. 148

[68] Stanton, Gerald B. "Will the Church Enter the Tribulation?" *The Church and End Times*. Los Angeles, CA: The Bible Institute Hour, n.d. p. 13

teachers would approach the gospels this way, as if there were four ministries of Jesus. We have four accounts of the same Shepherd at work--not four shepherds or four phases. This difficulty with the separation of the Second Coming into two events is the result of the issues which were under discussion in the Albury and Powerscourt meetings in England in the 1800s in which Edward Irving and J. N. Darby attended.[69] Since Irving had translated Manuel Lacunza's book on the return of Christ into English, he was aware of Lacunza's claim for the believers to be taken up and kept safe for forty-five days while the final judgments took place.[70] Somewhere in the process, the forty-five days became seven years.[71] This resulted in Darby's formulation of two aspects or phases of Jesus' return, when scripture states just one. His model included the introduction "of a secret rapture of the church and of the parenthesis in prophetic fulfillment between the sixty- ninth and seventieth weeks of Daniel."[72] Since then, there is often a subtle shift in wording from "stage" to "phase" or to "aspect" used by pre-trib teachers by which they hope to reduce their risk of actually being accused of promoting two second comings.[73] Yet, this is the result regardless of the dispensational nomenclature. This manipulation tells us that the idea was from men. It is not in the written Word. In Hebrews, we are told the Lord comes but "once."[74] Any deviation from God's word is unjustifiable and misleading. This unscriptural idea was never espoused by any Bible writer. Jesus never taught this. If this distinction is so critical to the dispensational rapture teaching, it is glaring by its absence

---

[69] Froom, Leroy. *The Prophetic Faith of Our Fathers*. Washington, DC: Review and Herald, 1954. Vol. III, p. 310-314, 529-520

[70] Thigpen, Paul. *The Rapture Trap*. West Chester, PA: Ascencion Press, 2001. p. 143

[71] See the chapter in this book, "History," for more detail on this issue.

[72] Sandeen, Ernest. *The Roots of Fundamentalism. British and American Millennariasm 1800-1930*. Chicago, IL: University of Chicago Press, 1970. p. 38

[73] Arnold Froese boldly embraces two second comings in his weak attempt to explain "the two phases." He even answers the question, "Are there two Second Comings" by emphatically saying, "Yes"! His further explanation does little to settle the matter, since as a pre-trib advocate, the teaching must be supported at all cost. Froese, Arno. *119 Most Frequently Asked Questions About Prophecy*. Columbia, SC: The Olive Tree Press, 2003. p. 65

[74] Heb 9:27-28

in scripture, since no Biblical text states a seven-year separation of Jesus' return to earth. The pre-trib assertion is an argument from silence.

4. **Two Groups**. Since Matthew twenty-four has already been mentioned, it will be helpful to clarify the issue of who is being addressed by the Lord Jesus. Most pre-trib authorities make a point that the Jews are the audience that Jesus is directing His message to--Israel at the end of the age. They know if the church is the audience, then the pre-trib rapture view is damaged beyond repair. Yet, this is the case. Jesus is not speaking to Jews--He has just condemned them in Matthew twenty-three saying, "...you will not see me again until you say, 'Blessed is he who comes in the name of the Lord'".[75] Their house was desolate. They had rejected Him. Shortly before, on the same day, Jesus informed the chief priests and the Pharisees that because they had rejected Him "the kingdom of God would be taken away from you and given to a people who would produce fruit."[76] He is obviously referring to the Church as the beneficiaries. He confirmed this two nights later when He said: "You did not choose me, but I chose you to go and bear fruit--fruit that will last."[77] There were no dissenting Jews present in the upper room when Jesus said this. Hence, the Apostles and others were the ones to take up Jesus' words, not the Jews who rejected Him. So in context, it was the Apostles and disciples who were the directed audience of the teaching of the Olivet Discourse--not Israel or Jews. It was four believers--Peter, James, John, and Andrew[78] who represented the Body of Christ--the church. It was they who asked Jesus privately about the end of the age and not Pharisees, priests, or unbelieving Jews. This issue must be considered carefully, since pre-trib teachers insist this discourse is for Israel. Notice verse nine of Matthew twenty-four where Jesus is very clear in His warning: "Then *you* will be handed over to be persecuted and put to death, and *you* will be hated by all nations *because of me*."[79] The

---

[75] Mt 23:39

[76] Mt 21:43

[77] Jn 15:16. The Great Commission affirmed that Christians would continue the work [Mt 28:18ff].

[78] Mk 13:3

[79] Mt 24:9 [emphasis added].

pronouns are directed to the Apostles present and, later, their followers who would come to know Jesus and openly confess their faith in Him.[80] This warning is for those who believe in Jesus only. This *cannot* mean the Jews or Israel, since they do not believe in Him. Pre-trib teachers, also, attempt to sidestep the church being the intended recipient of the warnings in Matthew twenty-four by saying Matthew was written to a Jewish audience. They brace their argument claiming the "elect" Jesus spoke of was Israel/Jews.[81] For the reasons above, this is not plausible. In addition, the term "elect" was understood by the church itself to mean Christians. Oswald Allis noted this point when he stated: "The *Didache* quotes Matt. xxiv. 31 twice and both times substitutes the word 'church' for 'elect.'"[82] The New Covenant was established for the church, and the writings are directed to believers. This encompasses the text from Matthew through Revelation. Primarily, one group is the audience.

5. **Two things**. Paul understood the order of events preceding the return of the Lord. This is what he taught everywhere. Evidence in brief form is found in 1 Corinthians fifteen and in both epistles to the church in Thessalonica. Because contradicting letters, messages, and reports were confusing the Thessalonians, Paul quickly sent word to them with reminders of his personal teaching. He restated the order of events clearly in the second letter. Chapter one covered the Second Coming, and chapter two dealt with our gathering to Him when He comes. Paul began this portion restating the context: "Concerning the coming of our Lord Jesus Christ and our being gathered to him."[83] He then notified them he knew of the false reports they had received regarding the day of the Lord. Next, Paul laid great emphasis on telling them again that *two things* must happen prior to the coming of the Lord. He linked both together as events to take place prior to our being gathered (the rapture, v.1). Paul plainly stated that the apostasy must occur and the man of sin must be revealed--before the Second Coming. Two things will be coincident with and precede the return of

---

[80] Acts 2:39
[81] Mt 24:24
[82] Allis, Oswald T. *Prophecy and the Church.* Philadelphia, PA: Presbyterian & Reformed Pub., 1947. p. 318
[83] 2 Thess 2:1

the Lord when He comes "in blazing fire with his powerful angels."[84] As noted by F. L Godet: "Paul reminds the Thessalonians of what he taught when amongst them, namely, that the glorious return of Christ must be preceded by a manifestation of a directly opposite nature, that of the *Man of Sin*."[85] This, of course, is the Antichrist. Accompanying this will be the rebellion (*apostasia*).[86] Hence, the Lord will return after the Antichrist is in view, the "man of sin" who will receive full Satanic power, and mankind, along with the church, rebels.[87] After these *two things* the church will see the coming of the Lord.[88] Bible teachers must not reconstruct and redefine these events.

6. **Two thieves**. Paul wrote to the church in Thessalonica and reminded them of his earlier instruction when he was with them. This included points that needed to be recalled about the return of the Lord. In 1 Thessalonians chapter five, he excluded the unnecessary information about "times and dates,"[89] since they were taught this in person.[90] He said they knew this very well. Consequently, the Thessalonians did understand the timing of Christ's return, and the world did not--which is Paul's point. Since the world was operating in darkness and in the futility of their thinking,[91] only those saints instructed by the apostles and other Godly teachers knew what to expect. The rest would be taken by surprise as if a thief had come in the night. They--the world--are the ones to be surprised and not true believers. The return of the Lord will occur when the world is saying, "peace and safety." Those who teach a pre-trib rapture often use this portion of 1 Thessalonians five to claim that the reference to "the thief" coming is the rapture.[92] Paul is saying nothing of the kind. He merely states

---

[84] 2 Thess 1:7

[85] Godet, Frederic. L. *Studies in Paul's Epistles*. 1889. rpt. Grand Rapids, MI: Kregel Pub., 1984. p. 28

[86] See "Apostasy and Falling Away" in the chapter "Some Little Words."

[87] Mt 24:15; Rev 13:1ff

[88] Mt 24:33

[89] 1 Thess 5:1ff

[90] Paul clearly defined the event with a reminder in his second epistle, because they had been the victims of false reports (2 Thess 2:1-2). See 2 Thessalonians 1:6-10 for Paul's overview on Christ's return.

[91] Eph 4:17-18

[92] Couch, Mal. *Dictionary of Premillennial Theology*. Grand Rapids, MI: Kregel Pub.,

that while the world is engaged in worldly business[93]and not paying attention to the signs of the return, the Lord will come and surprise *them* like a thief. Paul assured the Thessalonians that they will not be surprised by this, because "they are sons of the light."[94] The first eleven verses of this chapter must be read in context. Noticeably, the pre-trib rapture emphasis here is meaningless, since Jesus spoke of His return just as Paul did. In the Book of Revelation, Jesus announced His coming as "a thief" in chapter sixteen. This is near the end of the tribulation period, just as the kings were gathering for the last battle having been drawn into the heart of Israel by evil spirits as described by the Apostle John.[95] This is the time when the seventh angel pours out his bowl f wrath, and the kings of the earth are gathered at the place "called Armageddon."[96] This is near the end of the seven year tribulation when the Lord brings the enemies of Israel against her.[97] This period begins with "peace"[98] and will conclude with God's final judgment. F. F. Bruce's comment is relevant:

> One prophetic utterance thus made in his name is of special
> interest. When John sees the kings of the earth mustering for
> the battle of Har-Megedon "on the great day of God the
> Almighty," a voice declares: "Lo, I am coming like a thief!
> Blessed is he who is awake, keeping his garments that he may
> not go naked and be seen exposed!" (Rev 16:15).[99]

1996. p 333. Here, Couch connects "Imminence" directly to these verses relating to "the thief" and the rapture. Also, p. 349. Note earlier pre-trib exponent, I. M. Haldeman who stated in his defense of the "Two-fold Coming" that: "In the first part he comes as a *thief*." He befuddles his claim referencing "Rev. xvi:15" which is at the end when the bowls are poured out! Haldeman, I. M. *Bible Messages.* Greenville, SC: The Gospel Hour, n.d p. 7.Once again, it can be seen that context is ignored. M. R. DeHaan, also claims, "as a thief."

[93] Lk 17:25-30
[94] 1 Thess 5:4
[95] Rev. 16:13-16
[96] Rev 16:16
[97] Ezek 38:1-6, 14-16
[98] Dan 9:27
[99] Bruce, F. F. *The Time is Fulfilled. Five Aspects of the Fulfilment of the Old Testament in the New.* Grand Rapids, MI: William B. Eerdmans Pub. Co., 1978. p. 109

This observation by Bruce reflects the chronology as well as the point of the Lord's words. Here, the Lord speaks interjecting a reminder at the time of the final battle *just prior* to the Second Coming. This is chapter sixteen, near the end of the seven year tribulation. He uses the "thief" simile to bring encouragement to those listening in the churches He already warned them to stay awake and be alert.[100] Note: if He had already come to remove the church, these words would be meaningless. At this point in time, the Lord is still in heaven, and the church is awaiting the "loud command" and "the trumpet call of God" [1 Thess 4:16].

Peter the Apostle concurred with this: "...the day of the Lord will come like a thief. The heavens will disappear with a roar; the elements will be destroyed by fire, and the earth and everything in it laid bare."[101] He described this at the end and stated that believers are looking forward to this--not a pre-trib rapture. These verses by Paul, John, and Peter all look to the one event at the end of the tribulation. So, when a pre-trib teacher employs the "thief" in Thessalonians as a proof for the rapture, he inadvertently has created two thieves which contradicts scripture and the teaching of Jesus since He promised to return at the end of the seven years.[102] There are not two thieves, since there is but one Second Coming.

7. **Two plans**. Dispensationalism by definition espouses two plans--one for Israel and one for the Church. This is a central component of dispensational teaching proper. This idea separates the "church" from Israel which brings two distinct bodies into the relationship God has with men.[103] This gives support, according to them, to call this the "Church Age," which relegates Israel into a state of suspension. The claim is made that God is not dealing with them now but will commence His plan for them during the last seven years. They insist

---

[100] Rev 2 and 3, the seven churches.

[101] 2 Pt 3:10

[102] Mt 24:30 -31

[103] Couch, Mal. *Dictionary of Premillennial Theology*. Grand Rapids, MI: Kregel Pub., 1996. p. 94

that the church will be removed, so God can deal with His people, the Jews. Hence, they refer to this time as "Jacob's time of trouble" based erroneously on a text from Jeremiah where he states: "It will be a time of trouble for Jacob, but he will be saved out of it."[104] Of course, Israel will be present during this time, but so will the other nations who, also, will face this. Pre-trib theorists neglect Jeremiah's earlier words: "'The tumult will resound to the ends of the earth, for the Lord will bring charges against the nations; he will bring judgment on all mankind and put the wicked to the sword,' Declares the Lord."[105] These verses demand the understanding that all on the earth will be facing great tribulation[106] not Jacob alone. There is also no hint anywhere that this grants the church any exemption. This is similar to the position of Replacement Theology[107] which also separates the two groups. Another view which reflects confusion in this area is the Dual Covenant teaching.[108] It asserts that God has one salvation plan for the Gentiles and another one for the Jews. The Scripture itself refutes these ideas, as Paul writes to the church at Ephesus.[109] Also, the Bible defines God as one who is not a respecter of persons, and, once "in Christ," there is neither Jew or Gentile [Col 3:11]. Unquestionably, we are called to be vigilant with regard to Israel. This is especially important as we see events transpiring in the Middle East. What we must not do is omit half of God's plan--Israel--in the process, as dispensationalists do, when it is convenient to add Israel into their theology in an attempt to prove a point. George West brought focus to this when he published his thoughts on the book of Daniel. He connected Daniel 12:1 with Matthew 24:21, there being "great distress, unequaled from the beginning of the world to now," as one-and-the-same for both the church and for believing Jews. He noted from Daniel: "At that time thy people--the Jews-- shall be delivered, every one that shall be found written in the Book."[110] West

---

[104] Jer 30:7

[105] Jer 25:31

[106] Mt 24:21; Lk 21:35

[107] See Glossary

[108] See Glossary

[109] Eph 3:1-6; 4:4. See: Jocz, Jacob. *The Jewish People and Jesus Christ*. London: SPCK, 1954. p. 311ff

[110] West, G. W. [George W.]. *Daniel. The Greatly Beloved*. London: Marshall, Morgan, Scott, n.d. [c1930]. p. 121

continued to amplify the importance of this referencing the next verse (Dan 12:2) where it "speaks of the actual resurrection of the dead. Here I would add: (1) That resurrection is not a hope first revealed in the New Testament as some appear to think, (2) That the resurrection is one of the events of the last days, and is bound up with the other events and the hope of Israel."[111] In other words the resurrection at the last day[112] is the hope and promise of both Jew and Gentile as believers. There is but one plan, not two.

8. **Two brides**. Further complications arise when the scripture is manipulated as in the above examples. The pre-trib model has a tendency to lead people to do this. Jack Van Impe has created two brides of Christ. He did this unwittingly in order to support his any-moment ideas. In his haste to account for the elect in scripture with one being Israel and the other being the church, he defined one as "the wife of Jehovah."[113] He noted this to be Israel. He then stated the "Church is the bride of Christ."[114] Since Biblically the Church is the bride, this may on the surface go unnoticed. However, this leads to not only a scriptural contradiction and to confusion, but blasphemy. Just as there cannot be two Gods, there cannot be two brides. Why? Scripture is clear that God is one.[115] "I am the Lord there is no other."[116] Since the Lord Jesus affirmed Himself to be one with the Father, the same as the one true God,[117] the claim of two brides equates to two wives. This is polygamy. It opposes scripture and the very nature of God's purpose in redemption to have one people unto Himself. Harry Ironside noted this issue as he excoriated the Bullingerites and others[118] for this gross accusation of God being a polygamist.[119] Great care must be used when interpreting figures of speech. A word or two in haste can lead to heretical

---

[111] *Ibid.* p. 126-127
[112] Jn 11:24-26
[113] Van Impe, Jack. *The Great Escape*. Nashville, TN: Word Pub., 1998. p. 19
[114] *Ibid.*
[115] Dt 6:4; Mk 12:32; Gal 3:20
[116] Dt 4:35, 39; Is 44:8; 45:5-6; Acts 4:12
[117] Jn 10:30; 17:11
[118] Ultra-dispensationalists. [See Glossary for Ultra-dispensationalism].
[119] Ironside, H. A. [Harry]. *Wrongly Dividing the Word of Truth. Ultra-Dispensationalism Examined in the Light of Holy Scripture.* Philadelphia. PA: Approved-Books Store, n.d. p. 50ff

ideas. These blunders can lead to unfathomable results: two brides, two marriage suppers, two weddings, and many other complications caused by this unwarranted division of God's people. Van Impe's problem, as with other pre-trib teachers, is the narrow confinement caused by holding to the tenets of dispensationalism rather than following the word of God alone. Where did Van Impe cultivate this dangerous supposition? From C. I. Scofield and his footnotes on Revelation 19:7. Scofield forces the distinction here and with Revelation 21:9. In both verses, the wife and bride are mentioned. He has done this in order to maintain the two dispensational groups: the church and Israel. Overall, though, he has relegated Israel to a lesser status.[120] Orthodoxy tells us that there is but one body of those God has called. This includes saints from the Old Testament and those saved under the new covenant. Paul made this clear: we are "heirs together with Israel, members together of one body, and sharers in the promise of Christ Jesus."[121] In Hebrews, we are told that they--the chosen of Israel--"that only together with us will they be made perfect."[122] Van Impe also added confusion by having the marriage supper both in heaven[123] and on earth.[124] We mention this solely for the purpose of illustrating the path that a false premise leads to. Van Impe was also bold enough to set dates for the imminent return (rapture): "the actual timetable falls between 2001 and 2012."[125] We have now exceeded his limit. Consequently, all his prophetic prognostications are of no value.

9. **Two Holy Spirits**. This concept may seem incredulous, however the pre-trib scenario actually promotes this--or covers over the conflict once the idea is brought into play. This occurs when the restrainer is identified in verse six and seven of 2 Thessalonians two. Those who advocate this claim that it is a "he" and "can be no other than the Holy Spirit in the church."[126] This emphasis was taught by C. I. Scofield and taken up by many others in their haste to remove

---

[120] See the *The Scofield Reference Bible*. p. 1348 and 1351.
[121] Eph 3:6
[122] Heb 11:39-40
[123] Van Impe. *Ibid*. p. 23
[124] Van Impe. *Ibid*. p. 70
[125] Van Impe. *Ibid*. p. 6
[126] See the *Scofield Reference Bible*. p. 1272

the church prior to the revelation of the Antichrist. Arnold Froese illustrated this in attempting to answer questions with this problem. He claimed that Jesus could "physically not come back to earth before the Church has been removed." Why? Because Jesus, "the suffering servant and the Holy Spirit, in the office of the Comforter, cannot be on earth simultaneously. Therefore, the Comforter must be removed so that Jesus can return."[127]His pretentious claim is exposed as he later explained how it could be possible for people to be saved if the Holy Spirit has been removed. He wrote: "The Holy Spirit is removed as the Comforter for the Church, but the Holy Spirit is God, therefore omnipresent."[128] This kind of doublespeak from Froese created another spirit. He stated this knowing that (from his pre-trib view) many come to faith in the tribulation, and only the Holy Spirit can accomplish genuine salvation. Nevertheless, he created two Holy Spirits. He is also guilty of creating "two days" (see above) and two Second Comings.[129] All this contradiction is ultimately the progeny of John Nelson Darby in the 1800s, yet the invalid pre-trib rapture idea fosters confusion to the present hour. J Barton Payne from Wheaton College provided further insight with this text as he noted the restraint to "be identified with lawful government."[130] This was the view held by the early church. Rome and the Caesars were identified as the enemy. Paul used safe terminology so not to risk exposure as an enemy of Caesar. George Ladd infused the place of God behind this as "the power of God Himself."[131] In any case, the context and wording by Paul do not indicate the Spirit being removed. If so, the Greek would be very different, and the Thessalonians knew what Paul meant. It is expositors today who are troubled by this. Orthodoxy requires that there be only one Third Person in the Trinity who has many functions.

---

[127] Froese, Arnold. *119 Most Frequently Asked Questions About Prophecy.* p. 66. Froese foolishly ignored Jesus' baptism by the Holy Spirit [Mt 3:16-17, all three Persons of the Godhead are present!].

[128] Froese. *Ibid.* p. 145-146

[129] Froese. *Ibid.* p. 65

[130] Payne, J. Barton. *The Imminent Appearing of Christ.* Grand Rapids, MI: William B. Eerdmans, 1962. p. 110

[131] Ladd, George Eldon. *The Blessed Hope. A Biblical Study of the Second Advent and the Rapture.* Grand Rapids, MI: William B. Eerdmans, 1988. p. 95

10. **Two Witnesses**. In Revelation eleven, there are two servants of the Lord who are supernaturally brought into the events at the close of the age.[132] The discussion which surrounds them by Bible commentators and teachers primarily centers on their identity. There are basically two schools of thought: (1) they are Moses and Elijah; (2) they are Enoch and Elijah. The dispute on their personage has been longstanding. Some tend toward Moses and Elijah since both appeared at the Transfiguration.[133] Others favor Enoch and Elijah since both were taken up alive.[134] What is often overlooked is the issue of when they appear to undertake their divine mission. Their ministry extends for 1,260 days while the Gentiles trample on the courts of the temple. This is the three-and-one-half year portion of the tribulation during which they are empowered by the Lord to do their work. The important question is "when" they appear to begin their work. The way a person understands this affects their overall grasp of end times. Do they appear in the first half of the tribulation or the second? Pre-trib experts Tim LaHaye and Thomas Ice promoted these two men arriving in the first half of the tribulation.[135] John Walvoord and Mark Hitchcock advocated the witnesses appearing in the second half of the tribulation.[136] This in itself creates confusion, since all four of these prophecy authorities are vehement in their defense of a pre-trib removal of the church. Hence, if someone reads their material, ultimately confusion will result. Bible teacher I. M. Haldeman who preceded the four men above also held to a pre-trib rapture and was correct in his conclusion regarding the timing. In one of his sermons, he placed the witnesses' appearance at the mid-point connecting it with the revelation of the Antichrist as mentioned by Jesus in Matthew 24:15. Haldeman said: "At this time, two witnesses will appear in Jerusalem,

---

[132] Rev 11:3

[133] Mt 17:1-13

[134] 2 Kings 2:11; Gen 5:24; Heb 11:5

[135] LaHaye, Tim. *Revelation--Illustrated and Made Plain*. Grand Rapids, MI: Zondervan Corp., 1975. p. 151-152; Ice, Thomas. "Pre-Trib Perspectives." Vol. III. No. 52. January, 2008. p. 8

[136] Walvoord, John F. *The Prophecy Knowledge Handbook*. Wheaton, IL: Victor Book, 1990. p. 572-575; Hitchcock, Mark. *The Complete Book of Bible Prophecy*. Wheaton, IL: Tyndale House, 2000. p. 124

testifying of Jesus unto Israel."[137] He based his conclusion on Daniel 9:27, Matthew 24:15, and Paul's warning about the Antichrist in 2 Thessalonians 2:3-4. Though he erred with the early removal of the church, he was right with the witnesses' arrival in the final period of 42 months. George Eldon Ladd properly placed these men after the midpoint in the second half with the church still present. He connected their work to the time mentioned by Daniel in chapter nine where is seen "the domination of evil," and the forty-two months are "the period of the satanic power in the world, with particular reference to the final days of the Antichrist."[138] This begins at the mid-point mentioned by Jesus who also used Daniel as the reference.[139] Why is this important? Because those who teach the Second Coming as hope for those who belong to the Lord have a responsibility to get it right. Consider, now, a few reasons why the witnesses will appear in the second half of the tribulation: First, they will oppose the numerous false prophets whom Jesus said would appear before His return during this time.[140] This is the same time that Paul noted when "the work of Satan" will be displayed to deceive those who are perishing. The two witnesses will have great power: "fire comes from their mouth;" they can turn water to blood;" they can send "a plague as often as they want."[141] The truth will be proclaimed, also, at this time encompassing the testimony of the two witnesses and others.[142] This all occurs after the mid-point, since up until this time, there is peace and safety,[143] prior to the Antichrist's grandiose claim at the temple to be God. As noted by Daniel, the church is present at this time under heavy persecution.[144] Second, the witnesses will have the charge to refute the claims of Antichrist to be God. There is no purpose for them to appear until the boasting and exultation of the man of sin commences.[145] It is at

---

[137] Haldeman, I. M. *Bible Messages.* Greenville, SC: The Gospel Hour, Inc., n.d. p. 27

[138] Ladd, George Eldon. *A Commentary on the Revelation of John.* Grand Rapids, MI: Wm. B. Eerdmans, 1996. p. 153

[139] Mt 24:15; Dan 9:27

[140] Mt 24:5, 11, 23-26

[141] Rev 11:5-6

[142] 2 Thess 2:9-12; Mt 24:14

[143] 1 Thess 5:1-3

[144] Dan 7:25

[145] Dan 11:36-37

this time that his wrath begins and will require strong opposition from those who know their God.[146] Third, the two witnesses will be needed to remind the believers of the Lord's promise to come and to encourage them in the face of extreme evil. During this time, the beast and the false prophet will be forcing compliance upon all men under a death penalty.[147] There will be counterfeit signs and wonders to deceive even the elect.[148] This will be a time unlike any other for God's people. The witnesses will be confirmation for God's faithful ones that their redemption is very near.[149] They will point to signs in the heavens and issue final warnings to repent.[150] The heralding of the two witnesses will encourage believers who will relate to the Lord's own words about these last of the last days.[151] This tells us that the church will be here, and that the presence of these two servants of God will come during the final forty-two months--when needed most. Grant Osborne offers in-depth understanding of the timing involved with the two Godly messengers placing them in the second forty-two months. He connected their deaths and being taken up to the final portion of the tribulation preceding the Lord's return (*parousia*). He likened their resurrection to be "a proleptic anticipation of the 'rapture'" which occurs at the end of this period and not prior.[152]

11. **Two Last Trumps**. This is another point of conflict within pre-trib circles. In Paul's first letter to the Corinthians, he described the Second Coming and the timing of the resurrection of the dead. He did this to refocus the thinking of the Corinthians as they discussed the Faith. Their ideas were being influenced by other voices. There were divisions among them, since they considered the teaching of unregenerate wise men, scholars, and philosophers on equal footing with the Apostles.[153] They were distracted from the pure Gospel. So Paul

---

[146] Dan 11:32
[147] Rev 13:1-18
[148] Mk 13:22; 2 Thess 2:9
[149] Lk 21:28
[150] Mt 24:29
[151] Is 13:6-10; Joel 2:1-2, 30-32
[152] Osborne, Grant R. *Revelation. [Baker Exegetical Commentary on the N. T.].* Grand Rapids. MI: Baker Academic, 2002. p. 432
[153] 1 Cor 1:10-12, 20-25

restated it throughout chapter fifteen. This included the order of resurrection and exactly when it would occur. Paul said it will take place "in the twinkling of an eye, at the last trumpet."[154] He was emphatic that this is the time. There is no hint here or elsewhere that Paul held to a previous resurrection. This is where pre-trib teaching slips and cannot remain faithful to the text. Tim LaHaye and Ed Hindson connected the trump in 1 Corinthians 15:52-53 with the resurrection in 1 Corinthians 15:22-24. They also noted this as the time Paul instructed the Thessalonians of the rapture [1 Thess 4:14-17].[155] This scenario is accurate and is an admission that the last trump, the Second Coming, and the rapture all take place at the same time. However, the Apostle John also noted a trumpet, the final of seven, when "the mystery of God will be accomplished."[156] This is the same mystery which Paul aligned with the trump in First Corinthians fifteen. Again, this is orthodox. There is but one last trump, and it has been described correctly and chronologically by these apostles. The problem arises when pre-trib advocates attempt to separate the trumps. This, then, yields two last trumps which violates the teaching of scripture. When LaHaye and Hindson reviewed the eleventh chapter of Revelation, they totally ignored the connection of Paul's two clear references[157] and sidestepped the unity of what was taught in the early church. They connected it to another "mystery" in Ephesians chapter three.[158] Paul had already cleared the air of mystery.[159] Here, two pre-trib writers bring it back. In the process by omission, they created two trumps. Scripture does not support this. Robert Mounce correctly linked the "mystery" found in Revelation eleven to the "mystery" in 1 Corinthians fifteen which reinforces the singularity of the trumps, that they are one and the same.[160] J. Oliver Buswell is more emphatic. He noted that John,

---

[154] 1 Cor 15:22-24, 52
[155] LaHaye, Tim, & Ed Hindson. *Exploring Bible Prophecy from Genesis to Revelation*. Eugene, OR: Harvest House, 2011. p. 413-415
[156] Rev 10:7
[157] 1 Cor 15:52 and 1 Thess 4:16-17
[158] LaHaye/Hindson. *Ibid.* p. 520-521
[159] A "mystery" is no longer a mystery once it is explained—except by those who have other motives.
[160] Mounce, Robert. *The Book of Revelation. [NICOT]*. Grand Rapids, MI: Wm. B. Eerdmans Pub., 1980. p. 212

writing years after Paul, would have known what was contained in the Corinthian and Thessalonian epistles. Buswell thoroughly reviewed all of the uses of "mystery." He wrote that John's use of the word in Revelation 10:7 was a special use of the Pauline term.[161] Buswell went on to say that this is when the mystery of God is completed: "At the great trumpet it will be a secret no more." And, on the basis of this, the mystery "is finished at the sounding of the seventh trumpet," and this is "an indication that the rapture of the true church takes place at this point."[162] The evidence from scripture is clear. There will be one trump at the Second Advent when the resurrection and the rapture occur.

12. **Two Resurrections**. The Resurrection is the doctrinal keystone of the faith once delivered. It is the event which secures the hope of the resurrection of believers when Christ returns at the end of the age. This truth was firmly established by the Lord Jesus when He spoke.[163] This was confirmed by Paul and the other apostles when they taught and preached.[164] The event is directly connected to the Second Coming with Jesus appearing in glory at the time He judges men and creation. In his later years, the apostle John defined for the church, the two components. He noted the fact of two resurrections, one for the righteous and another 1,000 years later for the wicked.[165] The righteous are the redeemed of the Lord who will be with Him in the age to come; the wicked will be cast into the lake of fire. Scripturally, this limits the resurrections to two. However, a number of pre-trib teachers promote a *third resurrection*.[166] John Walvoord in an attempt to refute the amillennial view insisted "there will be a number of resurrections."[167] This broad statement is unsupportable, since

---

[161] Buswell, J. Oliver. *A Systematic Theology of the Christian Religion*. Grand Rapids, MI: Zondervan, 1979. Volume II. p. 450.

[162] *Ibid.*

[163] Jn 5:24-25; 11:25

[164] 1 Cor 15:1-58

[165] Rev 20:4; 20:11-15

[166] Dave Hunt claims Revelation 20:4-5 is "only a partial resurrection," and that the earlier rapture is a "general resurrection" for those in Christ. With this, he has made three resurrections when the resurrection of the wicked is included. See: Hunt, Dave. *How Close Are We?* Eugene, OR: Harvest House, 1993. p. 239

[167] Walvoord, John F. *End Times. Understanding Today's World Events in Biblical*

the scripture itself and its earliest interpreters limited it to two. To add to the single, first resurrection and the second is risky, indeed. This increase by Dr. Walvoord and others who repeat this error openly contradicts what the Bible states will occur. As an example, in a question and answer period in a prophecy conference, Dr. Thomas Ice insisted that there would be three events. He was in dialogue with Richard Perry, a preterist, who challenged Dr. Ice and his incongruities. Dr. Ice agreed there was a resurrection in 1 Corinthians 15:51. He confirmed this, but only in the light of his false premise that the rapture takes place at the beginning of the last seven years. Realizing he was being pressed into admitting an unsupportable claim, he then denied the rapture and the resurrection occur together. He attempted to avoid exposure by saying: "the rapture is the translation of the living believers and the resurrection can only happen to dead people."[168] In Paul's words, they happen simultaneously.[169] Dr. Ice, then, compounded his blunder stating that the rapture is only for those "who are in Christ." He insisted this excluded the Old Testament saints, and then said those saved during the tribulation and the Old Testament saints will be "resurrected at the end of the seven-year tribulation."[170] With this claim, he established *three resurrections*: one with the rapture, a second at the Second Coming, and a third at the end of the Millennium.[171] This distortion of truth can be traced back to J. N. Darby when he created two second comings with his new brand of eschatology: one return and resurrection at the rapture and a second event later per Matthew twenty-four.[172] Scripture supports none of this. In the ninth chapter of Hebrews, it states Jesus returns just once--"a second time, not to bear sin, but to bring salvation to those who are waiting for him."[173] No previous return is indicated. No third return is mentioned anywhere. This is

---

Prophecy. Nashville, TN: Word Pub., 1998. p. 153
[168] htttp://www.lastdaysmystery.info/rapture_debate.htm, accessed 10-24-03
[169] 1 Thess 4:16-17
[170] Debate, accessed 10-24-03; note Dan 12:1-2; Jn 11-24-26
[171] LaSor, William Sanford. *The Truth About Armegeddon. What the Bible Says About the End Times*. New York, NY: Harper & Row Pub., 1982. p. 172
[172] Sandeen, Ernest. *The Roots of Fundamentalism. British and American Millenarianism 1800-1930*. Chicago, IL: The University of Chicago Press, 1970. p. 63
[173] Heb 9:27-28

the Second Coming. The Old Testament saints are to be raised and rewarded also at this time--"together with us."[174] This is a promise set into context by Paul as he addressed the church in Ephesus. He wrote: "This mystery is that through the gospel the Gentiles are heirs together with Israel, members together of one body, and sharers together in the promise in Christ Jesus."[175] This is the good news heralded by Jesus as He "led the captives in his train" when He ascended "on high."[176] These are the Old Testament saints, who held out hope for their Messiah and were honored for their faith. Jesus will bring them with Him at the time of the Second Coming. All who belong to the Lord will be raised at that time. John Newton, the author of *Amazing Grace*, and a sound preacher in his own right, clarified this in a message in 1789. His text was 1 Thessalonians 4:16-17. He connected the rapture and one-time return of the Lord together with *all* the saints being gathered. He said: "This will constitute his train. The redeemed from the earth; they who lived and died in the faith of his name, through a course of successive generations; and they who shall be alive at his coming, shall be *all* collected together, and be prepared to welcome Him."[177] With this, he assured his hearers and us that when the King returns, all of His subjects will be present to welcome Him. There will be no third event. When Jesus comes, all who believed in God and His eternal promise to send the Redeemer will be resurrected.[178] The only other resurrection is that for the wicked who will spend eternity in the lake of fire.

We will look into some of these concerns and others elsewhere in this book. But, suffice it to say, the weaknesses of dispensational pre-tribulation teaching are numerous when examined and compared to Scripture. Biblical scrutiny is necessary and, also, what most believers fail to apply which enables this teaching to continue on in error.

---

[174] Heb 11:39-40
[175] Eph 3:6
[176] Eph 4:8
[177] Newton, John. *The Works of the Rev. John Newton*. New Haven, CT: Nathan Whiting, 1826. Vol. III, p. 590 [emphasis added].
[178] Job 19:25-27; Jn 11:25-27; Dan 12:1-2; Mk 3:16-18

THE PROBLEM OF PRESUPPOSITION

Many people come to the table with thoughts and ideas regarding Bible prophecy. Some of their beliefs may be grounded in fact being obtained from sound Biblical sources. Their grasp of eschatology[1] may be rational, logical, and also may be correct. However, with the overwhelming popularity of pre-trib teaching, many who attend conservative, evangelical churches have been exposed to only one view. Otherwise orthodox believers have been exclusively brought into agreement with the teachings of Dispensationalism[2] without knowing it. Many have never heard--accurately and in detail--other views. They have also for the most part never pursued the subject by studying the related scriptures personally and have instead taken the word of so-called prophecy experts. Also to be noted is the tendency for the writer or teacher of Bible prophecy to be merely presenting pre-trib views without any consideration of the conflict between the Bible and their own statements. Often, this is nothing more than the result of private interpretation. When reading through commentaries, articles, and other statements by these exponents of pre-trib ideas, we find that one person is often repeating the ideas of another person or their favorite Bible teacher without giving it a second thought. Key sections, verses, and context from the Bible are ignored. Everything is filtered through their presupposition.

Ernest Best cautions in this regard, so a problem might be recognized before we become entangled by presumptive ideas or unfounded new ones. He says we all come to Scripture with our own presuppositions, that "they are part of our world view, part of our personal theology." His cautionary advice should help us to recognize that "our minds are not empty when we read or listen to Scripture." We must rationally deal with this, so our reading and interpretation become "consistent" and not tainted by notions accepted previously without the safeguard of genuine truth.[3] Anytime we are predisposed through a personal

---

[1] Study of the last things. [See Glossary].
[2] See Glossary

preference, we become potential targets of further deviation, since we have not investigated all the ramifications of a text as it applies to Biblical doctrine or a newly encountered question about that doctrine.

D. A. Carson extends this line of thought in his masterful treatise on challenges surrounding the Christian confrontation with pluralism. His preliminary look into the difficulties in this area of theological interest begins with hermeneutics. He is crystal clear about the hardcore presuppositions that effect everyone and, like Best, warns of the underlying prejudices and traditions--the prejudgments that are invariably brought into our interpretation of scripture.[4] Carson underscores the issue by saying: "Long-defended interpretations may be nothing other than manipulative displays of power exercised by some group that is trying to enforce conformity to its heritage. Previously held criteria such as coherence and internal consistency are judged largely inapplicable."[5] In the simplest terms, these maneuvers are mere slights of hand which in the end will justify the position held by the Bible teacher with an agenda. With Bible prophecy, it becomes dangerous to the Body of Christ when preaching and teaching take on an air of authority built on a shaky premise. By comparing the claim to Scripture, uncovered will be a statement that uses the Bible to justify the claim by the same Bible that is being contradicted. End times' teaching in particular has this tendency to exceed rational thinking, since the events have not yet occurred. As noted by C. S Lewis: "We must admit at once that this doctrine, has in the past, led Christians into very great follies."[6] Lewis was commenting on the Second Coming in his reflection on the failures of William Miller who was a date setter. Miller's claims did not materialize. Jesus did not return in 1844. This became known as the Great Disappointment.

Dr. Cyril Barber included a valuable reference with the problem of an open or

---

[3] Best, Ernest. *From Text To Sermon: Responsible Use of the New Testament in Preaching.* Atlanta, GA: John Knox, 1978. p. 97-99.

[4] Carson, D. A. *The Gagging of God. Christianity Confronts Pluralism.* Grand Rapids, MI: ZondervanPublishingHouse, 1996. p. 68

[5] *Ibid.* p. 74

[6] Lewis, C. S. *The World's Last Night.* New York, NY: Harcourt Brace Jovanivich, 1973. p. 106

closed mind in his excellent commentary on the book of Job. He brought to light the thoughts of Dr. Milton Rokeach from his work on this very topic. Dr. Barber wrote:

> The dogmatic or closed-minded person fails to discriminate between relevant and irrelevant factors. They hold their views in isolation, fail to engage in logical integration with other data, and in the final analysis tend strongly to reject and be ill-informed about belief systems other than their own. Such an individual becomes close-minded and manifests an inflexibility when confronted with other belief systems.[7]

This describes the challenge in succinct terms. All pre-suppositions must yield to the truth. No individual's version of it can be permitted to alter or set aside what scripture states. Even difficult passages must be weighed carefully and not melded into a pre-fabricated notion when a congregation or an interested inquirer's soul is at stake.

The danger of this should be obvious. However, a great number of church-goers like what they hear and accept it. Then, when they repeat the scenario, they are passing along the identical message without doing the labor to investigate. The borrowed presupposition is then handed on to others who are unlikely to measure carefully what is promoted. They are supposing that this is true, that this is sound doctrinally, and that this is what the church always believed. If someone questions what is said, and scriptures are searched, the pre-suppositional grid is in place, and the conclusions are filtered through the previously assumed conclusions which may not be true at all. Many times the context and the intent of the Bible writer are ignored. Again, the filter is in place, and we find the pre-suppositional matrix at work. Most of those young in the faith open the Bible without knowledge or understanding and are ripe for any help that comes along--sound or otherwise. They trust those who teach and do not question much of what they hear. Overlooked is the caution from Isaiah:

---

[7] Barber, Cyril J. *Job. The Sovereignty of God and the Suffering of Man.* Eugene, OR: Wipf & Stock, 2013. p. 125

"Come let us reason together...."[8] Church-goers are not told to reason directly with the Lord, and because the eschatological area of Bible study is difficult, conclusions are left with the experts. When a Bible teacher brings up the Apostle Paul who reminded them of the Bereans who searched the scriptures daily to see if it were so,[9] it seems to be a subtle seal of approval on what the teacher just said, so the details do not have to be verified. Sadly, the unwary listener is led astray and left in a pre-suppositional quagmire. Once *serious* investigation occurs, a believer has a valuable opportunity to learn that the Bible presents an entirely different view which will expose the error of pre-trib teaching. Then the presuppositions should become recognizable, and the soundness of scripture now visible in context will have a fresh, sensible meaning.

Walter Kaiser warned of pre-suppositional diversions within his discussion on methods and their importance: "...the warning must be reissued once again against all premature impositions of assorted generalizations or allegedly heightened and contemporaneous meanings of the text."[10] The risk should be clear, that presuppositions will provide the basis for adjusting the meaning of the text. Kaiser said further: "In no way should such a half-baked theologizing substitute for that diligent search for an internally derived principle of unity."[11] James Stalker, well known for his biographical masterpiece on the life of Christ said: "The first duty of an interpreter is to find out what the writer meant to convey at the moment he wrote."[12] This same responsibility applies to the Bible expositor, teacher, or preacher as well. Darrell Bock, a dispensationalist from Dallas Theological Seminary, writing about "preunderstandings" explains that "certain approaches to questions often draw us in favorably almost by default, not because we have examined the issues carefully, but because we are almost predisposed to accept a certain orientation over another."[13] This candid

---

[8] Is 1:18
[9] Acts 17:11
[10] Kaiser, Walter C., Jr. *Toward An Old Testament Theology.* Grand Rapids, MI: Zondervan, 1978. p. 18
[11] *Ibid.* p. 18
[12] Stalker, James. *The Psalm of Psalms.* Edinburgh: T & T Clark, 1912. p. 10
[13] Bock, Darrell L; Craig A. Blaising; Kenneth L. Gentry; Robert B. Strimple;. *Three*

reflection shows that presupposition can act like a lodestone drawing someone to a predetermined view which could be orthodox or outright heresy. Ramesh Richard, writing in Dallas Seminary's publication, "Bibliotheca Sacra," candidly offered the same warning: "Some people twist Bible passages in an effort to make them relevant."[14] This revelation also tells us that dispensationalists may know the rules and still violate the purpose for established safeguards. For some, the end justifies the means. D. Martyn Lloyd-Jones, an amillennialist, cautioned vigorously as he detailed the difficulties of reading and interpretation. With regard to Paul's epistles, he said: "You can easily read these Epistles and be no wiser at the end than you were at the beginning because of what you have been reading into what Paul says, wresting them to your own destruction."[15] He further amplified the danger by stating that we often "approach the Bible with a theory, and everything we read is controlled by it."[16] Seeking to pinpoint the source of this in general, he called attention to expositors and teachers who were honest men, but also "mistaken men."[17] In identifying more carefully their problem, he said it was not their sincerity in question, but that "they evolved a theory and they were rather pleased with it; then they went back with this theory to the Bible, and they seemed to find it everywhere."[18] While he was not solely pointing out dispensationalists here, he clearly was not in favor of C. I. Scofield's ideas as expressed in his study Bible.[19] Lloyd-Jones' primary concern for believers was their Bible reading, and how they approach it. He placed great emphasis on this and warned that: "There is nothing so dangerous as to come to the Bible with a theory, with preconceived ideas, with some pet idea of our own, because the

---

Views on the Millennium and Beyond. Grand Rapids, MI: Zondervan, 2002. p. 285 (Bock's "Summary Essay").

[14] Richard, Ramesh P. "Bibliotheca Sacra." Volume 143. April – June 1986. Number 570. p. 123

[15] Lloyd-Jones, D. Martyn. *Studies in the Sermon on the Mount.* Grand Rapids, MI: Wm. B. Eerdmans, 1979. Vol. I, p. 11

[16] *Ibid.*

[17] *Ibid.*

[18] *Ibid.*

[19] Sargent, Tony. *The Sacred Anointing. The Preaching of Dr. Martyn Lloyd-Jones.* Wheaton, IL: Crossway Books, 1994. p. 225

moment we do so, we shall be tempted to over-emphasize one aspect and under-emphasize another."[20] And this is a major concern with the pre-trib rapture theory. We must read with great care and not be tempted to interject our preferences or transpose the ideas of the writer into a modern idea. This doctrine of the end-times events must be approached with great caution.

Noted Greek scholar and founder of the Institute for Antiquity and Christianity, Ernest Cadman Colwell, was well aware of the attempts to modernize Bible interpretations and to conform them into a more contemporary setting. He recognized: "A rich vocabulary has grown up around the effort to read modern meanings into the Scriptures."[21] He noted the use of "allegory, typology, numerology, tropology, and the anagogical sense"[22] as tools which would be used to distract from the Bible writer's primary purpose. He raised the concern, since latter-day modernizing made it appear that the first readers of the Scriptures did not understand what was written to them. He used the Scofield Reference Bible as an example of this problem. Colwell pointed to C. I. Scofield and an exaggerated claim regarding Ezekiel 38:2-3, referring to Rosh, Meshak, and Tubal. Scofield claimed, "in the opinion of all interpreters" this means Russia, Moscow, and Tobolsk. Colwell pointed out that this kind of claim infers that Ezekiel's readers could not possibly understand what Ezekiel was talking about.[23] He noted that some of the church's early interpreters also became victims of this. Because the danger of drawing something from the text that is not there is a perennial danger, Bible readers and students must be vigilant today and utilize a safeguard whenever questionable doctrines are examined. Pre-trib teaching falls into the arena of teachings to be examined carefully.

Phillip E. Johnson who authored *Darwin On Trial* taught law for more than thirty years. He obviously has experience in the rules of evidence and the tools

---

[20] Lloyd-Jones. *Studies in the Sermon on the Mount.* Vol. 1, p. 11
[21] Colwell, Ernest Cadman. *The Study of the Bible.* Chicago, IL: The University of Chicago Press, 1976. p. 106
[22] *Ibid.*
[23] *Ibid.* Colwell demonstrates the fallacy of ignoring the Bible writer's primary intent for the sake of pressing the interpretation of the hour.

of research which are necessary to render a sound foundation for a case. As a former Supreme Court law clerk and an attorney, he knew arguments are won on the basis of facts. Through the years, he noted the change in the way data is gathered and used. In Johnson's later work, *The Wedge of Truth*, Dallas Willard expressed this thought succinctly in the Foreword. He wrote: "Now, sadly, the method is judged by whether it brings you to the 'right' conclusion, as determined by institutional consensus congealed around glittering personalities. If you don't come to the 'right' conclusion, your method is wrong, and you are probably a bad person. Derisive terminology will be used to describe you."[24] While Willard's field was philosophy and Johnson's was law, both observed the shift in the prudent adherence to faithful examination of facts which will determine the resulting verdict. This downgrade is also shared in theological circles. Hence, basic hermeneutical rules can be totally ignored when seeking to determine when the rapture occurs. For pre-trib advocates, it is the conclusion that matters and not the facts. In the process, simple contextual guidelines are set aside. For them, the result of any investigation is a forgone matter: it will be pre-trib. This directly affects those who sincerely desire a true understanding of what the scripture says.[25] When they seek more help and better resources, the books and material found will be lacking the orthodox foundation of truth, and the innocent reader may be led astray.

While not every denomination or church holds a dispensational, pre-trib statement of faith, we only have to peruse the shelves of many Christian book stores to see that the majority of books dealing with end times are in the pre-trib mode. To find opposing views you have to search diligently--libraries, used book stores, and the internet. If we investigate carefully, we will find that the pre-suppositional attitude of the pre-trib theory has been dealt with and refuted in the past. This is to the credit of those who recognized its danger and then taught, preached, and wrote to dispel the error--primarily by facing off against the false teaching itself. Some of them were the English contemporaries of John Nelson Darby, the originator and popularizer of this end-time theory.[26]

---

[24] Johnson, Phillip E. *The Wedge of Truth. Splitting the Foundations of Naturalism.* Downers Grove, IL InterVarsity Press, 2000. p. 9-10

[25] See Appendix for "Recommended Reading List."

[26] The influence of John Nelson Darby and his dispensationalism has been major.

Notably, the writings of B.W. Newton, Samuel Tregelles, Robert Chapman,[27] and the man of faith, George Muller,[28] all stand in opposition to the pre-trib idea and are thorough in their orthodox use of scripture to expose the fallacious teachings.[29] Their efforts reveal the overt use of pre-suppositional thinking from the outset. These men were side by side with Darby in the 1800's. Their books and pamphlets are still available and reflect an obvious effort on the part of some of those associated with Darby's own group, the Plymouth Brethren, to correct the faulty teaching of its leading voice. Many have written and spoken out since their day, yet because this idea of a pre-trib rapture is appealing, the pre-suppositional train rolls on. The error has been continued through the writing of C. H. Mackintosh, William Kelly (who edited Darby's works), F. W. Grant, and William E. Blackstone. Further popularization has come to us through Arno C. Gaebelein, C. I. Scofield, Lewis Sperry Chafer, H. A. Ironside, I. M. Haldeman, Clarence Larkin, William R. Newell, and more recently, John F. Walvoord, E. Schuyler English, Charles C. Ryrie, J. Dwight Pentecost, along with a host of other contemporary pre-trib advocates. These men are to be given credit where they have held to the cardinals of the faith, but must be identified and renounced for misleading many innocent truth-seekers with dispensational ideas.

Here is a further problem and the key to surmounting this difficult obstacle: It is only when a believer is seriously concerned enough about this issue that clarity starts to emerge. It is when the earnest heart under conviction seeks answers to questions that the light of truth begins its work.[30] It is when the Holy Spirit connects us with truth as revealed in the scripture that the unsound claims become clearly opened up--exposed as error. The Spirit does this for us, as commissioned by Jesus: He is the Spirit of Truth who will guide us into all truth.[31] When Jesus prayed that we would be sanctified, it was to be through the

---

[27] See Appendix for Robert Chapman.

[28] See Appendix for George Muller. Also, note that a number of A-mill and Post-mill advocates have refuted pre-trib teaching.

[29] See the chapter "History" for additional information regarding these men.

[30] This is the testimony of numerous former Dispensationalists who abandoned the pre-trib theory.

[31] Jn 14:26ff

word of Truth: "Thy word is truth."[32] We are called to work our way through the scriptures ourselves--with the Holy Spirit--and not take the word of others.[33] Consequently, the light of truth comes when a believer searches out the Bible for the evidence directly from the texts where they appear.[34] This means weighing the statements of Jesus, Paul, John, Peter, and looking back to the words of the prophets. Jesus spoke clearly when He said, "until heaven and earth disappear, not the smallest letter, nor the least stroke of a pen, will by any means disappear from the Law until everything is accomplished."[35] Everything is not accomplished. All is not done. Heaven and earth are still here. We would do well to compare our ideas with those of the prophets Jesus mentioned and the Law He fulfilled. Peter stated clearly that "we have the word of the prophets made more certain,"[36] and we will do well if we pay attention, thereby avoiding pre-suppositional pitfalls.

There are a number of dynamic factors which directly contribute to the continuance of presupposition. One is the premise of employing only a certain number of Bible references to the *exclusion* of others. Relevant evidence is either ignored, reinterpreted, or minimized. This places undue weight on a few critical pre-trib references which at first glance would seem to support the view. When examined in the light of other passages, though, the fallacy becomes clear. The addition of other verses assists in presenting an orthodox statement about the Second Coming. "The Golden Rule of Interpretation" is a reasonable directive in this regard. It was drawn up by David L. Cooper. He wrote:

> When the plain sense of Scripture makes common sense, seek no other sense; therefore, take every word at its primary, ordinary, usual, literal meaning unless the facts of the immediate context, studied in the light of related passages and axiomatic and fundamental truths, indicate otherwise.[37]

---

[32] Jn 17:17
[33] 1 Cor 2:10ff; Col 2:4, 8
[34] Ps 119:97-100, 105, 130
[35] Mt 5:18
[36] 2 Pt 1:19

It is interesting to note that Cooper was a staunch believer in the dispensational teaching of J.N. Darby and C. I. Scofield. It is rather fascinating to note that Dr. Tim LaHaye who was influenced by Cooper, when quoting this, conveniently omitted the latter portion where we might be encouraged to check these matters more carefully. He edited the statement, omitting "ordinary, usual" and cut off the quote at the point Cooper suggests checking "related passages" that might "indicate otherwise":

> When the plain sense of Scripture makes common sense, seek no other sense, but take every word at its primary, literal meaning unless the facts of the immediate context clearly indicate otherwise.[38]

This subtle edit leads us away from careful study and, unfortunately, helps to maintain the bias that pre-trib teaching is valid. This also casts a bad light on pre-trib teachers who claim to take scripture literally, when in reality their presuppositions force them to add and adjust as they go.

Another error that contributes to the continuance of presupposition is similar and equally important. This is simply *assumption*. The conclusion is assumed based on only a limited number of references. This uses just parts of the whole to make up the whole. This is like "connecting the dots"--but with only a few of the dots. With pre-trib teaching, some truth is employed and then extended into the whole to form the premise. Because the little pieces are true, then the grand pre-trib statement must be also. This is a fallacy not to be ignored. It forces a conclusion on limited evidence and assists the prophecy teacher to bring us to a forgone conclusion. This methodology is a component of *apriorism* which does not afford us a look at all the facts. The published works of John F. Walvoord show him to be a masterful exponent of numerous

---

[37] Cooper, David L. *What Men Must Believe.* Los Angeles, CA: Biblical Research Society, 1953. fronticepiece

[38] LaHaye, Tim. *No Fear of the Storm. Why Christians Will Escape All the Tribulation.* Sisters, OR: Multnomah Press Books, 1992. p. 240

assumptions regarding the rapture. Many of his conclusions are mere presupposition crafted to divert attention from context and original intent. This is a significant issue as noted by George Eldon Ladd. He encouraged the use of caution when hearing pre-trib claims which leave a believer to assume a statement is valid. He wrote, it may seem all right on the surface, however "if we are to interpret Scripture by assumption, we can find almost anything we desire in the Word of God by assuming it is there."[39] When the Apostle Paul wrote, "What saith Scripture?"[40] in his appeal to the church in Rome, it was to encourage a good, long look at truth and not men's conclusions emanating from incomplete investigation.

A third area which confounds this pre-suppositional theory is one of **distinction**. With this, we have to look at the way a pre-tribulationist teaches the position at large. Careful observation will show us that the concept of the pre-trib view (Dispensationalism) is presented so as to appear to be pre-millennialism proper (Historic Pre-millennialism). This is not the case at all. In reality, pre-trib is a distinct teaching and should be termed separately as "dispensational pre-millennialism" for the sake of clarity. The historic pre-millennial view is able to stand alone in the sense that it defines itself as Christ returning before the millennium. Other millennial views place the Lord's return at the end of the millennium or reject the idea of a millennium altogether.[41] The pre-millennial view was brought to the forefront again in the nineteenth century due to a renewed interest in eschatology in general and, more specifically, as a reinvigorated defense against the a-millennial teaching which had resurfaced. As this debate grew, J. N. Darby emerged as a major proponent spreading the pre-trib theory as if it were a legitimate part of pre-millennialism. He labored first in Britain and then traveled to the United States. C. I. Scofield popularized it for thousands of Bible readers from the early twentieth century on with his

---

[39] Ladd, George Eldon. *The Blessed Hope*. Grand Rapids, MI: Wm. B. Eerdmans Pub., 1973. p. 97

[40] Rm 4:3

[41] Post-millennialism and A-millennialism, respectively. Note that Robert Clouse's work, *The Meaning of the Millennium: Four Views*. Downers Grove, IL: InterVarsity Press, 1984, adds the pre-tribulation position as a *fourth* view, distinct from historic pre-millennialism.

well-known Scofield Reference Bible.[42] Hence, Dispensationalism came to America--"the happy hunting ground for all kinds of isms."[43] Harry Ironside in writing of the mystery of Christ and the church says:

> In fact, until brought to the fore through the writings and the preaching and teaching of a distinguished ex-clergyman, Mr. J. N. Darby, in the early part of the last century, it is scarcely to be found in a single book or sermon throughout a period of sixteen hundred years! If any doubt this statement, let them search, as the writer has in measure done....[44]

Dr. Ironside employs the distinction of this "mystery," joining it with that of the rapture in a subsequent chapter, and by inference connects the explanation of these "mysteries" to Darby and Scofield who appeared on the scene in the latter part of the 1800s. These admissions aid in exposing the sources of this theory as Darbyist. Obviously, this frames the idea as a later, nineteenth century addition--not first-century Apostolic at all!

In addition, notice that pre-trib teachers for two succeeding generations have subtly employed **term switching** to redefine "dispensational pre-tribulationalism" as if it were "pre-millennialism." Today they use the term freely and interchangeably, superimposing a term where it does not match the proper definition. These terms are not the same at all. The distinction between

---

[42] Walvoord, John F. *The Rapture Question*. Findlay, OH: Dunham Pub. Co., 1957. p. 15. Here, Walvoord traces the pretribulational position and says, "This teaching was espoused by Darby and the Plymouth Brethren and popularized by the famous *Scofield Reference Bible*." His subtle admission is an honest credit to the two men for their instrumental part in introducing this new theory. This fact is confirmed by Dr. John Warwick Montgomery as he stated: "Certainly, J. N. Darby and the Scofield editors introduced the church to Dispensationalism as a special brand of millennialism." See: Armerding, Carl E., and W. Ward Gasque. *Handbook of Biblical Prophecy*. Grand Rapids, MI: Baker Book House, 1978. p. 181

[43] Berkhof, L. *Aspects of Liberalism*. Grand Rapids, MI: Wm. B. Eerdmans, 1951. p. 111

[44] Ironside, H.A. *The Mysteries of God*. New York, NY: Loizeaux Bros., n.d. p. 50-51

them has been masked by all the dust stirred up by the feet of teachers who use pre-suppositional approaches to engage their audience with pre-trib ideas. The fallacy here can be cleared up by any sound theological dictionary or an orthodox systematic theology.[45] A good definition always improves the value of a word and protects its use in context. This is true with the use of all language in any field of study. As former President Grover Cleveland noted with regard to "self" and citizenship: "…it is time to forbid the prostitution of the word to a sinister use."[46] This is not to insinuate a sinister connection with dispensationalism, but moreover to point to the word as it applies in context being misused. Rearranging words, connecting verses not directly related, and adding meaning unintended by the Biblical writer only add to the confusion. Clear definitions of terms are a must. "Pre-trib" plainly means Jesus returns at the commencement of the seven year tribulation; "Pre-mill" means Jesus returns at the beginning of the 1,000 year millennium referred to in the Apocalypse. They are very different, indeed.

This takes us is to an arena where logic is discarded, and the basic hermeneutical principles are pressed toward *a conclusion that does not exist*. The offered proof becomes like a simple demonstration of a magnet and its effect on a compass. The person holding the magnet can make the needle point anywhere he wishes. The claims made by dispensational pre-trib teachers and so-called prophecy experts assuring us that they take the Bible literally are pure nonsense. A simple study employing careful reading of the texts in question will determine who employs literalism and who does not. Like the oil leak from a car in a driveway, we find the culprit once again is faulty pre-suppositional thinking. The answer for serious inquirers is simple: examine the scriptures; read and read until understood. R.A. Torrey, himself a dispensationalist, boldly advocated this, yet held to his pre-trib position. He said, "Do not study commentaries, lesson helps or other books about the Bible: study the Bible itself. Do not study *about* the Bible, study *the Bible*."[47] It is

---

[45] See: Erickson, Buswell, Grudem, etc.; also, Unger, Brown, Smith, etc.

[46] Cleveland, Grover. *Good Citizenship*. Philadelphia, PA: Henry Altemus Co., 1908. p. 28

[47] Torrey, R.A. *The Importance and Value of Proper Bible Study*. New York, NY:

most unfortunate that he was under the dispensational influence of D.L. Moody and other early supporters of dispensational ideas. He could have heeded his own advice and undertaken a closer look at the author of Thessalonians and his plain statements on this subject. When Paul called us in the Body of Christ to an orthodox faith and a Biblical understanding of doctrine, he directed us to Scripture and not outside authorities. He expounded this in the first chapter of First Corinthians.[48] He, also, pointed to our mind being a critical instrument in the needed change saying, "...be transformed by the renewing of your mind."[49] This is a process. It also demands that we have--each of us--input from the Word of God, not presumption from others who may only repeat erroneous theories. This is a key reason for Paul's second letter to the church at Thessalonica--a warning about false letters, a prophecy, or report supposedly from him.[50] When concerned believers investigate the Biblical context of what pre-trib teachers promote, a clear understanding will emerge about the warnings for us not to be deceived. We must not be misled by pre-suppositions. This is not to suggest that theological works should be set aside. Many of the commentaries and studies from past masters are worthy of consultation. Yet, scripture must be thoroughly studied first, and then, commentaries and other reference works can be consulted. This was the method of Arthur W. Pink who developed his form of study over many years. He labored through the text itself seeking its meaning in context. "To state Pink's method of study and writing very simply, he was a deep student of his primary text, the Bible."[51] This model has also been followed by many other pulpit masters and divines through the years. It is the Bible itself that must take pre-eminence in our study. The opinions of good men may contain error, and a sincere teacher can be sincerely wrong. Yet, all must yield to scripture in context. The Lord Jesus warned us about deception at the end of the age for good reason.[52]

George H. Doran, 1921. p. 33   [emphasis in the original].

[48] e.g., 1 Cor 1:19-21. Paul directed this church to follow the "preaching"--the word, not personalities.

[49] Rm 12:1-2

[50] 2 Thess 2:2; also, 2 Pt 2:2

[51] Belcher, Richard P. *Arthur W. Pink. Born to Write. A Biography.* Columbia, SC: Richbarry Press, 1980. p. 34-35

[52] Mt 24:4, 5, 11, 24; Mk 13:5, 6, 9, 22-23; Lk 17:23; 21:8

Another point to remember when reading through the most commonly used pre-trib Bible references is to be keenly aware of what is left out. When we lay the Scripture verse side by side with the theory offered by the pre-trib interpretation, the omissions become obvious. The error of *omission* is likely the most glaring aspect of how we are led astray. A primary example of this is found in John 14:1-3. This is a favorite proof-text of all pre-trib teachers. Note that there is no hint whatsoever of *when* this occurs. The Lord says He will come back--for us--but He does not describe this as part of a first-phase rapture of the church. So, when a prophecy expert uses John 14:1-3 to support the pre-trib view, the statement is just an argument from silence, since Jesus did not say anything about before, during, or after a return from heaven at the end of the age. He simply states that He will come back. The pre-trib assumptions and their pre-suppositions should be obvious and weakened considerably by this oversight. Further as an example: when the Apostle Paul wrote to the Thessalonian church regarding the Lord's return, we find another serious omission on the part of those holding the pre-trib position. Note that in context, 1 Thessalonains 4:13-18 does not include any chronological reference. Paul is not placing a fix on the timing of this event within these verses--only that it will occur. It is the pre-trib teacher that adds in the timing to set this event to take place before the tribulation. As a defense of this fallacy, we may hear words to the effect that the timing is in the next chapter--we are "not appointed to wrath,"[53] implying we must be removed prior to "wrath," hence, taken out (raptured) in 1 Thessalonians 4:16-17 before trouble begins. However, Paul never states this. In fact, he says just the opposite in the verses that follow. He says *that day* will come as a thief--destruction for them and salvation for us.[54] In other words, believers are all here, and it should not take a Christian by surprise. He confirms the identical scenario in second epistle to the Thessalonians.[55] Today, attention must be paid to these omissions. In order to

---

[53] 1 Thess 5:9

[54] Read carefully through 1 Thess 5:1-11. Paul's further explanation of "the Day of the Lord" is comprised of the two events together. The first being described in 1 Thess 4:13-18, then amplified for encouragement in chapter five.

[55] 2 Thess 1:3-10. Note Paul's vivid description of their current persecution and how he describes the brilliant return of the Lord to resolve all of this for them. He is specific

clarify the gross error caused by pre-trib teaching and see the true picture of Paul's intent, all an inquirer needs to do is read the passages (and those related) a few times in context. Again, we see the dangerous effect of *eisegesis*[56] at work. Something was *added*, because something was *left out*. This is all too common with the popular exposition involved with end-times explanations.

Yes, a little presumption goes a long way. Clear thinking and rational reasoning are important safeguards when weighing the importance of claims made by prophecy teachers. Conclusions must not only be sound, they must agree totally with Scripture. False application of logic leads to false teaching. All Christians are at risk from errant views. Hence all of us must be diligent in testing for the Truth.[57]

---

in his use of pronouns and time words (when). There is *no* hint of any relief until the Lord comes "in blazing fire with his powerful angels." He reinforces this in chapter two, stating two things must happen *first* [2 Thess 2:1-3].

[56] Reading into the text; putting in place what is not there; adding to what the writer intended.

[57] For additional insight on false claims, see: Carson, D. A. *Exegetical Fallacies. Second Edition.* Grand Rapids, MI: Baker Books/Paternoster, 1998.

SOME LITTLE WORDS

It is very important to pay attention to words as they appear in presentations offered by pre-trib advocates. Often, these words are misused in order to garner credibility. Obviously, their teaching centers around concepts associated with a rapture. This inordinate emphasis of the church's early removal has caused this theory to take on a life of its own. Consequently we find that the pre-trib rapture idea takes precedence over the truth which New Testament writers actually place before us. The pre-trib view has been promoted heavily for less than two hundred years.[1] Many of the ideas advanced today follow the same pattern as set by the early followers of John Nelson Darby in England and, later, by C. I. Scofield in America. Because this theory was new in the nineteenth century,[2] the early advocates were developed a system of teaching based on Darby's thoughts and other early Plymouth Brethren teachers. This led to a pattern of teaching for the pre-trib rapture which gradually evolved into what is known today commonly as "Pretribulationalism."[3] It is openly admitted by some pre-trib teachers that the post-tribulation view is the oldest view of the church.[4] John Walvoord affirmed this as he commented of the church's place in prophecy. He wrote: "In the church of the second and third century, it was commonly believed that the church was already in the great tribulation predicted by Christ. For this reason, they believed in the imminency of Christ's return as an event which could happen any day."[5] In spite of this--the church's

---

[1] Ladd, George Eldon. *The Blessed Hope*. Grand Rapids, MI: Wm. B. Eerdmans Co., 1973. p. 35-60

[2] Hindson, Ed. *Earth's Final Hours*. Eugene, OR: Harvest House, 1999. p. 54-55. Hindson, a pre-trib advocate, admits the pre-trib rapture being "unique" to Darby's teachings. See chapter "History" for additional information; also, consult the "Recommended Reading List."

[3] One of the primary components of Dispensationalism which Darby promoted. Commonly, "Pre-trib."

[4] Hocking, David. *What Christians Believe*. Tustin, CA: Hope For Today Pub., 1998. p. 159; Ross, Randall. *The Next 7 Events of the Future*. Orlando, FL: Creation House, 1997. p. 134

post-tribulational stance--pre-trib teachers continue to actively promote pre-trib views ignoring church history and, more important, what the Bible says in context. Often, these teachers muddy the waters by inaccurately referring to pre-trib as premillenialism. This is unwarranted and adds to the confusion about the Second Coming.[6] For some time, current events in the Middle East seem to add credibility to their proposition, especially in light of the re-establishment of Israel in 1948. However, this premise can be misleading, and by using this event many prophecy teachers willfully continue to emphasize the church being raptured at the expense of scripture.

The add-on feature of the removal of the church at the beginning of the tribulation period was a codicil brought to the table by J. N. Darby which was novel to premillennial thinking. His interpretation was radically new to those who supported premillenialism. This feature is one of the distinctives of Dispensationalism.[7] Because of this, and the fact that end-times events were often neglected or misunderstood prior to Darby, his embryonic concept allowed some ministers the option of taking up this teaching without examining the full range of scripture. In other words, the idea took on its own life, and the flea has ended up wagging the dog. It is John Nelson Darby's pretributional*ism* that founded a new doctrinal perspective--all *isms* have a tendency to do this. In addition, the early phases of Darby's theological development of this notion separated the church from Israel. Once that was established, he drew together the plan for Israel and then the plan for the church. "Darby will find few writers, outside of his own group of followers, who will admit the absolute distinction which he maintains between Israel and the church."[8] According to Darby's followers, the future for Israel meant great tribulation, and the church would be removed prior to this by a pre-trib rapture.

The irony of contemporary pre-trib teaching is that it is likeable. It permits the

---

[5] Walvoord, John F. *The Church in Prophecy.* Grand Rapids, MI: Zondervan Pub. House, 1964. p. 114

[6] See Glossary for the proper definition of these terms.

[7] See Glossary; also see chapter: "History."

[8] Bass, Clarence. *Backgrounds to Dispensationalism.* Grand Rapids, MI: Wm. B. Eerdmans Pub. Co., 1960. p.126

church to face off against the worst time imaginable in all of human history and not have to be a participant. Christians can now deal with the end of the age and the horrific threats of wrath and judgment thinking they are no longer a menace. People are led to believe they are insulated from the Antichrist, the false prophet, and judgment. Yet, when a serious inquirer reads through the New Testament and encounters certain words in rapture proof-text passages and questions them, something happens. Either they stop and rethink what they have been taught, or they move on thinking erroneously that what they heard from a "prophecy expert" must be right. Often important *little words* are not even noticed. But if a seeker honestly returns to those chapters and sections, looking again at the verses in question, certain words will be a puzzle. These are the very words ignored or mistreated by the "experts" who surround us. This has not changed since Darby's day. In fact, this pattern of bypassing points in certain texts was once known as "grasshopper exegesis"[9] and continues to the present hour. This standard has become part of the Calvary Chapel network of churches as admitted by Pastor Chuck Smith, the founder. He confirmed his pattern of glossing "over certain passages of Scripture," admitting his critics in this area are "correct."[10] Other teachers do not make the admission but proceed anyway with their avoidance of not only many controversial passages, but key words. This is not limited to eschatology. We find it in ministries where shepherds lack the knowledge or the conviction to present the full message.[11]

This pattern can be noted when we scrutinize pre-trib comments and see important words being neglected or passed by. It is important in basic reading to observe *who, what, where, how, why,* and *when* in order to establish the veracity of the message presented. These are common steps to gain a clear

---

[9] This means certain verses are hopped over, being either reinterpreted or ignored. "If it stood in the way of an 'any moment expectation of the Advent,' it was instantly leaped over." Fromow, George H. *B. W. Newton and Dr. S. P.Tregelles. Teachers of the Faith and the Future.* London: The Sovereign Grace Advent Testimony, 1969. p. 44

[10] Smith, Chuck. *Calvary Chapel Distinctives.* p. 53

[11] Acts 5:20

understanding of a story, report, novel, or in this case to determine the purpose of the message in a New Testament book. Even in a single verse, this carries through, so we can take hold of the basic imperatives as established by the Lord and the Apostles. Jesus set the pattern when He said, "Man does not live by bread alone, but by *every word* that comes from the mouth of God."[12] He articulated this from Deuteronomy[13] as the model for those who were His disciples to follow. Not *one word* was to be tampered with. What He would not fulfill in His first advent would certainly be fulfilled in the second.[14] His followers were responsible for every word. And today we find the playground is vocabulary, with key words--little words--left wanting, and the body of Christ is left deficient in its doctrinal foundation. The parsing of words has become a serious matter for some. The words of Jesus, as with the rest of scripture, carry the weight of truth. All Scripture is inspired.[15] We must consider every word from God to be important. Jesus spoke with full authority. His words exposed hearts and challenged men with regard to the Truth. He said if He had not spoken, "they would not be guilty of sin."[16] Yet, because he had, they had no excuse. It is the same for the doctrinal concerns under discussion today, especially eschatology. Jesus did come and lay out these precise events. We have no excuse for attempting to sidestep the truth about the end of the age. Every word He uttered in this regard must be understood just as He meant it. Note, also, Jesus made a point of alerting us to the difference between the "teaching" of men[17] and His own--and what we should follow after He returns to heaven. All believers must walk in His light--from the teaching He gave and hold to it.[18] As Christians unreservedly hold to and continue in His teaching, the Holy Spirit will teach the Truth just as Jesus did.[19] We must not run off on our own.

---

[12] Mt 4:4 [emphasis added].
[13] Deut 8:3
[14] Mt 5:17-18
[15] 1Tim 3:16-17
[16] Jn 15:22
[17] Mt 16:12; also, Paul, Rm 16:17
[18] Jn 8:30-31
[19] Jn 14:26

When we read or hear key pre-trib verses, we must be careful to actually look at the verse ourselves. The noble ones in Berea[20] examined the Scriptures with care to confirm what was being taught by Paul--an Apostle. We must follow their example. If words are altered, omitted, added, or redefined, then a red flag should appear. We must watch for words that are given a different meaning or being taken out of context. We must carefully compare the text in context to the soundness of the teaching by measuring it by scripture. This examination will assist us to receive and understand the original intent of the writer. With the pre-trib usage of certain verses, we must take great care and note: (1) **time words**; (2) **pronouns**; (3) **context**. When this is done, many verses will appear with more clarity and read more naturally in *context* the way the writer intended. We must pay attention to *time words* and the *personal pronouns* just as they appear in place as used by Paul, John, Matthew, Peter, and the others. They knew what they meant, and we must not draw conclusions which are in opposition to their understanding as they wrote--even if it places us in the path of persecution and danger.[21] Their *context* must be ours, also.

Little Words

Consider some simple examples in the following Scriptures.

Trust Me

****[John 14:1-3] "Do not let your hearts be troubled. Trust in God; *trust also in me*. In my Father's house are many rooms; if it were not so, I would have told you. I am going there to prepare a place for you. And if I go and prepare a place for

---

[20] Acts 17:11
[21] See 1 Thess 3:4; 2 Tim 3:12; and Heb 10:32-39

123

you, I will come back and take you to be with me that you
also may be where I am."[22]

These verses in John's gospel are used as a major proof text for pre-trib
teaching. The proponents of this theory establish the pre-trib rapture as a
doctrine here. But as you look and read carefully, notice there are no *time
words* at all. There are no hints that this plain truth--the Lord to "come back
and take you"--is before, during, or after any specific event. Our popular
prophecy teachers enforce their claim within a fabricated context, reading into
it a pre-tribulational application. Notice, the Lord does not do this. He is clear
about the fact that he will come again, but leaves the details to be established
by other Scriptures. As you can see, there is an absence of chronology in these
verses. The words here are to set to affirm the coming, but not details of the
taking. The thrust of His statement is a call to the disciples to *trust Him* just as
they trust in God. Also, the real-time chronology of the Lord's final week of
ministry on earth tells us that He delivered the Olivet Discourse just a few days
before. There would be no need here in this context to repeat what these men
previously heard. Jesus' teaching on His return was fresh in their minds. They
possess understanding from the same detail we read in Matthew twenty-four,
which simply says He will return after "the distress of those days."[23] Note,
Jesus did not want hearts troubled by his departure and, so, encouraged these
men to be of good cheer,[24] since He is coming back.[25] In the meantime, no
matter what happens, His own will be "with me." This was clearly designed to
increase their faith at a time they would need it most. We tend to forget that in
a few hours He would not only be arrested but condemned and put to death.
The disciples needed encouragement and strengthening from Him, their
Teacher. This is why Jesus said: "Consider carefully what you hear."[26] He also
was clear about deception being rampant at the end of the age.[27] The well-

---

[22] [emphasis added].
[23] Mt 24:29-30.
[24] Jn 16:33, "take heart."
[25] Acts 1:10-11, the disciples were told this again by "two men dressed in white."
[26] Mk 4:24
[27] Mt 24:4, 24 ; Mk 13:5, 9, 21, 23; Lk 21:8, etc.

meaning intention of some of our favorite teachers has altered the purpose of this text putting a blindfold on the sincere truth seeker. Distortion is the result. Every Bible student must be sure to consider the *context* in this portion of John. Jesus' lesson here is to *trust Him*--no matter what. And, yes, for us, also, it is encouragement--He *is* coming. And He said, "Trust **me**"!

Another facet within this portion of Jesus' words of encouragement is the sense of *where* He will be. He does mention the Father's house, and, yes, He is looking toward the time when these disciples will join Him there. He had just told them that they cannot follow Him now but will follow Him later.[28] They will soon be commissioned, empowered with the Holy Spirit, and commence a lifetime of ministry.[29] At some future time, they will join Him. When that occurs, they will be in the Father's house in heaven. There will be plenty of room for them there. They will not be outcasts in heaven as they soon will be unwelcome at the Jerusalem Temple, also known on earth as the Father's house--God's house. Once these men begin to speak out in power, the Jerusalem authorities will make vicious attempts to stop them. Those who will shortly oppose these representatives of Christ and imprison them are members of the ruling council on Temple Mount. The disciples' familiarity with them-- the corruption and opposition from the priests, rulers, and leaders who governed Israel--gave them concern about their own safety. They are being reminded to trust only God. Hence, Jesus offers this admonition. We must remember that as soon as the Holy Spirit comes upon them at Pentecost, each of these men will be risking their lives. Yes, they will join Him later. Also, we must sense the two distinctives here. First, Jesus assures them (trust me), so they know He will be part of their continuing work. This means if one of them is put to death, that disciple will immediately go to be with the Lord in heaven, the true Father's house. This is something to consider, since the Lord previously told them that they would be flogged, arrested, and hated because of Him.[30] He, also, had just reminded them in the upper room of this when He warned that "a time is coming when anyone who kills you will think he is

---

[28] Jn 13:36
[29] This in itself cancels the thought of an imminent return.
[30] Mt 10:16-33; Lk 21:12-19

offering a service to God."[31] Second, the Lord leaves these disciples with the sense that wherever He will be, they will join Him there. This is a very subtle shift by Jesus from the "Father's house" to the assurance that "you also may be where I am." This is important in as much as the Lord wanted these men to grasp the reality that they will be with Him forever no matter where He is. This leads back to His explanations previously as to what will happen when He does return for the second time. He will gather them as described in Matthew thirteen, Matthew twenty-four, and later described by the Apostle Paul.[32] Noticeably absent from these verses in John is the mention of a rapture or a snatching away. Those who employ this section to support the pre-tribulational removal of the church must first consider the full context. This is relevant for us today, since these disciples are presently in the Father's house, and we must carry on with the expectation of the Lord's Second Advent. Jesus does not state here that He is coming to rapture us before trouble commences. He is broadly laying out our place with Him forever once He comes to resurrect the dead and redeem fully the corrupt bodies of His own who "are alive and remain."[33] Location is the key here. We will be with Him forever when He returns to rule and reign. If we perish before that, we will be with Him in heaven,[34] until the Day He comes to judge the world. In either case, we will see His glory.[35] Yes, we will be there.

We

Consider these favorite verses from Paul's first epistle to the Thessalonian church:

> ****[1 Thess 4:16-18]. "For the Lord himself will come down
> from heaven, with a loud command, with the voice of the

---

[31] Jn 16:2
[32] 1 Cor 15:22-24, 50-57
[33] 1 Thess 4:14-17
[34] 2 Cor 5:6-8
[35] Jn 17:24

archangel and with the trumpet call of God, and the dead in Christ will rise first. After that, *we* who are still alive and are left will be caught up together with them in the clouds to meet the Lord in the air. And so *we* will be with the Lord forever. Therefore encourage each other with these words."[36]

This portion of First Thessalonians is another of the primary proof-texts for pre-trib teaching. Again, read carefully. You will not find any reference to chronology. There are no *time words* at all in Paul's explanation as to the disposition of believers who are alive when the Lord returns. He does not say this will occur at the beginning of the tribulation or at any specific time. He merely states that the "dead in Christ will rise first" when the Lord comes. This answers the Thessalonians' concern about their deceased brothers, many of whom perished because of Caesar and their confession of Christ, a capital offense.[37] Continue reading, and the *pronoun* "we" has prominence. Paul makes special note that some of *us* will remain alive at the coming of the Lord. At that time, "we" will be caught up (raptured)--not before or after. Paul is simply stating that some of "us" will be here when the Lord comes to judge. The reason Paul does not emphasize judgment in these verses is his prior mention of this in chapter three. In verse thirteen,[38] he highlighted the graphic sense of the Lord's visible return to include all the "holy ones." These are the same holy ones the Lord spoke of in Matthew thirteen as those who carry out His retribution.[39] The Lord reiterated this in the Olivet Discourse when He taught us to expect to see "the sign of the Son of Man" in the heavens followed by the same holy ones, as He "will send his angels with a loud trumpet call," and then the elect will be gathered.[40] Paul redirects us to this reality in Second Thessalonians chapter one. A reading of verses six through ten will amplify the

---

[36] Compare this passage to Isaiah 4:2-6 which presents this at the end of the last seven years. [emphasis added].

[37] See comments elsewhere in this book regarding these martyrs.

[38] 1 Thess 3:13. Paul had taught them fully when he was there; both epistles are reminders, 2 Thess 2:5.

[39] Mt 13:4-50; also, note Rev 19:11-15. This comparison places this event at the end of the age.

[40] Mt 24:30-31

picture of the Lord's return at the end of the age in "blazing fire with his powerful angels."[41] These verses which appear in context in various places in Scripture are a safeguard for us. We can compare these statements and see the full picture. There is real danger in settling a doctrine on just two or three verses in First Thessalonians[42] alone. We must contemplate what is clearly stated in other places in the Bible as well. Also, note in this section that there is no hint of a quiet event where the Lord will secretly remove His people. This will be a thunderous, brilliant, multi-faceted event with the heavenly host participating. The "we" who are still alive will not be taken by surprise.[43] Why? Because all of the verses relating to this event prepare us for what is to come, and as Paul says, so we can be alert.[44] The Lord said, "See, I have told you ahead of time."[45] As He spoke those words, He continued with several illustrations at the end of the Olivet Discourse, so we would be alert, watching, and ready.[46] Another point to keep in mind is the fact that a return to heaven is never in focus. Paul does not state returning because he knew the Lord would come to earth and set up His kingdom. This is why Paul writes of our being caught up "to meet the Lord in the air." The Greek word Paul uses is *aeer* which specifies the lower atmosphere.[47] There is no mention of the second heaven or the third, just the immediate atmosphere where the clouds are. This correlates directly with the Lord's departure as noted by Luke in Acts 1:11. The Lord will return as the disciples saw Him leave--visibly. This will be at the Second Coming, and those alive will be changed along with those resurrected to join Him here on the earth. Within the context, there is only one coming to the earth in view. This agrees with Paul's vivid description of this in 2 Thessalonians chapter one where he indicates the time of judgment of those on the earth and what happens to the church which is still here.[48] Notice, too, that

---

[41] 2 Thess 1:6-10

[42] 1 Thess 4:16 and 17

[43] 1 Thess 5:4-6

[44] *Ibid.*

[45] Mt 24:25; Mk 13:23

[46] Mt 24 and 25.

[47] Thayer, Joseph Henry. *The New Thayer's Greek-English Lexicon of the New Testament.* Peabody, MA: Hendrickson Pub., 1981. p. 13

[48] 2 Thess 1:6-10

this Pauline reference is analogous to the Lord's words in John 14:1-3 that we will be with Him no matter what--words of encouragement to continue to trust Him.

So

Consider the following verses from Jesus in the Olivet Discourse:

> ****[Mt 24:15] "**So** when you see standing in the holy place 'the abomination that causes desolation, spoken of through the prophet Daniel—let the reader understand...."[49]

This is the first "sign" for believers to watch for. "So" is in place like "therefore." The reader is to take note of this and check further. The Lord even mentions "Daniel"--the only place in the N.T. where Daniel is mentioned by name. This means it is significant and must be considered with care. The Lord did not merely raise this prophet's name as a simple footnote. The text says: "Let the reader understand." When the Book of Daniel is consulted in context, it points to the direct reference found in Daniel nine. There Daniel writes of the man of sin--Antichrist--first confirming a covenant and allowing worship at the temple in Jerusalem, then breaking his word in the middle of the "seven" [years], and in short order putting "an end to sacrifice and offering." In combination with this, he will cause desolation and place "abominations on a wing of the temple."[50] He with an armed force will carry this out, again the "desolation."[51] This will occur at the mid-point of the final years with "1,290 days" to the end.[52] With this citation from the Lord Himself regarding Daniel's prophecy, we learn that this will occur at the half-way mark of the final seven years, and that we will see this when it happens. Alva J. McClain, former president of Grace Theological Seminary, connected this directly to Daniel

---

[49] [emphasis added]. In the KJV, the word "therefore" denotes the same urgency.
[50] Dan 9:27
[51] Dan 11:31
[52] Dan 12:11-12

129

9:27, the mid-point of the final seven years. He based this on the "desolations" mentioned by Daniel.[53] Dr. McClain wrote: "Since this period of 'desolations' begins in the middle of the last week and lasts 'even unto the full end' (9:27), obviously it will continue for three and a half years."[54] Hence, the revelation in *toto* of the man of sin occurs at the mid-point as He demands worship and begins to subjugate Christianity and Judaism.[55] Dr. McClain connected this directly to Daniel 7:25 and Revelation 13:5-7 at the time the Antichrist begins persecution in earnest.[56] Though he is a pre-trib advocate and related these events to be for Israel, Jacob's time of trouble, Dr. McClain set the chronology correctly as to Matthew 24:15. He affirmed this by writing: "Daniel's contribution to the prophecy was to provide the chronology of the period of persecution."[57] Dr. McClain, then, directly connected this Matthew 24:15 and Jesus' warning.[58] The verse itself tells us Jesus was clearly warning us of the abomination which will be visible ("So, when *you* see..."). The context of the Olivet Discourse shows us the Lord was speaking to the Church which would be present at the end.[59] Jesus is directing this to believers. Peter, James, John, and Andrew asked Him about the end of the age. Jesus' reply is for them and for us. Those alive when this begins will see the abomination caused by "the man of lawlessness."[60] The Lord is openly saying: "Therefore, you will see this." This underscores the reality of the church's presence throughout this time. Within this example, there is confirmation of the importance of every word that has come from God.[61] We must understand what is being said in the language here. The Lord does not employ complex terminology, nor does He frustrate us with mystical distraction. His usual, daily vocabulary was by design a tool to state simple truth and reach out to us so we can comprehend it

---

[53] Dan 9:26
[54] McClain, Alva J. *Daniel's Prophecy of the Seventy Weeks.* Grand Rapids, MI: Zondervan Pub., 1965. p. 56
[55] 2 Thess 2:3-4
[56] McClain. *Ibid.* p. 56
[57] *Ibid.* p. 57
[58] *Ibid.*
[59] Apostles asked Him about His *parousia*, not Jews. Hence, His words are for His own: believers .
[60] 2 Thess 2:3-4
[61] Mt 4:4

all. Our "experts" have brought confusion here. It is unwarranted. The Olivet Discourse, of course, continues and contains a wealth of valuable information. The Lord pursues this subject of the end through chapter twenty-four and twenty-five.

From and *ek*

Consider the warning to the church in Philadelphia in the Book of Revelation:

> ****[Rev 3:10]. "Since you have kept my command to endure
> patiently, I will keep you *from* the hour of trial that is going
> to come upon the whole earth to test those who live on the earth."[62]

Those who attempt to reinforce the pre-trib theory consistently reference this verse from John's Apocalypse. It is one of a number of warnings included in the beginning of John's message to those who are known to be God's servants.[63] This, of course, is directed to the church. Pre-trib teachers attempt to remove the church in chapter four. However, this does violence to the language there. We treat this issue separately.[64] Yet, notice in this short discourse the critical nature of the subject: "the hour of trial."[65] This is overlooked by those teaching the rapture idea, since any word or verse that seems to work in favor of an early removal of the church is favored and promoted. This verse fails them, and they do not know it. Usually, their claim is made referencing the Greek word *ek* which has been translated as "from." It can mean a number of different things depending on the context. It may mean "out of," "from," or "through."[66] Here, again, the *context* is "the hour of trial." Yet, pre-trib advocates erroneously insert the seven year tribulation instead of the "hour" mentioned by the Lord

---

[62] [emphasis added].

[63] Rev 1:1

[64] See our comments on the word "Come" in this chapter.

[65] Rev 3:10

[66] Morris, Leon. *The Book of Revelation.[Tyndale N. T. Commentary]*. IVP/Eerdmans, 1989. p. 79. Morris states *ek* "might mean 'keep you from undergoing the trial' or 'keep you right through the trial. The Greek is capable of either meaning."

who is speaking here.[67] They proceed with the assumption that this verse is another proof of believers being raptured before the tribulation. Dr. Thomas Ice assured readers that this verse is an explicit promise "that the church will escape the tribulation,"[68] meaning the final seven years. His assertion is mere speculation. Jesus painted a different picture in the Olivet Discourse.[69] Paul described this in graphic detail to the church in Thessalonica.[70] Dr. Ice continued the confusion by enlisting Dr. Charles Ryrie to support this error. Dr. Ryrie assured us this escape is a guarantee for us "being kept from the Tribulation itself." He even quoted the verse and restated the importance of the "hour" by saying: "It is 'I will keep you from *the hour* of trials.'"[sic][71] It has always been a theological standard for establishing doctrine not to build a case on a single verse. The use of this verse exemplifies the danger with this approach. The context has been ignored by Dr. Ice, Dr. Ryrie, and a host of others. They fail to connect the "hour" under consideration which is a clear part of the wrath and judgment described later in the Book of Revelation. It is in chapter eighteen we find the graphic portrayal of the judgment of Babylon. It is there "the hour of trial" is presented in fullness. Revelation three was just a forewarning. The actual event is described for us by John near the end of his book. There we see the final fall of mankind under the banner of "Babylon" being destroyed by "fire" in "one hour."[72] This is what the church is promised to be spared from. Why? Because the church has kept His "command to endure patiently."[73] Over and through all of this, we find the Lord's admonition presented to the church in view, Philadelphia--and to all the rest of the churches--is to overcome.[74] The word of encouragement is for "him who overcomes."[75] There would be no need to overcome or wait patiently if the

---

[67] Rev 3:7, He "who holds the key of David."

[68] Ice, Thomas. "Pre-Trib Perspectives." *The Nature of the Church*. Volume VIII, No. 97. April 2012. p. 5

[69] See Mt 24 and 25.

[70] 2 Thess 1:6-10

[71] Ice. "Pre-Trib Perspectives." *The Nature of the Church*. p. 5; Ryrie, Charles C. *Come Quickly, Lord Jesus*. Eugene, OR: Harvest House, 1996. p. 135 [emphasis added]; "trials" (plural) alters the context.

[72] Rev 18:8, 10, 17, 19

[73] Rev 3:10

[74] Rev 3:12

church were gone. This verse spoken to the Philadelphia church would either not be in John's book or it would read differently. Jesus laid the warning before the church previously in the Olivet Discourse: "...he who stands firm to the end will be saved."[76] If the Lord intended to take them out (rapture), there would be no admonition for believers to "overcome." This cancels the premise of escape caused by the pre-trib misinterpretation of our English word "from" and the Greek word *ek*. The word itself and its meaning must be judged in the context. This is a safeguard against a false, secondary application which would lead believers astray. All Bible students must ensure that even simple words are looked at with care. British preacher, G. Campbell Morgan, broadly laid this in place with his comments on "The Philadelphia Letter." He stated:

> Recognizing the faithfulness of His people, He promises them exemption from the tribulation which is to come. While that promise may have had its partial fulfillment in the escape of the church at Philadelphia from some wave of persecution that swept over the district, its final fulfillment will undoubtedly be realized by those who, loyal to His word, and not denying His name, shall be gathered out of the world *at His Second Coming* before the judgment that must come in the setting up of His Kingdom on earth.[77]

Notice that Morgan places this gathering properly at the end when the Lord returns to establish His kingdom and not before. Note, also, within the context of these verses in Revelation and in Dr. Morgan's comments that there is the call to remain "loyal to His word" and not to deny "His name." If the church were removed prior to this devastating persecution of the saints,[78] there would be no purpose in warning them who are not here to "hold on."[79] Alexander

---

[75] *Ibid.* This is repeated seven times: note Revelation 2:7; 2:11; 2:17; 2:26; 3:5; 3:12; 3:21

[76] Mt 24:13

[77] Morgan, G. Campbell. *A First Century Message to Twentieth Century Christians.* Chicago, IL: Fleming H. Revell Co., 1902. p. 172 [emphasis added].

[78] Rev 13:1-18; Dan 7:25; 11:32-35

[79] Rev 3:11

MacLaren commented: "He will keep us in the midst of and also from the hour of temptation."[80] John Stott noted: "Had they kept His word? Then He would keep them. He would not spare them from suffering; but He would uphold them in it."[81]   Richard C. Trench expounding on the seven churches Revelation, noted that the promise to the church in Philadelphia did not exempt them "from persecutions which should come upon all other portions of the Church; that by any special privilege they should be excused from fiery trials which others should have to pass." He connected this as a promise to all the faithful alive at this time of trouble--"to be kept *in* temptation, not exempted *from* temptation."[82] Henry Frost noted that "it is plain that the promise is, not that they will be delivered *from* the great tribulation, but it will be preserved *in the midst* of it."[83] He related this term (*ek*) directly to the Lord's use of it in John 17:15. Frost wrote the confirmation: "I pray not that thou shouldest take them out (*ek*) of the world, but that thou shouldest keep them from (*ek*) the evil."[84] These faithful men recognized the proper use of this word in context. Today's pre-trib experts would like us to hang our hats on "from" or *ek* and not pay attention to other little words which correct their error.

Another serious difficulty is caused by the application of history to the seven churches that received the words of the Lord in chapter two and three.[85] While these churches were in existence at the time John wrote, dispensational teachers often employ a timeline with graphics which parallel the progress of the church age. According to dispensational teaching, the church age flows in

---

[80] MacLaren, Alexander. *The Epistles of John, Jude and the Book of Revelation. [Expositions of Holy Scripture].* New York, NY: A. C. Armstrong, 1910. p. 206

[81] Stott, John R. W. *What Christ Thinks of the Church. Insights from Revelation 2 – 3.* Grand Rapids, MI: Wm. B. Eerdmans Pub. Co., 1972. p. 104

[82] Trench, Richard Chenevix. *Commentary on the Epistles to the Seven Churches in Asia .Revelation II. III.* New York, NY: Charles Scribner, 1861. p. 237-238 [emphasis in the original].

[83] Frost, Henry W. *The Second Coming of Christ. A review of the teaching of Scripture concerning the return of Christ.* Grand Rapids, MI: Wm. B. Eerdmans Pub., 1934. p. 220 [emphasis in the original].

[84] Frost. *Ibid.* p. 220

[85] See comments by John R. Rice in the chapter: "The Error of Imminence."

seven stages from the church's founding up until the time when the body of Christ is removed by rapture. From the initial church mentioned by John, which is Ephesus, to the last, Laodicea, believers live in one of the stages of the advance of history. The idea itself is attractive, but crumbles under its own weight once the last two churches come into play. Keith Brooks[86] outlined this when he published his interpretation of Daniel and Revelation. He related the church in Philadelphia (where *ek* appears in verse ten) to the time when the "Puritans and Methodists came on the scene to stir up dead Christendom." He called this time of "general revival." "Missions and united evangelistic efforts marked this new epoch." He depicted Philadelphia and how "perfectly it describes this epoch."[87] He, then, proceeded to treat the church in Laodicea where "popular opinion" replaced the word of God, the result being neither hot nor cold. He expanded on this and concluded: "Do not these words describe the modern church?"[88] This general interpretation is used by many dispensational teachers. Yet, the collapse occurs, since they have assured us that the *ek* in connection with the Philadelphian church is our way of escape. It is not possible for the scope of this historical arrangement to allow for the church's removal when the dispensational template continues to have the church on earth through all seven stages. Brooks, by the way, does have the church removed in Revelation chapter four and "taken up."[89] Since the use of this historical model has been challenged, some pre-trib teachers have insisted the Laodicean church is the apostate church left behind after the rapture. However, in either case, it is fabrication, since neither option fits the context. The Apostle John never alluded to any connection to church stages. None of this sort of exaggerated typology was evident until dispensationalists applied it, courtesy of J. N. Darby in the late 1800s and C. I. Scofield in the early 1900s.

Many times pre-trib teachers will utilize examples which they claim are types of the early removal of the faithful. Noah and his family are employed as a type of the rapture. Enoch is used and Elijah. Also, we find Lot's removal from

---

[86] Brooks, Keith L. was editor of "Prophecy Monthly" in Los Angeles, California.
[87] Brooks, Keith L. *Prophecies of Daniel and Revelation. Verse by Verse.* Los Angeles, CA: Brooks, 1925. p. 35
[88] *Ibid.*
[89] *Ibid.* p. 37

Sodom as a pre-trib tool to influence our thinking. However, Noah was preserved from the judgment of the wicked on the very day that the Lord closed the door of the ship. Noah and his family were not removed seven years before, seven months before, or seven weeks before. It all commenced just as the Lord had said.[90] Seven days after the Lord told them to enter the ark, floodwaters "came upon the earth,"[91] since "all the springs of the great deep burst forth."[92] God was now judging the wicked, and none would be left. Jesus confirmed this event and its timing when He spoke to the disciples about the coming of the kingdom. He highlighted Noah as an historic reference. Jesus said life was routine for the wicked *up to the day* Noah entered the ark. Then the flood came and destroyed them all."[93] The same timing faced Lot in Sodom. The two angels arrived in Sodom "in the evening" and hastened Lot to get himself and his family away from the impending judgment. Lot was informed of the urgency in this matter. He was not given a seven-year or seven-month eviction notice. He was to gather his family and follow the angels without delay. Lot convinced the angels to have a meal. The evening was interrupted by the depraved Sodomites demanding sex, so the angels immediately commanded Lot to get moving. Around the time "the sun had risen over the land," the Lord "rained down burning sulfur" and the cities of Sodom and Gomorrah were destroyed.[94] This took place within twenty-four hours. A seven-year pre-trib removal is unsupportable within this example. Also, Jesus confirmed this event as the same type of immediate judgment as with Noah. The Lord said: "But the day Lot left Sodom, fire and sulfur rained down from heaven and destroyed them all."[95] The use of types with these two men for pre-trib support is a twisting of God's word unless read carefully in context. Please note that Noah and Lot were not taken up. They were protected on earth as the events happened. When we look at Enoch, we find an even weaker example, since there was no impending judgment as compared to Noah

---

[90] Gen 7:11-13
[91] Gen 7:10
[92] Gen 7:11. After seven days, there was no doubt what a "flood" was. Never before was this seen on earth.
[93] Lk 17:26-27 [emphasis added]
[94] Gen 19:1-28
[95] Lk 17:28-29

and Lot. In Genesis, Enoch is mentioned in the genealogy from Adam to Noah. He "lived 365 years." He "walked with God; then he was no more, because God took him away."[96] Again, there is no judgment at hand and no mention of any distinct chronology other than his genealogical placement. Enoch is mentioned by Jude in his epistle but only with a reference to a prophecy about the Lord coming with "thousands upon thousands of his holy ones."[97] However, these words of Enoch confirm the Second Coming at the time the Lord is going to judge the wicked, just as in the examples of Noah and Lot. There is no pre-trib association at all. These examples relate to judgment and not to a secret rapture. Another individual that is used is Elijah. He was taken "up to heaven in a whirlwind," but not before a judgment. He was not an example used by Jesus with any connection to retribution. We only see him reappearing with Moses to give approval to the impending death of Jesus at the time of the Transfiguration.[98] These "proofs" used by those who advocate a rapture prior to the seven year tribulation are riddled with flaws and must be discounted entirely by serious Bible students.

As these individuals above are valid for other examples, we must not ignore their importance overall. The key is to understand that God was with them through their trials. He safely saw them home to heaven. Hebrews eleven is replete with those faithful servants who faced multiple trials. They held on to the end, just as the saints at the end of the age will be required to do. In Revelation chapter two, the Lord reminds the church in Smyrna: "Be faithful, even to the point of death."[99] At the end of the age, with the Antichrist prevailing against the church, we will have little choice but to withstand all of the devices of the evil one.[100] Looking back to the earlier days of Israel, the Lord protected them as He poured out his judgment upon Pharaoh. God increased the judgments and sent the destroying angel to kill the first born of Egypt. With blood on the lintels and doorposts, the children of Israel were protected. They took God at His word, and He spared them because they were

---

[96] Gen 5:23-24
[97] Jude 14-15. Also, 1 Thess 3:13; Mt 24:30-31
[98] Mt 17:1f; Mk 9:2ff; Lk 9:28-36
[99] Rev 2:10
[100] Dan 7:21-22, 25; Rev 13:5-10

obedient. God did not take them out of this. He took them safely through it.[101]
This shows the Lord's ability to protect His own in the midst of the evil
produced by the foes of God and His power to preserve His own as He judges.
The Lord reminded them of this pointedly: "When I brought your fathers out of
Egypt, you came to the sea, and the Egyptians pursued them with chariots and
horsemen as far as the Red Sea. But they cried to the Lord for help, and he put
darkness between you and the Egyptians; he brought the sea over them and
covered them. You saw with your own eyes what I did to the Egyptians. Then
you lived in the desert for a long time."[102] The church should use this kind of
example as opposed to the dispensational extremes which distort scripture.

Another strong example for the church's presence throughout the final seven
years is found in Acts at the time Paul was heading to Rome. A violent storm
arose, and the ship was breaking up. The crew was in fear for their lives. Paul
told them on God's authority that they must stay with the ship: "…not one of
them will be lost; only the ship will be destroyed."[103] As the ship neared the
shore, some of the crew had thoughts of an "escape from the ship." Paul
informed the contingent of Roman guards aboard: "Unless these men stay with
the ship, you cannot be saved."[104] This demand from Paul is a parallel to the
Lord's words regarding the end of the age: "Because of the increase of
wickedness, the love of most will grow cold, and he who stands firm to the end
will be saved."[105] This agrees to the message to the seven churches in the book
of Revelation. In this light, it is evident that the church will remain on the earth
until the Lord appears at the Second Coming.

Us or Them

Consider another portion of John's Apocalypse where pre-trib authorities take

---

[101] See Ex 6:28 through Ex 12:32
[102] Joshua 24:6-7
[103] Acts 27:22
[104] Acts 27:30-32
[105] Mt 24:12

extreme liberty with the text:

> ****[Rev 5:9-10]. "And they sang a new song: 'You are worthy
> to take the scroll and to open its seals, because you were slain,
> and with your blood you purchased *men* for God from every
> tribe and language and people and nation. You have made
> *them* to be a kingdom and priests to serve our God, and *they*
> will reign on the earth.'" [NIV].[106]

Within these verses, those who wish to stress the church's presence in heaven will point to the twenty-four elders as representing the church. They would like us to think that the elders' place in heaven means we are too, courtesy of the rapture.[107] The basis for this claim is the mistranslation of the word "us" in verse ten as it appears in the King James Version.[108] Looking at the KJV text, it states: "And they sang a new song saying, Thou art worthy to take the book, and to open the seals thereof; for thou wast slain, and hast redeemed *us* to God by thy blood out of every kindred, and tongue, and people, and nation; And hast made *us* unto our God kings and priests: and *we* shall reign on earth."[109] However, the majority of more accurate translations employ "them," since the Greek usage is more exact. For instance, the New International Version verses read: "And they sang a new song: 'You are worthy to take the scroll and to open its seals, because you were slain, and with your blood you purchased men for God from every tribe and language and people and nation. You have made *them* to be a kingdom and priests to serve our God, and they will reign on earth.'"[110] As we know, context is critical in determining the use of a word. Here in this section of the Book of Revelation, the twenty-four elders have already been introduced. We find them in the previous chapter seated before

---

[106] [emphasis added].

[107] John MacArthur errs with this and proffers indirect references which do not support the actual Greek text. He follows the usual pre-trib claims. MacArthur, John F., Jr. *The Second Coming of the Lord Jesus Christ. Study Notes. Selected Scriptures.* Panorama City, CA: Word of Grace Communications, 1981. p. 68

[108] This error also appears in the New King James Version.

[109] Rev 5:9-10. From the King James Version [emphasis added].

[110] Rev 5:9-10. From the New International Version [1984] [emphasis added].

the throne on "twenty-four other thrones."[111] However, they are not alone. With them are "four living creatures" colorfully described by John as he sees them before the throne. They "never stop saying: 'Holy, holy, holy is the Lord God almighty, who was, and is, and *is to come.*'"[112] At this point, it is crucial to note that these creatures state that the Lord "is to come." This tells us He has not yet come. This means that the twenty-four elders cannot represent the church, since the Lord has not yet begun His descent to earth to gather the Church. Paul the Apostle wrote that on earth two things must happen first: the Man of sin revealed and the great falling away. With this in mind, the heavenly picture by John places the Lord Jesus yet on the throne and trouble brewing on earth. Further, John tells us that when the living creatures are glorifying God, the twenty-four elders "lay their crowns before the throne and say: 'You are worthy, our Lord and God, to receive glory and honor and power, for you created all things, and by your will *they* were created and have their being.'"[113] Notice, that before the argument about "us" and "them" in chapter five begins, these elders clearly relate that "they"--not themselves but those men on earth-- are "created." They are looking at those men who on earth need full redemption. These elders are eternal creatures, not fallen, and speak as observers of the sovereign plan of God about to come to its conclusion. If this is understood clearly from the context, then there is no way that the word "us" fits the sense of meaning in chapter five. These elders had no need for redemption.[114] Sinful, fallen men on earth do. This is the whole purpose for John's Apocalypse which portrays the soon coming judgment on those who will not repent and those who perish in rebellion against God. So, with the contextual structure of John's record in chapter four and five, it is impossible for the elders to be men--or the Church. The New International Version states clearly the elders' position: "...with your blood you purchased men for God"

---

[111] Rev 4:4

[112] Rev 4:8 [emphasis added].

[113] Rev 4:9-11 [emphasis added].

[114] Heb 1:14. The elders are like the angels, also created, not fallen, otherwise they could not be in God's presence. They, also, are those who minister to us "who *will inherit* salvation" [emphasis added]. The angels (and elders) do not need redemption. They are not flesh and blood. Christ did not die for them. Notice: With His blood, Jesus Christ "purchased *men* for God" (Rev 5:9)--not elders.

and "You have made *them* to be a kingdom and priests to serve our God."[115] The "them" is the Church still earthbound. Another point which is very important is the fact that the elders were not alone in glorifying God in verses nine and ten. No, the living creatures joined in and were in complete agreement with the elders. So, is it possible for the living creatures to be "the Church"? No. It is impossible. Both groups sang a new song not just the elders. Hence we have three instances in context which favor without question the use of the word "them." This defense for a pre-trib rapture is undone once these elders are properly seen in context.

Let us look a bit further into this section of Revelation. Notice the word "saints" in verse eight of chapter five. This is in the very same context. The elders are holding "golden bowls full of incense, which are the prayers of the *saints*."[116] This tells us that the saints are elsewhere and are not the elders. The saints remain on earth and continue to petition the Lord in heaven. This is restated in Revelation chapter eight, as the prayers from the believers on earth continue. This occurs just as the seventh seal is opened, and the seven angels are given seven trumpets.[117] The same procedure occurs with the incense, the smoke, the golden altar, and "prayers of the saints" being brought "before the throne."[118] The elders are not mentioned here, but they are noted present in chapter seven along with the angels and the four living creatures.[119] The scene is the same. The priority John sees is the trumpets which are about to sound. Meanwhile, the Body of Christ, yet on the earth, awaits His arrival from heaven to gather them from the four corners of the earth.[120] Some of the martyrs are already there before the throne.[121]

---

[115] Rev 5:9-10 [NIV, 1984] [emphasis added]. John correctly designates the "us" in chapter one making the distinction using the pronoun (us) for us believers who have been redeemed by "his blood" [Rev 1:6]. The elders were not redeemed--only men. Peter agrees [1 Pt 2:4-5, 9]

[116] Rev 5:8 [emphasis added].

[117] Rev 8:1-5

[118] Rev 8:3-4

[119] Rev 7:11

[120] Matt 24:31. This scene includes those waiting on earth for "the last trumpet" not yet given out. [Rev 11:15; 1 Cor 15:50-54; 1 Thess 4:16-17].

[121] Rev 7:13-14

Another interesting observation regarding those who are with the Lord at His throne is offered by Micaiah in the Old Testament. He was the son of Imlah and was a true prophet of God. He spoke against the false prophets who lied to Ahab. Micaiah's words were directly from the Lord and not well received by Ahab who preferred to have his false prophets tell him only what he wanted to hear.[122] In First Kings, these two men are face to face--at Ahab's request. Ahab wanted Jehoshaphat to join him in battle. Jehoshaphat was wise and asked for "a prophet of the Lord" to bring the truthful word of the Lord. Micaiah did just that. He went before the Lord for the right answer. Micaiah tells us that he "saw the Lord sitting on his throne with all the host of heaven standing around him on his right and on his left."[123] There is no mention of patriarchs or apostles. Pre-trib advocates often tell us that the twenty-four elders represent the twelve tribes and the twelve Apostles. This brief description by Micaiah discounts that, since he states clearly that it is a group of "the heavenly host" and not anything earthly. Pre-trib typology has its limits. At some point it becomes plain distortion. Micaiah settles the matter for Ahab, Jehoshaphat, and us.

Before we leave this portion of Revelation, let us look at some comments from a few of the authorities with language. First is Henry Alford. In his extensive work on the New Testament, he noted the appropriate changes from the Authorized King James Version to Revised Version regarding the difficulty over "us." He denoted the elders to be heavenly and not the church. He concluded the "object" of "and didst redeem [+ us] to God..." is not needed nor expressed. "Us" is omitted in the Alexandrian manuscripts (v.9).[124] Another well versed scholar is Marvin Vincent. In his examination of the language in the New Testament, he stated simply, "omit *us*, supply *men*" regarding verse nine, as in the Revised Version; likewise in verse ten, *them*.[125] Another scholar, Alfred Marshall, in his well-known Greek-English New

---

[122] Consider 2 Tim 4:3-5
[123] 1 Kings 22:19
[124] Alford, Henry. *The New Testament for English Readers*. rpt. Chicago, IL; Moody Press, n.d. p. 1826-1827
[125] Vincent, Marvin R. *Word Studies in the New Testament*. rpt. Hendrickson Pub., n.d. Vol. II. p. 491.

Testament denoted "men" and agrees with Alford and Vincent.[126] David Stern in his comments on the New Testament translated "persons" instead of "men," as he agrees with those above regarding verse nine; also, "persons from every tribe." In verse ten, he specified: he "made *them* into a kingdom...*they* will rule."[127] George Ladd dealt with this in his commentary on Revelation. He highlighted the textual problem with "us" in verse nine. He compared the Authorized Version with the Revised Version, stating the "King James Version was based on a late inferior text. It is surprising to find any modern commentary following the incorrect King James Version. The elders sing praise to the Lamb not for their own redemption but for the redemption of the church."[128] Another important source to consider is John Nelson Darby himself, since he is the primary individual responsible for formally advocating the pre-trib rapture. In his translation of the Bible, he is in agreement with those experts above and translates verse nine: "and hast redeemed to God" with no *us*. In verse ten, Darby translates: "...he made *them*...*they* shall reign."[129] William R. Newell noted Darby's reference to these elders, but was not satisfied and proceeded to add clarity. Newell went on to offer assurance that these elders were not symbolic, that they are not "human beings," and his conclusion is based on the text which says that "...the elders do not testify of their own *salvation* at all: although they celebrate that of *others*, as in v.5:8, 9 (R.V.)."[130] These comments on the text itself in *context* render the human association of these elders pointless and fabricated.

There has been needless confusion with these simple words surrounding the identity of the twenty-four elders in John's account of the beings that surround

---

[126] Marshall, Alfred. *Zondervan Parallel New Testament in Greek and English. [NIV/KJV]*. Grand Rapids, MI: Zondervan Bible Pub., 1977. p. 734-735

[127] Stern, David H. *Jewish New Testament*. Clarksville, MD: Jewish New Testament Pub., Inc., 1989. p. 339 [emphasis added].

[128] Ladd, George Eldon. *A Commentary on the Revelation of John*. Grand Rapids, MI: Wm. B. Eerdmans Pub. Co., p. 92

[129] Darby, John Nelson [J. N.]. *The Holy Scriptures. A New Translation from the Original Languages*. Lancing, Sussex, UK: Kingston Bible Trust, 1984. p. 1492 [emphasis added].

[130] Newell, William R. *The Book of the Revelation*. Chicago, IL: Moody Press, 1935. p. 374

the throne. We must read with care and not be led to a conclusion which confounds the reality of what the apostle saw and was told to write down.

Apostasy and Falling Away

Consider the word "apostasy" as it appears in Paul's second letter to the Thessalonians:

> ****[2 Thess 2:3]. "Don't let anyone deceive you in any way, for [that day will not come] until *the rebellion* occurs and the man of lawlessness is revealed, the man doomed to destruction."[131] [NIV].

In an attempt to pursue another "proof" of the early removal of the church, some prophecy experts have seized on the word "departure" in this verse written by Paul. Among them is Dr. J. Vernon McGee who said bluntly: "That's the Rapture of the church. The church is going to depart from the earth"[132] This is pure presumption on his part. In the verse above from the New International Version, we see "rebellion." This is the word in question which pre-trib advocates stumble over, since in the King James Version, it reads "departure." The English word for the Greek (*apostasia*) is translated in different forms depending on language usage at the time. The English language in colloquial use at the time the translators produced their work (Tyndale, Coverdale, KJV 1611) denoted "departure" as rebellion, meaning rebellion against God and His authority. Translator James Murdock used the word "defection."[133] Commentator George Milligan correctly related this to Joshua 22:22 with "the word directly applied to rebellion *against the Lord*."[134] He

---

[131] [emphasis added].

[132] McGee, J. Vernon. *On Prophecy: Man's Fascination with the Future.* Nashville, TN: Nelson Books, 2004. p.173-174

[133] Murdock, James. *The New Testament or, the Book of the Holy Gospel of Our Lord and Our God, Jesus the Messiah. A Literal Ttranslation from the Syriac Peshita Version.* New York, NY: Stanford and Swords, 1852. p. 377. Murdock includes a footnote for this word as "rebellion."

noted this to be a religious apostasy and a necessary event "preceding the Lord's Parousia" with the definite article (the rebellion) providing its "full consecutive force."[135] Commentator John Hutchinson offered additional clarity: "There is set before us here not a general indifference, but a fearful and widespread defection, a 'departing from the living God' (Heb 3:12)."[136] J. B. Rotherham in his Emphasized Bible used the word "revolt."[137] Hy Pickering, noted author and publisher of dispensational works, rendered the meaning in 2 Thessalonians 2:3 saying: "It refers to the utter abandonment of Christianity." He further stated this to include the timing: "This is public rejection of God, of Christ, and the Holy Ghost is yet future."[138] F. F. Bruce in his masterful work on the letters of Paul provided an alternate rendering of the falling away to be: "the Great Rebellion."[139] These variants help us to see how language has changed and, also, how some pre-trib teachers will tweak a word in an attempt to alter the meaning.

The older word "departure" denotes a departure from the Faith, not a departure as in "leave town." In 2008, Dr. Tim LaHaye proclaimed that "apostasia should not have been translated as 'apostasy,' or often 'the rebellion,' but a better translation, as many of the earliest English translators used, is 'departing.'"[140] He was attempting to redefine Paul's term as if it meant that Christians would be raptured in verse three. However, this is impossible, since Paul set the context and the meaning in verse one. The Apostle Paul stated that we would

---

[134] Milligan, George. *St. Paul's Epistles to the Thessalonians. The Greek Text with Introduction and Notes.* London: Macmillan and Co., Ltd., 1908. p. 98. [Emphasis in the original].

[135] *Ibid.*

[136] Hutchinson, John. *Lectures Chiefly Expository on St. Paul's First and Second Epistles to the Thessalonians. With Notes and Illustrations.* Edinburgh: T. & T. Clark, 1884. p. 288

[137] Rotherham, Joseph Bryant. *Rotherham's Emphasized Bible.* Grand Rapids, MI: Kregel Pub., 1994. N.T., p. 212.

[138] Pickering, Hy. *One Thousand Wonderful Things About the Bible.* London: Pickering & Inglis, 1946. p. 106

[139] Bruce, F. F. *The Letters of Paul. An Expanded Paraphrase.* Grand Rapids, MI: Wm. B. Eerdmans Pub. Co., 1965. p. 58-59

[140] LaHaye, Tim. "Pre-Trib Perspectives." *Rethinking The Rapture.* Vol. 8, No. 55. May 2008. p. 2

be "gathered" (v.1), but *first* there would be a "departure" (v.3). The "gathering" in verse one and the "departing" (using LaHaye's term) in verse three *cannot* be the same event, otherwise, following LaHaye's premise, we would have the rapture as a sign for the rapture.[141] Dr. LaHaye seems to be grasping at straws here. We must note, also, that in the same publication in the next column Dr. Thomas Ice defined apostasy "simply to depart from one's faith."[142] He restated this again in his article as "departing from the faith" and "doctrinal defection."[143] It would seem that Dr. LaHaye and Dr. Ice, the editor, never consulted one another on this. What makes this even more interesting is the position that Dr. LaHaye expounded in 1999 while continuing his *Left Behind* Series. He went to great lengths emphasizing that *apostasia* was rebellion, "a defection from the truth or a departure from that which was given at first." He quoted Robert L. Thomas, Donald Guthrie, J. A. Motyer, Alan Stibbs, D. L. Wiseman, and Ralph Earle in order to support this.[144] He was attempting to use the valid definition to point to the church's *apostasia* at the time he wrote the fictional book, *Left Behind*. It would seem for Dr. LaHaye that the definition shifts at will. Ultimately, his effort to explain conditions prior to the Second Coming directly confounded the intent of Paul who wrote to the Thessalonian church. Bible teacher and writer E. W. Rogers who espoused the pre-trib position in his books wrote: "In the papyri it means a bond of relinquishment, a contract of renunciation, a bill of ejectment. The suggestion that it means 'the rapture' is not tenable."[145] He related this to a specific event and to the word's usage elsewhere in Hebrews: "departing from." Rogers wrote this will be "a departure from everything Christian to make room for the Man of lawlessness."[146] Consequently, we must look at the

---

[141] Or worse, two raptures. Chuck Smith claimed a second rapture. See chapter: "The Error of Imminence."

[142] Ice, Thomas. "Pre-Trib Perspectives." *End Time Apostasy*. Vol. 8, No. 55. May, 2008. p. 1

[143] *Ibid.* p. 5

[144] LaHaye, Tim. *Are We Living in the End Times?* Wheaton, IL: Tyndale House Pub., 1999. p. 69-71ff. Note that he confirms the James Murdock translation ("defection") as noted above.

[145] Rogers, E. W. *Concerning the Future*. Chicago, IL: Moody Press, 1962. p. 115

[146] *Ibid.*

context carefully and read thoroughly all of a section of scripture as opposed to blindly focusing on a single word. Even John Walvoord admitted that most Bible "expositors have understood it as doctrinal departure, that is apostasy."[147]

D. Edmond Hiebert devoted time in his Thessalonian commentary to set aside the notion that the apostasy is the pre-trib rapture. This carries some weight, since Dr. Hiebert held to the pre-trib view. He concurred with Paul's intent to show this to be a specific event before the return of the Lord. Hiebert wrote: "It denotes a deliberate abandonment of a formerly professed position or view, a defection, a rejection of a former allegiance."[148] He noted that in the Septuagint, it was "used as rebellion against God."[149] Further, he negated the recent view that this word means the "rapture of the church" by referencing the absence of any other place in Scripture where the term applies to the church's departure. He also stated the important fact that Paul had already "referred to the rapture as 'our gathering together unto him' (v.1)." Dr. Hiebert inquired why Paul would now use such an "unlikely term to mean the same thing?"[150] This is the sensible answer and leaves in place the fact that the rebellion will occur first prior to the return of the Lord with no previous gathering or rapture. Robert Mounce made the application clearly in his shorter commentary on the Book of Revelation. In his remarks on chapter thirteen, he noted the beast and the false prophet appearing and causing great distress for the body of Christ, not raptured and still present on the earth. Mounce described the image of the beast being set up and being given breath to speak. This is followed by the demand for all to worship the image. "All those who refuse to worship the beast are to be killed."[151] This demand brings division between those who will accept this and those who reject and are willing to pay with their lives. As with the challenge from the first century Roman authorities, this is life or death. It

---

[147] Walvoord, John F. *The Thessalonian Epistles.* Grand Rapids, MI: Dunham Pub., 1967.
     p. 119
[148] Hiebert, D. Edmond. *The Thessalonian Epsitles. A Call to Readiness.* Chicago, IL: Moody Press, 1977. p. 305
[149] *Ibid.*
[150] *Ibid.* p. 306
[151] Mounce, Robert H. *What Are We Waiting for? A Commentary on Revelation.* Grand Rapids, MI: Wm. B. Eerdmans Pub., 1992. p. 68

will be your life forfeited or a pledge to embrace Satan's abomination. Mounce correctly stated: "This is the great apostasy that precedes the return of Christ (*cf.* 2 Thess 2:3)."[152] These comments by Dr. Hiebert and Dr. Mounce accurately portray the thought intended by Paul as he wrote the Thessalonians. It also is in conformity with Jesus' words in the Olivet Discourse when He warned of the "time many will turn away from the faith and betray and hate each other."[153] A pre-trib removal was never in the thoughts of the Lord Jesus or the Apostle Paul. This was well expounded by Thomas Newton, Bishop of Bristol, in his masterwork *On the Prophecies* which pre-dated all the latter-day dispensational tinkering. He noted the apostasy comes first, before the Second Advent, and that it was "not a revolt from the government but a defection from the true religion and worship."[154] He called this "a departing from the living God" in reference to Hebrews 3:12.[155] In reference to Paul's use of *apostasia*, Newton, referring to Erasmus and Ambrose, agreed that this was to occur before the Lord gathered His own, which Paul had used as one of the two conditions in 2 Thessalonians 2: the rebellion and the man of sin to be revealed before Christ gathers the church. It is unproductive for pre-trib theorists to convolute Paul's words and his pastoral concern for the believers in Thessalonica.

You, us, them

Take a closer look at Paul the Apostle's description of the Second Coming in his second letter to the Thessalonians:

> ****[2 Thess 1:6-10]. "God is just: He will pay back trouble to
> those who trouble *you* and give relief to *you* who are
> troubled, and to *us* as well. This will happen when the Lord

---

[152] Mounce. *Ibid.*
[153] Mt 24:10
[154] Newton, Thomas. *Dissertions on the Prophecies.* Philadelphia, PA: J. J. Woodward, 1838. p. 389
[155] *Ibid.*

Jesus is revealed from heaven in blazing fire with his powerful angels. He will punish those who do not know God and do not obey the gospel of our Lord Jesus. *They* will be punished with everlasting destruction and shut out from the presence of the Lord and from the majesty of his power on the day he comes to be glorified in his holy people and to be marveled at among all those who have believed. This includes *you*, because *you* have believed our testimony to **you**."[156]

Commentators agree that this is the Second Coming. Paul's description is brief, yet clear and precise. However, when pre-trib exponents look at this section, they cannot admit that the Apostle is writing of the same event in the next chapter.[157] Here in this first chapter, we find adequate language in place to bring to mind exactly what will occur when the Lord does come. Paul's terminology parallels the Lord's words in the Olivet Discourse. Yet, pre-trib teachers will avoid this Pauline outline as if it did not exist. You will be searching for a long time to locate these verses linked directly to those "proof texts" they liberally employ in the next chapter by Paul.[158] This tells us that the subject is taboo, since it might just cause a reader to reconsider Paul's encouragement in the light of the coming judgment. In the original letter, there were no chapters with numbers or verses enumerated as in our Bibles today. This aids our reading but also enables teachers to pass by important points we must know. This is exactly why Paul included these words here. It is *personal*. It is directed to the reader in Thessalonica or those who would hear it read. This is why the *pronouns* are so important. Notice that there are two groups in view. Seen are "us" and "them." Paul uses the term "they" to indicate those who oppose the Lord Jesus and have persecuted the believers in Thessalonica. The "trouble" Paul points to is the deliberate confrontation by the Roman authorities in their enforcement of Emperor worship along with the demand to revere the local gods.[159] The Thessalonians were confessing Christ and not

---

[156] [emphasis added].
[157] 2 Thess 2
[158] See comments above on 2 Thess 2:3

yielding to the demand from the local authorities to confess Caesar as god. Hence, their troubles were life threatening. With this in mind, Paul assures them that the Lord Jesus will pay them back--those who are causing this "suffering"--when He returns. Paul identifies "them" and "you." He also includes himself and the believers with him in the group the Lord will bring "relief" to. The Lord will "pay back" those who are doing the persecuting when He appears in glory. Those who are to be "punished" are the "them." The "you" and "us" are the believers who will see this happen. Paul is specific in identifying two groups: us and them. He is stating that all of the believers will be here when the Lord comes. In other words, he plainly writes that no one is leaving prior to the day when the Lord Jesus "comes to be glorified in his holy people." Those "people" are "us" who are alive and remain and believe.[160] This is the church that is called to stand firm to the end.[161] We will be "gathered"[162] just once; when He comes "in the majesty of his power" and not before. If Paul sincerely believed in some kind of two-stage coming, this epistle would read in a different way. This section would be written to include a removal before the Lord's Second Coming. It does not. Also, Paul knew very well what he taught them in Thessalonica when there. He also knew this subject well. He wrote a lengthy chapter in First Corinthians which included clear information about the Lord's return and the resurrection on *that day*.[163] These verses from six to ten must be read diligently. Paul writes of the event which will occur only once: when Jesus comes and is with us forever.

Come

Take a moment and think of the simple words the heavenly voice speaks to John the Apostle:

---

[159] See additional comments in the chapter "The Danger of Complacency."
[160] 1 Thess 4:16-17
[161] Mt 24:13; Rev 2:7; 2:11; 2:17; 2:26; 3:5; 3:12; 3:21
[162] 2 Thess 2:1
[163] Read 1 Cor 15 for Paul's teaching about the Gospel and what is to occur when the Lord comes and is present on "the Day."

****[Rev 4:1]. "After this I looked, and there before me
was a door standing open in heaven. And the voice
I had first heard speaking to me like a trumpet said,
'**Come** up here, and I will show you what must take
place after this.'"[164]

The voice speaking to John like a trumpet is the Lord.[165] This scene takes us to
the throne and those who are the heavenly host. The four living creatures are
present with the elders and angels. This chapter begins to unfold the task that
John has been assigned which is to write down what is yet to come. The
primary focus here is the simple heavenly call for John to "come up." This is
the Lord speaking to the Apostle alone. There is no one else present or anyone
else to accompany him as he is taken up. This is John's responsibility alone. As
a faithful servant, he writes all of it down, and we have the Book of Revelation
to read and ponder. However, many of those who ascribe to the pre-trib rapture
theory look upon this verse as a call to the Church to be removed from the
earth. The Church is not present in the *context* here. John stands by himself.
Only with the gross exaggeration of typology can anyone conclude that the
Body of Christ on earth is taken up at this point. Though the context does not
permit it, this is exactly how Clarence Larkin handled it. He wrote in 1919: "In
this 'Rapture' of John we have a type of the rapture of the church, and it is at
this place in the Book that the 'Rapture' of the Church takes place."[166] Bible
teacher and pre-trib advocate William R. Newell bluntly claimed "the Church
is represented here" without any supporting evidence.[167] He wrote this
regarding chapter four employing an errant, underlying premise that the church
does not appear after this until "the apocalypse is over!"[168] Again, we see that a
theory trumps the *context*. In his explanation of this, Tim LaHaye made an

---

[164] [emphasis added].

[165] Rev 1:9-18

[166] Larkin, Clarence. *The Book of Revelation.* Philadelphia, PA: Clarence Larkin
Estate, 1919. p. 33

[167] Newell, William R. *The Book of Revelation.* Chicago, IL: Moody Press, 1935. p.
90

[168] *Ibid.* The issue of the church not mentioned from chapter 4 until the end is treated
elsewhere in this chapter.

extra effort to embellish this verse in his commentary on the Book of Revelation. With regard to this passage, LaHaye wrote: "This has been given impetus to the suggestion that the Church will be raptured before the Tribulation." He admitted that this passage alone places this idea on "shaky ground" but then added to the claim referencing other passages "that make this point clear."[169] He continued to waffle though his claim using Revelation 3:10 and 1 Thessalonians 4:13-18.[170] Since this idea by LaHaye is truly stretching the *context*, his vain attempt to support it fails. He is not alone in causing problems with this passage. In a message entitled "A Jet Tour Through Revelation" given in 1982, John MacArthur boldly proclaimed the rapture when he arrived at the fourth chapter. He said: "Now we come to chapter 4 and leave the church age. People often ask, 'Where does the rapture come in?' *It's in the white spaces between chapter 3 and 4.* You have the church on earth in 2 and 3; all of a sudden we appear in heaven in chapter 4."[171] This is an astounding declaration. There is no hermeneutical basis for making this kind of radical claim. No one in their right mind should make a doctrinal affirmation from the "spaces" of "white" where no scripture appears. This rash assertion is from the president of a Bible seminary and a master preacher. The context, once again, along with the apostle's own distinct language trumps MacArthur and the others. In reference to a book on the Second Coming by Dr. MacArthur published in 1999,[172] he restated his incredible "in the white spaces" idea when promoting the book in a radio interview with Warren Duffy on KKLA in Los Angeles. Some years later, John MacArthur still holding to a pre-trib rapture, altered his position on this verse. He affirmed the orthodox interpretation on this verse by writing: "This is not a veiled reference to the Rapture of the church, but a command for John to be temporarily transported to heaven 'in the Spirit' to receive revelation about future events, things which must take place

---

[169] LaHaye, Tim. *Revelation. Illustrated and Made Plain.* Grand Rapids, MI: Zondervan Pub. House, 1975. p. 75

[170] *Ibid.* p.76-77. See our comments above on these passages.

[171] MacArthur, John. *Truth Endures. Commemorating Forty Years of Unleashing God's Truth One Verse at a Time, 1969-2009.* Panorama City, CA: Grace to You, 2009. p. 132 [emphasis added].

[172] MacArthur, John. *The Second Coming of Jesus. Signs of Christ's Return and the End of the Age.* Wheaton, IL: Crossway Books, 1999.

after this."[173] MacArthur's self-contradicting shift is the kind of bungling that only adds to the difficulties of an honest seeker of Truth. Charles C. Ryrie from Dallas Theological Seminary concurred that this does "not teach the rapture of the church," yet subtly left the event there with his sophistry.[174] This portion of Revelation chapter four is the scene just as the Apostle John experienced it. He surely knew what he was writing. He may have been utterly astounded when he was taken up, but the idea of him as a single person representing the "rapture" was not a viable premise for him to place before us. John was commissioned to write specifics, things he saw and heard, and not reel in dispensational additions which do not fit. The superimposing of the rapture here is another failed attempt to present an idea which is pure Dispensationalism at its worst. The natural reading of John's account will support him alone as the one person privileged to "come up"--and not the church. Dr. Robert Mounce confirmed this not to be the rapture, noting that some commentators have used this invitation to John "symbolically as the rapture of the church. Nothing in the verse, however, supports this interpretation."[175] Mounce explained that this simply was the event which allowed John to begin his written testimony of what was coming so he could report this to the churches. At no time, can this section support a pe-trib removal of the body of Christ.

144,000

****[Rev 7:3-4]. "'Do not harm the land or the sea or the
trees until we put a seal on the foreheads of the servants
of our God.' Then I heard the number of those who were
sealed: *144,000* from all the tribes of Israel."[176]

---

[173] MacArthur, John. *The MacArthur New Testament Commentary*. Nashville, TN: Thomas Nelson Pub., 2007. p. 912

[174] Ryrie, Charles C. *Revelation. [Everyman's Bible Commentary]*. Chicago, IL: Moody Press, 1982. p. 33-34

[175] Mounce. *Ibid*. p. 19

[176] [emphasis added].

This portion of John's Apocalypse has suffered much at the hands of false teachers and the cults. The Jehovah's Witnesses have used these verses to graft themselves into the kingdom of God. However, the *context* is entirely Israel. Our concern here, though, is the misuse of the 144,000 by dispensational teachers who force these sealed men from the twelve tribes into a new role as evangelists. Pre-trib exponents do this since they know there are believers still on the earth--after the secret rapture which, according to them, has already occurred. Because pre-trib teachers enforce a two-stage Second Coming, adjustments are made to cover the loose ends which they cannot explain without a full measure of distortion. One of the most vehement about this was Dr. C. I. Scofield who is well known for his reference Bible. In his footnotes for this section, he described the Great Tribulation outlining events as he interpreted them. When faced with the fact that believers (martyrs) have come "out of the great tribulation,"[177] he assigned these individuals as those being saved after the church has left. He even inserted an unwarranted section heading (within the text) for the verses that describe these martyrs which reads: "Vision of the Gentiles who are to be saved during the great tribulation."[178] These individuals are not specified as Gentiles in the text. They are martyrs given white robes as were the martyrs that were already in heaven. They are noted in chapter six.[179] Ignoring the importance of the martyrs, Scofield claimed that the second group is the result of converted Jews. He stated they are responsible for this and are an "election of Israel sealed for God"[180] linking this to the 144,000 who are named by John from the twelve tribes. Scofield swapped their place as true, undefiled sons of Israel and commissioned them into an evangelistic ministry. This is pure fiction. Nowhere does John report any activity of this sort. Since it is God Himself through the Holy Spirit who issues His call and then commissions individuals,[181] it appears that Scofield has supplanted the role of the Third Person of the Trinity with this wild idea. Also, in his footnote, with legalistic assurance, he says, in spite of "unexampled

---

[177] Rev 7:14
[178] Scofield, C. I. *The Scofield Reference Bible.* New York, NY: Oxford University Press, 1945. p. 1337
[179] Rev 6:9-11. Both groups were killed for their faith and were given white robes.
[180] Scofield. *Ibid.* p. 1337
[181] Heb 5:4; Is 6:8; Acts 13:2

trouble" in the great tribulation, it will be "a period of salvation."[182] Yes, there will be individuals saved during this time. However, it will not be as a result of anyone left behind or a special group of Israelites. It will happen because courageous Christians will risk their lives to tell the truth. The Church will be on earth to the end, and they will witness--at great cost. Again, looking at Scofield's invalid claims, he amplified this bogus assertion in his study course. This program was used extensively by the Moody Bible Institute in Chicago who published *The Scofield Bible Correspondence Course* in multiple editions beginning in 1907. It is in this material that the false notion was spread. After stating "the church is no longer on the earth," Scofield insisted: "Converted Jews are to be the preachers during the tribulation."[183] He denoted them to be a "saved remnant" that reappear in chapter fourteen. To avoid the context of chapter fourteen, he presented a risky hypothesis in order to lay his premise into what he thought to be safer territory: "Imagine the effect upon the Gentile world, of the simultaneous appearance of one hundred and forty-four thousand Pauls!"[184] Since Scofield's footnotes and comments influenced the thinking of many early dispensationalists, it is no wonder that pre-trib teachers continue to promote this gross error today. Nowhere in the book of Revelation does John record any action on the part of these individuals as soul winning work. He does identify them again in chapter fourteen, but there the 144,000 are with the Lord. They are sealed and appear first on Mount Zion and then appear quickly before the throne with the twenty-four elders and the four living creatures.[185] They are redeemed and go wherever the Lamb goes.[186] There is not a single statement in the Apocalypse or in any other book of the Bible that reflects an evangelistic effort by 144,000 converted Jews. Dr. Scofield continued to assert this false idea in his Sunday School lessons republished by Arno Gaebelein in 1920. He added a reference in addition to Revelation six in answering the question "Can the Lord Come at Any Time?"[187] Zechariah 8:23 was his

---

[182] Scofield. *Ibid.*
[183] Scofield, C. I. *The Scofield Bible Correspondence Course.* 1907. rpt. Chicago, IL: Moody Bible Institute of Chicago, 1934. Vol. II, p. 344
[184] *Ibid.*
[185] Rev 14:1-5
[186] *Ibid.*
[187] Scofield, C. I., *Things Old and New. Old and New Testament Studies.* New York,

additional proof, but he overlooked the previous verse in Zechariah which states the Lord was already present on the earth. This would place the individuals noted to be in the millennium and not in the final seven years. It appears Scofield failed to read his reference in context and created a blatant contradiction. Zechariah's verse indicates these are the remnant of the Jews[188] who have survived the tribulation and are among those who have "come to Jerusalem to seek the Lord Almighty and to entreat him."[189] Dr. Scofield introduced a major blunder here and elsewhere with his creative interpretations.

Looking at more contemporary statements, in 2007, in response to this question about the 144,000, the Pre-Trib Institute wrote: "During the first half of the tribulation, God will evangelize the world by means of the 144,000 Jews (Rev. 7:1-17) and thus fulfill the prophecy found in Matthew 24:14."[190] This in itself reflects the continuance of a hundred year error, since Scofield's study course included this in 1907. However, Thomas Ice and many others continue to teach this false idea. Note that in this quote Dr. Ice claims this select group of Jewish converts is to "evangelize the world."[191] Scofield limited it to Gentiles. Dr. Ice also connected it to the Olivet Discourse which does not specify Jews or anyone else by name who will evangelize. The Lord Jesus merely said that "...this gospel of the kingdom will be preached in the whole world as a testimony to all nations, and then the end will come."[192] This is likely a reference to the angel who "had the eternal gospel to proclaim to those who live on the earth"[193]--after the 144,000 were already in heaven.[194] This oversight is an embarrassment to Scofield and his teaching. Also, the absence of a named group in Matthew leaves the Pre-Trib Institute's answer without merit. The placement of the Lord's words, "then the end will come," leaves the

---

NY: "Our Hope," 1920. p. 299

[188] Zech 8:6-8

[189] Zech 8:22-23

[190] Ice, Thomas. "Pre-Trib Perspectives." [Prophecy Questions]: *What is the purpose for the seven-year tribulation?* Vol. 8, No. 44, April, 2007. p. 8

[191] Note that by connecting these two verses, Dr. Ice contradicts himself, since Jesus stated this would occur at the end and not in the first half of the tribulation!

[192] Mt 24:14

[193] Rev 14:6

[194] Rev 14:3

final preaching to be just that--at the end.[195] Notice that the response by Dr. Ice to the question stated the evangelization will be during "the first half of the tribulation." The Lord Jesus said at "the end." It can be seen from this question and answer about the 144,000 that "experts" are reading into the text what is not there. When this occurs, people cannot get real answers.

The Blessed Hope

> ****[Titus 2:11-13]. "For the grace of God that brings salvation has appeared to all men. It teaches us to say 'No' to ungodliness and worldly passions, and to live self-controlled lives in this present age, *while we wait* for *the blessed hope*-- the glorious appearing of our great God and Savior, Jesus Christ...."[196]

The little words here that Paul wrote to his fellow worker and apostle, Titus, are favorites for pre-trib teachers to bring into their argument for an imminent, secret rapture. Among them is J. Vernon McGee who connected the blessed hope to the rapture. He strongly made this claim: "'Looking for that blessed hope'--this is the next happening in the program of God: Christ is coming to take His church out of this world."[197] Tim LaHaye insisted the blessed hope is the rapture. He quoted the entire verse and then stated: "The Blessed Hope is definitely a reference to the rapture of the church."[198] He, then, assigned the "glorious appearing" to the Second Coming, avoiding the grammar and context. His presumptive maneuver forces two events where Paul denotes one. Blunt claims like Dr. LaHaye's are not rational, since Paul did not intend the two to be separate events. As we have noted with these "little words," *context* must be considered. Overall, this portion of the epistle must be considered in light of its greater intent. Paul's concern for Titus was doctrinally oriented[199]

---

[195] The Olivet Discourse provides the broad timeline.

[196] [emphasis added].

[197] McGee, J. Vernon. *Thru The Bible with J. Vernon McGee.* Nashville, TN. Thomas Nelson Pub., 1988. Vol V, p. 491

[198] LaHaye, Tim. *No Fear of the Storm.* Sisters, OR: Multnomah Press Books, 1993. p. 70

and not merely a quick reminder about a rapture. Titus was among the next generation of church leaders who would be carrying on the work of the kingdom. Paul wanted to be sure that Titus (and Timothy) were well prepared for this--the great and challenging work of the Gospel which would continue until Jesus returned. Hence, Paul says "while we wait." Since Titus was a traveling companion of Paul and a number of the other first-generation apostles, he would have been in agreement with the Gospel as stated by Paul and the others just as we read it in 1 Corinthians fifteen. The entire chapter includes the life, death, resurrection, and the Second Coming of Christ at which time believers are to be raptured--changed in the twinkling of an eye.[200] Paul reminded the Corinthians: "Whether, then, it was I or they, this is what we preach, and this is what you believed."[201] Paul's message was the same wherever he went. All the churches were privileged with the presence of these men who had been with Christ or taught by their associates. The Gospel was uniform everywhere and would include the true picture of the Second Coming, just as Jesus described it Himself in the Olivet Discourse. Jesus gave an illustration to indicate His return would be a long time in coming.[202] He encouraged us as believers to watch, be alert, and be ready even if he came in the second or third watch of the night.[203] The implication within the context of the core doctrine is that of *waiting*. Hence, Paul wrote "while we wait." Again, the wait is for the Second Coming. The rapture is not in view in this message to Titus, except that the change from corruptible to incorruptible will happen at the time Jesus returns. Paul never hinted to Timothy or Titus that there would be a secret removal prior to the Second Coming.

The point forced upon Paul's text is to make the "blessed hope" a different event from the "appearing." This problem emanates from the King James Version which has the conjunction in the verse. This word "and" (*kai* in Greek) does appear in the original Greek text. However, the inclusion of "and" in English was something for some pre-trib teachers to use to separate the two

---

[199] Titus 2:1
[200] Read the entire chapter and pay particular attention to verses 22 to 24.
[201] 1 Cor 15:11
[202] Mt 25:14-18
[203] Lk 12:37-39

subjects in view. Grammatically, the conjunction "and" joins the two subjects together denoting them to be the same. The broader subject in view is: Jesus Christ who is our God and Savior and is coming in glory. This is the Second Coming. The Greek conveys the meaning with a sharper focus by amplifying "the blessed hope" to be even more powerful by heightening our hope and expectation when it is realized when He comes--and we see Him--which is "the appearing." In other words, the blessed hope and His appearing are one-and-the-same event. His physical, visible appearing will confirm every hope of each believer as they see Him coming in the clouds.[204] The Greek word for "appearance" is *epiphaneia* which is His manifestation or brightness.[205] This is the same Greek word Paul used in his epistle to the Corinthian church indicating the Second Coming: "Therefore you do not lack any spiritual gift as you eagerly *wait* for our Lord Jesus Christ to be *revealed*."[206] Paul encouraged them as they will need to be "strong to the end."[207] This brief exhortation denotes the appearance to be at the end and not before. Paul uses the same Greek word to charge Timothy "until the *appearing* of our Lord Jesus Christ."[208] Certainly Paul knew what the return of Christ entailed. His use of language did not allude to any other phase within the return other than the final appearance when the Lord would come to judge. There is but one Second Coming. Kenneth Wuest, formerly professor of Greek with the Moody Bible Institute, concluded correctly with his analysis of this section of Titus. He wrote: "Granville Sharp's rule makes the blessed hope and the appearing of the glory to be one and the same thing, the blessed hope of the Church being the appearing of the glory of the Lord Jesus, and also makes it clear that our great God is the Lord Jesus."[209] He said this well even as a dispensational teacher. John MacArthur who also holds to a pre-trib rapture agreed that Paul intended

---

[204] Acts 1:11; Mt 24:30

[205] Zodhiates, Spiros. *The Hebrew-Greek Key Study Bible. [NAS]*. Chattanooga, TN: AMG, 1994. p. 1614; Greek Dictionary, p. 32

[206] 1 Cor 1:7 [emphasis added].

[207] 1 Cor 1:8

[208] 1 Tim 6:14

[209] Wuest, Kenneth S. *Wuest's Word Studies From the Greek New Testament*. Vol. III. *Prophetic Light in the Present Darkness*. "The Departure of the Church." Grand Rapids, MI: Wm. B. Eerdmans, 1966. p. 57

this to be the Second Coming: "It seems rather that the apostle is here referring to Christ's second coming in general, when He will appear in glory and power rather than in humility and submission as in His first coming."[210] The Greek text itself provides the key as it states "the blessed hope and the appearance." This will be one event--and visible.

Generation

> ****[Mt 24:34-35]. "I tell you the truth, this *generation* will certainly not pass away until all these things have happened. Heaven and earth will pass away, but my words will never pass away."[211]

Here Jesus is emphasizing the importance of all His preceding words in response to the questions from Peter, John, James, and Andrew.[212] They wanted to know what was going to happen at the end of the age when Jesus returned. The Lord's answer here in the Olivet Discourse covers the event and describes for us those things we must watch for. The word that creates a stir is "generation." Jesus applied it to those who will be alive at the very time these events are taking place. He indicated that all of these things must be occurring and not just an isolated incident here or there. There is a sequence reflected in this discourse, and Jesus lays it out for those who have ears to hear.[213] The simple word "generation" stumbles many.[214] Darrel Bock noted the challenge in general for those attempting to account for Jesus' use of this word. In his comments on the parallel passage in Luke, he offered a rational conclusion based on the context that those alive at the beginning of the signs mentioned

---

[210] MacArthur, John. F., Jr. *Titus. The MacArthur New Testament Commentary.* Chicago, IL: Moody Press, 1996. p. 212-213

[211] [emphasis added].

[212] Mk 13:3

[213] Compare Jesus' words in Matthew, Mark, and Luke regarding His return-- addressed to believers.

[214] See comments in the "Introduction."

will see the end.[215] The real danger occurs when a pre-trib teacher employs their definition of a generation as they press their claim for an early removal of the church. David L. Cooper in contemplating the effect of the length of a generation in his commentary on the Olivet Discourse, recognized the "thirty-five to forty year" time frame and then extended it.[216] He increased the length to "seventy or eighty years" based on his interpretation of Psalm 90:10.[217] Since a good portion of his rendering was a reliance on World War I as the sign of the end,[218] a thirty-five to forty year calculation appearing in his 1935 edition put his claims at risk. It was revised in 1983 with that portion rewritten.[219] Jack Chick employed the generation formula from Psalm 90:10 and attached the seventy years to the founding of Israel in 1948.[220] He added seventy to 1948 which would yield 2018 as the time for the return of Christ with the pre-trib rapture in 2011. This did not happen. Once again, this is a clear example of the faulty kind of assumption tied to the lure of date setting. And the body of Christ is still here. For the preterist,[221] "generation" means those people who were alive as Jesus was speaking. This enables them to support their theory that most or all of these things took place around 70 A.D. This teaching is not credible, since all of these things did not happen then, nor have they happened since. The pre-trib advocate will also use this same word, "generation," to denote Jews or Israel.[222] However, as we noted in an earlier chapter, this is presupposition and not viable, since Jesus had just condemned Israel for their rejection of Him as their Messiah and Redeemer.[223] He said to them: "...you

---

[215] Bock, Darrell. *Luke. Volume 2: 9:51-24:53.Baker Exegetical Commentary on the N. T.* Grand Rapids, MI: Baker Academic, 2002. p. 1692

[216] Cooper, David L. *Future Events Revealed. An Exposition of the Olivet Discourse.* Los Angeles, CA: Biblical Research Society, 1983. p. 106

[217] Cooper. *Ibid.*

[218] Cooper. *Ibid.* p. 48, 52

[219] *cf.* Cooper, David L. *Future Events Revealed. According to Matthew 24 and 25.* Los Angeles, CA: By the Author, 1935. p. 91, 94-98

[220] Chick, Jack. *Kings of the East.* [Gospel tract]. http://chick.com/reading/tracts/1067/1067_01.asp

[221] See Glossary.

[222] See *Scofield Reference Bible.* p. 1034, footnote links this directly to Israel. Sometimes: "race."

[223] Mt 23:33-39

will not see me again until you say, 'Blessed is he who comes in the name of the Lord.'"[224] Jesus left them to ponder this, which today's church, especially those who hold to a pre-trib rapture, fail to comprehend. The rest of the verse Jesus quoted is from Psalm 118. It says: "From the house of the Lord we bless you."[225] The Jewish rulers did not. Hence, the judgment for failing to "bless" Him--Jesus--came upon them and those they ruled. This is an example of the conditional requirements God had set before Israel generations before.[226] So, Jesus rightfully identified them as reprobate and unworthy of the promise of God to bless them. Hence, the kingdom would be taken from them and given to someone else.[227] As we look at the very next chapter, Matthew twenty-four, we find the Olivet Discourse. The *context* tells us that the generation Jesus spoke of could not be the Jews nor could it be a vague reference to destruction of the Temple in 70 A.D. as preterists claim. The Olivet Discourse was an answer to a question from believers[228] who accepted Him as their Lord and Messiah. This would exclude Israel until they saw Him return. It is also clear that the heavens did not alter in the first century as Jesus warned regarding the sun, moon, and stars. The celestial bodies are still in the heavens. They will remain there until the "lightning flashes" from east to west.[229] Jesus was firm in His resolve that all of this must happen: "When you see all of these things."[230] So, the generation He refers to is those who will be alive when all of these things are occurring. In context, it is "this generation"--a yet future generation and not any other. Those alive when these events begin to occur will see it all, even His glorious return: the Second Coming.[231] We have dealt with the subject of "generation" elsewhere in this book.[232]

---

[224] Mt 23:39
[225] Psalm 118:26
[226] *e.g.*, Dt 30:11-20; Zech 7:13
[227] Mt 21:43
[228] Peter, James, John, and Andrew [Mk 13:3].
[229] Mt 24:26-27
[230] Mt 24:33
[231] Mt 24:29-31
[232] See "Introduction."

The Restrainer

****[2 Thess 2:7]. "For the secret power of lawlessness is already at work; but ***the one*** who now holds it back will continue to do so till he is taken out of the way."[233]

A simple examination of this verse shows Paul to be reminding the Thessalonians about the unseen power behind the lawlessness which they were personally familiar with.[234] He did not have to fully explain something they were already acquainted with. Roman law was in force along with local regulations. This did not stop the opposition to Christians by individuals or various magistrates. Many people opposed the very idea of Christianity. At one point, Paul wrote to the Corinthians about his remaining in Ephesus, since "a great door for effective work" opened for him. He wrote: "there are many who oppose me."[235] Paul and many others in the local churches were well acquainted with opposition, hostility, and persecution. This included a variety of threats from the local authorities. At times, mobs confronted them, and their lives were seriously at risk.[236] Thessalonica was no different. The church that Paul wrote to knew about lawlessness. Paul also noted that "something" is holding back the advance and full outpouring of evil. He mentioned "the one" holding it back, and that it is a "he." This simple statement could relate to a number of possibilities. However, as Paul noted, he used to tell the Thessalonians these things when he was there. He did not repeat his in-person dialogue in the epistle. So we are left to wrestle with this and interpret the meaning of Paul's intention.

Many theories have been offered. Pre-trib advocates tell us that this restrainer is the Holy Spirit. Then, they apply the removal of the restrainer to the idea that this is the Holy Spirit in the church being removed. They employ this as a pretext for the rapture. Surely Paul would have used a few different words here

---

[233] [emphasis added].

[234] Milligan, George. *St. Paul's Epistles to the Thessalonians. The Greek text with Introduction and Notes.* London: Macmillan and Co., Ltd., 1908. p. 101

[235] 1 Cor 16:8-9

[236] Acts 17:5-7. This occurred in the city of Thessalonica!

if that was his intent. Obviously, the pre-trib theory has to be grafted into this, since it is not in the text. A careful reading of this entire epistle will set that teaching aside.[237] However, this pre-trib rendering can be traced back to footnotes by C. I. Scofield. Many others have capitalized on this novelty, since it adds some grit to the dispensational thought of an early removal of the church. Scofield included this claim in the footnotes in his reference Bible. He outlined the "order of events" as it related to "that day."[238] Within Scofield's "order" there is his personal solution to the "mystery." He wrote that the "restrainer is a person," and "this Person can be no other than the Holy Spirit in the church, to be 'taken out of the way.'" He linked this directly to verse seven and First Thessalonians 4:16-17.[239] Consequently, with the longstanding influence of his footnotes, we find an unsound idea that the church is removed at this point. This is an aberration and an addition to the thoughts of Paul which is not in the original. Paul knew what he meant. Scofield simply swallowed a camel.

Those who insist on following Scofield's model that the Holy Spirit is removed will find no support for this idea in the New Testament. His assumption is one among others in an attempt to resolve the "restrainer" issue. As noted by commentators C. F. Hogg and W. E. Vine, it is not "stated or implied that the Holy Spirit will leave the earth at the rapture of the saints, for after that there will be those upon the earth who will witness for God, see Rev 11:3-4; 13:7, etc., in the energy of the Holy Spirit, see Joel 2:28-29."[240] Hogg and Vine are notably pre-trib advocates who render the Scofield idea as unsupportable. Both of these commentators held to dispensationalism and have their own problems. But as noted here, even a dispensationalist at times will conclude what is sensible and in agreement with Scripture. Hogg and Vine went on to note the likelihood that the restrainer "is God" as evidenced by "the countless operations of His providence."[241] They listed this with several "possibilities,"

---

[237] Comments elsewhere in this book cover this issue.

[238] 2 Thess 2:3

[239] Scofield, C. I. *The Scofield Reference Bible*. p. 1272

[240] Hogg, C. F. and W. E. Vine. *The Epistles to the T hessalonians*. 1914. rpt. Grand Rapids, MI: Kregel Publications, 1959. p. 258-259

[241] *Ibid*. p. 259

yet avoided the obvious within their own statements, since their pledge was to hold to a pre-trib rapture. Commentator, D. Edmond Hiebert, repeated this proposal from Hogg and Vine that the restrainer "is God" and continued, as they did, to erroneously connect this with the Holy Spirit as "the indweller of the saints" to be removed before "the manifestation of the lawless one."[242] This contradiction in ideas--and a direct challenge to Paul who wrote the epistle--is repeated over and over by numerous pre-trib teachers, many whose names have already been mentioned. This shows once again that the end justifies the means for pre-trib claims, regardless of the intent of the Biblical author and the context.

There are a number of other suggestions as to who the restrainer is. As noted in the verse, the gender is male. We see a person in view. Yet some expositors have insisted that the restrainer is the government. Rome was an early contender, since the Apostle wrote this as the Roman Empire was governing throughout the west and east--from Europe on into the Middle East. However, Paul as a Roman citizen was familiar with the empirical authorities in various provinces, especially since he came from Tarsus and dealt with a variety of rulers on his extensive missionary journeys. While the government then and today restrains anarchy and full bore corruption, Paul's terminology did not reflect government in general or Rome in particular as what restrains.[243] It is true, as Paul writes to the church in Rome, that all government has "been established by God."[244] But Paul is foremost concerned with "submission" to the governing authorities and not that they are restraining the final revelation of the man of sin. Many governments are wicked and tyrannical, yet they keep people in line. So, Paul in Thessalonians is looking at the final government which will be headed by the "man of sin" and not a type of government as if it were socialist, democratic, or a system of regency. At the last of the last days,

---

[242] Hiebert, D. Edmond. *The Thessalonian Epistles. A Call to Readiness*. Chicago, Il: Moody Press, 1977. p. 313.

[243] Milligan, George. *St. Paul's Epistles to the Thessalonians*. p. 101. Milligan notes the early position that Rome was the restraining force. Also: Hutchinson, John. *Lectures on St. Paul's First and Second Epistles to the Thessalonians*. Edinburgh: T. & T. Clark, 1884. p. 293-294

[244] Rm 13:1-7

there will be a despotic regime headed by the Antichrist whose evil nature will be satanically empowered and deadly for those who oppose him. At some point after he proclaims himself to be God,[245] the restraining power will be removed and evil will increase exponentially.[246] Once the restrainer is removed (the power that keeps evil in check), then the identity of the Antichrist will be in full view. All men will be able to see him for who he is. Since, this entire shift from bad to worse cannot proceed unless God permits, the simple option for us is to accept the idea that God Himself is the restrainer. Jesus noted this heavenly point of control when He faced Pilate at the time of His trial. Jesus told the Roman governor that he would have no power "if it were not given to you from above."[247] The implication is simple, that God is in control, and no man or government can interfere with His sovereign plan of redemption--even at the final time of the end. It must be noted, too, that God holds all power and raises up and brings down leaders[248] according to His sovereign purpose. This would include the revelation of the man of sin. As seen in Paul's letter to the church in Rome, when men totally reject God and His testimony, He will give them over to further corruption. It is God who allows this--not halting it--even as men willfully move toward the full suppression of His truth.[249] The human embodiment of this will be incarnate in the Antichrist. God will permit him to continue to the extremes of blasphemy[250] in order that overwhelming evidence of evil will be in full view. At that time, the Lord will take out of the way the restraints in place now which prevent both the fullness of evil and the revelation of the man of sin. At the appointed time,[251] all of this will be in plain view.[252]

Within the possible options for the identity of the restrainer there are some who conjecture that the angels may be what Paul is referring to. William Hendriksen

---

[245] 2 Thess 2:4

[246] 2 Thess 2:9-10

[247] Jn 19:11

[248] Ps 75:6-7; Dan 2:21. Also, *cf.* Is 40:23-24

[249] Note in Romans 1:18-32, God gives them over (3 times) to allow the complete degeneracy of man to be seen.

[250] Dan 9:27; 11:36; Mt 24:15; 2 Thess 2:3-4

[251] Dan 11:35; Zeph 2:1-2; 1 Cor 4:5

[252] Mt 24:15, 33-35

made note of this and discounted the idea as the single solution. He mentioned Michael or another archangel who may be hindering the Antichrist, yet did not endorse fully this thought. He noted those who would draw their conclusions from Daniel 10:13, 20 and Revelation 20:1-3. Hendriksen waffled a bit when he attempted to leave the option on the table, as if the angels who influence rulers may be part of the event. He melded this with his personal preference that law or government will be the restraining force. We do not accept this in the manner Hendriksen laid out his case.[253] The Pauline language does not leave room for angels or an angel to be the restrainer. Government as we know it today also fails to meet Paul's criteria. Angels, as indicated by Jesus, will be involved at the very end of the age at the time the church is gathered.[254] Paul, also, mentioned angels to be included at the end as the "Lord Jesus comes with all his holy ones."[255] He gave no Biblical evidence in context here that their identity is the same as the "restrainer."

Noting the words of Asaph in Psalm seventy-five, we find the Lord defining the general parameters of His restraint and power. It is God alone, the omnipotent One, who holds all power and determines sovereignly the timing of major events. Asaph recorded God's statement: "'I choose the appointed time; it is I who judge uprightly. When the earth and all its people quake, it is I who hold its pillars firm.'"[256] These remarks indicate the power of God to control events throughout history.[257] This is most evident at the time of the birth and death of His Son, the Lord Jesus. As Paul wrote: "But when the time had fully come, God sent his Son, born of a woman, born under the law, to redeem those under the law, that we might receive the full rights of sons."[258] Likewise, as Paul wrote to the church in Rome: "You see, at just the right time, when we were still powerless, Christ died for the ungodly."[259] These critical events were

---

[253] Hendriksen, William. *Exposition of I and II Thessalonians. N. T.* Commentary. Grand Rapids, MI: Baker Book House, 1971. p. 182
[254] Mt 24:30-31; Mt 13:40-43, 49-50
[255] 1 Thess 3:13
[256] Ps 75:2-3
[257] Consider Cyrus [Is 44:28; 45:1, 13].
[258] Gal 4:4-5
[259] Rm 5:6

fully in God's hands. He engaged history and humanity at just the right time. The same will be true at the end of the age when He removes the restraining power which up to this point has held back the full exposure of evil. As John Eadie noted: "A set time is appointed by God for the manifestation of the Man of Sin--a time neither to be antedated or postponed, and the restraining power which prevents his immediate appearance is also in God's hand."[260] This does not mean the Holy Spirit will be removed from the world as pre-trib teachers claim. It simply indicates the shift from God holding back the full operation of the evil one at this point in the final seven years. As pre-trib advocates must admit, there will be people saved during the tribulation period. Only the Holy Spirit does this.[261] God will be present through it all: the Triune God.[262]

Parousia

> ****[1 Thess 4:15-17]. "According to the Lord's own word, we
> tell you that we who are still alive, who are left till *the coming*
> of the Lord, will certainly not precede those who have fallen
> asleep. For the Lord himself will come down from heaven,
> with a loud command, with the voice of the archangel and
> with the trumpet call of God, and the dead in Christ will rise
> first. After that, we who are still alive and are left will be
> caught up with them in the clouds to meet the Lord in the air.
> And so we will be with the Lord forever."[263]

This portion of Paul's Thessalonian epistle is the center of controversy within the discussion of the pre-trib removal of the church. Those who teach this idea hold dearly to their interpretation which they portray as foundational evidence

---

[260] Eadie, John. *Commentary on the Greek Text of the Epistles of Paul to the Thessalonians*. 1877. rpt. Grand Rapids, MI: Baker Book House, 1979. p. 276. Note, also Acts 17:31

[261] Jn 16:8

[262] Deut 31:6, 8; Josh 1:5; Heb 13:5

[263] [emphasis added].

for the rapture and its being a hasty, secret removal of believers prior to the tribulation. There is little question that Paul has referred to the event which is the rapture. However, his choice of words eliminates the possibility that the return he notes is secret. It is anything but. The loud command or shout, the voice of the archangel, and the blast of the trumpet are together the description of a major, heavenly revelation. Also, the flow of words and his reference to "the Lord's own word" tell us that Paul's understanding of the Second Coming is in full agreement with the Lord's, just as He detailed it in the Olivet Discourse. As the Lord Jesus taught specific signs to precede His return, so Paul's simple reminder here brings a clearer picture of the Second Coming. These verses are distinctly a synopsis of the Second Advent when the Lord comes in glory to judge and remove His own. Paul knew this according "to the Lord's own word"[264] from personal revelation.[265]

The words which are emphasized by the advocates of the pre-trib rapture are "the coming" found in verse fifteen. In the Greek text, the word in contention is *parousia* which has the definite article preceding it. This tells us it is a specific event to be measured by the text which surrounds it. Pre-trib teachers are obligated to reinforce the rapture of the church taking place before the tribulation, hence they attach a secondary meaning to the Greek word *parousia*. They add a connotation of "coming for" the church rather than coming to gather the church as a protective measure when the final judgment occurs. Since they have already proclaimed this to be the time when the Lord removes believers, the notion of a quick removal is added. The prevalence of this is confirmed by Millard Erickson: "The pre-tribulationist argues *parousia* refers to the rapture, the first stage of the return, the believer's hope of being delivered from the world when the tribulation begins."[266] This is the emphasis whether spoken or not. William Evans, formerly teaching at Moody Bible Institute and at Bible Institute of Los Angeles (BIOLA), was most blunt in his assertion that "there is nothing to hinder the 'rapture' or 'parousia."[267] In Mal

---

[264] 1 Thess 4:15

[265] Gal 1:11-12

[266] Erickson, Millard J. *Christian Theology*. Grand Rapids, MI: Baker Book House, 1986. p. 1191

[267] Evans, William. *The Great Doctrines of the Bible*. Chicago, IL: Moody Press,

Couch's pre-trib reference, *Dictionary of Premillennial Theology*, under the section on the "Biblical Study of the Rapture," it states plainly the "term *parousia* is used to describe the Rapture."[268] Among the verses listed that have been attached to this Greek word are 1 Thessalonians 4:13-18. This is done in spite of the editor's admission in "Major Rapture Terms and Passages"[269] that this word has additional meanings, in particular "arrival" and "presence." Dr. Couch then boldly stated: "Thus, when the word *parousia* is used in rapture passages, it in no way has to be understood as 'coming to stay.'"[270] He followed this claim with the thought that the word does not automatically designate the Second Coming. This is patronizing at best, since he showed no intention of honestly determining the usage by its context. The fact that the author has a well-defined bias in mind, his rhetoric is mere sophistry. Pre-trib teachers know the primary definition of this word means "presence," yet go to great lengths to adjust the sense of it as to appear to support the instantaneous removal of the church and a return to heaven. Paul knew this was not the case. He made sure the church in Thessalonica understood this when he was there and again in writing as he described visually the Lord's return in 2 Thessalonians chapter one.[271] Instructor in systematic theology, pre-trib advocate, Floyd Barackman, chided post-tribulationists who ignore the possibility of other interpretations and reject anything but "*parousia* as an ordinary word for 'coming' and 'presence'."[272] In other words, he knew the meaning of the word, its position in Paul's letters, and its threat to the pre-trib idea. This is not sound *exegesis* at all. What we find instead is a consistency to meld an un-Biblical idea into the text. This is unhealthy.

As noted by Alfred Plummer, *parousia* first appears as found in Matthew's gospel in the very place where its context is established.[273] This directly relates

---

1949. p. 243

[268] Couch, Mal. *Dictionary of Premillennial Theology*. Grand Rapids, MI: Kregel Pub., 1996. p. 333

[269] Ice, Thomas, and Timothy Demy. *When the Trumpet Sounds*. Eugene, OR: Harvest House, 1996. p. 50

[270] *Ibid.*

[271] See 2 Thess 1:6-10

[272] Barackman, Floyd H. *Practical Christian Theology*. Grand Rapids, MI: Kregel Pub., 1991. p. 437

to the question asked by the Apostles: "What will be the sign of your coming (*parousia*) and of the end of the age?"[274] Jesus was going away. These men were concerned and needed encouragement. Jesus answered assuring them He would return in glory. From this, these men understood *parousia* to mean the Second Coming and used the term in this manner with no other "return" prior to the one the Lord outlined for them in this discourse. Plummer noted: "It intimates that the return of the Messiah in glory will not result, like the First Coming, in a transitory stay, but will inaugurate an abiding *presence*."[275] David Williams correctly related the revelation (*apokalypsis*) of Jesus in 2 Thessalonians 1:6-7 to Paul's words of encouragement in 1 Thessalonians 2:19.[276] There Paul says: "For what is our hope, our joy, or our crown in which we will glory in the presence (*parousia*) when he comes? Is it not you?"[277] Paul directly connects the Lord's presence (*parousia*) with His revelation (*apokalypsis*). In other words, Paul used these terms for one-and-the-same event: the Second Coming. Richard Longenecker brought out the fullness of the return of the Lord as he harmonized Paul's thoughts from various epistles:

> The parousia in Paul's teaching, then, means first of all permanent union for the Christian with Christ (I Thess. 4:17) and the resurrection of the believer's body, completing the sonship to which the believer has been called by the transformation of the body "to be like his glorious body" (Rom. 8:23; I Cor. 15:12-58; Phil. 3:21). It also means judgment, though for the Christian the ultimate verdict is already known (Rom. 8:1); whatever else judgment may mean in terms of purgation and recompense, it cannot affect the salvation of those who have believed in Christ (I Cor. 3:13-15; 5:5; II Cor. 5:10). For those apart from Christ, however, the parousia can mean only "sudden

---

[273] Plummer, Alfred. *An Exegetical Commentary on the Gospel According to Matthew.* p. 329

[274] Mt 24:3

[275] Plummer. *Ibid.*

[276] Williams, David J. *1 and 2 Thessalonians. New International Bible Commentary.* Peabody, MA: Hendrickson Pub., 1992. p. 114

[277] 1 Thess 2:19

destruction," "wrath," and "condemnation" (I Thess 1:10b; 5:3; 9a, II Thess 2:10-12)."[278]

Dr. Longenecker clearly summarized the Second Coming with the broader inclusion of Paul's thoughts. He also properly highlighted the scene with the deliverance of the Lord's own and at the same time the judgment of the wicked. Ralph Earle defined Paul's use of the word as he described its use in Philippians 2:12 where Paul reminded them of his visit. Earle writes: "'Presence' is *parousia*, which literally means 'being beside,' while 'absence' is *apousia*, 'being away from.'"[279] Surely, Paul knew from his own experience that this word meant being physically present--just as he had been. The Apostle John used the same word (*parousia*) when he described the Lord's return: "...when he appears we may be confident and unashamed at his *coming*."[280] Certainly, John, the author of the Book of Revelation understood this word and its contextual relationship to the Lord's Second Advent. He was present to hear the Olivet Discourse. The Apostles knew what the Lord meant and always looked to His coming as the event to consummate this age and initiate the age to come without a previous rapture of the church. Bishop Thomas Newton clearly presented all of the Apostle Paul's language as supporting just one event when the Lord comes "to judge the world." He linked this to the future event: the "second coming in glory" to include our gathering, just as Paul laid it out in both Thessalonian letters. Lord [1 Thess 4:13-18; 2 Thess 1:6-10].[281] Newton understood exactly Paul's words which refuted the idea that the day of the Lord had come or that any of them would be left out when the Lord did return. Theodor Zahn in his monumental *Introduction to the New Testament* connected the *parousia* with the resurrection.[282] He correctly noted that the resurrection "must still be considered as simultaneous with the parousia, since it is the condition of participation in the kingdom."[283] There is one Second Coming and

---

[278] Longenecker, Richard. *The Ministry and Message of Paul.* Grand Rapids, MI: Zondervan, 1973. p. 113-114

[279] Earle, Ralph. *Word Meanings in the New Testament.* Peabody, MA: Hendrickson, 2002. p. 339

[280] 1 Jn 2:28 [emphasis added]. The *parousia*.

[281] Newton, Thomas. *Dissertions on the Prophecies.* p. 388-389

[282] Rev 20:4-6

one first resurrection. Any deviation from this corrupts the texts and distorts the author's meaning.

"No argument for the two-stage coming can be derived from the use of the New Testament words for the Second Coming." This is the statement of Anthony Hoekema in his analysis of the nature of the Second Coming.[284] He referenced three terms used to relate to the Second Coming: *parousia* (literally, presence), *apokalypsis* (revelation), and *epiphineia* (appearance).[285] Hoekema compared the pre-trib use of the English word "rapture" to Paul's use of *parousia*. In 1 Thessalonians 4:15, pretribulationists connect this to the rapture. In 1 Thessalonians 3:13, *parousia* is again used by Paul, and the pre-rib advocate will assign this to the second phase of Jesus' return. This is the Second Coming when the Lord returns with all his saints. Notice that Paul uses the same word in both verses for the same event--the Second Coming--while pre-trib teachers do not. They redefine the word to fit their dispensational bias. Paul never separated the Lord's return into phases. Hoekema reminds us that Paul used the same word (*parousia*) in 2 Thessalonians 2:8. There he applied it to the coming "at which Christ shall bring the antichrist to nought--which is not supposed to happen, according to pretribulationists, until the second phase."[286] Hoekema then shows Paul's use of the word *apokalypsis* in 1 Corinthians 1:7, which pre-trib interpreters call the rapture, ("as you eagerly wait for our Lord Jesus Christ to be *revealed*") is the same word he uses in 2 Thessalonians 1:7-8 ("the Lord Jesus is *revealed*") which they apply to the Second Coming.[287] This is the time the Lord comes to judge "in blazing fire." Notably, Peter used the same word when he addressed the elders as they awaited the Lord's return and "the glory to be *revealed*."[288] As you can see, pre-trib interpretation is fluid and is not compatible with the context or the N. T. writer's intent. The third Greek term is

---

[283] Zahn, Theodor. *Introduction to the New Testament*. 1909. rpt. Minneapolis, MN: Klock & Klock, 1977. Vol. 1, p. 224

[284] Hoekema, Anthony A. *The Bible and the Future*. Grand Rapids, MI: Wm. B. Eerdmans Pub. Co., 1982. p. 165 [italics in the original].

[285] *Ibid.*

[286] *Ibid.* p. 166

[287] *Ibid.*

[288] 1 Pt 5:1 [emphasis added].

epiphineia which relates to the Lord's appearing. Pre-trib teachers will apply the rapture to Paul's words to Timothy: "...the *appearing* of our Lord Jesus Christ." In 2 Thessalonians 2:8, Paul used the same word to describe the Lord's return at the time He "will overthrow" the "man of lawlessness" The Apostle stated this will occur "by the *splendor* of his coming." This is the manifestation or appearance of the Lord at the end of the tribulation when He destroys Antichrist. Pre-trib teachers relate this to the Second Coming, yet fail to see that Paul reckons this to be the singular return of Jesus.[289] In relating these three Greek terms to the Second Coming, L. J. Kreitzer in an extensive article on eschatology, noted the terms used by Paul to be in conformity with the "Day of the Lord" at the end of this age. This is the Second Advent and the time of judgment. Kreitzer noted *apokalypsis* and *epiphineia* to be in context with Paul's use of *parousia* to suggest "a future manifestation of the glory of Lord Jesus Christ."[290] This is not a secret event. It is the day the Lord appears to judge one and all. Even Thomas Ice, staunch pre-trib advocate, freely admitted this was the Lord's coming in Messianic glory. He wrote: "Our Lord's use of *parousia* demands His physical, bodily presence."[291] Dr. Ice's affirmation also placed him in agreement with Paul who, as we noted above, used *parousia* just as the Lord had in the Olivet Discourse to signify His glorious return. Further, C. I. Scofield correctly defined these three Greek words in his footnote for 1 Corinthians 1:7 in his reference Bible. A careful reading of his explanation yields the conclusion that he used all three words to refer to the Second Advent with the Lord's "personal presence" at the time of His coming when the rapture [1 Thess 4:16-17] occurs, and He destroys the Antichrist [2 Thess 2:8]. Scofield's own scripture references are clearly portraying a single event which is the Second Coming of Christ in glory.[292]

In his extensive commentary on 1 Corinthians 15, Spiros Zodhiates dealt with

---

[289] Hoekema. *Ibid.* p. 165-166; Mc Reynolds, Paul R. *Word Study Greek-English New Testament.* Wheaton, IL: Tyndale House, 2003. p. 1034, 1224

[290] Hawthorne, Gerald F.; Ralph P. Martin; Daniel G. Reid. *Dictionary of Paul and His Letters.* Downers Grove, IL: InterVarsity Press, 2004. Kreitzer, L. J., "Eschatology," p. 259

[291] Ice, Thomas. "Pre-Trib Perspectives." Vol. VIII, Num. 99. April, 2012. p. 4

[292] See *The Scofield Reference Bible.* p. 1212, footnote 1.

this word as it appeared in context. He wrote:

> The word *parousia* in the New Testament, when used in reference
> to the Lord Jesus, always means the second coming of Christ. In
> ecclesiastical writing this is called "the second coming" (*hee
> deutera parousia*). (See Matt. 24:3, 27, 37, 39; I Cor. 15:23; I
> Thess. 2:19; 3:13; 4:15; 5:23; II Thess 2:1, 8, 9; James 5:7, 8; II
> Pet. 1:16; 3:4, 12; I John 2:28).[293]

Zodhiates continued to explain this term and its contextual importance:

> The word *parousia* implies more than the word e*leusis*. The latter
> word stresses more the act of arrival and coming--as when Christ
> was born in Bethlehem--while the *parousia* of Christ stresses more
> the continuity of His staying. The Lord in His *parousia* is not
> coming merely temporarily, as He did the first time in His
> incarnation, when He remained for a relatively short period of time.
> We never find His incarnation or first coming, referred to as His first
> *parousia*. Only His second coming is referred to as a "presence."
> And that is because He will always be present.[294]

Dr. Zodhiates brought together a number of the locations for this word as used
by the New Testament writers. They all were looking at a single return of the
Lord which will occur at the end of this age. At that time, the resurrection will
take place, and the Lord will remain here with us who believe.[295] John Stott
addressed the implications of Paul's words answering the question *when* this
will take place. His comments are framed in the context of Paul's second letter
to the church in Thessalonica. Dr. Stott underscored Paul saying this will occur
when the Lord is revealed in flaming fire from heaven. Stott wrote:

---

[293] Zodhiates, Spiros. *Conquering the Fear of Death. An exposition of I Corinthians
15, based on the original Greek text.* Grand Rapids, MI: Wm. B. Eerdmans Pub.,
1970. p. 315
[294] Zodhiates. *Conquering the Fear of Death.* p. 317
[295] Dr. Zodhiates commented on 1 Cor 15:23. You will find 1 Cor 15:22-24 covered
elsewhere in this book.

The *parousia* (official visit) has now become the *apokalypsis* (unveiling) of Jesus Christ. The basic affirmation of his coming is almost identical in both letters:

1 Thes. 4:16 'the Lord himself will come down from heaven'.

2 Thes. 1:7 'the Lord Jesus is revealed from heaven'.

According to both statements his coming will be personal (the same Lord Jesus, he himself and no other, who lived, died, rose and ascend, will come again), visible (having disappeared from sight at the ascension, he will reappear) and glorious (first coming having been in weakness and obscurity, his second will be in power and public magnificence). [296]

Consequently, Dr. Stott affirmed the description of the Second Coming to be one-and-the-same in both of Paul's letters, the *parousia* (physical presence) being described in each. He noted, instead of the "loud command, the voice of the archangel and the trumpet call of God, we now read of *blazing fire*, a regular symbol of the holy, consuming nature of God's presence."[297] This leaves no room for a previous return or removal of the church.

It must be noted here that J. H. Thayer in his *Greek-English Lexicon* defined *parousia* with great precision. He stated it to mean "presence;" "the presence of one coming, hence *the coming, arrival, advent*;" "the future visible *return* from heaven of Jesus, the Messiah, to raise the dead, hold the last judgment, and set up formally and gloriously the kingdom of God."[298] Alfred Edersheim in his monumental work on the life of Christ directly noted *parousia* to be the Second Advent.[299] As noted by J. Barton Payne: "The stress of *parousia*, however, falls

---

[296] Stott, John. *The Gospel and the End of Time: The Message of 1 & 2 Thessalonians.* Downers Grove, IL: InterVarsity Press, 1991. p. 147-148

[297] Stott, John. *Ibid.* p. 148 [emphasis in the original].

[298] Thayer, John Henry. *A Greek-English Lexicon of the New Testament.* 1901. rpt. Grand Rapids, MI: Baker Book House, 1983. p. 490 [emphasis in the original].

[299] Edersheim, Alfred. *The Life and Times of Jesus the Messiah. Vol. II.* Grand Rapids, MI: Wm. B. Eerdmans Pub. Co., 1962. p. 432, note.

not so much upon coming as upon the arrival and resultant presence."[300] Even Kenneth Wuest, an ardent dispensationalist, stated: "The word means literally "the being beside," thus "the personal presence."[301] More recently, Robert Van Kampen defined this to be the Lord's arrival "when He will rescue His subjects and destroy the enemy." He said, "…the Greek noun *parousia* refers to Christ's coming as an event, not as an activity."[302] James Gray, past president of Moody Bible Institute, wrote: "There are also certain Greek words associated with the second coming of Christ, which are translated thus: 'The *appearing* of our Lord Jesus Christ,' 'The *Coming* of Jesus Christ,' 'The *Revelation* of Jesus Christ,' and which mean in every case His bodily presence."[303] The evidence is soundly in favor of the Greek terms pointing a single event at which time the Lord appears in glory to bring relief and rescue to His own and, also, retribution to those who are unrepentant foes of God.

The Missing Church

****Revelation 5 through 19….

There are many prophecy teachers who emphasize the so-called absence of the church in the Book of Revelation after chapter four. The usual byline employed states that the church is addressed directly in chapters two and three. Then, John is called to "come up" in chapter four, and after that there is no mention of the church. Hence, this becomes another "proof text" for the rapture since they do not see the church present in John's Apocalypse after the fourth chapter. Robert Jeffress of the First Baptist Church of Dallas, Texas, used this as one of his primary reasons for believing in a pre-trib rapture. He does not see the church present "during the description of the Tribulation (Rev 6-18)," stating, "…there is no mention of it." He claims the church is "not present during that horrific period of time."[304] This is the standard approach. Bible

---

[300] Payne, J. Barton. *The Imminent Appearing of Christ.* p. 45
[301] Wuest, Kenneth S. *Bypaths in the Greek New Testament for the English Reader.* Grand Rapids, MI: Wm. B. Eerdmans Pub. Co., 1954. p. 33
[302] Van Kampen, Robert. *The Rapture Question Answered.* p. 95
[303] Gray, James M. *My Faith in Jesus Christ. A Personal Testimony.* Chicago, IL: Fleming H. Revell, 1927. p. 124

teacher J. Vernon McGee stated: "Then after chapter 3, the church is not mentioned anymore. The church is not the subject again in the entire Book of the Revelation."[305] He continued to press the absence by stating: "When we see her in the last part of Revelation, she is not the church but the bride."[306] Dr. McGee affirmed his view with his comments on chapter four: "From here on you will not find the word *church* mentioned." He continued: "The church has gone to heaven--that is what happened to it."[307] This is the general outline followed by many pre-trib teachers. John Walvoord wrote "...the rapture may be viewed as having already occurred in the scheme of God before the events of chapter 4 and following chapters of Revelation unfold." With regard to the church he stated: "She is not a participant in the scenes of the tribulation which form the major content of the book of Revelation." Further: "At the beginning of chapter 4, then, the church may be considered as in heaven and not related to events which will take place on earth in preparation for Christ's return in power and glory." He noted the word "church" not appearing again until chapter twenty-two.[308] Paul Benware, author of a number of commentaries, simply stated regarding Revelation six through nineteen, "...the church (*ekklesia*), the Body of Christ, is never mentioned."[309] This, then, is the general approach to the difficulty of attempting to account for the church being elsewhere and not present in John's Apocalypse. The pre-trib view requires that the church already be in heaven, so those who teach this theory cannot allow for the church to still be on earth. The exception they make for this is the recognition of believers whom they claim will come to Christ after the church is removed, some being martyrs. The problem with this disjointed theory lies in the fact that everything John wrote is to and for the church. The dispensational, pre-trib idea

---

[304] Jeffress, Robert. *As Time Runs Out: A Simple Guide to Bible Prophecy*. Nashville, TN: Broadman & Holman Pub., 1999. p. 63-64

[305] McGee, J. Vernon. *Thru The Bible with J. Vernon McGee*. Vol. 5. Nashville, TN: Thomas Nelson Pub., 1988. p. 881

[306] *Ibid*.

[307] *Ibid*. p. 926 [emphasis in the original].

[308] Walvoord, John F. *The Revelation of Jesus Christ. A Commentary*. Chicago, IL: Moody Press, 1989. p. 103

[309] Benware, Paul N. *Understanding End Times Prophecy. A Comprehensive Approach*. Chicago, IL: Moody Press, 1995. p. 205

cannot accommodate this, so they bypass the natural flow of John's writings which they do not do in his Gospel. This is dangerous. J. Barton Payne provided a simple rebuttal for the riddle of the "missing" church when he stated: "*Ekklesia* is not found anywhere in six of the books of the New Testament, and yet these epistles are undeniably directed to the church."[310] Believers must think carefully and not be sidetracked by Biblical adjustments which are un-Biblical.

Think about this carefully. The word "church" does not appear in the text of the Book of Revelation after the third chapter.[311] But it does appear in chapter twenty-two. You will see "the churches" in Revelation 22:16.[312] Here, Jesus is summarizing the concern He has for the message in the previous twenty-one chapters. Since the books and verses were numbered for our convenience many years later, Jesus is actually commending the entire book to the church.[313] This is always overlooked by those who attempt to enforce their pre-trib idea. It is not surprising that they would not know this from the broad context, since at all cost they must get the church out completely (rapture) from chapter four on. Notice in this verse at the end of the book (Rev 22:16), Jesus speaks directly to the "churches" with His "testimony." This tells us that the entire book was written to the church. Since these events have not yet unfolded, it means it was written for us. This is not perceived by those who have been misled with pre-trib teaching, since they are simply told the church will not be here. Hence, when they read through these chapters, they have an ingrained bias that no church is included in the events after the fourth chapter. This premise is unsound, since it is an argument from silence. It is interesting to note the difficulty in supporting the thought of an absent church. Robert Jeffress, noted above, illustrated this when he identified the "harlot" as the "world church" and its head, "the false prophet." He stated: "This apostate church will have the appearance of a legitimate church, but will deny the basic tenets of

---

[310] Payne, J. Barton. *The Imminent Appearing of Christ.* Grand Rapids, MI: Wm. B. Eerdmans Pub., 1961. p. 80

[311] Rev 3:14, 22, Laodicea, the seventh church.

[312] Rev 22:16, "I, Jesus, have sent my angel to give you this *testimony to the churches.*" [emphasis added].

[313] Rev 1:1. Written for His servants, the church.

Christianity."[314] He, then, moved his focus to the mid-point of the tribulation (after the rapture, of course) and quoted from the Book of Daniel: "I kept looking, and that horn was waging war against the saints and overpowering them (Dan. 7:21)."[315] With this reference, he acknowledged there will be saints on the earth during the final seven years who face the Antichrist. The question for us then becomes, who are these saints? The pre-trib accommodation defines them as Jews or others who convert during this time, but Daniel does not specify this to be the case. He writes "saints." He would not have used the word "church," since the word was not part of his vocabulary. But it was employed in context by Jesus and the Apostles. Jesus addressed His warning to the *church* in the Olivet Discourse to include believers seeing the "abomination that causes desolation," the same one Daniel writes of who will war against the saints.[316] Jesus was speaking to believers, Apostles who were saints and represented other saints. Paul wrote addressing "saints" who were the church.[317] The term is synonymous with all who belong to God whether under the old covenant or the new. Jude wrote that the Lord was to return with "ten thousands of his saints."[318] This is inclusive of all of the believing departed and will include all those still living when the Lord Jesus descends from heaven with a shout to gather His elect--"saints"--the church.[319] In Merrill Unger's definition, included are "every NT believer" and *pious* Israelites."[320] It is not helpful for pre-trib teachers to misapply the identity of the saints just to support their notion. Further, the prophet Daniel mentioned "saints" six times within the same chapter as his dream and its explanation. He noted regarding the activity of the horn which came from the fourth beast, that it not only waged war against the "saints,"[321] it spoke against the Most High and oppressed the

---

[314] Jeffress, Robert. *As Tine Runs Out*. p. 79

[315] *Ibid.* p. 81

[316] Mt 24:15

[317] Rm 1:7; 1 Cor 1:2; 2 Cor 1:1; Eph 1:1, etc.

[318] Jude 14 [KJV]

[319] 1 Thess 4:16-17; Matt 24:30-31

[320] Unger, Merrill F./Harrison, R. K.; Howard F. Vos; Cyril J. Barber, eds. *The New Unger's Bible Dictionary*. Chicago, IL: Moody Press, 1990. p. 1112 [emphasis in the original].

[321] Dan 7:21

"saints."[322] The "saints" are handed over to him for "a time, times and half a time." This agrees with Jesus' warning in Matthew 24:15. Daniel also noted that the "saints" will possess the kingdom when the "ancient of Days" defeats "the horn" and they--the "saints"--possess the kingdom.[323] Daniel wrote looking ahead to the time when the "sovereignty, power and greatness of the kingdoms under the whole world will be handed over to His saints, the people of the Most High."[324] This occurs at the end, once Jesus has come to judge and establish His everlasting kingdom. Clearly, the "saints" in view are God's own from all the ages. This includes the "church" as it is identified in John's Apocalypse, named or not.

At this point, it would be good to look at chapter one as it relates to chapter twenty-two. In the first verse of chapter one, John is writing "to show his servants what must soon take place."[325] John is writing as a servant, and his message is likewise for all other servants. This would include the seven churches mentioned by name in chapter two and three, plus each one who "reads the words of this prophecy." Not only that, John states that all those who "hear it and take it to heart" will be blessed.[326] In this simple formula, it means no believer is excluded from learning or understanding this book. The message is for all in the Body of Christ through all the ages until these events begin to unfold. The term "servants" in the first chapter and the same word ("servants") in chapter twenty-two identifies those who are the recipients, beneficiaries, and concerned participants in what John writes of in advance. This same focus is what is contained in the brief admonition in the Olivet Discourse as Jesus looked ahead to these events which are recorded with more detail by John.[327] The direct participants are noted by John as he commences to write. He then is given specific warnings to seven churches. These were real churches functioning in the locations mentioned at the time he wrote. It was directed to them severally but sent to each one individually. This should be clear since

---

[322] Dan 7:25
[323] Dan 7:22
[324] Dan 7:27
[325] Rev 1:1
[326] Rev 1:2-3
[327] Mt 24:3-35

Paul's Ephesian letter was sent to a number of churches with the name "Ephesus" omitted from the text. Many manuscripts were copied and circulated to other churches as well. In the context of Revelation, it was directed to seven churches, so the book would be guaranteed to arrive in seven locations and not be lost. This is so we "his servants" would be warned.

The seven churches in chapters two and three are used by the dispensational teacher to represent the church ages.[328] This becomes a distraction because someone may think the church is brought into view in these two chapters and then disappears. They are not told the entire book is written to them--the church. So, we must look at what John wrote as he began to preserve this revelation about the last days and, also, read the words of Jesus at the end of John's book. The conclusion is that this book has been written to us, and there is no part of it which does not affect us directly or indirectly. This is for our edification, so we can understand what is coming and prepare. Those who mislead others by teaching a pre-trib idea are merely repeating the influence that they received from another pre-trib source. Bible teacher, J. Vernon McGee, claimed to avoid this pitfall but stated: "Many works on Revelation are merely carbon copies of other works. In my own library I have more commentaries on the Revelation than any other book of the Bible, and most of them are almost *copies* of those that have preceded them."[329] This admission explains why the distortion continues.

Let us look further into John's writings. As a point of interest, in Revelation 11:18, the seventh angel has sounded his trumpet. The twenty-four elders proclaim this to be the time God's wrath has come. They state: "The time has come for judging the dead, and for rewarding your servants the prophets and your saints and those who reverence your name, both small and great--for destroying those who destroy the earth."[330] This is a brief synopsis of the complete judgment of God with retribution for His enemies and rewards for

---

[328] Note our comments on this elsewhere in this book, since this theory contradicts imminency.

[329] McGee, J. Vernon. *Thru The Bible with J. Vernon McGee.* Vol. 5. p. 881 [emphasis in the original].

[330] Rev 11:18

His servants--believers, the faithful, the church. There is no evidence prior to this anywhere that the church has been removed. This is the final trumpet which John the Apostle mentions in chapter ten at which time he says "the mystery of God will be accomplished."[331] This is the same "mystery" that Paul refers to in his letter to the church in Corinth as he described the rapture.[332] Paul even states this to be the "last trumpet." There are no other last trumpets. There are no saints removed before the mention of the "mystery" in Rev 11:18. The actual procedure begins here when this angel who has been given his trumpet by God[333] sounds his instrument. This relates directly to Paul's words in 1 Thessalonians 4:16-17 which is consummated in Revelation 19:1-6. It should be noted here that this all occurs at or near the end of all things--not in the beginning of the final seven years. This trumps any thought of the church being taken out before the end of the Apocalypse. Hence, the event Paul reminds the Thessalonians about, the time we are "caught up" along with the "dead in Christ," occurs just as John states it with the "trumpet call" which is the final event bringing change to the mortal bodies of those who are alive--His servants--believers, the faithful, the church. The overall thrust of John's Apocalypse upholds this and agrees with Paul's description of this event and the Lord's words in the Olivet Discourse. As the events during the second half of the tribulation period proceed, these final portions will happen quickly at the end.[334]

The reason we do not see the term "church" used by John after the third chapter is because in the early chapters he is addressing and warning believers in specific, physical locations. However, believers who are part of the church--the faithful who look to their Creator, fear Him, and believe[335]--are noted in various portions of the Apocalypse. The terms "saints," "elect," "church," "churches," and "servants" are synonymous. There are pre-trib teachers, like Gerald Stanton, [336] who have attempted to refute this, but in the process only

---

[331] Rev 10:7
[332] 1 Cor 15:50-57. Read this carefully.
[333] Rev 8:1-2
[334] Note Rev 18:4, 8, 10, 17, 19.
[335] Malachi 3:16-18; John 17:3; Rom 8:9; 10:9-10. They are those "who reverence your name" [Rev 11:18].

add confusion and end up complicating what John presents for us. Remember, the Lord is addressing His "servants" throughout this book. He emphasizes this at the end as the angel reminds John: "These words are trustworthy and true. The Lord, the God of the spirits of the prophets, sent his angel to show his *servants* the things that must soon take place."[337] The Lord Himself affirms just a few verses later that this testimony is "for the churches."[338] Within the body of John's writing, his record of the Lord revealing things to come, we find the church. Carefully notice "saints" in Revelation 5:8; 8:3; 8:4; 11:18; 13:7; 13;10; 14:12; 16:6; 17;6; 18:20; 18:24; and finally in Rev 19:8 at the time believers (the church) are given "fine linen" to wear. Up to that point, the church is on earth, and each picture that John presents in those verses shows the church yet earthbound. The term "elect" is not used by John here, but is readily defined by the Apostle Peter as he writes to the churches. Note: "To God's elect, strangers in the world, scattered throughout Pontus, Galatia, Cappadocia, Asia and Bythnia, who have been chosen according to the foreknowledge of God the Father, by the sanctifying work of the Spirit, for obedience to Jesus Christ and sprinkling by his blood."[339] Surely this is the church. Certainly the locations Peter mentions include the churches in Asia where John directs his words. Obviously the "elect" and the "church" are one and the same. The term "servants" is used in Revelation as we have already noted. You will find it in a few places. However, notice in Revelation 6:11 where John writes of them, they are on the earth as some of those in heaven inquire "how long" until their number is completed. This confirms the believers' presence in heaven--those who have departed, identified by Paul[340]-- who will be joined by others during the tribulation period. None mentioned by John were raptured. They perished and are in heaven awaiting their number to be completed. In Revelation seven, we find "servants" once more. These happen to be the Jews who will be sealed for redemption to fulfill God's promises given under the former covenant.[341] There is but one body of

---

[336] Stanton, Gerald. *Kept From The Hour. Biblical Evidence for the Pretribulational Return of Christ.* Miami Springs, FL: Schoettle Pub. Co., 1991. p. 65
[337] Rev 22:6 [emphasis added].
[338] Rev 22:16
[339] 1 Pt 1:2
[340] 1 Thess 4:13-15

believers.[342] Jews and Gentile believers will make up the faithful. Some are with the Lord now. Others will join them during the last seven year period. Therefore, the simple words we have discussed here should not be separated into special groups to distract us from seeing God's one purpose in redemption, to bring us all together--the one body--so His house will be full. As the Book of Revelation closes, all those who believe are promised to be with the Lord forever in His city where His throne is, "and his servants will serve him." We will see His face and will have His name on our foreheads.[343] This will be the full Body of Christ joined together on the earth as the age to come begins. Please note that Peter, James, John, Paul, and other Biblical authors use these terms above interchangeably. Their words include each of us who believe. We are the Body of Christ with an array of names to describe us who believe.

It should be noted also that the Antichrist will be warring against the saints defeating and killing them.[344] This takes place on the earth just as John notes it in Revelation thirteen. The Lord also warned of this in the Olivet Discourse. Nowhere in the context of these portions of scripture is there any sense that the church has been removed. We are looking at the great contest of good and evil at the end of the age. On the last of these days, the Lord Himself will resolve all facets of this, and we will see it.[345] There will be saints on the earth in the midst of this time of stress never to be equaled again. Pre-trib teachers know that there will be "saints" on the earth, yet they attempt to disqualify them as the true church by denoting them as "tribulation saints." Some teach they are not part of the church.[346] But no New Testament writer makes this distinction. This is a clear signal that some pre-trib advocates prefer to confuse their followers with an unfounded alternative. John the Apostle who wrote the Book of Revelation had no doubt that the Antichrist would be facing the church. When he wrote his first epistle, he made this clear: "...as you have heard *the*

---

[341] Rev 7:3

[342] Eph 3:6

[343] Rev 22:3-4

[344] Dan 7:21; Rev 13:7

[345] Mt 24:33-35

[346] See *Scofield Reference Bible.* p. 1337 ; Walvoord, John F. *The Rapture Question.* p. 35-36, 38

antichrist is coming, even now many antichrists have come."[347] John penned this many years after Paul's identical warning[348] and affirmed for us the idea that his readers knew they would face the man of sin. This shows that the span of roughly forty years from Paul to John's words did not alter the expectation for the church to face the Antichrist. John Law, writing in his masterful commentary on First John, noted that this information was well circulated through the churches, and John's "readers were well acquainted with, and probably concurred in, the belief as commonly held."[349] Surely, John understood that believers would remain on the earth until the Lord appears in glory at the end. His words in the Book of Revelation are directed to the church so Christians will know what to expect. In examining this portion of the epistle, John Law noted: "In the New Testament the time immediately preceding the Second Advent is regarded as one of much and various tribulation, both *for the Church* and for the world."[350] The church is part of the Book of Revelation. The Church is present within the context of John's warnings and his encouragement. At the conclusion of his apocalyptic description, the Lord comes in glory. We will see this. We will see Him and be with Him forever.

A final thought might help resolve this issue. John addresses the recipients of this book in the very beginning. He is addressing saints, believers, and those in the church. Since those hearing this know it is for them, there is no need to mention them by name in every chapter or paragraph. We do not repeat a person's name again and again when we speak to someone or write to them. Neither does John. He was commissioned from on high to write down the critical events he was shown and to lay out in words events coming in the future. It should be simple logic that the apostle had no need to add names where the Lord did not. John included a very specific warning about adding or taking away from this book. The Lord did not add or take away. Neither did John. We must not either, unless we wish to lose our eternal inheritance.[351]

---

[347] 1 Jn 2:18 [emphasis added].
[348] 2 Thess 2:3-4
[349] Law, John. *The Tests of Life. A Study in the First Epistle of St. John.* Edinburgh: T & T Clark, 1914. p. 319
[350] Law, John. *Ibid.* p. 318 [emphasis added].
[351] Rev 22:18-19

Language means things. When overlooked or reinterpreted, some little words can alter the plain meaning of scripture. We must read carefully and think in the vein the author intended. Our understanding must conform to the Faith and the Truth.

HISTORY

Where does history begin regarding the return of Christ? While there are many threads which lead us back to Old Testament references, it is the more contemporary popular view based on portions of the New Testament that causes so much controversy. It will be beneficial to look into a good deal of this, but also to narrow our examination to enough information sufficient to support a late rather than early view of the origin of a pre-trib rapture teaching. In much of the evangelical church today, the pre-trib rapture has been assumed to be the orthodox, long-standing position held by the Apostles. This idea is without justification and is not upheld by scripture or by the records of those who have seriously looked into the Second Coming through the years. Absent is a sound, church-held, scripturally-based pre-trib teaching from the first century on to the nineteenth century when Dispensationalism[1] became popularized through the Plymouth Brethren and others. We will review some of this as it relates to the unwarranted conclusions of Bible expositors and teachers who espouse the pre-trib theory. Some of them are known to be experts in the field of Bible prophecy. They are dedicated men and are fine Christians, yet have veered off in their interpretation of certain particulars with eschatology. A sincere Bible student today will be helped by considering this, since unjustifiable theories abound, and only the clear position established by scripture matters.

The Second Coming[2] is the name given to establish doctrinally the return of Jesus Christ when He comes to judge the earth. He proclaimed this Himself in several areas of His teaching as He ministered among us during His First Advent. He said He would go away[3] return to earth[4] and judge those who are living at the time, plus the deceased.[5] In essence, Jesus proclaimed this future

---

[1] See Glossary
[2] Also known as the Second Advent. See Glossary
[3] Jn 14:2-3; 16:5-7; also, Acts 1:11
[4] Mt 24:27-31; 16:27
[5] Jn 5:24-25, 28-29

event, and once the Holy Spirit came upon the disciples and Apostles at Pentecost, the message of the Lord Jesus' return was set into the fabric of church teaching. This continued unchanged throughout the Apostles' ministries and was carried forward by others who followed them. In recent years, much distortion has become evident.

Immediately after the ascension of Jesus, two men in white were emphatic about Jesus' return which would be visible--seen in the same way the disciples saw Him leave.[6] This event was another astounding part of the mystery of the incarnation of God's Son. The disciples were not prepared for His death, or His resurrection, and now He is about to depart with a promise to return. This is overwhelming in context, since these men were not just eyewitnesses to an unusual occurrence but were participants in scripture being fulfilled and history unfolding before their eyes. This entire three year adventure was filled with amazement and its share of disappointment. These men had earlier thought that Jesus the Messiah would remain and establish His kingdom. This was not part of His plan at that time. After Pentecost, they recognized more fully what Jesus explained about this in the upper room the night before His arrest.[7] It was the Holy Spirit who engaged them and aided them to remember what the Lord had said.[8] This would include all His teaching--even about His return in glory.

As Jesus' ministry unfolded, people were affected by His teaching and miracles. His public display of power and authority gave credence to Him being the long promised Holy One of God, Israel's redeemer. As a result, many thought He would begin to rule as King as the earlier prophets stated. This was not to be. This in itself shows us the difficulty in grasping the clear meaning of certain passages of scripture that speak of future events. Prior to the incarnation, those who were standing by faith had great hopes that Jesus would fulfill all things in their day without a death[9] and with the glory of God to return to Jerusalem, the city of God. Simeon expressed this when Mary and Joseph brought Jesus to the temple to be consecrated. Simeon saw personally

---

[6] Acts 1:11
[7] See John 13 through 17; note Jn 14:3 and Jn 16:7
[8] Jn 14:26
[9] Mt 16:21-23. Note Peter's objection to Jesus' death.

189

God's "salvation" and His "light for revelation to the Gentiles and for glory to your people Israel."[10] Anna the prophetess was there and affirmed for Jesus' parents that this child was the one whom "all who were looking forward to the redemption of Jerusalem" had anticipated.[11] This is a clear testimony as to who Jesus was, yet one that did not include the thought that this was just His first coming. The Old Testament was their hope, and it expressed the Messiah's advent but without a distinct separation between Jesus coming in the flesh and later His return in glory at the end of the age. It was Jesus who explained this. We find the core of it in the Olivet Discourse. Jesus came first as the Redeemer. Then, in the future at the end of the age, He will come once more, but as King. At the time Jesus ministered, there was a noticeable misunderstanding among the general population with regard to the truth about this in the scripture. The people were poorly instructed by teachers of the Law who rejected Jesus and overall misinterpreted the scriptures.[12] This is one reason that Jesus spent three years as the teacher of the disciples. They must know without question the entire plan of God for redemption.

After the Holy Spirit descended at Pentecost, the ministry of the disciples and Apostles changed to include things yet to come.[13] This is evident in Acts two with Peter's message to the men of Israel. But a few weeks prior, when Jesus entered Jerusalem and fulfilled the words of Zechariah, the people responded in accord with the prophet's call to rejoice for the king entering Jerusalem.[14] They openly shouted their recognition of Him and their hope that His kingdom would be established at that time when He made His final entry into the city. They shouted: "Hosanna" and continued to shout: "Blessed is he who comes in the name of the Lord. Blessed is the King of Israel."[15] Mark recorded in his gospel this crowd with even more direct acclamation: "Blessed is the coming kingdom of our father David."[16] The texts in the gospel record show us the

---

[10] Lk 2:25-32
[11] Lk 2:36-38
[12] Mt 22:29; Jn 5:39-40
[13] Jn 16:13
[14] Zech 9:9
[15] Jn 12:12-14
[16] Mk 11:10

hope of the people and their understanding of its potential for fulfillment as they observed Jesus. Their comprehension led them to believe the kingdom was being established then in its fullness. When Jesus was put to death, many who had hoped He was the predicted one were greatly disappointed. This is expressed in Luke's gospel, where Cleopas encountered the risen Jesus. Cleopas and his companion, both disciples, conversed with Jesus and expressed this hope: "...but we had hoped that he was the one to redeem Israel."[17] This is the broad hope of the kingdom which did not come to fruition at that time. It would be in the distant future.

This is the basis for the theology of their day. Scripture stated that the Lord would come and dwell with His people. This was to be a personal presence with Him ruling in the city of David. It was a long held promise for Israel which they anticipated. The idea of God's presence where He would be living among them takes us back to Moses and the children of Israel after they had left Egypt. Moses was given the law, and the Lord was dealing directly with him as the provisions were being made for Israel to be governed by the law from on high. This included regulations for offerings and worship. At that time, the Lord indicated He would live with them at the tabernacle. The Lord said, "Then have them make a sanctuary for me, and I will dwell among them."[18] This initiated the promise, some of which was fulfilled as the Israelites proceeded to distance themselves from Egypt and headed towards Canaan. At that time they were led by a pillar of cloud and a pillar of fire.[19] But this presence was not intended to be a lasting arrangement. Later in their history, after a permanent temple was erected by Solomon in Jerusalem, "the ark of the Lord's covenant" was brought to the inner sanctuary. At that time, the glory of the Lord came. When the priests came out from the sanctuary, the cloud filled the temple, and "the glory of the Lord filled his temple."[20] Again at Solomon's dedication, this scene repeated: "the glory of the Lord filled the temple."[21] At the time Jesus was ministering, the people knew the shekinah glory was not

---

[17] Lk 24:21
[18] Ex 25:8
[19] Ex 13:21-22
[20] 1 Kings 8:1-11; 2 Chron 5:13-14
[21] 2 Chron 7:1-3

191

present in the temple. They knew the glory had departed.[22] Their hope was not lost nor was it cancelled.[23] It was just postponed. The people received prophetic encouragement along the way through the voices of the Godly men who called Israel to account. They were bold in charging the people, the rulers, and the priests with their shortcomings and their evil practices. Yet, hope was not omitted with regard to the future expectation of the Lord living among His people. Zechariah reminded them as he delivered the Lord's own words: "Shout and be glad, O Daughter of Zion. For I am coming, and I will live among you."[24] Zechariah confirmed this: "The Lord Almighty will inherit Judah as his portion in the holy land and will again choose Jerusalem."[25] The scripture is clear with this future promise from the Lord: "I will live among you...."[26]

In the first century, Paul the Apostle reminded the church in Corinth of this promise in a similar manner: "As God has said: 'I will live with them and walk among them, and I will be their God, and they will be my people.'"[27] Since Paul's words were written after the Lord Jesus had come the first time and ascended back to heaven, this Apostle was confirming for us that all of the previous promises are still in force and are yet future. The Lord will come and will dwell with men. This is the *parousia*[28] mentioned in the gospels and the epistles.[29] This Greek term indicates a physical presence which corresponds exactly to the Old Testament predictions. The church looks at this as the Second Coming. It is the long held "primary view of church history."[30] Hence, the New Testament writings as a whole affirm Jesus' return in glory. Because

---

[22] Ezek 9:3. A fuller description of this departure is found in Ezekiel 10:1-22.

[23] Note Paul in Rm 11:1ff

[24] Zech 2:10

[25] Zech 2:12. Also note: Ezek 37:27; Lev 26:12

[26] Zech 2:11

[27] 2 Cor 6:16

[28] Meaning "presence," or "being beside," *i.e.*, "standing beside." Earle, Ralph. *Word Meanings in the New Testament.* Peabody, MA: Hendirckson Pub., 2002. p. 338

[29] Robinson, Wm. Childs. *Christ--the Hope of Glory. Christological Eschatology.* Grand Rapids, MI: Wm. B. Eerdmans Pub. Co., 1945. p. 205

[30] Hocking, David. *The Case for Pre-Tribulationalism. The Rapture of the Church.* Tustin, CA: HFT Pub., 2005. p. 2

believers through the ages waited with great anticipation for the Lord's return, at times of distress, especially with wars, famines, and pestilence occurring, numbers of erroneous predictions were made. The accumulation of these miscalculations is reflected in the history of eschatology for two thousand years. This in itself is reason to carefully weigh history, so believers will not repeat past mistakes.

In consideration of the Apostles passing off the scene, we must note where the teaching traveled along its historical timeline. There were those who learned the orthodox doctrines of the faith from the Twelve and other of the first disciples. Timothy and Titus are notable in this respect. Titus was told by Paul: "You must teach what is in accord with sound doctrine."[31] This would include all he learned from Paul and the others.[32] Paul wrote to Titus to remind him of this responsibility to live righteously awaiting the Lord's return at the end of "this present age." Paul broadened this to include other believers, succinctly including them "while we wait for the blessed hope--the appearing of our great God and Savior, Jesus Christ."[33] As Paul described this, it is one event. Timothy, also, was the benefactor of Paul's instruction and knew well his stand on the return of Christ. He received a direct charge from Paul in this regard: "In the presence of God and of Christ Jesus, who will judge the living and the dead, and in view of his appearing and his kingdom, I give you this charge: Preach the Word."[34] Paul is careful to connect the dynamic of the Second Coming with its various components. He reminds Timothy that the Lord's appearing and His kingdom will be a simultaneous event and that this will be at the time He judges the living and the dead. Paul places all four of these major parts of the return of Christ together.[35] The whole is equal to the sum of its parts. Hence, it is natural for Paul to express the Second Coming this way to Timothy, since Timothy had heard Paul teach this before.[36] To these leaders, it

---

[31] Titus 2:1

[32] Acts 2:42; 1 Cor 15:11

[33] Titus 2:13

[34] 2 Tim 4:1-2

[35] Four parts: (1) His appearing; (2) His kingdom; (3) judge the living (immortality); (4) judge the dead (retribution). Those who are God's own (deceased or living) will receive eternal life; the "dead" will be swept away to await their fate.

was a single event. These men were to stand and preach to the very end when Christ would appear once at the end of the present age.[37] They also well knew that the Lord's return in glory would be "preceded by the rebellion" and the appearance of the Antichrist.[38] This formula of unity with its four components of the Second Advent was carried forward into the thoughts and writings of the early church fathers and on into later creeds. Timothy and Titus represent the next generation of teachers in the body of Christ who would influence others who would follow in their footsteps. Remember, also, John the Apostle continued to live and teach until the last decade of the first century.

Following the Apostles, we find notable teachers and preachers during the next three hundred years of the church. These are the Church Fathers. The first group is known as The Apostolic Fathers who were ministering up to the second century. Associated with them were The Second Century Apologists. They were followed by The Third Century Church Fathers. The Greek and Latin Fathers came later.[39] Well-known names appear throughout these centuries: Clement, Ignatius, Hermas, Papias, Polycarp, Justin Martyr, Irenaeus, Tertullian, Origen, Cyprian, and others. Some of them wrote objectively with clarity. Others were allegorical or mystical. They must be read with care, since they wrote with the knowledge they possessed at the time. We must keep in mind, too, that they were human and not infallible. In an address at Calvary Baptist Church in the City of New York, William F. Kerr noted: "We must be careful not to read present-day viewpoints and interpretations into the writings of the Church Fathers. Rather, we must let them speak for themselves as clearly as possible in the light of their own theological background and environment."[40] Dr. Kerr held to the pre-trib view, yet was

---

[36] 2 Tim 1:13

[37] Heb 6:11-12

[38] Keener, Craig S. *The IVP Background Commentary: New Testament.* Downers Grove, IL: InterVarsity Press, 1999. p. 602; Lightfoot, J. B. *Biblical Essays.* p. 260; 2 Thess 2:3-4

[39] Jackson, George Anson. *The Apostolic Fathers and the Apologists of the Second Century/The Fathers of the Third Century. [Early Christian Literature Primers].* 2 Volumes. New York, NY: D. Appleton & Co., 1879, 1881.

[40] Culbertson, William, and Herman B. Centz, eds. *Understanding the Times. PropheticMessages Delivered at the 2nd International Congress on Prophecy, New*

succinct with his admonition here. Among other Bible teachers in the dispensational camp, we find a number who reject an honest approach with their conclusions about what these Church Fathers said.[41] Some of today's prophecy experts have twisted their words and have deliberately omitted key statements. We will deal with this problem in the course of our look into the historical record of the Second Coming's teaching. It is highly recommended for further study to read the Church Fathers themselves.[42] As Bible expositor Wilbur Smith noted, the Fathers through "the second century gave a great deal of attention to eschatology and Biblical prophecy," while later divines maintained "a spirit of indifference" regarding this area of study.[43] The words of these early writers must not be ignored.

One of the earliest non-canonical writings is the *Didache*. This work was the vital source of church doctrine and orthodoxy for the fledgling churches. It was written sometime during the second century "immediately after the NT period,"[44] though some believers in the third century thought the Apostles themselves may have contributed a portion.[45] By the end of the first century, the forces of Gnosticism were challenging orthodox Christianity. Hence the

---

York City. "The Lord's Return in Patristic Literature," William F. Kerr. Grand Rapids, MI: Zondervan Pub., 1956. p. 85

[41] William Kelly, prolific Plymouth Brethren writer and editor of J. N. Darby's works, promoted overt disdain for the Church Fathers. This is evident in an article, "The So-called Apostolical Father on the Lord's Second Coming," where in mocking tones he denoted their writing to be "relics" and "trumpery." In particular, he considered the *Didache* "spurious." Kelly's conclusion was due to the fact that these writings upended his pre-trib view. Published in: Kelly, W. *The Heavenly Hope*. London: T. Weston, 1910. p. 75ff

[42] Roberts, Alexander, & James Donaldson. *The Ante-Nicene Fathers*. 1884. rpt. Grand Rapids, MI: Wm. B. Eerdmans, 1977; Lightfoot, J. B. & J. R. Harmer. *The Apostolic Fathers*. 1891. rpt. Grand Rapids, MI: Baker Book House, 1987; Wake, William. *The Genuine Epistles of the Apostolic Fathers....* Manchester: W. Shelmerdine & Co., 1799.

[43] Smith, Wilbur M. *Egypt in Biblical Prophecy*. Boston, MA: W. A. Wilde Co., 1957. p. 239-240

[44] Brown, Colin. *The New International Dictionary of New Testament Theology. Vol. I.* Grand Rapids, MI: Zondervan Pub., 1993. p. 51, 55

[45] Fisher, George Park. *History of Christian Doctrine. [Int'l. Theological Library]*. New York, NY: Charles Scribner's Sons, 1896. p. 71

Didache was "the authoritative source of Christian knowledge" and the key for fundamental truths.[46] It also is entitled: *The Teaching of the Lord to the Gentiles Through the Twelve Apostles*.[47] This important work was written in Greek and located in a Constantinople library along with other manuscripts.[48] Its discovery was announced in 1875[49] and then published in English in 1884.[50] Its reputation was known early on, since it had been referenced by some of the Church Fathers. Because of the close proximity in time with this document and the New Testament itself, some theologians along the way thought it might belong in the New Testament due to the "content."[51] Others in the church before the close of the second century regarded this document "as Scripture."[52] As noted by James Orr, it was quoted as Scripture by Clement of Alexandria about 170 A.D.[53] The date of its composition "may be put between 80 and 120 AD."[54] Within this valuable work, there is material relating to liturgy, practice, and doctrine. Dr. Orr noted this document to be "important historically as a witness to the church's beliefs" during this period.[55] Within the eschatological content of the *Didache*, there are clear references to the Second Advent with signs preceding. In particular, there are vivid warnings of false prophets, persecution, and the rise of the Antichrist, "who is designated as the World-deceiver."[56] At no time is there any hint of an expectation of Jesus' return being a pre-trib event without any signs. The writer of this document, echoing

---

[46] Fisher. *History of Christian Doctrine*. p. 70
[47] There are abbreviated titles used for this same work.
[48] Douglas, J. D. *The New International Dictionary of the Christian Church*. Grand Rapids, MI: Zondervan Pub., 1983. p. 297
[49] Lightfoot, J. B., & J. R. Harmer. *The Apostolic Fathers*. p. 216
[50] Hitchcock, Roswell D., and Francis Brown. *Teaching of the Twelve Apostles*. New York, NY: Charles Scribner's Sons, 1884. [Includes the Greek and the English texts].
[51] Brown, Colin. *Ibid. Vol. 2*. p. 219-220
[52] Brown. *Ibid. Vol. 3*. p. 402
[53] Orr, James. *The International Standard Bible Encyclopedia. Volume III*. Grand Rapids, MI: Wm. B. Eerdmans, 1939. p. 1898
[54] Orr. *Ibid.*
[55] Orr. *Ibid.*
[56] *Ibid.* p. 1899

Jesus and the Apostles, restated the basic position of the faith once delivered that the Antichrist will be in view first. The following is Part 16:

> Be watchful for your life; let your lamps not be
> quenched and your loins not ungirded, but be ye ready;
> for ye know not the hour in which our Lord cometh.
> And ye shall gather yourselves together frequently,
> seeking what is fitting for your souls; for the whole
> time of your faith shall not profit you, if ye be not
> perfected at the last season. For in the last days the
> false prophets and corrupters shall be multiplied, and
> the sheep shall be turned into wolves, and love shall be
> turned into hate. For as lawlessness increaseth, they
> shall hate one another and shall persecute and betray.
> And then the world-deceiver shall appear as a son of
> God; and shall work signs and wonders, and the earth
> shall be delivered into his hands; and he shall do
> unholy things, which have never been since the world
> began. Then all created mankind shall come to the fire
> of testing, and many shall be offended and perish; but
> they that endure in their faith shall be saved by the
> Curse Himself. And then shall the signs of truth
> appear; first a sign of a rift in the heaven, then a sign
> of a voice of a trumpet, and thirdly a resurrection of
> the dead; yet not all, but as it was said: The Lord shall
> come and all of His saints with Him. Then shall the
> world see the Lord coming upon the clouds of heaven.[57]

Notice the clear distinction of the order of events. Believers will be present while the Antichrist is causing severe problems for those who belong to Christ. Warnings abound regarding false prophets, the increase of evil, false signs and wonders, persecution, betrayal, and that many shall perish. The words in this

---

[57] Lightfoot, J.B. *Ibid.* p. 235. Also in Roberts & Donaldson. *The Ante-Nicene Fathers.* Vol. 7. p. 377-383

document parallel exactly the words of Jesus in the Olivet Discourse and, later, the writers of the New Testament, especially Paul. The timeline is here, and the sequence is plain: the church is on the earth when the Antichrist is revealed, it suffers, then, at the end, Christ appears with all His saints. In the Lightfoot English translation, all of the direct scripture references are in italics. There are many. We have omitted them here for the sake of easy reading.[58]

This early church reference is not favored by pre-trib dispensational advocates as written. It is in direct contradiction to their theory. Consequently, it is either ignored or distorted. As an example, when Grant Jeffrey decided to employ the *Didache* as a reference, he transformed its intent by omitting the entire middle portion where the Antichrist and persecution are detailed. Here is his version:

> Watch for your life's sake. Let not your lamps be
> quenched, nor your loins unloosed; but be ye ready,
> for ye know not the hour in which our Lord
> cometh…And shall appear the signs of truth; first, the
> sign of an outspreading in heaven; then the sign of the
> trumpet; and the third, the resurrection of the dead; yet
> not all, but as it is said: The Lord shall come and all
> His saints with Him. Then shall the world see the
> Lord's coming upon the clouds of heaven."[59]

It is easy to see the missing section. Just look at the *ellipsis* after the second sentence. This is not a case of faulty editing. It is a major case of deliberate distortion. It is one thing to omit unnecessary details. It is quite another to rearrange supporting facts and evidence to arrive at your pre-conceived idea. Jeffrey also took liberties with other portions of his prophetic writing which when exposed does nothing to help his credibility and demeans the work of

---

[58] Refer to the original in Lightfoot/Harmer. *The Apostolic Fathers.* p. 235. The patristic quotations of the New Testament were extensive. Within the writings of seven of the Fathers, more than 36,000 citations are identifiable. See Geisler, Norman L, and William E. Nix. *A General Introduction to the Bible.* Chicago, IL: Moody Press, 1986. p. 430-431

[59] Jeffrey, Grant R. *Heaven—The Mystery of Angels. Revised and Expanded Edition.* Toronto, ON: Frontier Research Pub., 1996. p. 53

others who attempt to honestly present Biblical truth. Jeffrey has fabricated a different document with a different message which leads someone to think the return of Christ occurs earlier than scripture states. So, in essence, he twisted scripture along with his re-manufactured "evidence." This is unscrupulous. Jeffrey continued this delusion in his next paragraph as he connected his edited *Didache* to a rapture and "an imminent resurrection of the believers."[60] It is evident that for him the end justifies the means. This is not scholarship.

The origin of the twisting of truth can be traced back to the Garden.[61] However, when ample truth has been proclaimed and recorded since that time, we lack any excuse for either repeating the error or initiating new ones. Regarding the corruption of the *Didache* above, we find others doing likewise. In his work on a systematic study of the rapture, we observe another case of blatant editing by Gerald Stanton. He is held in high regard by many pre-trib exponents, since he presented his claims with rhetoric crafted to exclude the facts. He included a short quotation in a chapter where he attempted to refute the post-tribulational position. Stanton quoted:

> Watch for your life's sake. Let not your lamps be
> quenched, not your loins unloosed; but be ye ready, for
> ye know not the hour in which our Lord cometh.[62]

You can see that the balance of Part 16 of the *Didache* was totally excluded. This would lead a reader to think that there was nothing else following this portion or nothing of further importance to consider regarding the return of the Lord Jesus. This is dishonest. This is the type of teaching model that causes confusion and misunderstanding in unnumbered people who might read Stanton's work for further knowledge of the Second Coming. Gerald Stanton was a professor at Talbot Seminary at Biola [Bible Institute of Los Angeles] for many years.[63] John Walvoord at Dallas Theological Seminary employed the

---

[60] *Ibid.*
[61] Gen 3:1
[62] Stanton, Gerald B. *Kept From The Hour. A Systematic Study of the Rapture in Bible Prophecy.* Grand Rapids, MI: Zondervan Pub., 1956. p. 221
[63] Now, BIOLA University in La Mirada, California.

identical abbreviated quote used by Stanton and boldly asserted this was "belief in the imminency of the Lord's return.[64] One year later, J. Dwight Pentecost, also at Dallas Theological Seminary, employed the same shortened format as he inexcusably attempted to support imminency.[65] Others since Stanton's time, and the days of Walvoord and Pentecost, have repeated this error. The recent recurrence of this by Grant Jeffrey supports the conclusion that the pre-trib theorists will not go to the primary source and correct their views, especially by admitting their errors and publishing the orthodox standard based on the actual words of the writer.[66] This example is from just one early church document. Distortion and omission with others is also common. When pre-trib teachers reference the Fathers, it is advisable to verify the claim with the original. This is the Berean attitude. It must be followed today.

Let us look at Clement who was ministering in Rome and may have been with Paul in Philippi.[67] He anticipated the return of Christ in the same manner as the Apostles. His letter to the Corinthians included important exhortation to the brothers there to continue to stand firm in the faith in spite of trials and persecution. This letter was composed shortly after the Domitian persecution, about 96 A.D. [68] He was careful to offer encouragement that in spite of the present hardships, the Lord Jesus would come once again. These believers were in the center of the Roman Empire's iron hand. Their lives were at risk. Hence, their real-time concern was that this may be the approach of the end. Naturally, they would need as much assurance as possible that the Lord would deliver them as promised. Clement reminded them with an illustration of timing: "the vine" must first shed its leaves, "then it buds, next it puts forth leaves, and then

---

[64] Walvoord, John F. *The Rapture Question.* Grand Rapids, MI: Zondervan Pub., 1972. p. 53-54

[65] Pentecost, J. Dwight. *Things To Come. A Study in Biblical Eschatology.* Grand Rapids, MI: Zondervan Pub., 1972. p. 169

[66] It is curious that Arno Gaebelein employed the *Didache* to reinforce his dispensational claims and quoted this section in full. He included the "world deceiver" to appear before Christ returns just as it is stated in the original. See: Gaebelein, Arno C. *Meat in Due Season.* New York, NY: Arno C. Gaebelein Inc., n.d. p. 45-46

[67] Phil 4:3. Also: Roberts & Donaldson. *The Ante-Nicene Fathers.* Vol. 1. p. 1

[68] Douglas, J. D. *Ibid.* p. 235

it flowers." He continued: "after that comes the sour grape, and then follows the ripened fruit."[69] He, then, related this to the need to be patient as "a tree comes to maturity." Next, he directed them to a scriptural truth as recorded by the prophet Malachi and the Apostle Paul. Since Clement was a respected teacher known to them, his words in his chapter twenty-three would have been quickly understood:

> Of a truth, soon and suddenly shall His will be
> accomplished, as the Scripture also bears witness,
> saying, "Speedily will He come, and will not tarry;"
> and, "The Lord shall suddenly come to His temple,
> even the Holy One, for whom you look."[70]

The thought Clement is passing on to these believers is the promised return and physical presence of the Lord (*parousia*) at the end of the age. Facing the reality of persecution directly, like the Thessalonians Paul wrote to, they would have expected the Lord Jesus to appear bringing relief for them and retribution for those who were causing their suffering.[71] There is absolutely no mention of the church being removed. There is no hint of a rapture event or some form of a removal from harm's way. As a matter of fact, Clement then continued his encouragement by reminding these saints of the resurrection. This, of course, is the promised event which occurs at the last day, just as Jesus affirmed.[72] Clement assured them "there shall be a future resurrection, of which He has rendered the Lord Jesus Christ the first-fruits by raising Him from the dead."[73] Notice that the supporting evidence for the comfort of these believers who are undergoing trials is not a pre-trib rapture but the hope in the resurrection at the end--not an early removal at all. Clement, obviously, would have written this portion of his letter very differently if his view was akin to the dispensational interpretation which evolved many centuries later. Clement is affirming that the

---

[69] Roberts & Donaldson. *Ibid.* p. 11
[70] *Ibid.* References to Habakkuk 2:3; Mal 3:1; Mal 4:1-3; Heb 10:37-39; 1 Thess 4:13-15
[71] 2 Thess 1:6-10
[72] Jn 6:44, 54; 11:24-25
[73] Roberts & Donaldson. *Ibid.* p.11

church will continue to be on earth until the very end when all the elect are gathered.[74]

The Epistle of Barnabas was written around 100 A.D. and also warns of the Antichrist. It is apparent from his words that believers were under the stress of persecution and were concerned about the return of the Lord. Barnabas wrote to encourage them in the same manner as Paul did with the believers at Thessalonica. He was focused like his readers on the "events at hand" and the "present time."[75] This is reminiscent of Paul's words to the Corinthians with respect to "the present crisis"[76] and his recognition of the trials, severe suffering, and persecution that faced the Thessalonians.[77] In chapter four of his epistle Barnabas wrote the following:

> The last offence is at hand, concerning which the
> scripture speaketh, as Enoch said. For to this end the
> Master hath cut the seasons and the days short, that
> His beloved might hasten and come to His inheritance.
> And the prophet also speaketh on this wise; Ten reigns
> shall reign upon the earth, and after them shall arise a
> little king, who shall bring low three of the kings under
> one. In like manner Daniel speaketh concerning the
> same; And I saw the fourth beast to be wicked and
> strong and more intractable than all the beasts of the
> earth, and how there arose from him ten horns, and
> from these a little horn an excrescence, and how that it
> abased under one three of the great horns.[78]

These words from Barnabas closely parallel those in the Olivet Discourse where Jesus spoke of the time at the end: the tribulation period. He informed the Apostles then with Him that this time would be like no other ever before or

---

74 Mt 24:30-31; 2 Thess 2:1
75 Roberts & Donaldson. *Ibid.* p. 138
76 1 Cor 7:26
77 1 Thess 1:6; 3:3, 7; 2 Thess 1:4
78 Lightfoot. *Ibid.* p. 271

again, and that time would be shortened "for the sake of the elect."[79] Jesus had just told them that believers alive at that time would see the Antichrist. He also reckoned this directly to the words of the prophet Daniel. This is exactly what Barnabas does in his epistle. In other words, Barnabas is in full agreement with Daniel,[80] Jesus, and Paul who all forecast the church being on the earth to see these things. Jesus said: "When you see all these things, you know it is near, right at the door."[81] Since Jesus outlined clearly the composite events prior to His arrival in glory, we find the same understanding in Barnabas' epistle. In his chapter six, he wrote: "Understand ye. Set your hope on Him who is about to be manifested to you in the flesh, even Jesus."[82] This obviously has nothing to do with a removal of the church prior to a seven year tribulation period. Barnabas knew well that Jesus would return in glory and be present (*parousia*) for all to see. He reminded believers then to set their minds and hearts on that-- not on anything else--otherwise this epistle would have been worded much differently. Like Clement and the author of the *Didache*, Barnabas expected to see Antichrist, then the Lord Jesus Christ.

The Shepherd of Hermas is another important work which was circulated and loved in the early church. It was written around 150 A.D. and was considered to be the "Pilgrim's Progress of the Early Church."[83] Its popularity continued through the third and fourth centuries.[84] In the first book which deals with visions, there is a section sometimes used by dispensationalists to support an early teaching of a pre-trib rapture. A vision may be a risky source for doctrinal support, especially if the conclusion contradicts scripture. Henry C. Thiessen insisted that chapter two of the Second Vision validated his view "the church would escape the Great Tribulation and that this is not a doctrine that was unknown, as it has been charged, until it was popularized by the Plymouth Brethren."[85] His conjecture is based on these words:

---

[79] Mt 24:22
[80] Dan 7:24, etc.
[81] Mt 24:33
[82] Lightfoot. *Ibid.* p. 274
[83] Jackson, George Anson. *The Apostolic Fathers.* p. 100
[84] Roberts & Donaldson. *Ibid.* Vol. 2. p. 6
[85] Thiessen, Henry C. *Lectures in Systematic Theology.* Grand Rapids, MI: Wm. B.

Now after I had passed by the wild beast, and had moved forward about thirty feet, lo! a virgin meets me, adorned as if she were proceeding from the bridal chamber, clothed entirely in white, and with white sandals, and veiled up to her forehead, and her head was covered by a hood. And she had white hair. I knew from my former visions that this was the Church, and I became more joyful. She saluted me, and said, 'Hail, O man!' And I returned her salutation, and said, 'Lady, hail!' And she answered and said to me, 'Has nothing crossed your path?' I say, 'I was met by a beast of such size that it could destroy peoples, but through the power of the Lord and His great mercy I escaped from it.' 'Well did you escape from it,' says she, 'because you cast your care on God, and opened your heart to the Lord, believing that you can be saved by no other than by His great and glorious name. On this account the Lord sent His angel who has rule over the beasts, and whose name is Thegri, and has shut his mouth, so that it cannot tear you. You have escaped from great tribulation on account of your faith, and because you did not doubt in the presence of such a beast. Go, therefore, and tell the elect of the Lord His mighty deeds, and say to them that this beast is a type of the great tribulation that is coming. If then ye prepare yourselves, and repent with all your heart, and turn to the Lord, it will be possible for you to escape it, if our heart be pure and spotless, and ye spend the rest of the days of your life serving the Lord blamelessly. Cast your cares upon the Lord, and He will direct them. Trust the Lord, ye who doubt, for He is all-powerful, and can turn His anger away from you, and send scourges on the doubters. Woe to those who hear

Eerdmans, 1974. p. 476

these words, and despise them: better were it for them
not to have been born.[86]

At first glance, someone might think Thiessen was correct. However, the word "escape" does not mean rapture. This work was written in Greek, and another word would have been in place to infer a removal from the earth as dispensationalists claim. Within this portion of the vision is the indication that the Church ("a virgin") will face the beast. Escape is possible for those blameless--by the beast's mouth being shut by an angel sent from above--not by being taken up. Once again, a pre-trib rapture is not indicated--just a form of Godly protection. There is notably a resonance here akin to the Lord's own admonition to the seven churches in Asia for each believer to stand firm and "overcome" what is to come.[87] Also, in the next portion, chapter three, we find this:

> For as gold is tested by fire, and thus becomes useful,
> so are you tested who dwell in it. Those, therefore,
> who continue stedfast, and are put through the fire,
> will be made purified by means of it. For as gold casts
> away its dross, so also will ye cast away all sadness
> and straitness, and will be made pure so as to fit into
> the building of the tower. But the white part[88] is the
> age that is to come, in which the elect of God will
> dwell, since those elected by God to eternal life
> will be spotless and pure. Wherefore cease not
> speaking these things into the ears of the saints. This
> then is the type of the great tribulation that is to come.[89]

This portion indicates that the elect will be purified by the "great tribulation that is to come." The words clearly specify the elect's presence and for their

---

[86] Roberts & Donaldson. *Ibid.* Vol. 2. p. 18
[87] Rev 2:7; 2:11; 2:17; 2:26; 3:5; 3:12; 3:21
[88] The Shepherd has indicated that the "black" is the world in which we now dwell [chapter three].
[89] Roberts & Donaldson. *Ibid.* p. 18

need to be "spotless and pure." There is no hint whatsoever that the elect are leaving the earth prior to this. The Shepherd is recounting his fourth vision which deals directly with "a representation of the tribulation that is to come."[90] In addition, in the second vision, in chapter one, it states:

> You will tell, therefore, those who preside over the
> church, to direct their ways in righteousness, that they
> may receive in full the promises with great glory.
> Stand stedfast, therefore, ye who work righteousness,
> and doubt not, that your passage may be with the holy
> angels. Happy ye who endure the great tribulation that
> is coming on, and happy they who shall not deny their
> own life.[91]

This is obviously encouragement to stand to the end through the tribulation. The mention of "passage" with the angels is directly connected to the return of Christ when He, the Son of Man, sends forth His angels to gather.[92] It is clear that the Shepherd is not presenting an imminent event which would remove the Body of Christ prior to the final seven years and escape the tribulation. He directs his readers to the reality of facing evil and being purified as they wait for the appearing and presence (*parousia*) of the Lord. Consequently, Dr. Thiessen's claim is not valid. Those who have repeated his error are adding to the confusion regarding the Second Coming of Christ. This is unwarranted and dangerous. Gerald Stanton whom we have noted above also offered a corrupted interpretation regarding the Shepherd. He forced his pre-trib conclusion narrowly by concluding the Greek word for escape (*ekphugo*) meant "complete exemption" from God's judgment--not "patient endurance in tribulation."[93] Absent from Dr. Stanton's reference is the extended quotation (as above) which would expose his fallacy. Since he openly promoted this error in his book published in 1956, it is likely that Dr. Thiessen merely modeled his conclusion on the faulty presentation by Dr. Stanton. This is the danger of

---

[90] *Ibid.* p. 17
[91] *Ibid.* p. 11
[92] Mt 13:49-50; 24:31; 25:31; 1 Thess 3:13
[93] Stanton. *Ibid.* p. 221

forcing a theory further along theological paths when the supporting evidence is altered or omitted. Those who teach or preach using these references as "proof" only compound the problem. Many current pre-trib authorities do just this and carefully omit the complete quotations from the Fathers. This is dangerous, indeed.

Another of the Fathers who held the clear, simple understanding of Christ's return is Polycarp. He lived from the latter part of the first century and into the second with his *Epistle to the Philippians* being written around 135 A.D. He is well known for the circumstances of his martyrdom[94] and was noted for the "conversations he had held with John and with others who had seen the Lord."[95] His pupil was Irenaeus who later wrote *Against Heresies*. In writing the Philippians, Polycarp noted the glorious benefit they had in days past from Paul who came among them and "taught face to face." [96] We have evidence of what Paul taught embodied in his epistle as he called the Philippians to stand firm "until the day of Christ Jesus." He wanted them "blameless" on "the day of Christ."[97] In Paul's experience, he was thoroughly acquainted with Roman hostility. The Philippians faced it, also, and dealt with "suffering" and the "same struggle" Paul himself faced, as did the other churches. Paul encouraged them to maintain the same attitude "of Jesus Christ," being obedient even "to death."[98] This admonition was in light of Paul's words of encouragement regarding the Second Coming when the Lord returns from heaven, as "we eagerly await a Savior from there."[99] Paul framed this with the resurrection[100] at the time the Lord comes and brings "everything under his control" and "will transform our lowly bodies so they will be like his glorious body."[101] In this light, nothing Polycarp wrote could be in contradiction with Paul's letters or the balance of the New Testament. Hence, Polycarp addressed the same

---

[94] Roberts & Donaldson. *Ibid*. Vol. 1, p. 37-44
[95] *Ibid*. p. 31
[96] Lightfoot. *Ibid*. p. 178
[97] Phil 1:6, 10; 2:27-28
[98] Phil 2:5, 8
[99] Phil 3:20
[100] 1 Cor 15:35-57; Rev 20:5
[101] Phil 3:21

Philippian church warning them: "For every one who shall not confess that Jesus Christ is come in the flesh, is antichrist."[102] This is the same warning the Apostle John issued who warned in his letter that "the antichrist is coming."[103] This simple reference by Polycarp, a martyr, lends itself to a firm call for believers to stand in the face of suffering, persecution, and death until the Lord appears in glory.[104] He reminded them that the Lord "comes as the Judge of the living and the dead."[105] He continued to encourage the Philippians to be like Christ: to "become imitators of His endurance" and to "glorify Him" if we suffer.[106] He went on to beseech the Philippians to pray for those who persecuted and hated them who were "enemies of the cross."[107] He encouraged them to stand firm in the face of increasing evil without a hint of relief except for the Lord's return in glory. These are not the words of someone expecting an imminent secret rapture. We see the testimony of a man willing to die for his Master-- and he did--as a martyr!

Papias was an associate of Polycarp, also the beneficiary of face-to-face contact with those who had "seen the Lord." He was bishop in Hierapolis, Phrygia, and was a "hearer of the Apostle John."[108] Like a number of the other Fathers, he is mentioned by Eusebius. In Papias' writings, as noted by Eusebius, we find the affirmation of his orthodox view on the Second Coming and the age to come: "...he says there will be a millennium after the resurrection from the dead, when the personal reign of Christ will be established on this earth."[109] This reference is obviously clearly stated and orthodox. Again, we have the testimony of a man who was a beneficiary of the Apostles [70-155 A.D.].[110] Papias affirmed he is sound in his eschatology, a true pre-millennialist.

---

102 Lightfoot. *Ibid.* p. 179
103 1 John 2:18; 4:3
104 Mt 24:30-31
105 Roberts & Donaldson. *Ibid.* Vol. 1, p. 33; Acts 17:31; Mt 24:30-31
106 Lightfoot. *Ibid.* p. 180
107 Lightfoot. *Ibid.* p. 181
108 Roberts & Donaldson. *Ibid.* Vol. 1, p. 151
109 Roberts & Donaldson. *Ibid.* Vol. 1, p. 154.
110 Roberts & Donaldson, *Ibid.* Vol. 1, p. 151

Justin Martyr was a contemporary of Papias and Polycarp. He was a Gentile from Samaria and his Apologies are some of the earliest extant in the church.[111] His exposition was a sound defense of Jesus as the Messiah, the one prophesied to come as written in the Old Testament. Embedded in his writing there is much color and insight into the interaction between Christians and pagans. In his *Dialogue with Trypho the Jew*, Justin affirmed the orthodox position on the Second Coming and what follows. He wrote: "But I and others, who are right-minded Christians on all points, are assured that there will be a resurrection of the dead, and a thousand years in Jerusalem, which will then be built, adorned, and enlarged, [as] the prophets Ezekiel and Isaiah and others declare."[112] Justin continued to reason with Trypho employing Micah 4:1-5ff reflecting on the time the Lord will be present on earth in His temple. He insisted that all this will happen and continued: "O unreasoning men! Understanding not what has been proved by all these passages, that the two advents of Christ have been announced: the one, in which He is set forth as suffering, inglorious, dishonoured, and crucified; but the other, in which He shall come from heaven with glory, when the man of apostasy, who speaks strange things against the Most High, shall venture to do unlawful deeds on the earth, against the Christians, who having learned the true worship of God from the law, and the word which went forth from Jerusalem by means of the Apostles of Jesus, have fled for safety to the God of Jacob and God of Israel...."[113] Note that Justin incorporated a number of Old Testament references within his broad statement, including the picture in Daniel of the Antichrist who speaks against the Most High and oppresses the saints.[114] This occurs after the man of sin is revealed at the mid-point of the final seven years.[115] This is the time of great persecution for the church which is still on the earth, just as Justin described it to Trypho, saying: this will come "against the Christians." These are not the thoughts of a confused Bible teacher. He was well trained in the Scriptures proven in his extensive writing. He described the two advents with the second preceded by

---

[111] Roberts & Donaldson. *Ibid.* Vol. 1, p. 160
[112] Roberts & Donaldson. *Ibid.* Vol. 1, p. 239
[113] Roberts & Donaldson. *Ibid.* Vol. 1, p. 241-242
[114] Dan 7:25
[115] Mt 24:15; 2 Thess 2:3-4

the revelation of the man of sin. His language clearly denotes the church present at the time the Antichrist begins to exact extreme measures of cruelty, and there is no hint of a previous removal of believers through a pre-trib event. Justin, also, perished as a martyr, beheaded in Rome.

Irenaeus was a student of Polycarp. He lived from 120 to 210 A. D. and ministered at the time the church had spread through the Western outposts of Rome. Heretics were flourishing, and the Gnostics were causing much trouble for the church.[116] Irenaeus recalled the warnings of Jesus and the Apostles who spoke of the time when men would embrace error and infiltrate the church. He was militant in his defense of the faith. He wrote *Against Heresies* in order to refute the gross mishandling of the truth and to render a death-blow to Gnosticism. In this extensive treatise, he covered many areas of theology in depth. Regarding John's Apocalypse and Daniel's prophetic writings, he remarked on "the ten kings who shall arise" who will "give their strength and power to the beast. They shall make war with the Lamb, and the Lamb shall overcome them."[117] Irenaeus also noted in context that these ten kings "shall give their kingdom to the beast, and put the Church to flight."[118] This is not an endorsement of a notion of early removal. Irenaeus was anticipating the Church's presence and persecution when the Antichrist appeared. He reiterated this by incorporating a portion of Revelation where John saw the time: "If any shall lead into captivity, he shall go into captivity. If anyone shall slay with the sword, he must be slain with the sword. Here is the endurance and the faith of the saints."[119] Irenaeus noted the mark of the beast and amplified the danger to the Church continuously. In his explanation of the number and name of the beast, he was clear in his reference to John writing just "the number of the name now, that when this man comes we may avoid him, being aware of who he is."[120] There was no hesitation in the mind of Irenaeus as he confirmed his sound, orthodox position that the church will see the Antichrist first, then Christ when He comes in glory.

---

[116] Roberts & Donaldson. *Ibid.* Vol. 1, p. 309-310
[117] Roberts & Donaldson. *Ibid.* Vol. 1, p. 554
[118] Roberts & Donaldson. *Ibid.* Vol. 1, p. 555; *cf.,* Rev 17:12ff
[119] Roberts & Donaldson. *Ibid.* Vol. 1, p. 557
[120] Roberts & Donaldson. *Ibid.* Vol. 1, p. 560

Hippolytus who labored later [170-236 A. D.] was direct in his position that the church would face the tribulation and see the Antichrist. He wrote: "Now, concerning the tribulation of the persecution which is to fall upon the Church from the adversary, John also speaks...."[121] He continued with exposition from the Apocalypse and proceeded to note the length of the church's persecution to be "...one thousand two hundred and threescore days (half of the week) during which the tyrant is to reign and persecute the Church."[122] He went on to note this to conform to Paul's warning in Thessalonians that the "man of sin be revealed, the son of perdition, who opposeth and exalteth himself above all that is God, or that is worshipped: so that he sitteth in the temple of God, showing himself that he is God."[123] These words are not those of a present-day dispensational teacher promoting a pre-trib rapture. Hippolytus writes truth!

Tertullian, in writing Marcion (*The Five Books Against Marcion*), presented a vigorous defense of the First Advent of Jesus. He, also, commented on the Second Advent in the process of combating the false notion of Marcion that the resurrection would be spiritual in nature and not physical. In writing *The Resurrection of the Flesh*, Tertullian placed the resurrection at the time of Christ's return in the same manner as the Apostle Paul noted it to the church in Thessalonica. In other words, he placed the Second Advent at the time the Lord comes in glory and as a singular event in concert with the first resurrection. He wrote: "But we do confess that a kingdom is promised upon the earth, although before heaven, only in another state of existence, inasmuch as it will be after the resurrection for a thousand years in the divinely-built city of Jerusalem, 'let down from heaven,' which the Apostle Paul calls 'our mother from above'...."[124] He clarified this further in *The Resurrection of the Flesh* by quoting extensively from Paul's letters to the Thessalonians and noting that the rapture (1 Thess 4:16-17) will not precede the unveiling of the Antichrist. He made the assumption that the Roman state would "fall away," then the man of sin would appear once the ten kings assumed power and gave allegiance to the world ruler. He noted that these ten kings would "introduce Antichrist" whom the

[121] Roberts & Donaldson. *Ibid.* Vol. 5, p. 217
[122] Roberts & Donaldson. *Ibid.*
[123] Roberts & Donaldson. *Ibid.* Vol. 5, p. 218; 2 Thess 2:3-4
[124] Roberts & Donaldson. *Ibid.* Vol. 3, p. 342

Lord Jesus will "consume with the spirit of His mouth, and destroy with the brightness of His coming...."[125] Tertullian had no illusions about the church facing this time of great tribulation, and he noted it to be a privilege to face the "oppression of the Antichrist" and be found alive at the coming of the Lord, being "found in the flesh." Those who go through this, he said, will experience "sudden change, to become qualified to join the rising saints...."[126] In his writing *Scorpiace*, he warned openly of the martyrdom of believers once Antichrist appeared, that they would share in the blessings of the martyrs who preceded them. He indicated that they, too, would "fully share in their glory," and this would be their "triumph over Antichrist."[127] It must be understood that his comments were made in the context of refuting heresy and misconception which the church faced at that time. His plain statements regarding the resurrection of the saints as being physical were paramount in setting aside the false notions of Marcion and others. However, Tertullian's statements are natural in context and support emphatically the orthodox pre-millennial view and lend no credence to the theory that the church will not face the Antichrist. He agrees with Paul and the Lord Jesus that we will see all of this.[128]

Cyprian who came on the scene later [200-258 A.D.] held to the same position as those who preceded him. He echoed the emphasis of Irenaeus and, like the other Fathers, employed a wealth of scripture references as he presented his case. In one of his epistles, he openly affirmed the coming appearance of the man of sin who would face off against the church. He wrote: "For even Antichrist, when he shall begin to come, shall not enter into the church because he threatens; neither shall we yield to his arms and violence, because he declares that he will destroy us if we resist."[129] He continued to encourage the believers he addressed to accept martyrdom as a reality. He wrote regarding the martyrs who preceded his day: "It is shown that none is free from the peril of

---

[125] Roberts & Donaldson. *Ibid*. Vol. 3, p. 562-563
[126] Roberts & Donaldson. *Ibid*. Vol. 3, p. 575
[127] Roberts & Donaldson. *Ibid*. Vol. 3, p. 645-646
[128] Mt 24:15, 33
[129] Roberts & Donaldson. *Ibid*. Vol. 5, p. 346. He could only write this in expectation of the Antichrist.

persecution, when even these accomplished martyrdoms."[130] He referenced past history as evidence and also looked ahead to the time the beast and false prophet would openly persecute the church. He called for these Christians not to be fearful of what was coming: "Nor let any one of you, beloved brethren, be so terrified by the fear of future persecution or the coming of the threatening Antichrist, as not to be found armed for all things by the evangelical exhortations and precepts, and by the heavenly warnings. Antichrist is coming, but above him comes Christ also."[131] We do not hear these warnings today. The pre-trib authorities of our day are telling the church no harm will come to them, since they will be raptured prior to the man of sin being revealed. This is heretical. It is a false assurance that Cyprian and these other Ante-Nicene Fathers stood against. Cyprian said very simply, first Antichrist, then Christ. Through this, he looked forward to the glory of Christ's return: "Oh, what and how great will that day be at its coming, beloved brethren, when the Lord shall begin to count up His people, and to recognize the deservings of each one by the inspection of His divine knowledge, to send the guilty to Gehenna, and to set on fire our persecutors with the perpetual burning of a penal fire, but to pay to us the reward of our faith and devotion!"[132] Once more, Cyprian is in full agreement with the Apostle Paul, the Apostle John, and the Lord Jesus pertaining to the Biblical doctrine of the Second Coming. There is no evidence that Cyprian entertained any of the contemporary illusions about the church being taken out of the world prior to the final seven year tribulation period. He expected the church to face the evil of the Antichrist. So should we.

Another of the writers who came on the scene later was Cyril of Jerusalem [315-386 A.D.]. He was appointed bishop there in 348 A.D. and wrote his extensive *Catechetical Lectures* around 350 A.D. As he commented on Daniel 7:9-14, he clearly presented the Second Coming to include the events just as the Lord described them in the Olivet Discourse. "Lecture XV" covers 32 sections and provides a lucid picture of the Lord's return. All of the sections should be read. However, Cyril asserted the fact that the Lord's coming would

---

[130] Roberts & Donaldson. *Ibid.* Vol. 5, p. 349
[131] Roberts & Donaldson. *Ibid.*
[132] Roberts & Donaldson. *Ibid.* Vol. 5, p. 350

be preceded by the Antichrist whom he referenced to be "the abomination of desolation" from Daniel and the very one Jesus said we would see. He wrote the Antichrist will have "beguiled the Jews, as though he were the expected Christ." He will then undertake a program "to outdo all unrighteous men who have gone before him" committing "crimes of inhumanity" against "all men, but especially against us Christians."[133] "After perpetrating such things for three years and six months only, he shall be destroyed by the glorious second advent from heaven of the only-begotten Son of God, our Lord and Saviour Jesus, the true Christ, who shall slay Antichrist with the breath of His mouth, and shall deliver him over to the fire of hell."[134] This agrees totally with Jesus' teaching and that of the Church Fathers who came before Cyril. There is only one second coming identified here. Cyril made this point as he began this lecture stating there are only two comings: the first, when He "was wrapped in swaddling clothes in the manger" and the second when He "comes attended by a host of Angels, receiving glory."[135] Cyril described this as the time of judgment with no reference to some prior relief for the church. This is evidence of the orthodox pre-millennial return of the Lord fully embraced through the fourth century. Nowhere is a secret removal in view. Cyril affirmed the church will be here when Antichrist comes on the scene and face him for three and one-half years. His lecture is in conformity to the post-trib position today. Read this lecture for yourself. Cyril states the case well.

Another important voice in the early years was John Chrysostom, Archbishop of Constantinople [349-407 A.D.]. He was a major influence in the Eastern Church and was known for his eloquent manner of preaching. He was referred to as "golden mouthed" (Chrysostom). His works are readily available today in printed form and online. He was prolific with comments throughout the New Testament, devoting a number of homilies to the Thessalonian epistles. In his comments on 1 Thessalonians 2:13-16, regarding the persecution and suffering

---

[133] This lecture can be located in the *Nicene and Post-Nicene Fathers, Second Series*, or as reflected above at: http://www.biblestudytools.com /history/early-church-fathers/post-nicene/vol-7-cyril-and-gregory/cyril/lecture-xv.html#P2010_556467 Note: Section 12

[134] *Ibid.*

[135] *Ibid.* "Lecture XV, Section 1."

they faced, he said those who were now persecuting them "are to be punished" referring to "*THE wrath*, showing again that it was due, and predetermined, and predicted."[136] His comments affirmed the attitude of Paul expressing comfort to these believers in the face of danger. Their current troubles would cease when the Lord comes and brings wrath upon the wicked. Paul made this point clear in his second epistle when he reminded the Thessalonians they would be present to see this.[137] In Chrysostom's comments on the well-known rapture passages, 1 Thessalonian 4:15-17, he denoted the "trumpet" to be "the last trumpet,"[138] that there might be others preceding it, but "at the last the Judge descends."[139] He proceeded to remind readers of the comfort intended by Paul, knowing the Lord was to come and bring relief and rescue at the time of judgment.[140] He illustrated this using the example of a king entering a city: "those in honour go out to meet him" while those who are condemned await the judge within."[141] He noted this to occur when there were "earthquakes in cities," and they would see "the heaven shriveled up."[142] This, obviously, sets the timing at the end of the tribulation period. In his comments, Chrysostom reminded readers that Antichrist will appear just as Paul wrote. In his remarks on 2 Thessalonians two, he pointed to Paul's emphasis of this fact that the man of lawlessness was to come, hence Paul offered them consolation that he would be judged, and they had "good things prepared for them." Chrysostom wrote that Paul was not "revealing the time itself, but shewing the sign of the time, namely, Antichrist."[143] These warnings in advance from Paul were for the benefit of the Thessalonian believers and for us as well. When dealing with 2 Thessalonians 2:1-2, Chrysostom made clear that the "Coming of Christ" and "our gathering together…will happen at the same time" just as Paul stated it.[144]

---

[136] Chrysostom, John. *The Homilies of S. John Chrysostom, Archbishop of Constantinople, on the Epistles of St. Paul the Apostle to the Philippians, Colossians, and Thessalonians.* Oxford: John Henry Parker, 1843. p. 362 . [emphasis in the original].

[137] 2 Thess 1:6-10

[138] 1 Cor 15:52

[139] Chrysostom. *Ibid.* p. 415

[140] Is 30:27; 40:5, 10

[141] Chrysostom. *Ibid.* p. 415-416

[142] Chrysostom. *Ibid.* p. 417

[143] Chrysostom. *Ibid.* p. 464

This is in the context of facing the Antichrist once he reveals himself. As Paul wrote concerning our gathering: "that day will not come until the rebellion occurs and the man lawlessness is revealed."[145] Chrysostom noted that the Antichrist will cause the falling away (rebellion/*apostasia*) by his "numberless mischiefs."[146] As Paul wrote, emphasized by Chrysostom, the Antichrist will proclaim himself to be God and demand worship--not only in Jerusalem at the temple but throughout the world to the harm of every believer. Nowhere in the writings of the Archbishop of Constantinople is there any reference to some event prior to the time of the Lord's arrival in glory when He judges the wicked and rescues us who are alive and remain to greet Him.

These Ante-Nicene and later references are sufficient to show the early church was not only premillennial but held to a post-tribulational position which is in accord with scripture. As a good number of prophecy experts in the past two generations have promoted dispensational ideas, their thrust has been to make these Fathers say what they did not. "The only significant matter that early theologians didn't develop appears to have been a pretrib rapture!"[147] We have noted some of the promoters of distortion in this chapter. John Walvoord, Grant Jeffrey, Dwight Pentecost, Henry Thiessen, Tim LaHaye, Thomas Ice, and a host of others have caused great harm, not just with their revisions to the history of the church, but they also have muddied the waters[148] of our present-day need to know what is coming. The church of this hour is closer to the time of the Second Coming than the Fathers. It becomes even more imperative to apply common sense along with the Holy Spirit's guidance, so our understanding of what approaches at the end of the age is clear and without conflict. This will prepare believers for a real event--not something that is make believe.

---

144 *Ibid.* p. 484
145 2 Thess 2:3-
146 Chrysostom. *Ibid.* p. 485
147 Gundry, Bob. *First the Antichrist.* Grand Rapids, MI: BakerBooks, 1997. p. 157-158
148 Ezek 34:19

Before moving on, another historical reference has caused much controversy between those who hold to the pre-trib rapture theory and those who are post-trib. Ephraem the Syrian [c306-373 A. D.] has been promoted as the ultimate proof that the imminent, pre-trib rapture was taught by the church many years prior to J. N. Darby who brought it to the table in the 1830s. Grant Jeffrey, who is mentioned above, claimed that he made the discovery in 1994.[149] He then provided quotations of Ephraem's writings which he blatantly and erroneously claimed affirmed the church would be removed by rapture prior to the Antichrist and his waging of war against the church. Jeffrey fashioned his "proof" in the same way he corrupted the *Didache*, by either omitting or reinterpreting the portions which did not agree with his pre-trib speculation. It is interesting to note that Ephraem's writings were well known long before.[150] In his work published in 1916, *The Death of a Nation*, Abraham Yohannan noted Ephraem was "widely read" and that "his works" were "extensively translated into Greek, Armenian, Coptic, Arabic, and Ethiopic."[151] There is no hint from any of these writings of a pre-trib event. Leroy Froom included some excerpts from Ephraem in his monumental work, *The Prophetic Faith of Our Fathers*, published in 1950. In the first of four volumes, Froom presented Ephraem as expecting the Antichrist to appear after the Roman Empire broke apart: "For things which have been written have now been fulfilled, and the signs which had been predicted, received their end; nothing remains then, except that the coming of our enemy, antichrist, appear (or, be revealed). For when the empire of the Romans meets its end (literally, receives an end), all things will necessarily be consummated."[152] This statement by Ephraem plainly lays out his clear belief which was the expectancy of the appearance first of the

---

[149] Jeffrey, Grant R. *Final Warning*. Eugene, OR: Harvest House, 1996. p. 466

[150] See: Jackson, George Anson. *The Post-Nicene Fathers*. New York, NY: D. Appelton & Co., 1883; Also: Roberts & Donaldson. *Nicene and Post-Nicene Fathers*. Peabody, MA: Hendrickson, 1989; Swete, H. B., *Patristic Study*. London: Longmans, Green, and Co., 1909; Kurtz. *Church History*.Three Volumes. New York, NY: Funk & Wagnalls, 1879; *et al*

[151] Yohannan, Abraham. *The Death of a Nation or The Ever Persecuted Nestorians or Assyrian Christians*. New York, NY: G. P. Putnam's Sons, 1916. p. 81-82

[152] Froom, Leroy. *The Prophetic Faith of Our Fathers*. Vol.1. Washington, DC: Review & Herald, 1950. p. 405- 406

Antichrist, then Jesus Christ. He did not embrace any type of early departure. In this regard, and in spite of the fabrication of "the Rapture as an imminent event"[153] by Jeffrey, Thomas Ice, LaHaye,[154] and others who repeated this error, Ephraem was in agreement with the earlier Fathers. For a full, clear commentary of Ephraem's *On the Last Times, the Antichrist, and the End*, it can be located in Robert Gundry's *First the Antichrist* with important references regarding Ephraem and Pseudo-Ephraem.[155] It is recommended to obtain Dr. Gundry's book for further insight with this rearrangement of Ephraem's words and intent.

We must proceed with this brief overview of history to see how the early Church Fathers' interpretations became altered into a quagmire of distortion. For three hundred years, the church was premillennial in its stance with eschatology. By the fourth century, things began to shift. Origen [184-253 A. D.] had already set in motion the allegorical interpretation of the Scripture through the Alexandrian school in Egypt. This had a negative effect on millennial hopes and led to the idea that *chiliasm*[156] was heretical.[157] Augustine [354-430 A. D.] embraced this approach as an alternate view and, as a result, initiated the idea that the millennium is not in the future, "but has already begun."[158] This view continued through the Middle Ages. Symbolism and allegory became prevalent tools for interpretation. The millennium in Augustine's rendering was under way. When Christ did not return in 1000 A. D., adjustments to the particulars of this position altered the 1,000 years to an

---

[153] Jeffrey, Grant R. *Heaven--The Mystery of Angels.* p. 52, This claim was made in direct reference to and support of Ephraem whom Jeffrey took out of context. Ephraim expected Antichrist, then Christ.

[154] LaHaye, Tim, and Jerry B. Jenkins. *Perhaps Today. Living Every Day in the Light of Christ's Return.* Wheaton, IL:Tyndale House, 2001. p. 51. LaHaye deliberately ignored the full translation and quoted a select portion with omissions.

[155] Gundry, Bob. *First the Antichrist.* Grand Rapids, MI: BakerBooks, 1997. p. 161-188

[156] Chiliasm: another term for millennialism. See Glossary

[157] Berkouwer, Louis. *The History of Christian Doctrines.* Grand Rapids, MI: Wm. B. Eerdmans Pub., 1949. p. 270-271

[158] Erickson, Millard. *Christian Theology.* Grand Rapids, MI: Baker Book House, 1986. p. 1206

indefinite period.[159] This shift favored the amillennial position, since much of its interpretative method is symbolic and allegorical. This is how they looked at the Book of Revelation, a view held by a number of groups today. "The Reformers held mostly to the old Augustinian conceptions, except in so far as they rejected Purgatory."[160] When the Church in Rome became the primary spiritual influence among the territory of the fallen Roman Empire, postmillennialism began to be the favored view.[161] Augustine's thoughts were claimed by both camps, and the end result is that neither school of thought conforms to the scripture.[162] History as seen in the eyes of the interpreter became the measure of interpretation. This is the source of many problems today, since both amillennialism and postmillennialism are still with us.

When the Reformation took place, Rome became the enemy of the Protestant church. The reformers, of course, separated themselves from its authority. The Pope became the Antichrist, and world events added fuel to the fire, leading to a historicist interpretation taken up by the Protestants. This was carried into the interpretation of the Book of Revelation which was then spread out chronologically like a chart of history. Futurism had not yet resurfaced, though it was not far off. Here is an overview of the different views of eschatology:

1. Futurist: Most events are future and will occur close together at the end of the age.
2. Preterist: Most or all of the events occurred at the time written.
3. Historical: Most of the events are future and occurring over the life of the church.
4. Symbolic: Events described are not sequential but timeless truths.[163]

---

[159] Erickson. *Ibid.* p. 1206-1207
[160] Farrar, Frederic W. *Eternal Hope. Five Sermons.* London: Macmillan & Co., 1901. p. 171
[161] Gundry, Robert H. *The Church and the Tribulation.* Grand Rapids, MIL: Zondervan Pub., 1973. p. 184
[162] Erickson. *Ibid.* p. 1205-1217. See also: Bethune-Baker, J. F. *An Introduction to the Early History of Christian Doctrine.* London: Methuen & Co., Ltd., 1954. p. 68-71
[163] Erickson. *Ibid.* p. 1154

When events predicted by those from the historicist school failed to take place, the view began to lose favor. This led to an opportunity for futurists to become an influence. Futurism, then, became a center of interest and much discussion followed. The future anticipation of the Second Coming returned to the realm of theological acceptance. Premillennialism, then, offered an acceptable option. This was not without problems, though. Some premillennialists held to their historicist application and became entangled with the setting of dates.[164] Yet, the futurist view became a viable alternative. During the seventeenth and eighteenth centuries, interest and discussion intensified. During the 1800s, the active discussion led to substantive assertion of new ideas. Ernest Sandeen noted: "The modern revival of millenarianism originated in the era of the French Revolution, and there has seemed no need to retreat further."[165] There were those that thought Napoleon was the expected Antichrist.[166] The seeds had been planted, and the futurists were seeking better answers.

This brings us to the issues surrounding the origin of pre-tribulational thinking. There are a number of persons connected with the formulation of the dispensational pre-trib view popular today. Looking back to time of the Reformation, a Jesuit from Spain, Francisco Ribera [1537-1591 A. D.] presented a fresh approach to set aside the claim that the Pope was the Antichrist. He was responding to the reformers' identification that Rome was the source of evil, and its head was the man of sin. Ribera pressed his construct into the future and laid out a scenario with a man to appear claiming to be God, who would be received by the Jews, rebuild their temple, persecute the saints, rule the world, and accomplish this all within three and one half years. Then, Christ would return.[167] In Ribera's commentary on Revelation, he placed most of the chapters to the end of the age in contrast to the historicists.[168] His

---

[164] Many errant predictions by those who set dates are noted in Leroy Froom's *The Prophetic Faith of Our Fathers*.

[165] Sandeen, Ernest. *The Roots of Fundamentalism. British and American Millenarianism 1830 - 1930*. Chicago, IL: The University of Chicago Press, 1970. p. xviii

[166] Weremchuk, Max S. *John Nelson Darby. A Biography*. Neptune, NJ: Loizeaux Bros., 1992. p. 117

[167] Froom, Leroy. *Ibid*. Vol. II, p. 486-493; Vol. III, p. 533, 655

[168] Historicist: taking place over the life of the church.

thoughts were not in total agreement with today's dispensational theory, yet some of the primary components were present. Note that this was a Jesuit endeavor, not a prototype from a Protestant authority. The Protestants did not bring forth a pre-trib dispensational proposition at this time--or confirm its prior existence. The flow of this doctrine went through changes from the time of the Fathers, but nowhere is there evidence of an early departure of the church. There was no imminent, pre-trib thought until much later at the time Edward Irving and John Nelson Darby became proponents of the additional alterations which in the process evolved into a secret rapture. As noted by Wayne Grudem, this idea is of recent origin and was "unknown in the history of the church before it was proposed in the last century by John Nelson Darby."[169]

After two hundred years another Jesuit came on the scene, Manuel de Lacunza [1731-1801 A. D.]. He was a student of the Church Fathers and numerous other historical works. He sought either to confirm the Fathers' teachings or to refute them. Lacunza determined that the Second Advent would occur at the beginning of the millennium. This conformed to the Church Fathers' views which we have discussed above. Lacunza held to the two comings of Christ, one past, and a single event yet to come. The Second Advent, he said, would be His return in glory. He described this proposition in his work: *The Coming of the Messiah in Glory and Majesty*. He labored twenty years to produce this. He used a pen name when this was published, Juan Josafat Ben-Ezra, being fearful of reprisal from the Vatican. Nonetheless, the book was circulated in Spain and South America. Spanish speakers took interest since it was controversial and stood against Roman teaching.[170] Lacunza was opposed to the earlier allegorical, mystical interpretations held by Rome. He insisted that the Lord will return at the time the Father has set, and that the Antichrist would appear first. He noted that the advent of Christ would end the reign of terror of the Antichrist. This agrees to Scripture and holds to a literal understanding which is also a claim held by those promoting the dispensational pre-trib theory today. The difference, however, is that Lacunza never proposed an earlier

---

[169] Grudem, Wayne. *Systematic Theology*. Grand Rapids, MI: Zondervan, 2006. p. 1100
[170] Froom. *Ibid*. Vol. III, p. 307-309, 317

return of Christ as defined by dispensationalists to remove the church some seven years prior to His glorious Second Coming. He did entertain a period of protection "much before" the end.[171] But, the thought of a secret removal of the church would be a later feature courtesy of others.

In 1812, a Spanish edition of this work was acquired by Edward Irving, a dynamic Scottish preacher who translated it into English. Lacunza's ideas affected him greatly since he spent a number of years completing the translation. Irving had his two volume edition published in 1827.[172] The subject of this work became a pivotal point of discussion at the Albury Prophetic Conferences.[173] These gatherings were hosted by Henry Drummond in Albury Park, Surrey, England, who invited laymen and clergy to discuss issues relating to the future millennium and the return of Christ. Edward Irving was present. Many millenarian scholars attended. The meetings were held from 1826 to 1830. It was through these discussions and others that followed that the formulation of a rapture preceding the tribulation became tenable with the feature of a "secret rapture"[174] Also in attendance at Albury was Lady Theodosia Powerscourt who held great interest in the discussion of the Second Coming. Her enthusiasm led her to establish meetings at her estate with the same theme beginning in 1831. Edward Irving and John Nelson Darby were active participants.[175] At these conferences, this new theory of the rapture preceding the final tribulation as connected to 1 Thessalonians 4:17 became a notable centerpiece.[176] It was Darby who introduced the secret rapture at the 1833 meeting.[177] Also participating in these Powerscourt gatherings were early

---

[171] Thigpen, Paul. *The Rapture Trap.* West Chester, PA: Ascencion Press, 2001. p. 143. Thigpen and others, say 45 days.

[172] Carlisle, Gavin. *The Prophetical Works of Edward Irving.* London: Alexander Strahan Pub., 1867. Vol. I, p. x; Froom. *Ibid.* Vol. III., p. 307-309

[173] Consider the fact that Irving labored on the translation of Lacunza's book for a dozen years. Hence, he had roughly a decade to contemplate the ramifications of the Antichrist appearing first, and then Christ at the end of the tribulation.

[174] Froom. *Ibid.* Vol. IV, p. 421

[175] Froom. *Ibid.* Vol. III, p. 585

[176] Froom. *Ibid.* Vol. IV, p. 422-423

[177] Sandeen. *Ibid* p. 38; Reid, Daniel G. *Dictionary of Christianity in America.* Downers Grove, IL: InterVarsity Press, 1991. P. 973-974; Weremchuk, Max S.

Plymouth Bretheren leaders: B. W. Newton and Samuel Tregelles. Both Newton and Tregelles[178] were not in agreement with Darby's novel idea and spoke out against it. Their later writings reflect their stance and sharp opposition to a pre-trib removal of the church as an unfounded idea unheard of by the early Church Fathers.[179] It must be weighed carefully that once the notion of a pre-trib event is brought into the return of Christ, this divides the Second Coming into a multiple of returns which is contrary to scripture and was never proposed by any New Testament writer.

As noted in the book of Hebrews, the Lord Jesus returns just once.[180] This occurs at the end of the age and will introduce the eternal state which includes the Millennium. Darby, however, promoted an option which altered the Biblical standard. "He emphasized the Lord's coming for His own (the so-called rapture) before a seven-year period of tribulation."[181] This created another return by the Lord which became a "gap" or "parenthesis"[182] never entertained before--except through the discussions at Albury and Powerscourt. Edward Irving and John Nelson Darby were active among the attendees. A variety of subjects were considered. As noted above, Irving was the translator of Manuel Lacunza's work, which entered into the discourse.[183] Lacunza noted a period of time between the removal of believers (1 Thess 4:16) "much before" the Lord returned to judge. He did not specify the time period; however this thought (*much before*) became amplified by those discussing his work. A number of more recent commentators have defined this as a unique removal of

---

John Nelson Darby. A Biography. p. 117, 133; Bebbington, David. *Evangelicalism in Modern Britain. A History from the 1730s to the 1980s.* Grand Rapids, MI: Baker Book, 1992. p. 86

[178] Tregelles is well known as a Greek scholar and his critical edition of the New Testament; also, his translation of Gesenius' *Hebrew Lexicon.*

[179] Froom. *Ibid.* Vol. IV, p. 423; Weremchuk, Max S. *John Nelson Darby. A Biography.* p. 122

[180] Heb 9:27-28

[181] Weremchuk, Max S. *Ibid.* p. 117

[182] Allis, Oswald T. *Prophecy and the Church.* Philadelphia, PA: The Presbyterian and Reformed Pub. Co., 1947. p. 287

[183] *The Coming of the Messiah in Glory and Majesty.* Reprinted in the UK by J. G. Tillin; or, available online.

the church to be taken out of harm's way for forty-five days. This was to occur while the Lord's judgments were taking place.[184] While Lacunza left the door open for an exact time, others at the time of Darby and Irving were considering the issue.[185] It was a thought incorporated by Darby into his thinking which lengthened to seven years. Darby with his self-assured attitude accredited his liberty with the texts to 2 Thessalonians 2:1-2 which he claimed "made me understand the rapture of the saints before--*perhaps a considerable time before*--the Day of the Lord (that is before the judgment of the living, Matthew 24:31-46)."[186] Absent from Darby's new addition to the Second Coming was any direct support from scripture that a two-part second advent had any basis. It has not changed since his day and has created multiple problems for dispensational teachers who blindly follow the pre-trib theory. William Kelly who edited Darby's writings wrote a pamphlet, *The Rapture of the Saints: Who Suggested It, or Rather on What Scripture?* Kelly was never present at Powerscourt and wrote years later often as a defense of the theory. It was he who wrote attributing the idea to Darby's understanding of 2 Thessalonians 2:1-2 by which Darby called for the rapture "perhaps a considerable time before" the Day of the Lord and judgment.[187] G. H. Lang, commenting on this, followed Kelly's timeline back to about 1830 but had no definite date for Darby's assumption. He did, though, place the claim at the time of the Powerscourt conferences.[188] This conforms to the 1833 date noted above. In any event, Kelly's account affirms Darby's admission that he formed the theory at this time as *his* "discovery," and it was not a re-discovery of early church teaching. The new idea was opposed, and the controversy did not subside. This is because "the only coming of Christ known to the Gospels and the Revelation is accompanied by power and great glory, being as brilliant and

---

[184] Olson, Carl E. *Will Catholics Be "Left Behind."* San Francisco, CA: Ignatius Press, 2003. p. 153-154; Thigpen. *The Rapture Trap.* p. 143

[185] For helpful background on this challenging point, see: MacPherson, Dave. *The Great Rapture Hoax.* Fletcher, NC: New Puritan Library, 1983. p. 181-186. The issue revolves around the 45 days noted in Daniel chapter 12 [1290/1335 days].

[186] Weremchuk. Max S. *Ibid.* p. 132-133 [emphasis edded].

[187] Quoted in; Lang, G. H. *The Disciple. Vol.1, No. 3.* 1954. rpt. Miami Springs, FL; Conley & Schoettle, 1984. p. 53

[188] Lang. *Ibid.* p. 53

visible as a flash of lightning, and that these portions of Scripture do not speak of a Pre-Tribulation coming of Christ."[189] Powerscourt was the planters' field for vibrant discussion of new ideas. Many historicists held to a year/day theory and also placed their ideas into the conferences discussions. This, too, made for fodder in the pensive mills of speculation. Nevertheless, "we find the idea of this seven-year period as a deferred seventieth week fully expressed in the Powerscourt Conferences."[190]

The respected Adrian Rogers fell into this trap in his commentary on the Book of Revelation. He divided up the return by comparing the event to a harvest: "The general harvest" being the rapture, and "The gleanings" being the resurrection of the tribulation saints.[191] This, of course, makes a claim for two unbiblical Second Comings.[192] It was Darby who integrated this fallacy into the return of the Lord once he adjusted the removal of the church into an earlier timeframe. This drew disapproval from his own contemporaries in the Brethren, including George Muller and Robert Chapman.[193] The position which was retained by the Albury gathering was historicist and was in expectation of Antichrist "to be soon revealed."[194] The Powerscourt group through the influence of Darby injected the futurist view with his secret rapture being a central feature. Darby was not clear on all of the particulars of his view, since he was still working on his premise. "Yet in spite of these steps in the development of his understanding of prophetic Scriptures, we are safe in saying that, on the united testimony of B. W. Newton and William Kelly, Darby came

---

[189] Lang. *Ibid.* p. 55
[190] Froom. *Ibid.* Vol. IV. p. 1224-1225
[191] Rogers, Adrian. *Unveiling the End Times in Our Time.* Nashville, TN: Broadman & Holman Pub., 2004. p. 246
[192] The most common device employed by pre-trib teachers is: the Lord first comes *for* the church, then returns *with* them at the Second Coming. This scripturally is impossible as noted by the word *as written* and those who are honest with it.
[193] See Appendix for Muller's and Chapman's statements. Both men are noted as influential writers in Plymouth Brethren history. See: Miller, Andrew. *Miller's Church History. From First to Twentieth Century.* Fincastle, VA: Scripture Truth Book Co., n.d. p. 1063
[194] Dallimore, Arnold. *The Life of Edward Irving. The Fore-runner of the Charismatic Movement.* Edinburgh: The Banner of Truth Trust, 1983. p. 63

to understand the rapture in the early 1830s."[195] This clearly reflects the fact that Darby and others at this time did not discover a lost doctrinal point from the early church but rather invented it. Master expositor D. Martyn Lloyd-Jones affirmed the origin saying this teaching "was not known before 1830," noting that it was "first taught" at the Powerscourt Conferences.[196] He went on to expound on the fallacy demonstrating from scripture the error and called his congregation to look for the single appearing of Christ, "our blessed hope."[197] In 1837, Darby traveled to Europe to bring his message to a number of congregations there, beginning in Switzerland. After returning to England, in 1845 he revisited Plymouth and found that they had departed from the basic Brethren teaching, including the "secret rapture."[198] This congregation was led by B. W. Newton who had continuously maintained the orthodox view that Christ returns at the end of the tribulation, and the church will see the Antichrist. Darby was wounded personally by this and rejected the rational, Biblical position maintained by Newton and others. Darby refused to amend his idea and pressed it further in the years to come.

There is an ongoing debate as to who at that time truly conceived the idea of the secret rapture. The pre-trib adherents of our day are violently opposed to this having a human origin. While some are openly favorable to crediting Darby with placing the teaching into a systematic form, they are not willing to give any favor to Irving.[199] They ardently attempt to undergird their view with scripture or the Church Fathers, but as we have shown, this is not possible. It was Samuel Tregelles, the contemporary and fellow Plymouth Brethren leader, who recognized that this feature was introduced, and it was "some time before a secret advent of the Lord and a secret rapture of the Church had a systematic place."[200] Dr. Tregelles recalled that there was nothing definite "until this was

---

[195] Weremchuk, Max S. *Ibid.* p. 131
[196] Lloyd-Jones, D. Martyn. *The Church and the Last Things.* Wheaton, IL: Crossway Books, 2003. p. 136
[197] *Ibid.* p. 138-141
[198] Pickering, Hy. *Chief Men Among the Brethren.* London: Pickering & Inglis, n.d. p. 13
[199] Froom. *Ibid.* Vol. IV, p.1223-1224. Darby resisted any attempt to connect his idea with a human source, *i.e.*, Irving.
[200] Tregelles, S. P. *The Hope of Christ's Second Coming.* 1886. rpt. Chelmsford, UK:

given forth as an 'utterance' in Mr. Irving's Church."[201] He placed this at the time of the Powerscourt gatherings. The utterance referred to is the speaking in tongues, a practice in Irving's meetings. This would place the origin in the hands of a person and negate a direct Biblical source. The individual who has been identified for laying this free-thinking curiosity into a church setting was a person whose name has the two most despised words in pre-trib eschatology: Margaret Macdonald. The historical account of the beginning of this diversion has been taken up and documented elsewhere.[202] However, it should be noted that the Macdonald family, including Margaret and her brothers, James and George, plus two sisters, Jane and Mary, came under the charismatic influence of Edward Irving and others. Soon, they were participating in tongues and "the gift of prophecy."[203] A friend of the Macdonalds, Mary Campbell, had already begun these public utterances in 1830. Irving testified of this when he was in London as did others.[204] This was an early occasion of the gifts and prophecy occurring in the Irvingites.[205] Margaret Macdonald and her two brothers were speaking in tongues. At that time, James interpreted the utterances as: "Behold He cometh--Jesus cometh."[206] It can be said that with this type of influence and the nature of some believers who exaggerate and abuse the gifts of the Spirit that the Macdonalds, Margaret in particular, are prime candidates for introducing an unbiblical idea which became topics in the discussions at the conferences. Irving's influence as a major participant was a viable source, along with the writings of Ribera and Lacunza.[207] Notably, it was Darby who exercised leadership at the Powerscourt gatherings while in discussion with

---

The Sovereign Grace Advent Testimony, n. d. [c1978]. p. 35; See: Grudem, Wayne. *Systematic Theology.* p. 860, footnote

[201] Tregelles. *Ibid.* p. 35

[202] MacPherson, Dave. *The Incredible Cover-Up. The True Story of the Pre-Trib Rapture.* Plainfield, NJ: Logos Int'l., 1975.

[203] Dallimore, Arnold. *Ibid.* p. 105

[204] *Ibid.* p. 104-105

[205] Additional background on Edward Irving, Mary Campbell, the Macdonalds, and the use of the gifts can be found in: Strachan, Gordon. *The Pentecostal Theology of Edward Irving.* Peabody, MA: Hendrickson Pub., 1988. p. 61ff

[206] Dallimore. *Ibid.* p. 106

[207] Bass, Clarence B. *Backgrounds to Dispensationalism.* Grand Rapids, MI: Wm. B. Eerdmans Pub., 1960. p. 146-147

Irving and the others. The open promotion of the secret rapture emanated from there.

G. H. Lang recorded a reference from Richard Baxter who wrote Irvingite history at the time [1833].[208] Lang noted Baxter's account that "it was in August 1831 that he himself first fell under the 'power' energizing that movement; but he mentions that *some time before this* his sister had 'heard several utterances from Miss E. C. [the chief prophetess among the Irvingites] in which she most emphatically pronounced that Christ would come at an hour when even His own people would not be looking for Him--that the time of His coming would not be known to His own people.'" Lang's conclusion: "Certainly that would be a secret coming."[209] This is another distinct account for the source of the secret rapture idea from an individual--and not from Scripture. The Plymouth Brethren did not want any connection to the Irvingites as source for this novel doctrine now ensconced in Brethren teaching. Not surprisingly, Darby wanted his followers to think it was derived solely from the Bible. He held to the Scripture as noted above [2 Thessalonians 2:1-2] and claimed "his doubts were removed by a Mr. Tweedy, who had no connection with Irvingism."[210] William Kelly also reported the Tweedy account which "cleared up the difficulty previously felt with this question," noting Tweedy "was the one who first suggested, as decisive proof from scripture, II Thes. ii. 1, 2."[211] Robert Cameron also affirmed the Tweedy account: that the church would be caught up "*secretly, before* the tribulation."[212] So now with Tweedy added into the mix, we have three separate sources from which the birth of this idea came.[213] All three of them reflect a human hand and a timing which can be traced to circa 1830. The 1833 date referenced above is viable. Whether Darby or someone else was the first to utter the words at these conferences the reader

---

[208] Baxter, Richard. *Narratives of Facts; Characterizing the Supernatural Manifestations in Members of Mr. Irving's Congregation and Other Individuals.* 1833. rpt. Rarebooksclub.com, 2013.

[209] Lang. *Ibid.* p. 55-56 [emphasis in the original].

[210] Froom. *Ibid.* Vol. IV, p. 1224

[211] Lang. *Ibid.* p. 57

[212] Cameron, Robert. *Scriptural Truth About The Lord's Return.* Chicago, IL: Fleming H. Revell, 1922. p. 70-72 [emphasis in the original].

[213] (1) Lacunza, Irving, Macdonald; (2) Miss E. C., Irving; (3) Tweedy, Darby.

can decide. Nevertheless, it was Darby who openly promoted it and gained from this unscriptural excursion into unorthodoxy. Soon he would travel to America with his unfounded message. He would influence unsuspecting ministers and others who held an earnest interest in Bible prophecy.

In addition to his European trips, John Nelson Darby traveled to North America, the West Indies, and New Zealand.[214] He made seven trips to Canada and the United States between 1862 and 1877.[215] During his time in the states he was welcomed by those who were seeking a system to set aside postmillennialism. Darby's message appeared to satisfy this concern. Soon, Bible conferences commenced which centered on prophecy. The first conference was held in Chicago in 1878 at the suggestion of Nathaniel West. Others which were more significant were held in "Niagara on Lake Ontario" from 1883 through 1897.[216] Many of the most notable evangelical voices attended. In 1898, William E. Blackstone published his well-known treatise, *Jesus Is Coming*, which in years following influenced many. His treatment of the Second Coming with the early removal of the church answered questions for those who had taken hold of dispensational pre-millennialism.[217] It also was one of the effective tools used to stand against liberalism.[218] Yet, the results from Niagara were mixed. Many of the participants were, or through the discussions became, post-tribulational. A few did accept Darby's new theory. Charles Ryrie noted the conferences were "not called to promote dispensationalism but to oppose postmillennialism." Dealing with the millennium was the issue. Hence, there was "little, if any, connection originally between dispensationalism and the earliest prophetic conferences in America."[219]

---

[214] Douglas, J. D. *The New International Dictionary of the Christian Church*. p. 282-283

[215] Couch, Mal. *Dictionary of Premillennial Theology*. Grand Rapids, MI: Kregel Pub., 1996. p. 83; Sandeen. *Ibid*. p. 71

[216] Ladd, George Eldon. *The Blessed Hope*. p. 43-44

[217] Blackstone, William E. [W. E. B.]. *Jesus Is Coming*. Chicago, IL: Fleming H. Revell, 1898. Revised editions appeared in 1908 and 1932.

[218] Marsden, George M. *Fundamentalism and American Culture .The Shaping of Twentieth-Century Evangelism: 1870-1925*. New York, NY: Oxford University Press, 1982. p. 51

[219] Ryrie, Charles C. *Dispensationalism. Revised and Expanded*. Chicago, IL: Moody

The consequences came later.[220] These meetings led to a conference in 1901 held in Sea Cliff on the north shore of Long Island, New York. At this time, Darby adherents, Arno C. Gaebelein and C. I. Scofield discussed the plan to produce a Bible with reference notes which would support the revolutionary views of Darby.[221] A first edition was issued in 1909 with the better known edition appearing with revisions in 1917. Oxford University Press has continued to print this. A later revision was published in 1967 with a new team of contributing editors who were fully committed to the dispensational pre-trib idea. Two of the consulting editors of the 1917 edition, William G. Moorehead and William J. Erdman, were adamant that the church would see the Antichrist and endure the tribulation. Others who were involved from the early conferences were also post-trib and were vocal in making the case known. They include Nathaniel West, Henry W. Frost, James Stifler, and Robert Cameron.[222] They were firmly opposed to the idea of a secret rapture.[223] This is reminiscent of the earlier opposition in England that came against Darby from B. W. Newton and others who held firmly to the scripture. Charles R. Erdman, noted by Scofield in the original introduction in the Scofield Reference Bible for his suggestions, strongly held the orthodox position that the falling away must occur, that the man of sin be revealed before Jesus Christ would return, and there will be no "secret rapture."[224] However, Darby's teaching was welcomed by D. L. Moody and other popular voices. So, Darby's dispensational theory and Scofield's adaptation marched ahead into the twentieth century.

The influence of the Scofield Bible cannot be underestimated. It became the

---

Press, 1995. p. 146

[220] Note that Ryrie's comment is an admission that Darbyism and his version of dispensationalism were imported.

[221] Sandeen. *Ibid.* p. 222

[222] See Appendix for Robert Cameron's testimony regarding the error of the rapture prior to the tribulation.

[223] Sandeen. *Ibid.* p. 211

[224] Erdman, Charles R. *The Return of Christ.* New York, NY: George H. Doran Co., 1922. p. 53-56

standard reference book for those adhering to and promoting the dispensational program. Even with dissenting voices which exposed the errors inherent within the theory itself, it still is favored by many Christians. Likely, they prefer to think they have an exemption from tribulation thanks to well-known, popular teachers. But, since this teaching fails to agree with Scripture, they will face the horrific reality of truth once the Antichrist appears. Nevertheless, Scofield along with Lewis Sperry Chafer labored to found Dallas Theological Seminary in 1924 which became the center for dispensational study in America. Many other Bible institutes were founded, also, including the Bible Institute of Los Angeles, Philadelphia School of the Bible, and Moody Bible Institute in Chicago. America's denominational seminaries did not welcome dispensationalism, hence new ground was broken with the institutes which produced thousands of graduates teaching Darby's views. The theory continues to be promoted even as we have shown here that it contradicts the historic, orthodox doctrinal position of the church, and more important, it violates Scripture. There is a great deal more history which offers insight into the development of Darby's views and how it has affected popular thinking regarding the last days. For those who wish to pursue this further, see our recommended reading list in Aids to Further Understanding elsewhere in this book.

Summary: Since the time of Jesus and the Apostles, including the Church Fathers who were students of those Jesus commissioned, none of them ever believed that there would be two separate stages or returns of the Lord at the end of the age. None held to imminency which embraced a "secret rapture." All of them were in agreement with the Olivet Discourse expecting to see the man of lawlessness prior to the Second Coming at which time Jesus would judge all the wicked and establish His kingdom forever.[225] Those who perpetuate the distortion of an early removal of the church prior to the final seven years are risking the fire of judgment since they mislead others with a false teaching.[226]

---

[225] Mt 24:15; 2 Thess 2:3-4; Rev 19:11-16
[226] Titus 2:1; Prov 21:28; Is 9:16

SCRIPTURAL EVIDENCE

As we have emphasized throughout this work, it is the scripture itself which must take pre-eminence when evaluating the value of a claim of orthodoxy. The record of history has been firmly laid in place through the ages and can be examined. Conclusions which result are based on evidence noted along the way.[1] With Biblical prophecy, events in the future, the challenge is of a different kind since the events have not yet occurred. This leaves room for discussion and further investigation, yet the potential outcome may be conclusions which do not agree at all with the facts. The Scripture must be the foundation. Questions about what is written are good, but the process of interrogation must never be slighted to undermine the results. Paul the Apostle said: "Test everything. Hold on to the good."[2] The Berean attitude of searching the scriptures must prevail. Sincerity must be the lifeblood of the search. Honest inquiry is of great value, since we all have questions. "If believers like John the Baptist could have problems of this sort with predictions about Christ's first coming, what guarantee do we have that believers will not have similar difficulties with predictions about Christ's second coming?"[3]

The following section is essentially topical and will look at the nature of the return of the Lord through the descriptions which various Biblical writers have laid in place. The promise of the Redeemer and Messiah of Israel was accepted as a future event since the law and the prophets gave advance notice. It is recommended that all scripture verses that follow in this section be read with an open Bible to allow for the full context to be examined.

---

[1] It is true that history can be adjusted and rewritten to conform to an ideology or a political agenda. But, the facts of history yet stand and cannot in themselves be altered. It is the tinkering that confounds true understanding.

[2] 1 Thess 5:21

[3] Hoekema, Anthony A. *The Bible and the Future.* p. 133

Judgment and the Second Advent

Judgment is a fact established by scripture in various places. It is shown to be an accounting for individuals, nations, and, one day, the world. The basis for this is God's requirement that evil be dealt with. At the end of the age, all evil will be eliminated. This will be the final retributive act from the Lord as He holds mankind to account for its blatant rejection of Him from the time man was created. In the course of Israel's history, the Lord instructed them to purify themselves and to purge evil from among them. He said: "You must purge the evil from among you."[4] Later, the prophet Isaiah identified the Lord Himself working on behalf of them to do this: "...I will purge away your dross."[5] Within this judicial approach to ungodly behavior and acts forbidden by the Mosaic Law is the concern for the Lord's people to be righteous and untainted by the evil that surrounded them. The same criterion is laid in place for the church, as Paul noted for them to "come out and be separate...touch no unclean thing."[6] The Apostle wanted the church to be blameless at othe Lord's coming.[7] Within the parameter of these admonitions, both from the Old Covenant and the New Covenant, is the key to understanding all of this: "the fear of the Lord." [8] The reason in both covenants is identical: the Lord is coming to judge. He is coming. "Behold, I am coming soon! My reward is with me, and I will give to everyone according to what he has done."[9] Rational thinking should lead to reverence and fear of our true source for wisdom,[10] especially in light of the fact that the Lord is going to hold men accountable for ignoring this. Consider, now, some of the components of the promised judgment.

1. [Ps 9:7-10]. ***His throne has been established for judgment***. In the previous verses in this psalm, David notes that the Lord has been on His throne "judging righteously."[11] David knows this having seen the Lord rebuking nations and

---

[4] Deut 13:5
[5] Is 1:25
[6] 2 Cor 6:17
[7] 1 Cor 1:8; Phil 1:10; 1 Thess 5:23
[8] Is 33:5-6
[9] Rev 22:12
[10] Pr 9:10
[11] Ps 9:4ff

judging the wicked. This will all culminate at the end of the age. The prophet Zephaniah emphasized this as he foretold the Lord's assembly of the nations, gathering the kingdoms, to pour our His wrath on them. At this time, the whole world will be consumed. The Lord will do this by fire.[12] This will happen suddenly, as He makes "a sudden end to all who live on the earth."[13] At this same time of judgment, when He deals with those who oppressed His people, He will "rescue the lame," "gather" the scattered, "bring them home, and restore their fortunes.[14] Within Zephaniah's declaration is the future promise which includes judgment and rescue at the same time. The wicked will be eliminated. God's people will be restored. This is brought out in Psalm two as the Lord states He will terrify them in his wrath and will "dash them to pieces."[15] In Psalm five, David tells us He will "destroy those who tell lies."[16] He gives us the reason: God cannot dwell with the wicked; they cannot stand in His presence.[17] In other words, as Zephaniah and David indicate, the wicked will be removed by fire, just as Peter notes elsewhere.[18] All this will be done in love, faithfulness, and justice by the Lord, the "one from the House of David."[19] He is the very one Isaiah foretold would come: "a child is born, a son is given…" who will sit on David's throne and uphold it "with justice and righteousness."[20] It is from this throne that justice will prevail and the final judgment will be initiated. Elsewhere we are told the Lord "comes to judge the earth."[21] He is coming here to do this. At this time, all things will be "exposed" when He "takes vengeance" on all, and He spares no one.[22] These verses outline briefly the fact of judgment and that when the Lord does this, all of the wicked will be eliminated. None of them will survive. Only the righteous will remain and be rewarded.

---

[12] Zeph 3:8
[13] Zeph 1:8
[14] Zeph 3:19-20
[15] Ps 2:5, 9
[16] Ps 5:6
[17] Ps 5:4
[18] 2 Pt 3:10
[19] Is 16:5
[20] Is 9:6-7
[21] 1 Chron 16:33
[22] Is 47:3

2. [Isaiah 13:6-13]. ***His wrath will bring judgment.*** Isaiah describes the day of the Lord in graphic terms which parallel the Olivet Discourse, the prophet Joel, plus the apostles Paul and Peter.[23] He notes this to come "like destruction from the Almighty" with "wrath" which will "make the land desolate" and "destroy the sinners within it." At this time, the cosmos will be affected: the stars, sun, and moon. There will be darkness, not light. The world will be punished "for its evil." All the arrogant and those who are ruthless will be brought to their end. Pride will be judged as men are "seized by terror." Isaiah warns that this will be universal in nature as "the heavens tremble" and "the earth will shake from its place." This will be the day when the Lord's wrath is poured out--"the day of his burning anger." This obviously leaves no room for anyone to survive except for the righteous. This act of full and complete judgment is supported elsewhere. Note in Psalm one that "the wicked will not stand in the judgment, nor sinners in the assembly of the righteous."[24] The Lord will remove them by fire. The reason for this retributive act will be judicial. Isaiah records in chapter twenty-four: the "people must bear their guilt."[25] In chapter thirty, the prophet tells us the Lord will shake "the nations in the sieve of destruction," and at the same time He will "shield Jerusalem; he will shield it and deliver it, he will 'pass over' it and rescue it."[26] This portion of Isaiah makes clear that the Lord is going to come once to judge and will rescue at the same time.[27] In other words, rescue and wrath are simultaneous. Zephaniah tells us that He will "assemble the nations" to pour out His "wrath on them" He will purify the lips of those who call on Him and remove "those who rejoice in their pride." The wicked will be judged, and the Lord "will leave within you the meek and humble," the ones "who trust in the name of the Lord."[28] This prophet clearly shows the wrath being poured out on the Lord's enemies while His own are rescued. Isaiah also speaks of the wrath to come upon the nations--"Oh, the

---

[23] Mt 24; Joel 3:30-31; 2 Thess 1:6-10; Acts 3:19-20; 2 Pt 3:10-13

[24] Ps 1:5; See also Ps 21:8-10

[25] Is 24:6. Read the entire chapter for the description of this complete judgment: Isaiah 24:1-23.

[26] Is 30:27-30; 31:4-5

[27] Notably, a second Passover, as in Egypt when the Lord's own were protected while the destroying angel judged.

[28] Zeph 3:8-13; Is 65:6-7

raging of many nations" and "the uproar of the peoples."[29] This prophet notes the Lord's rebuke of them as they attempt to escape and become like chaff "before the wind" He describes "sudden terror" in the evening and before the morning, they are gone."[30] This is a future warning and the fate of those who come against God's people. They will face His wrath and be eternally judged. Isaiah adds to this later stating retribution will come upon God's enemies, as the Lord puts on "garments of vengeance" at the same time He puts on "righteousness as his breastplate" and wears "the helmet of salvation."[31] This is described as a single event when the Lord repays His foes and comes to Zion as the Redeemer "to those in Jacob who repent of their sins."[32] Even those in distant islands far from Israel will be affected in this full judgment. Yet, it is a comprehensive event to include both wrath for the wicked and salvation for those who turn to Him. Again, one event is seen. Previously, Isaiah noted the Lord coming to "judge the people of the earth for their sins."[33] The instructions for His people--who notably are still present on the earth--are to enter their rooms and shut the doors behind them. They are told: "hide yourselves for a little while until his wrath has passed by."[34] This occurs at the same time they are told "your dead will live; their bodies will rise."[35] Once more, we find a single event portrayed in plain terms.[36] Later, Isaiah reinforces the picture of the coming wrath when the Lord comes with fire to "execute judgment upon all men."[37] At this future time, His hand "will be made known to his servants" and "fury will be shown to his foes." Both groups are present. Isaiah states plainly: "When you see this, your heart will rejoice."[38] This places His people on earth to see the wrath of God coming upon the wicked. Earlier, Isaiah wrote: "Tell

---

[29] Is 17:12

[30] Is 17:13-14

[31] Is 59:17

[32] Is 59:17-20

[33] Is 30:21

[34] Is 26:20

[35] Is 26:19

[36] Some pre-trib advocates attempt to use these verses to support the church being in heaven (*i.e.*, the "rooms" being in the Father's house in heaven). However, a careful reading of all the verses in context does not allow for this.

[37] Is 66:15-16

[38] Is 66:14

the righteous it will be well with them, for they will enjoy the fruit of their deeds. Woe to the wicked!"[39] This is the time the Lord "rises to judge the people." He will also judge the elders and leaders of His people who have taken advantage of and misled them. It is clear from this that the Lord will not be remiss in carrying out full judgment upon those who have failed as shepherds of the flock.[40] There is no indication from these passages that any of God's people are either exempt from or are removed from the earth prior to the execution of God's wrath.

3. [Isaiah 14:3-17]. ***Satan is to be judged***. Since Satan is behind all sin, evil, and iniquity, he will face harsh judgment. Jesus exposed him openly in the eighth chapter of John, "being a murderer" and "a liar and the father of lies."[41] These words were directed at the Pharisees and others who opposed Him and were victims of Satan's deceptive devices. Satan is the one who has been behind every system of evil since the beginning. He is responsible for "the blood of the prophets and of the saints, and all who have been killed on the earth."[42] He has accomplished this through a variety of political systems, *e.g.*, mystery Babylon. History records millions perishing as a result of the destructive ambitions of dictators and ruthless leaders, all empowered from the master deceiver who controls the dominion of darkness. In the Book of Ezekiel, the King of Tyre is compared to Satan. The latter was "the model of perfection," once in Eden, and "a guardian cherub." He was blameless until "wickedness was found" in him.[43] Caused by his pride, he was "expelled" and was thrown "to the earth" where he initiated his career of deception.[44] Further detail on the root of Satan's fall is found in the Book of Isaiah. There he is titled "the King of Babylon" which alludes to his mystery systems and his later demise in the Book of Revelation. He is referred to with a touch of sarcasm as the "morning star"--the one who has "fallen from heaven." His pride is noted as the prime cause of this, since he desired to be "like the Most High."[45] Since

---

[39] Is 3:10-11
[40] Is 3:10-15
[41] Jn 8:44
[42] Rev 18:24
[43] Ezek 28:11-15
[44] Ezek 28:16-19

God will not share His glory with another, Satan was removed from his post in heaven and left to wander and cause trouble.[46] Though Satan is blamed for many things that man has done without his direct help,[47] he will pay severely in the end. He will be thrown "into the lake of burning sulfur."[48] His torment will be for all eternity. His fate has been assured by the same act that guaranteed our salvation: Jesus' death and resurrection. Jesus said this was the very reason He came: to secure the promise of the judgment to come and assure us that "the prince of this world will be driven out."[49] In the Book of Hebrews we are told that Jesus' death was purposed to "destroy him who holds the power of death-- that is, the devil."[50] Regardless of anyone's position on eschatology, the final disposition and judgment of Satan is sure.

4. [Isaiah 2:12-18]. *The Lord has established a day for judgment*. Isaiah deals with the subject of judgment often as the prophet who looked beyond the challenge of his day. His future prophetic words must be taken just as seriously as those foretelling the birth of Christ.[51] This prophet's words were fulfilled when Christ came into the world as Savior. In like manner, they will be consummated when He returns in judgment of the wicked. This will occur once at the end of the age. Jesus reminded us of this in Luke's gospel: "I have come to bring fire on the earth, and how I wish it were already kindled. But I have a baptism to undergo, and how distressed I am until it is completed."[52] As Isaiah pointed ahead to the day of judgment, so did the Lord Jesus. When He spoke in His synagogue in Nazareth, He abbreviated His reference to this as He quoted Isaiah. His next words were the proclamation of "the day of vengeance of our God"[53] which was not yet to occur. First will be the Cross--later, the judgment.[54] The fullness of "the Lord's favor" will take place when the day of the Lord and

---

[45] Is 14:4, 11-15
[46] Job 1:6ff
[47] Jas 1:14
[48] Rev 20:10
[49] Jn 12:31
[50] Heb 2:14
[51] Is 7:14; 9:6-7
[52] Lk 12:49-50
[53] Is 61:2; Lk 4:18-19
[54] Lk 17:24-25

His retribution are complete. Then, the "age to come" will be the time when is seen the completion of His "treasured possession."[55] As Isaiah recorded, the Lord has a day in store for "the proud and lofty, for all that is exalted" in opposition to Him.[56] They will all be humbled in that day. "For the Lord has a day of vengeance, a year of retribution, to uphold Zion's cause."[57] It will be the time that all of Israel's enemies will face justice, and not overlooked will be all who have oppressed any of His saints: the church. The wicked will be eternally judged, no longer being able to slander Him or His own people. Ezekiel has recorded: "I will make known my holy name among my people Israel. I will no longer let my holy name be profaned, and the nations will know that I the Lord am the Holy One in Israel. It is coming! It will surely take place, declares the sovereign Lord. This is the day I have spoken of."[58] This is the time when He sends fire upon Magog and those even "in the coastlands."[59] This the final battle between good and evil while flesh is on the earth, Armageddon.[60] This is the end.[61] This is the time of the Second Advent when the Lord appears and He sends fire upon the earth. Malachi records, "'Surely the day is coming; it will burn like a furnace. All the arrogant and every evildoer will be stubble, and that day that is coming will set them on fire,' says the Lord Almighty."[62] Since the Lord is coming to earth, to His own, there is no reason to think anyone has left before He makes up His "treasured possession."[63] Some will perish at the hands of Antichrist and the beast.[64] Those who survive will be "purified and made spotless until the time of the end, for it will still come at the appointed time."[65] This is why the Lord encouraged the church to stand firm to the end[66] and the promise to "him who overcomes and does my will to the end--I will

---

[55] Mt 12:32; Eph 1:21; Mal 3:17
[56] Is 2:12
[57] Is 34:8
[58] Ezek 39:7-8
[59] Ezek 39:6
[60] Rev 16:16
[61] Ezek 7:6
[62] Mal 4:1
[63] Mal 3:17-18
[64] Rev 13:10, 15
[65] Dan 11:33-35
[66] Mt 24:13; James, also: Jas 5:8

give authority over the nations."[67] There is a time, a place, and a day for judgment for all nations.[68] It will be a day of darkness, a day unlike any other before or ever again. This is the day of the Lord.[69] The sun will be darkened and the moon turned to blood "before the coming of the great and dreadful day of the Lord."[70] Nowhere is there a sign of a departure by the Lord's people before this day.

5. [Psalm 102:13-18]. ***This is a future event***. This psalmist looks ahead to the time of compassion on Zion when the Lord appears in glory. This brings together the day of judgment and the time of restoration: "the appointed time has come."[71] At this time the Lord will rebuild Zion and the kings and rulers who have survived the judgment will revere Him and worship Him. Clearly, this is a future event when His name is no longer despised and surviving nations gather to praise Him in Jerusalem.[72] This is a guarantee for "a future generation, that a people not yet created may praise the Lord."[73] The prophet Daniel received explanation regarding the future on a number of occasions. Michael responded to his prayers for insight explaining that the visions concerned "a time yet to come."[74] Daniel was told that the full understanding is reserved for "the time of the end."[75] He pressed the concern and learned it "will be completed" after three and one half years "when the power of the holy people has been broken."[76] This indicates God's people will be present through the final portion of the tribulation (3 ½ years) which will be ended when the Lord comes "after the distress of those days."[77] Daniel was also told again these "words are closed up until the time of the end," and "those who are wise will understand."[78] It should be obvious that the words of these prophets

---

[67] Rev 2:26
[68] Is 41:1
[69] Joel 2:1-2; Mt 24:21
[70] Joel 2:31
[71] Ps 102:13
[72] Ps 102:21-22
[73] Ps 102:18
[74] Dan 10:14
[75] Dan 12:4
[76] Dan 12:5-8
[77] Mt 24:29-30

broadly point to this event, the return of the Lord and the judgment, to be future.

Scripture informs us that God alone has the authority to judge men and creation. It is He who is coming to judge the earth. He is the righteous judge[79] who will judge all "the peoples with equity." He will "judge the world in righteousness and the peoples in his truth."[80] The one who will carry this out is the Lord Jesus. He is the "God who judges the earth"[81] and has been appointed. Paul the Apostle made this clear when he was in Athens and informed his hearers that God formerly overlooked their ignorance, but now "commands all people everywhere to repent. For he has set a day when he will judge the world with justice by the man he has appointed. He has given proof of this to all men by raising him from the dead."[82] The righteous judgment of men will occur when the Lord Jesus returns at the Second Advent.

Kinds of Judgment

There will be wrath for the wicked and rewards for the righteous. These are the only two classifications of people that scripture identifies. Men are either lost or saved. There is no category in between. This is why the Gospel must be preached, so men will come under conviction and be converted--changed from death to life. This must be done prior to the death of a person, since there is no opportunity for anyone to change their mind in the afterlife.[83] The consequences of a person's acceptance or rejection of Christ are eternal.[84] This truth is one that is basic to the Faith and should not be neglected in orthodox teaching. Instruction about "the resurrection of the dead, and eternal judgment" are considered to be "elementary."[85] The church and its individual members should know this and be able to relate this reality to others so they will repent

---

[78] Dn 12:9-10
[79] Ps 7:11; 76:1-10
[80] Ps 96:10-13
[81] Ps 58:11
[82] Acts 17:30-31; also, Jas 4:12; 1 Pt 4:5
[83] Ecc 9:10. [See Glossary for "Doctrine of the Second Chance"].
[84] Jn 5:24-30; Jn 17:3
[85] Heb 6:2

of sin and not face harsh eternal judgment. Heaven's justice is assured for all. After death, the final state is unalterable. It is appointed to man to die once and "after that face judgment."[86] All have sinned, so all will be judged.[87] All will give an account.[88] There are two groups to be considered. The righteous and the wicked, but there are a number of judgments, either primary or inter-related.

1. [Romans 14:10]. ***The bema seat judgment***. This judgment is exclusively for the Lord's people. No unbelieving, unrepentant soul will participate. Those who belong to God and have turned to the Lord for salvation will be rewarded at this time. Those who are believers and have somehow fallen short will also appear and receive what is due. The term *bema* references the judgment seat which is the dais or platform upon which a judge is seated as cases are heard and decided.[89] This picture of judicial reference was known to the early church which was under the jurisdiction of Rome and subject to its laws. In the case of Paul's reference, he was reminding the believers in Rome that we will "stand before God's judgment seat." At this time, Jesus will be the judge, since the Father has entrusted this to His Son.[90] The affirmation of the Lord Jesus being the judge is reflected in the parabolic illustration when He comes in glory with all His angels and the nations are separated like "sheep from the goats."[91] This is a portion of the Olivet Discourse in which Jesus emphasized the finality of judgment. However, it is illustrative and not a separate judgment as taught by some. His point is clear that He, the Son of Man, will be the final judicial authority, and when He comes, the destiny of all men will be set for eternity. Paul reminded his co-worker, Timothy, of this noting Christ Jesus to "judge the living and the dead" at the time of "his appearing and his kingdom."[92] The fact of judgment is realized when He comes, but the sentence for the wicked comes later.[93] The righteous, though, will receive their due when the Lord comes. Paul

---

[86] Heb 9:27
[87] Rm 3:23
[88] 2 Cor 5:10; Rm 2:5, 16
[89] Mt 27:19; Jn 19:13
[90] Jn 5:22, 26-29; Acts 10:42
[91] Mt 25:31-32.
[92] 2 Tim 4:1

243

notes the nature of our standing before Him, and "each of us will give an account of himself to God."[94] Paul evoked more clarity to the Corinthians: "For we must all appear before the judgment seat of Christ, that each one may receive what is due him for the things done in the body, whether good or bad."[95] He had previously written to them that the Lord will bring hidden things to light--exposing the underlying motives in men's hearts: "At that time each will receive his praise from God."[96] This will take place after the arrival of Jesus, the Second Advent, and the wicked will have been removed. The Lord will deal judicially with His own first. Peter notes this, stating judgment will begin with the household of God, because we have obeyed the gospel of God.[97] He was reminding them of Ezekiel's words warning of judgment when the man clothed in linen marked those who were righteous, and the idolaters were judged. The sentence was carried out at the Lord's sanctuary, and it began "with the elders who were in front of the temple."[98] God's people should reflect on this. Judgment is serious.[99] The Corinthians received insight from Paul's own concern as he assured them he was not building on anyone else's foundation. He was only building on Jesus Christ. Paul called for care in building, whether someone builds with "gold, silver, costly stones, word, hay or straw," it will be "revealed with fire" on "the Day" when the Lord comes.[100] In other words, the judgment of men will commence as soon as the Lord comes down from heaven.[101] The Lord Jesus also made this point clear when he began to predict His death. He spoke to His disciples and told them, the "Son of Man is going to come in his Father's glory with his angels, and then he will reward each person according to what he has done."[102] Believers will appear before the

---

[93] Rev 20:12-15

[94] Rm 14:11-12

[95] 2 Cor 5:10

[96] 1 Cor 4:5

[97] 1 Pt 4:17

[98] Ezek 9:6; Is 3:13-14

[99] Heb 10:30-31

[100] 1 Cor 3:10-15

[101] 1 Thess 4:16-17; Rev 19:11-21

[102] Mt 16:27

bema seat. This also indicates that all believers will be present on earth when this occurs--not having left beforehand.

2. [Revelation 20:11-15]. ***The great white throne judgment.*** This judgment is for all others--those who have remained unresponsive to God's testimony through creation, who have rejected His witness through the word--both written and that given by His called servants--and those who have had the opportunity to yield their lives to His Son either directly or through those Christian voices since the Cross. No believer will appear at this time for judgment. This will take place 1,000 years after the first resurrection.[103] John the Apostle records this scene in advance as he penned the book of Revelation. He saw this and proceeded to give us a simple but plain rendering of the finality of the verdict and its sentence. The dead both "great and small" were resurrected and appear before the throne of God. Books were opened, and then another book. Deeds were recorded in the books. The single book was "the book of life." Judgment will be based on what they had done. In this case, all present had demonstrated enmity toward God and never sought His forgiveness for sin.[104] Their acts of violence, corruption, and evil are all recorded there with special notation indicating the thought and motive behind each willful display of wickedness.[105] Hence, none of their names appear in the book of life. The one good thing they needed to do to prevent this was never done: to confess sin and repent. The conviction brought upon the multitudes at this time will be beyond comprehension, since their sentence will be immediately carried out.[106] Those-- all present--will be cast into the lake of fire. The Lord Jesus, the Alpha and Omega, affirmed this: "This is the second death."[107] He is the just Judge.[108] In his reference to the judgment of Sodom and Gomorrah the Apostle Peter, noted the rescue of Lot and the ability of the Lord "to hold the unrighteous for the day of judgment."[109] They will be those who despise God and His authority--all

---

[103] Rev 20:5
[104] Note Paul warning the Romans of all being "under sin" and being "accountable": Rm 3:9-20; Ecc 3:15
[105] Heb 4:12-13
[106] Ecc 8:11
[107] Rev 21:8
[108] Jn 5:30

rebels. He went on to offer the assurance of the word of the Lord to preserve heaven and earth until "the day of judgment and the destruction of ungodly men."[110] Peter's comments briefly inform us that the Lord knows how to "rescue" His own and to "judge" the ungodly at the same time. He in no way alludes to anyone being removed from the earth prior to these simultaneous events. Those who are a part of Israel and have forsaken Him will also be judged.[111] Those who have assumed they were His--using His name--and never turned to Him for life will be judged, while they lament and say: "Lord, Lord, didn't we...."[112] This will all occur quickly.[113] This entire event, beginning with the Second Coming will take these infidels by surprise.[114] As it was in the days of Noah, they will be busy with their own affairs and then were taken away.[115] This day will come upon them while they are unaware of its serious threat. The Lord will come all of a sudden, "in an instant" and be accompanied with "thunder and earthquake and great noise, with windstorm and tempest and flames of devouring fire."[116] This will overtake them "in a moment, in a single day."[117] At this point, it is over for them, unless they have come "to love the truth and be saved"[118] in their last moments. For them, the wicked of all stripes, their next contact with God will be at the great white throne. The pronouncements there are eternal.

3. *Associated judgments.* There are other judgments which expositors identify as separate from the two above. We do not find this valid. Other judgments noted in scripture are related to the judicial acts described above in one way or another. *Israel.* The nation of Israel, past and present, will be accountable. Their heritage is great, and as a people they have a testimony like no other nation on earth.[119] The Lord will judge them according to His former method of

---

[109] 2 Pt 2:9
[110] 2 Pt 3:7
[111] Jer 1:16
[112] Mt 7:21-23
[113] 2 Pt 3:9
[114] 1 Thess 5:1-4
[115] Mt 24:37-39; Lk 17:26-37
[116] Is 29:5-6
[117] Is 47:9
[118] 2 Thess 2:10

calling attention to their failings. In the story offered by Jesus about the rich man and Lazarus, "Father Abraham," told the rich man who was concerned for his brothers: "They have Moses and the Prophets; let them listen to them."[120] Consequently, those Jews who have died prior to the Second Coming, who have rejected God's testimony[121] or Christ, will be judged according to the Law of Moses. They will be considered as unfaithful and be rejected. For those Jews alive at the end of the age, the Lord will use His prophets just as He had used them in the past. He will send two witnesses to be in their midst. This will begin during the tribulation period and continue from the mid-point to the end when "suddenly the Lord you are seeking will come to his temple."[122] During the final forty-two months, all Israelis (Jews) will have the testimony of the Lord's power in their midst. It will be like the days of old when the God of Israel displayed His power in full view of His people. The two witnesses will be in the holy city of Jerusalem in sackcloth prophesying for 1,260 days.[123] They will have power to shut up the sky and bring down fire. The Jewish people will have a prime opportunity to turn to the Lord as they watch this display of power and the witnesses' open opposition to Antichrist and the beast. Christians will be able to relate to this since the New Testament describes this in a number of places.[124] The Jewish people will be required to consider this by faith as they recall the words of the prophets and Moses.[125] The Lord will surely get their attention when the purging of evil begins.[126] Israel will have this time to repent and turn to God or face judgment like all others when Jesus the Messiah appears visibly. The oaths, promises, and covenants made with Abraham, Isaac, and Jacob have not been revoked,[127] and

---

[119] Ps 147:19-20; Dt 7:6; Amos 3:2

[120] Lk 16:29

[121] Eligibility is based on them (Jew or Gentile) coming to God through faith and obedience [Gen 15:6].

[122] Mal 3:1

[123] Rev 11:1ff

[124] Mt 24:15; Rev 11:1-13; Rev 13:1ff; et al. The counterfeit will be at work simultaneously, 2 Thess 2:9-12

[125] Moses or Enoch may be one of the witnesses. Certainly, Elijah [Mal 3:1; 4:5]. [See "The Pitfall of Eagerness."].

[126] Is 1:24-26; Ezek 20:36-37; 33:20; Mal 3:2-5

[127] Rm 11:1, 28-29

each Jew's salvation will be secured in accord with their repentance and acceptance of Jesus as their Messiah and Redeemer. No one comes into the kingdom except through Jesus Christ.[128] It is imperative that men turn to Christ before the door is closed, be they Jew or Gentile. Some commentators indicate Israel will have a separate judgment, however once someone either accepts or rejects Jesus Christ, their future will fall into accord with either of the two judgments above. *Nations*. The nations are groups of people who are aligned politically, culturally, or by their tribal heritage. The roots of the nations can be traced to their beginnings which are noted in Genesis chapter ten. Many alterations have since occurred. Yet, the Lord knows every distinction in their historic bloodline. Broadly, the judgment will cover all mankind. "Nations" indicates that none will be overlooked.[129] The idea of a separate judgment of nations apart from the two primary judgments noted above has been created by those who teach a pre-trib removal of the church and then do not perceive the picture of judgment as described by Jesus in Matthew twenty-five. A careful reading of this portion of the Olivet Discourse shows it to be a parabolic illustration and not a separate event. The Lord uses the term "as" to denote a picture of the separating of people (nations). He says "*as* a shepherd separates the sheep from the goats."[130] This is a simile. It is clear from the previous verse that this happens when He "comes in his glory, and all the angels with him"[131] and is not a separate event. The interpretation of this portion of Matthew is only a difficulty if someone embraces a rapture prior to this. The Lord has previously described this event in Matthew thirteen when the angels come and separate the wicked, and they are burned.[132] We are not sheep or goats. We are men and women and will face this at the Second Coming, both believers and non-believers.[133] *Satan*. The devil and his minions will face severe judgment. This will include demons, fallen angels, the beast out of the sea (Antichrist/man of sin), the second beast (false prophet), and Satan (the dragon). It is very clear that Jesus will exact retribution on them when He

---

[128] Jn 14:6. Note Mt 3:8-9; Rm 2:17-29

[129] Is 34:1-4

[130] Mt 25:32 [emphasis added].

[131] Mt 25:31

[132] Mt 13:40-43

[133] Mt 16:27, the Lord is coming; His reward is with Him, for "each person."

comes at the end of the tribulation period. He does this in conjunction with the various other events which occur in close proximity to each other. As written by Isaiah: "Zion will be redeemed with justice, her penitent ones with righteousness. But rebels and sinners will both be broken together, and those who forsake the Lord will perish."[134] When the Lord comes upon His white horse with the armies of heaven, the final confrontation is at hand.[135] This is the great battle when the kings of the earth are gathered. At this point, "the beast was captured, and with him, the false prophet who had performed the miraculous signs on his behalf."[136] Both were hurled into "the fiery lake of burning sulfur."[137] This is their judgment, swift and sure--at the Second Coming. At this point, an angel descends, seizes the dragon (Satan), and he is bound for a thousand years in the abyss to prevent further deception of the nations.[138] This judgment notably is a portion of the fast-moving activity in the final hours of the present age. There is no need to establish a multiplicity of "judgments" when they all are dependent on the visible return of the Lord in power and glory. It would seem that lists of judgments merely distract from the fact that the Lord returns once and once only at the end of the age.[139] Those who hold to the pre-trib position forcibly encumber the simplicity of the judgments, since they have removed the church some seven years before, thereby creating another resurrection and another judgment. Both alterations are unwarranted and not supported by scripture. When faced with the "first resurrection" in Revelation twenty, they then claim this is for "the Old Testament and Tribulation saints."[140] However, as distorted as their assertion appears, it further supports the single resurrection of the just which is in accord with the word of God. Why? There is only *one* first resurrection and only *one* second resurrection. The first is for those who belong to God and the second is for those who do not. After the first resurrection, the redeemed will have

---

[134] Is 1:27-28
[135] Rev 19:11-16ff
[136] Rev 19:19-20
[137] Rev 19:20
[138] Rev 20:1-3
[139] Heb 9:27-28
[140] Couch, Mal. *Dictionary of Premillennial Theology.* p. 226-227

received their immortal bodies. They will return and walk in Zion.[141] This will be the initiation of the millennial age.[142]

The Second Advent

The Second Coming is the monumental event culminating the end of this age and initiating the next. Significant scriptural particulars should be noted here. This is important because many Christians hold to the "popular view" which is kind to the ears but short on truth. Most believers have never thoroughly examined the Biblical texts to see if it is so. We know the Second Advent will occur, because the Lord Jesus did promise to return.[143] We also know that Jesus and the writers of the New Testament were concerned about false teaching, especially with regard to His return. Jesus expressed a clear warning not to let any man deceive us. Paul warned about false prophecies, letters, and reports which were not genuine. Peter warned about false teachers and those who distort the scriptures. Yet, the scripture is able to speak to us, and Paul said he had not written anything we could not read or understand.[144] So the basics of eschatology are within the reach of most if they read carefully. Also, the Second Coming is only going to happen one way, since God is not the author of confusion.[145] The bottom line? Jesus will return once at the end of the age to bring relief to us and retribution to His foes.[146] In John fourteen, He promised to return. In Acts chapter one, the two men in white gave us assurance He would come back exactly as He left--visibly. Jesus prayed that we not be taken out of the world but would be kept from harm from the evil one.[147] In short order this affirms our presence at the end of the age and the need to be prepared to stand firm to the very end.[148] Believers must also be ready to testify even in the face of hostility and persecution. Knowing that Jesus will come and bring relief from this at the end is the kind of encouragement Paul wrote of.[149]

---

[141] Is 35:8-10
[142] Rev 20:4-6
[143] Mt 16:27; Jn 14:1-3
[144] 2 Cor 1:13
[145] 1 Cor 14:33
[146] 2 Thess 1:5-10; Ps 50:2-6
[147] Jn 17:15
[148] Mt 24:13

During this time, God's righteous remnant will be sealed and protected from retributive acts which are to fall upon the wicked alone. This has been His way in the past as noted by Ezekiel[150] and also by John in the Apocalypse.[151] Paul, also, was confident the Lord will protect His own.[152] The church will be present. As Jesus said: "For it will come upon *all* those who live on the face of the whole earth."[153] When this event starts to unfold, there will be confusion, primarily in those who have been misled by differing views on the end times. There will be great danger from false prophets who will appear and the temptation to listen to them.[154] The church must be vigilant at this time and reject any false notions from men or angels.[155] Deception will be rampant.[156] Relief will come when the Lord arrives. Judgment and rescue will take place at the same time.[157] "At that time those slain by the Lord will be everywhere-- from one end of the earth to the other."[158] The Body of Christ, however, will be safe--forever.[159]

The Event

The time of Jacob's trouble--culminating in the great and terrible day of the Lord--is clearly spoken of in the Old Testament.[160] The scriptures available at the time of Jesus affirmed the facts surrounding this, including Messianic expectations. Israel was the beneficiary of the written word which noted a comprehensive judgment, the hope of resurrection, the kingdom of God being established with the Lord ruling, and that this would be a visible event. As Jesus worked publicly during His first coming, so He will engage the world

---

[149] Mt 5:11-12; Jn 16:33; 1 Thess 4:18
[150] Ezek 9:4-6ff
[151] Rev 9:4-6
[152] 2 Thess 3:3; Phil 1:6; 1 Cor 1:8
[153] Lk 21:35 [emphasis added].
[154] Mt 24:4, 11, 23-27; Jer 23:11-32
[155] 2 Cor 11:4, 13-14; Gal 1:8-9
[156] 2 Thess 2:9-10
[157] Ps 50:2-6
[158] Jer 25:33; 30:7
[159] 1 Thess 4:17
[160] It is also the time for trouble for all the nations--"all who live on the earth"--"all mankind" [Jer 25:30-33] .

and preserve His own faithful ones when He comes the second time. The prophets spoke of these things. The Old Testament is not silent.

Resurrection. Jesus confirmed this in John 11:24-25, "I am the resurrection and the life."

1. [Is 26:19]. "But your dead will live; their bodies will rise."

2. [Ps 71:20-21]. "...you will restore my life again; from the depths of the earth you again bring me up."

3. [Ps 68:20]. "From the sovereign Lord comes escape from death."

4. [Ps 49:15]. "But God will redeem my soul from the grave...."

5. [Ps 86:13]. "You have delivered my soul from the depths of the grave." Also, Ps 56:13

6. [Job 19:25-27]. "...in the end he will stand upon the earth... in my flesh I will see God...."

7. [Dan 12:1-3, 13]. "...a time of distress. Multitudes who sleep in the dust of the earth will awake some to everlasting life, others to shame and everlasting contempt." "...at the end of days you will rise to receive your allotted inheritance."

See also Ps 11:7, "...upright men will see his face;" Is 61:3; Ps 73:24, "...take me into glory." Note the affirming references in the Gospel of John: Jn 5:24; 6:44; 11:24-26, "the last day;" Jn 14:1-3. There is ample proof that there will be a resurrection of the dead. Note Dan 12:2.

Judgment & Gathering at the Same Time. Jesus confirmed this in Matthew 13:37-43; 16:17; 24:30-31; Luke 17:24-35

1. [Ps 50:2-6]. "Our God comes and will not be silent; a fire devours before him...judge his people... Gather to me my consecrated ones...."

2. [Is 26:19-21]. "Go, my people…hide yourselves…until his wrath has passed by." Note Is 24:21-23, "In that day the Lord will punish the powers…the kings on the earth…. The moon will be abashed, the sun ashamed." All this is at the end. There is no pre-trib rapture in view here.

3. [Is 35:4]. "…he will come with vengeance; with divine retribution he will come to save you." Both will be at the same time. Once complete, "only the redeemed" will be present (v.8-10).

4. [Is 61:2b]. "…day of vengeance…comfort all who mourn." Jesus read this portion of Isaiah in his hometown synagogue but cut off His words just short of this [Lk 4:17-19]. Note Heb 9:27-28.

5. [Is 40:5]. "And the glory of the Lord will be revealed, and all mankind together will see it." This event will be visible!

6. [Is 40:10]. "See, his reward is with him, and his recompense accompanies him."

7. [Is 46:4b]. "…I will rescue you." We must wait for Him [Is 30:18].

8. [Is 60:15-22]. "…in its time I will do this swiftly." Note Is 59:20.

9. [Is 63:3-6]. Salvation and wrath are at the same time. Compare to Is 61:2-3

10. [Is 59:14-19]. Salvation and wrath/retribution at the same time.

11. [Zeph 9:14-16]. "…assemble the nations…pour out my wrath…leave within you the meek and humble who trust in the name of the Lord." Note Zeph 2:1-3, "sheltered."

12. [Zech 9:14-16]. "The Lord will appear…shield…save…." This occurs at the end of the age. Read Zechariah chapters 9 through 14 for the full picture of "the Day." See Isaiah 30:5

See also Ps 96:13; Hosea 4:9; Is 24:1-3, it will be alike for judge, priest, and people. Ps 145:17-20, the Lord is near and saves, but "the wicked he will destroy." Further emphasis is found in Ps 33:18-22; 34:17-20; 7:10; 18:30-31.

Note David's assurance: "For in *the* day of trouble he will keep me safe in his dwelling; he will hide me in the shelter of his tabernacle" [Ps 27:5]. David was not speaking of an early removal. The tabernacle here (v.6) is in the city of David. See Ps 31:23, "preserves...pays back." Also, Ps 140:7; 145:20. The compilation of these verses reflects the Lord's determination to bring judgment upon the earth with retribution for the wicked and rescue for his faithful ones. This will occur at the same time. No portion of these verses or others leads to a seven-year gap for any of the peoples mentioned. This holds true in the New Testament, also.

Visible Event. Jesus was pointed in His description of the Second Coming in the Olivet Discourse. He fully answered the disciples' questions about His return and gave them the signs for us to watch for. He said: "Even so, when you *see* all these things, you know that it is near, right at the door."[161] This tells us that all of His words just spoken will be taking place while we are yet here and can verify that it is the end of the age--and that He will return--very soon. This was also confirmed by the two men in white saying Jesus would return just as He left: visibly.

1. [Ps 21:8-10]. "At the time of your appearing you will make them like a fiery furnace."

2. [Is 26:19-21]. "See, the Lord is coming out of his dwelling to punish the people of the earth for their sins."

3. [Is 40:5]. The glory of the Lord will be revealed, and "all mankind together will see it."

4. [Is 52:8]. "When the Lord returns to Zion, they will see it with their own eyes."

5. [Is 66:14-16]. "When you see this...."

6. [Hos 6:3]. "As surely as the sun rises, he will appear, he will come to us...."

---

[161] Mt 24:33 [emphasis added].

7. [Micah 7:7]. "But as for me, I keep watch for the Lord...."

8. [Zeph 3:20]. "At that time I will gather you... I will restore your fortunes before your very eyes."

9. [Zech 9:14ff]. "The Lord will appear...."

10. [Zech 10:7]. "Their children will see it and be joyful."

11. [Zech 12:10]. "The will look upon me, the one they have pierced...."

12. [Mal 3:1-2]. "Then suddenly the Lord you are seeking will come to his temple...." "Who can stand when he appears?"

The visible nature of the Lord's appearing and His judgments cannot be disputed. It will be visible and observed globally, yet with a special emphasis on Zion. This is "the day of the Lord" as described by Joel and preached by Peter.[162] As those in Jerusalem saw the working of the Holy Spirit at Pentecost, so shall men see "wonders in the heaven above and signs on the earth below." This will be seen before the great day of the Lord. It will all be visible.

The Wicked at Judgment

The wicked will not survive the judgment which is to come upon the earth. Though, pre-trib teachers insist there will be people in the millennium in their natural bodies, this is impossible. No flesh will survive the fiery judgment to come.[163] Only those who belong to God will be able to stand through it until changed "in the twinkling of an eye, at the last trumpet."[164] Those who have died in faith will be resurrected at this time.[165] All others will come under the penalty for sin which is death, and as reprobates will face the second death. All the wicked will be taken away never to be seen again.[166] Consider the following:

---

[162] Joel 2:1-2, 29-30; Acts 2:16-21
[163] 1 Cor 15:50
[164] 1 Cor 15:52
[165] 1 Thess 4:16-17
[166] Pr 24:19-20; Ps 37:10

1. [Lk 17:24-37]. *Noah and Lot*. Examples are given using "Noah and Lot" as signs to represent men and their activity at the end of the age. Often a pre-trib teacher will apply Noah and Lot as types of the rapture since both were taken out of harm's way. Yet, the illustration used by Jesus focuses on the wicked--and them being taken for judgment. Rapture is not the point of the Lord's teaching in the least. We are called, though, to be mindful of the degeneration of the culture around us as it becomes more and more perverse. The people described are evil and debauched having rejected God's standard for living on the earth at this time. For many, much will appear normal, since the new, lower standard is tolerated by all but the elect remnant. When God's judgment does come, the wicked are all taken in judgment and removed. The Lord destroys them all.[167] In the example used with Lot, his wife was judged—taken--while Lot and his surviving family were not "taken out" but moved out of the immediate area of danger. They were permitted to reach Zoar which was nearby.[168] In the example in Luke, verses thirty-four and thirty-five, the ones "taken" are going to be judged. The implication is that this will come "as a thief" to those who are not prepared.[169] As Paul the Apostle noted, we are "children of the light" and this should be understood by us. Those who take these examples to heart will not be taken by surprise at the end of the age. The Lord's use of Noah contains the same warning. The people in Noah's day did not take his words seriously. They were eating, drinking, and carrying on as if no danger existed and were ignoring God's messenger. Then, they were all taken in judgment.[170] Jesus remarked that it would be like this when He returns: when He comes, the wicked will be destroyed and the righteous will be spared and preserved.

2. [Prov 10:25}. *The Wicked are Gone*. Solomon looked forward to the final day at the end of the age when all of the wicked will be held to account. Judgment might seem fitting when the corruption is first noticed, but God has His purposes and leaves time for many to repent. He also wants there to be no sense of haste when He brings down His right hand to judge.[171] Solomon was

---

[167] Ps 73:27; 145:20; Zech 12:9
[168] Gen 19:16-23
[169] Rev 16:15; 2 Pt 3:10-14; 1 Thess 5:4-5
[170] Gen 7:4-13, 21-23

clear, that "when the storm has swept by, the wicked are gone, but the righteous stand firm forever." He anticipated the fulfillment of all the promises from the Lord made to his father, David. The psalms which David penned are replete with examples. In Psalm thirty-four, David wrote: "...the face of the Lord is against those who do evil, to cut off the memory of them from the earth."[172] In Psalm thirty-four, he wrote: "A little while, and the wicked will be no more; though you look for them, they will not be found."[173] David affirmed this later in the same psalm: "But all sinners will be destroyed; the future of the wicked will be cut off."[174] He later wrote in Psalm fifty-eight: "Before your pots can feel the heat of the thorns--whether they be green or dry--the wicked will be swept away."[175] What is the conclusion? The wicked will "vanish like smoke."[176] David and other Old Testament writers pronounced the same truth.[177] This reinforces two facts. First, the Lord will judge thoroughly at the end of the age; second, He will remove all of the wicked. None will be left. This in itself sets aside any notion of unsaved men entering the millennium in their natural bodies. Only the righteous will survive this judgment.

3. [Mt 13:36-43]. *The Parable of the Weeds*. The Lord explained this parable early in His ministry. The simple picture shows the weeds and the wheat growing together. The illustration emphasized them both growing together until the harvest. Jesus explained this to His men. First, the harvest "is at the end of the age." There is no hint here about an earlier harvest. Just one is taught. We are told that the enemy, the devil, has corrupted the harvest. Jesus states "the harvesters are the angels." He, the Son of Man, will send out the angels to harvest. They will weed out "everything that causes sin and all who do evil." It is a simple picture, distorted by some, but clearly all the wicked will

---

[171] Gen 15:16; Rev 14:15, 18

[172] Ps 34:16

[173] Ps 37:10

[174] Ps 37:38

[175] Ps 58:9

[176] Ps 37:20. Note, also, Ps 73:19, "How suddenly they are destroyed, completely swept away by terrors!"

[177] Ps 1:4-5; 9:5; 11:6; 21:9-10; 73:18-19; 75:8; 91:7-8; Pr 14:11; 16:4; Is 1:28; 13:9; 14:20; 29:20; 33:18-19; 65:15; Jer 25:30-31, 33; Zeph 1:2, 7-9, 18; 3:6-12; Zech 9:7; 14:12, 21, etc.

be removed at the end of the age. They will be thrown into "the fiery furnace" for eternity. Then, "the righteous will shine." This is a description of the Second Coming when the Lord returns and sends wrath upon the wicked. The Lord repeated the intent of this lesson in the same discourse in the Parable of the Net. The outcome is the same. The righteous are redeemed and the wicked are judged. The evildoers will face an eternity without God, the One they rejected while alive. Those who are the Lord's people will be with Him forever. Jesus describes one event here and not one divided into two, years apart. The separation and subsequent judgment will be final with no option for an appeal. The wicked will be gone.

4. [Ps 1:4-5]. ***The Wicked Will Not Stand in the Judgment.*** The writer of this psalm sets the tone for the path of the righteous and that of the wicked. One follows the words of the law, the counsel of God. The other follows the advice and influence of the wicked that produced sinners and mockers. These are the enemies of God. The righteous man is rewarded by his study and meditation on God's word and is promised a blessing. The wicked seize their rewards while continuing their madness. The disposition of the wicked is clear: they are "like chaff that the wind blows away." Further, they "will not stand in the judgment." As sinners, they will not be "in the assembly of the righteous." These two verses tell us that when the corporate body of those who revere God and belong to Him is brought together, the wicked will not be present, having failed to measure up to God's standard. When the righteous elect are assembled, the wicked will have been removed. This takes place at one time when the Lord's righteous dead are raised and living believers are changed putting on immortality.[178] The wicked are gone but will reappear at the great white throne judgment--accountable and sentenced for what they had done.[179] As the psalmist says, "the Lord watches over the righteous, but the way of the wicked will perish." It is plain from this first psalm that the unrepentant foes of God will never enter His kingdom. They will be judged for all eternity.[180] This

---

[178] 1 Cor 15:53-54; 1 Thess 4:16-17
[179] Rev 20:12
[180] Rev 21:8

affirms the fact that only the righteous will be eligible to be in the millennial age.

Note also the orderliness exacted in the judgment of God's people described by Ezekiel in his chapter nine.[181] This portion of the prophet's words shows that God does judge His people. First, the faithful are dealt with (those who grieve and lament, v.4) by the guards of the city. They are marked and under the Lord's protection.[182] Then, the other guards execute judgment on all who do not have the mark. This mark seals the righteous and protects them while the judgment falls. The judgment begins at "my sanctuary" (v.6) with the elders. Clearly, the outpouring of God's wrath was upon Jerusalem and His people. They were not exempt from wrath. The wicked were dealt with first while those who were truly righteous were protected. This is similar to the Passover when the children of Israel were in Egypt preparing to leave. In other words, the Lord well knows how to deal with the wicked and at the same time protect His own who belong to Him. All were present when this occurred. As recorded in principle by Zechariah, "those who are left belong to our God...."[183] Consider, too, Psalm five, "the arrogant cannot stand in your presence...."[184] This warning was issued to Israel directly.[185] All men must heed the Lord's disdain for human pride.[186] It precedes destruction and will be in full bloom at the end of the age.[187] David answered the question in Psalm twenty-four: "Who may ascend the hill of the Lord? Who may stand in his holy place? He who has clean hands and a pure heart, who does not lift up his soul to an idol or swear by what is false."[188] David's words were not just for his day. They are akin to the Lord's words: "Blessed are the pure in heart, for they will see God."[189] There is a distinction between the righteous and the wicked, seen clearly by the

---

[181] Ezek 9:1-11
[182] *e.g.*, the Passover when the Israelites were protected as the Lord struck down the firstborn of Egypt [Gen 12:1-30].
[183] Zech 9:7
[184] Ps 5:5
[185] Is 2:11-18
[186] Pr 8:13
[187] Pr 16:18
[188] Ps 24:3-4
[189] Mt 5:8

Lord now, but obvious to all at the end of the age when the wicked are gone. David inscribed the Lord's words promising the future for the blameless: His eyes are on them, "the faithful in the land, that they may dwell with me; he whose walk is blameless will minister to me."[190] All others will be "brought down when they are punished."[191] These are the ones today who have no shame and claim there is "peace" when there is no peace. The Lord will "sweep them away."[192] All the wicked will be eternally punished.[193] "You will see the arrogant no more."[194] It will be quick.[195] Scripture is clear that the wicked will be judged completely, and none will survive.

Additional Thoughts on the Second Advent

Many of the scripture references above are from the Old Testament. This is foundational for interpreting what the New Testament writers preserved for us. It also helps us to understand the firm position the Lord Jesus espoused when He dealt with this topic. As suggested above, it will be helpful to review the scriptures that follow with an open Bible.

The return of Christ is an essential component of our faith. We almost take this teaching for granted without investigating the texts involved or their context. Many Christians just accept what they hear, especially if the source is a well-known personality. It is better to question as the Bereans did than to be misguided and drawn into error. Scripture itself will bear witness to itself. Christians must examine texts that are important, especially regarding the Second Coming.

1. [Acts 1:9-11]. The two men in white indicate the Apostles were looking "intently up into the sky" as Jesus was "taken up before their very *eyes*." This tells us that they were eyewitnesses. They saw this take place. The two men then said, "This same Jesus will come back in *the same way* you have seen him

---

[190] Ps 101:7
[191] Jer 8:11-12
[192] Hos 4:19
[193] See Pr 21:7; Is 13:11; 17:14
[194] Is 33:19
[195] Mal 3:5

go into heaven." The importance denoted is Jesus' return will be just alike: visible. As there was eyewitness exposure at His ascension, so there will be eyewitness exposure at His return. It will *not* be secret or invisible. Note Rev 1:7, "every eye will see Him" and "He is coming in the clouds." Isaiah confirmed, they "will see the salvation of our God."[196]

2. [Acts 2:14-21]. Peter preaches and explains the "tongues" on the Day of Pentecost. In the process, he confirms Joel's prophetic words in which the Lord promises to pour out His Spirit on His servants in the last days. Peter, also, confirmed that the Lord will "show wonders in the heaven above and signs on the earth below, blood and fire and billows of smoke." Further: the "sun will be turned to darkness and the moon to blood before the coming of the great and glorious day of the Lord." All at that time will be saved, if they call on His name. This occurs *before* the "delusion"[197] after which no one can be saved. The Lord's servants are present at this time and will see the coming of the Lord. According to Joel and Peter no one leaves early.

3. [Acts 3:19-21]. Jesus must remain in heaven until "the time comes for God to restore everything." He *cannot* return before Elijah comes to restore all things.[198] The Lord confirmed that Elijah must come *first*.[199] He comes to prepare the way for the Lord. Then, the Lord will "come to his temple."[200] Since most evangelical teachers agree that Elijah is one of the two witnesses, there should be no controversy as to when the Lord actually returns. He will come after Elijah and not before which excludes a pre-trib rapture. When Elijah appears, he will restore the testimony of the living God before the people by speaking the Truth. He will call men to repent much as he did ages before when he called the people to choose either Baal or God.[201] This time, it will be a choice between the Antichrist and the Lord who is soon to appear.[202] Elijah

---

[196] Is 52:8
[197] 2 Thess 2:11-12
[198] Mt 17:11
[199] Mk 9:12; Mal 4:5-6
[200] Mal 3:1
[201] 1 Kings 18:21
[202] Rev 11:3ff

and his companion will be able to send fire on the opposition and close up the sky. Once, Elijah was called the "troubler of Israel." In the future, he will trouble every people, tribe, language, and nation. All of this takes place before the Second Coming--before "that great and dreadful day of the Lord comes." He will turn hearts of the fathers to their children and the children to their fathers.[203] Jesus will remain in His heavenly place at the throne until Elijah finishes his work.[204] Then, Jesus will commence His final battle against evil and rescue His faithful ones.

4. [Acts 10:42]. Peter, an eyewitness, as were the others of the Twelve, provides testimony that Jesus is the one "appointed as judge of the living and the dead." This confirms Jesus' words that the Father had given Him "authority to judge because he is the Son of Man."[205] Paul, also, gave assurance that Jesus is "the Lord of both the living and the dead."[206] These brief, simple words tell us that the disciples knew what Jesus meant when He spoke of judgment. They looked forward to the time when this would take place without any false notion of departing early.

5. [Acts 17:30-31]. Paul preached in Athens and introduced the philosophers there to God's claim on them. They knew not the living God. Paul informed them, they must repent. He announced that God has "set *a day* when he will judge the world with justice by the man he has appointed. He has given proof of this to all men by raising him from the dead." These learned men knew nothing of resurrection and less about being accountable to the God who created man.[207] Paul alerted them as Gentiles, just as Peter had proclaimed this to the friends of the centurion, Cornelius.[208] The message was simple: repent of your sin, Jesus is coming to judge.

6. [Acts 24:25]. Paul, who was held under guard in Caesarea, presented his defense to the court. Felix, the governor, heard his response to his accusers. In

---

[203] Mal 4:5-6
[204] Rev 1:4-5; 19:11ff
[205] Jn 5:27
[206] Rm 14:9
[207] Acts 17:24ff
[208] Acts 10:34-43

a few days, Paul spoke again about the charges against him with Felix and his wife, Drusilla. They now heard distinctly about Paul's faith in Jesus Christ. He discoursed on "righteousness, self-control and *the judgment* to come." This sent fear into Felix, since judgment was an ominous consideration, and he was well acquainted with the teachings of these early believers.[209] The judgment to come was the core of the message from Paul and not a rapture. He had previously reminded Felix of the resurrection and the implications of it. Note that the encounter was focused on resurrection and judgment, not resurrection and rapture. The resurrection is our hope. Some believers hope to obtain "a better resurrection" with no concern about a departure prior to the Second Coming.[210]

7. [Rm 2:5]. The unrepentant will be judged on "*the day* of God's wrath, when his righteous judgment will be revealed." This is the same day Paul mentioned in Acts seventeen, and it will be a visible event. Believers will participate in the judgment.[211] This happens "on the day of the Lord" and not before.[212] On that very same day a believer's work "will be shown for what it is, because the Day will bring it to light." [213] No one has departed prior to this which confirms that the *bema* seat judgment[214] only occurs at the Second Coming and not before.

8. [Rm 2:16]. They will be judged on the day [Rm 14:12].

9. [Rm 8:17-25]. We wait for "the sons of God to be revealed" (wheat and tares will be together at the end of the age, Mt 13:30, 39-40), when He is revealed in His glory.[215] These events all coincide at the end of the age. We wait eagerly (v.23) and patiently (v.25)--sharing in His suffering first (v.18) before the "redemption of our bodies" (v23). This takes place when the Lord returns in glory--not before.

---

[209] Acts 25:22
[210] Heb 11:35
[211] 1 Cor 6:2-3
[212] 1 Cor 5:5
[213] 1 Cor 3:13
[214] See above: "The bema seat judgment."
[215] Mt 25:31-32

10. [Rm 9:28]. The Lord will come quickly[216] and "carry out his sentence" [Rev 22:20; Acts 17:30-31]. The day is set--not spread out over seven years. "I will do this swiftly."[217]

11. [Rm 11:7]. The "elect" is not Israel. What they sought, they did not obtain—"the elect did." All Israel will not be saved--only the remnant.[218] They *must* believe.[219] As Paul noted, "not all who are descended from Israel are Israel."[220] Likewise, there is controversy over who is--and who is not--"the elect." The "elect" are those Christ has chosen.[221] This stands against any notion of universalism. The Lord has made the choice.[222] All who are alive and remain when the Lord descends must believe, whether Jew or Gentile.[223] When combined, they are the complete Body of Christ--the true elect of all the ages.[224] As Paul wrote, the "full number of gentiles must come in."[225] These, all together, are the saints of the Most High. They "will receive the kingdom and will possess it forever--yes, for ever and ever."[226] All others will face the second death.

12. [Rm 13:11-14]. Paul says to "wake up." Many were asleep and not thinking clearly about the salvation to come. He wrote: "our salvation is nearer now." This aligns with the statement in Hebrews: Jesus "will appear a second time...to bring salvation to those who are waiting for him."[227] The "night" that Paul reminds the Roman saints of is the perilous time before the Lords's coming (*parousia*).[228] He also calls them to: "clothe themselves with the Lord

---

[216] Is 60:22
[217] Is 60:15-22
[218] Rm 9:27. Paul expounds on this in Romans 11:1-32, defining "Israel."
[219] Jn 14:6
[220] Rm 9:6
[221] Mk 13:20
[222] Rm 9:15; Jn 15:16; Eph 4:1-6
[223] Rm 11:23; Gal 3:29
[224] Dan 12:1-2; Eph 3:6
[225] Rm 11:25
[226] Dan 7:18
[227] Heb 9:28
[228] See discussion on *parousia* elsewhere in this book. *para* = with; *ousia* = being— being with.

Jesus Christ," because "the day is almost here."[229] This is like Paul's call to "put on the full armor of God, so that when *the day* of evil comes, you may be able to stand your ground."[230] There is no suggestion in either letter for these believers to expect a rapture prior to the Lord's return.

13. [1 Cor 1:7-8]. We "eagerly wait for our Lord Jesus Christ to be revealed." Paul assures the Corinthians that the Lord is going to come. In the meantime, He "will keep you strong to *the end*, so that you will be blameless on *the day* of our Lord Jesus Christ." If Paul had notions of a pre-trib event, he would not have worded this encouragement with the need to be strong to *the end*. He also reminded them, the Lord "is faithful." This occurs at the revelation when He comes in glory, just as He taught His disciples.[231] Paul confirmed this to the Thessalonians[232] and Titus.[233]

14. [1 Cor 3:13]. It will be on "the Day" that the true foundation of "each man's work" will be brought to light. Paul says this "will be revealed with fire." Since the Lord returns in the fire of judgment,[234] this event can only take place at the Second Coming. Paul affirms the judicial nature of this to be at the "appointed time" when "the Lord comes."[235] Again, there is no hint of a separate event removing believers before "the Day."

15. [1 Cor 4:5]. When the Lord comes, He will "bring to light what is hidden in darkness and expose the motives of men's hearts." It will be then that each man (believer) will "receive his praise from God." The broad spectrum here is judgment and praise. Paul distinctly employs the terms, "judge" and "praise." This occurs at the appointed time when the Lord is coming to judge. It will be relief and rescue for Christians and retribution for all others--comfort for the righteous and condemnation for the wicked. [236]

---

229 *cf.* Rm 13:14 and Rm 13:12
230 Eph 6:14 [emphasis added].
231 Mt 16:27
232 1 Thess 5:23-24
233 Titus 2:13
234 Mal 3:2-3
235 1 Cor 4:5
236 1 Cor 3:13; 5:5; Rm 14:12; 2 Cor 5:10

16. [1 Cor 5:5]. Paul, even dealing with a grossly immoral brother in the church, affirms that the sinful nature will "be destroyed" and the man's "spirit saved on the day of the Lord." One is the result of judgment of sin (the flesh) and the other is salvation. Both occur at the same time.

17. [1 Cor 11:26]. Paul has great concerns about the Corinthians' negligence with the Lord's Supper. He rightly berates them for this, since the bread and the cup have eternal significance. The participation in the elements is a participation in the body and blood of Christ.[237] Paul insists that they do this as instituted by the Lord in the upper room "until he comes." The Lord was clear in the upper room that He would "not drink of this fruit of the vine from now on until *that day* when I drink it anew in my Father's kingdom."[238] Luke records that He will not drink it again "until the kingdom of God comes."[239] This upper room announcement tells us that only after the Second Coming, when all disciples and all of God's people are assembled, and the kingdom is here on the earth will He take up the cup *with us*. This confirms the church being gathered at the end of the tribulation and excludes the idea that the marriage supper takes place in heaven.[240] It is apparent that Paul connected this directly to the Second Coming and the judgment of the wicked, since he offered his remarks as a caution, so "we will not be condemned with the world."[241]

18. [1 Cor 15:22-24]. Paul briefly outlines the sequence of resurrection. He first designates Christ as "the firstfruits,"[242] since He "was raised on the third day according to the Scriptures,"[243] and He Himself affirmed for us that He is "the resurrection and the life."[244] So, Christ is first in the order, and this is finished. The second part for "those who belong to him" occurs "when he comes."

---

[237] 1 Cor 10:16-17
[238] Mt 26:29 [emphasis added].
[239] Lk 22:18
[240] Rev 19:9. Notice that this announcement is made at the end of the Book of Revelation!
[241] 1 Cor 11:32
[242] 1 Cor 15:20
[243] 1 Cor 15:4
[244] Jn 11:25

"*Then*, the end will come when he hands over the kingdom to God the Father after he has destroyed all dominion, authority and power." This succinct portion of Paul's thoughts on the resurrection to come indicates the Second Coming and our resurrection will happen at the time He comes to destroy all the wicked and every evil authority.[245] This occurs at the last trumpet[246] and will be "at the last day."[247] Paul describes "each in his own turn." There is no consideration in these verses or in the rest of this important chapter on our resurrection that there is an earlier event with a rapture and a resurrection. There is but one first resurrection[248] at the Second Coming and Paul details it here. Charles Hodge in his comments on verse twenty-three affirms just one resurrection. He wrote: "There is no indication of any further division or separation in time in the process of the resurrection. The resurrection of the people of Christ is to take place *at his coming*, 1 Thess. 3, 13. 4, 14-19."[249] Hence, there will be only one coming with one resurrection.

19. [1 Cor 15:50-54]. In continuing his comments on the Gospel and the resurrection, Paul assures us that the dead in Christ will be raised when "the last trumpet sounds." He is very clear that "we all will be changed." At that time, we will "inherit the kingdom." The "dead will be raised imperishable." It will be at the time He comes: the Second Coming, just as described in the earlier verses by Paul.[250] There are not two events alluded to in this chapter. Paul denotes one Second Coming and one resurrection when we will be changed and put on immortality. The entire chapter fifteen leads to this single event and the conclusion that this all occurs "when he comes." Verses twenty-two through twenty-four inform us what happens when He comes, and verses fifty through fifty-seven tell us what will happen *to us* when He comes. Jesus does not return before the last trumpet which according to Paul is when the

---

[245] Ps 2:10-12; 97:3. See comments on judgment above.

[246] 1 Cor 15:52; Rev 10:7; 11:15-18

[247] Jn 6:44; Mt 24:30-31; Dan 12:1-2

[248] Rev 20:5-6

[249] Hodge, Charles. *Commentary on the First Epistle to the Corinthians*. 1857. rpt. Grand Rapids, MI: Wm. B. Eerdmans, 1994. p. 326 [emphasis in the original].

[250] 1 Cor 15:22-24

resurrection and rapture take place.[251] There are no multiple events. All are to occur once, at the last trumpet.

20. [1 Cor 15:54-57]. Here, the pronouncement of victory over death is affirmed by Paul. When the Lord said, "It is finished," the proof of His power to conquer death would stand or fall on the discovery of the tomb on the third day. It was empty. He rose. Paul reminds us of our victory over the grave which will be equally affirmed when Christ returns and we receive imperishable bodies. This is why this entire chapter underscores the core of the Gospel and our blessed hope.[252] This portion by Paul also affirms that there will be no more death [Rev 21:4].

21. [2 Cor 5:1-10]. Paul reminds us of our accountability. Believers will appear before the *bema* seat. Also noted is our "heavenly dwelling" (the immortal body) to be received at the time of the resurrection. This is fully guaranteed. The Holy Spirit indwelling, the "deposit," is the proof of the promise from heaven. Paul offers encouragement while we wait for the return of the Lord: we must walk by faith, even as we go through the tribulation period. This is another reason the Holy Spirit is with us and in us, to comfort us while we wait for the "blessed hope."[253]

22. [Gal 1:4]. Paul reminds the Galatians that Christ "gave himself for our sins to rescue us from the present evil age." This is broad and general, yet confirms again that the Lord Jesus will come and rescue us from the gross wickedness of this age. Paul included accountability and judgment when he preached and taught. This is evident as he dealt with Felix and Drusilla. He discoursed "on righteousness, self-control and the judgment to come."[254] Paul, the other apostles, and numerous other disciples would have been uniform regarding judgment and the Second Coming, holding to the same message.[255] None of them expressed thoughts of a two-stage coming.

---

[251] 1 Thess 4:16-17; Ps 50:5
[252] Titus 2:11-14
[253] Titus 2:11-14; Eph 1:11-14
[254] Acts 24:25
[255] 1 Cor 15:11

23. [Gal 5:5]. Paul reminds the Galatians that we *wait*--"we eagerly await through the Holy Spirit the righteousness for which we hope." This echoes his words to the church in Rome: "as we wait eagerly for our adoption as sons, the redemption of our bodies."[256] In both cases, he is seeking the Holy Spirit's increase of patience for these believers. There is no place here for the sense of some kind of imminent pre-trib removal. Otherwise, the church would not need to patiently await the redemption of their bodies which takes place only at the Second Coming.

24. [Gal 6:9]. Paul reminds the believers that "at the proper time we will reap a harvest if we do not give up." Again, there is no hint of a rapture event. The focus is on the "harvest" which occurs at the time of the Second Coming.[257] Those in view here, like us, are called to "stand firm to the end."[258]

25. [Eph 1:14]. The Holy Spirit as the deposit is the guarantee of our inheritance which will be realized fully on the day of our redemption.[259] It is the Holy Spirit who has sealed us for "the day of redemption."[260] Our redemption was secured by the blood of Christ shed on the Cross[261] which will be actualized in its fullness when He comes.[262] This assurance from Paul is the same one provided by Malachi regarding those who are the Lord's "treasured possession." At that time, on that day, "you will again see the distinction between the righteous and the wicked."[263] The words of Paul and Malachi substantiate that there will be just one event at which time the righteous are gathered and the wicked culled out for judgment. Hence, a two-phase adjustment by pre-trib advocates fails. This all occurs together at the last day.

26. [Eph 4:30]. Paul stresses once again the purpose of the sealing by the Spirit which has been done "for the day of redemption." This is *the day* when the

---

[256] Rm 8:23-25
[257] Mt 13:37-39; 24:30-31
[258] Mt 24:13
[259] Rm 8:23; Lk 21:28
[260] Eph 4:30
[261] Gal 3:13-14
[262] Heb 9:27-28
[263] Mal 3:17-18

Lord gathers His people and not before. It occurs when He is "revealed from heaven in blazing fire with his powerful angels."[264] At that time, He brings "relief" from the persecution of Antichrist and judges the wicked.[265] No one is redeemed until the Lord comes with His Holy angels and delivers us from the devices of the wicked and delivers them over for destruction. This is one event.

27. [Eph 6:13]. Paul draws our attention to "the full armor of God." He reminds believers twice of the need to put on God's armor in this chapter. It will be required at this time--the end of this age---in order to stand against all the forces of evil. All the devil's schemes will be unleashed. The church will need supernatural armor to stand "when *the day* of evil comes." This is not just an "any day" or "every day" caution, though the devil is relentless. This is the end of the age when Satan is playing for keeps using "counterfeit miracles, signs and wonders" and "every sort of evil" is unleashed.[266] The church will be here to see this.[267]

28. [Phil 1:6]. Paul encourages these believers that the Lord who began His work in them would continue to do so and "carry it on to completion until the day of Christ Jesus." This is a direct reference to the day of redemption, the day He brings salvation to those who are waiting.[268] There is no other day when all these events are brought together. Paul's terminology here would differ if that were the case. Instead, he points to the end when Christ returns to complete it all.

29. [Phil 1:10]. Paul, for a second time in his opening remarks, mentions *the day*. He reminds the church here of the importance of insight and discernment which will be much needed when the full program of deception commences during the tribulation. Jesus, too, warned. Paul, especially, wants them "pure and blameless until the day of Christ." At the time "many will turn away from

---

[264] 2 Thess 1:7; 1 Thess 3:13
[265] 2 Thess 1:6-10
[266] 2 Thess 2:9-10
[267] Mt 24:33
[268] Eph 4:30; Heb 9:27-28

the faith and will betray and hate each other."[269] Paul does not want these Christians to slip.

30. [Phil 1:29]. In the course of encouraging these believers, he reminds them to stand and contend for the faith, even if it results in suffering. Paul writes from prison explaining that his own suffering was not to be thought unusual. He tells them they were granted not only to believe on Christ, "but also to suffer for him," with no hint of an imminent return for their relief.

31. [Phil 3:20-21]. Paul reminds the Colossians that they are waiting for the Lord to appear. Their citizenship is in heaven,[270] and He will come from there for those who believe. At that time, by His "power" He will "bring everything under his control" and "transform our bodies so they will be like his glorious body." Paul's words here negate any possibility of two phases of the Lord's return. He says: (1) we are waiting for Him to come; (2) He will bring all things under His control (judgment); (3) transform us. This is the Second Coming and the rapture--one event!

32. [Col 1:28]. Paul emphasizes their need to be strong in the faith and blameless, so when the Lord comes they may be presented to Him "perfect." The Lord will come in glory, raise the dead, and change the living believers into their immortal state. Paul wants all to be perfect, without stain, wrinkle, or blemish when He comes.[271] The Lord said, "Be perfect."[272]

33. [Col 3:4]. When Christ appears--not a secret arrival--but is seen visibly, believers will see His glory. They, too, will be taken up in that glory when He appears. This was a portion of Jesus' prayer in the Gospel of John and His promise in the Olivet Discourse.[273] At that time, we also "will appear with him in glory." This is also the time of God's "wrath," but we are safe.[274]

---

[269] Mt 24:10
[270] 1 Pt 1:4
[271] Eph 5:27; Phil 2:14-16
[272] Mt 5:48
[273] Jn 17:24; Mt 24:30-31; Mk 13:24-27; Lk 21:27-28; Is 40:5
[274] Col 3:7; 1 Thess 4:14, 17

34. [1 Thess 1:9-10]. Paul states that part of our serving "the living and true God" is to "wait for his Son from heaven. We are waiting for the one who will rescue "us from the coming wrath." This is God's wrath (judgment) and not the wrath of men.[275] The context here tells us that we cannot go anywhere until He arrives. In the meantime, the church in the world today faces the wrath of Satan. Just ask Christians in Iraq, Syria, Nigeria, China, North Korea, etc. The devil specializes in all forms of persecution using many devices. Paul notes believers suffering, trial, hardship, persecution, and death. This is not God's wrath but that of man. Paul warned these believers in Thessalonica that they would be persecuted for their faith--but never face the wrath of God. He kept telling them they would be persecuted.[276] When the Lord comes bringing His retribution, "the earth and sky will tremble," but He "will be a refuge for his people" and "a stronghold for the people of Israel."[277] Both judgment and relief will be at the same time.[278] Vengeance and salvation will occur together.[279] Paul says: "the coming wrath." This tells us he was expecting wrath to come from men, and that we would be spared from God's wrath.[280]

35. [1 Thess 2:19]. Paul expected believers to revel in God's glory when He comes. There is no sense here of a departure before we share in His glory. This is not a reference for a secret coming. He will come with the loud command, the voice of the archangel, and the trumpet call.[281] This negates the thought of a quiet affair. The sounds incorporated here resonate with a battlefield rescue. Every eye will see Him.[282]

36. [1 Thess 3:13]. Since Paul taught them of the Second Coming previously and had warned them about the persecution from the evil one, he now asks the Lord to "strengthen their hearts." They will need strength to stand and

---

[275] See discussion on this in the chapter "The Pitfall of Eagerness." Note: Dan 7:21-22, 25; 8:12
[276] 1 Thess 3:4
[277] Joel 3:16
[278] Zech 9:14-16
[279] Is 35:4; 34:2ff
[280] Rm 5:9. The fire of judgment is reserved for God's enemies [Is 26:9-11].
[281] 1 Thess 4:16-17
[282] Rev 1:7

persevere under the Antichrist.[283] Paul reminded them of the source of the strength needed in his second epistle: the Lord "will strengthen you and protect you from the evil one."[284] He encourages them to "be blameless and holy" when the Lord comes. Notably, the two epistles reflect the basic fact that Paul taught them to expect Antichrist. Then, the Lord would come and with Him will come "all his holy ones." Paul made certain that they knew the order: that before our "gathering," the man of sin must be revealed and the rebellion must take place.[285] Then, the Lord will appear with His angels (holy ones) to judge and to retrieve us. No secret event is part of this. Paul does not say the Lord will "come for you--take you out." He says, He "comes with." This is directional. He is coming here from heaven--coming to us--to be with us (*parousia*). This is affirmed by Zechariah that following the "battle" and the great "earthquake," the "Lord my God will come, and all the holy ones with him."[286] Paul confirmed the fullness of this arrival saying "that God will bring with Jesus those who have fallen asleep in him."[287] The scene Paul portrays here is the Lord coming with the angels, then the gathering, and the judgment with angels assisting.[288] No suggestion is found within this context that the church leaves at an earlier time.

37. [1 Thess 4:13-18]. Paul includes in this epistle the comfort these believers need since some of the brethren had "fallen asleep." Their deaths were not from illness or old age. This church was young, and attrition was not a factor. Those who were exposed as Christians and did not recant their faith were executed.[289] Paul reminded them of the hope we have--that we are not to grieve. Our hope is in the resurrection. As Christ rose, we will also be raised-- when He comes. At that time, "we believe that God will bring with Jesus those who have fallen asleep in him." The "we" is Paul, the Thessalonians, and the entire church--all the faithful. The ones Jesus brings with Him are those whose

---

[283] 1 Thess 3:4; 2 Thess 2:1-4
[284] 2 Thess 3:3
[285] 2 Thess 2:1-4
[286] Zech 14:5; Dan 4:17; Is 13:3
[287] 1 Thess 4:14; Col 3:4
[288] See Zech 14:5; Mt 25:31; 24:30-31; 13:41; 13:49; 13:30; Is 13:3
[289] See comments in chapter: "The Danger of Complacency."

spirits were at home with the Lord.[290] This in simple terms indicates He is coming *to* us. At that time, the righteous dead will be raised. This is a needed reinforcement of the order of events with the second Coming, since some men were teaching the resurrection had already taken place,[291] and others said "the day of the Lord had already come."[292] The words here to the Thessalonians agree with the same order that Paul briefly noted to the Corinthians: (1) Christ, the firstfruits; (2) then, when He comes, those who belong to Him; (3) then, the end will come, when He hands over the kingdom to God the Father.[293] This is at the very end of the age when the resurrection occurs for the departed faithful. At this same time, the living faithful will be transformed in the twinkling of an eye. This is the rapture which Paul includes here and is an event concurrent with the Lord's revelation. Paul asserts this is "according to the Lord's own word" which means there is no conflict with his sequence or timing of the events as described by Jesus in the Olivet Discourse. Those of us who are alive and remain after the bloody, ungodly reign of the Antichrist will be caught up after the man of sin and his false prophet oppress and plunder the believers.[294] Paul states we will be caught up "with them in the clouds to meet the Lord in the air." This "meeting" is akin to the disciples going out to meet Paul as he approached Rome when they accompanied him into the city.[295] This is the glorious return, and believers will greet Him, being changed immortal as He approaches. Dean Henry Alford states the "to meet" used here "implies meeting one who was approaching--not merely 'meeting with' a person."[296] Paul describes the Lord's advent: "come down" (v.16), "after that" (v.17), "caught up" (v.17), "meet" (v.17). Then, we are with Him forever. Paul clearly portrays the Lord coming with His holy ones (1 Thess 3:13) to judge (Mt 13:30, 41, 49) and to gather His own at the same time (Ps 50:2-3; Is 13:3, 9-13; Mt 24:31). Never is there a reference to anything other than a single event as

---

[290] 2 Cor 5:6

[291] 2 Tim 2:18

[292] 2 Thess 2:2

[293] 1 Cor 15:22-24

[294] Dan 7:25; 11:33

[295] Acts 28:14-16

[296] Alford, Henry. *The New Testament for English Readers.* Chicago, IL: Moody Press, n.d. p. 1331

described thoroughly in the Old Testament as judgment. The Second Coming will be judgment for the wicked with rescue, relief, redemption, and salvation for the righteous ones of God.

38. [1 Thess 5:1-5]. We, as redeemed believers, "are not in darkness." We have been informed about this return by the Lord Himself and the New Testament writers. But, we must "be alert." Paul wants all Christians to be watching, ready, and blameless. We will need the full armor of God and must stand in "the day of evil."[297] Peter calls believers to "prepare their minds for action" in order to deal with the upheaval prior to the time "when Jesus Christ is revealed."[298] The concern about "times and dates" is only a priority with misinformed date-setters and false prophets. We see them today.

39. [1 Thess 5:9]. The day of the Lord comes "as a thief" to those who are unprepared. In an unregenerate, unrepentant state, they are not aware of the full implications of what is coming. Like those in Noah's day, they will be caught off guard. Paul, Peter, and the others would not issue these warnings if we were not going to be here. While the unsaved are saying (falsely) "peace and safety," this will come upon them. But we are not appointed to suffer God's wrath. He is coming to us to bring salvation. If Paul was looking to remind these Thessalonians that they would be removed prior to the Lord coming as "a thief," he would have written this differently. The Lord comes late in the tribulation period as "a thief" and not in the beginning of the seven years.[299] This portion of chapter five is assuring us that we will be present up until the time of the full "destruction" coming upon the wicked, and then we will receive "salvation."

40. [1 Thess 5:23]. Paul exhorts us to "be kept blameless at the coming of the Lord Jesus Christ." This, once again, is phrased with the picture of us being here until His Second Coming. These believers in Thessalonica were facing heavy, life-threatening persecution and were becoming unsettled. Paul

---

[297] Eph 6:13
[298] I Pt 1:13
[299] Rev 16:15. Note: The Lord does not come twice as a thief. He appears once at the end [Heb 9:28]

encourages them by saying: "the one who calls you is faithful" to keep you blameless until He comes. Those alive at the end of the age will need to understand the fact that the Lord will keep them strong to the end--in the face of massive evil.[300]

41. [2 Thess 1:5-10]. This portion of Paul's second epistle to this church is often overlooked for the simple reason that it does not help the claims of those who insist on a pre-trib rapture. Note that Paul states that at the time the Lord comes in glory, He will "pay back trouble" and "give relief." The Thessalonians were suffering tremendous persecution, and some had been put to death for their faith. The thought of this increasing in intensity was overwhelming. So Paul reminded them that when the Lord comes, they will get relief and not before. He gives a clear picture of the "when." "This will happen when the Lord Jesus is revealed from heaven in blazing fire with his powerful angels." The judgment ("pay back") and "relief" (rescue/rapture) occur at the same time--one event. He will "punish" (v.8) those who are disobedient with "everlasting destruction" (v.4) "on the day he comes to be glorified in his holy people and to be marveled at among all those who have believed. This includes you, because you believed our testimony to you." Note the pronouns Paul employs. The "you" is the church he writes to. They are not going anywhere until the Lord comes in glory. If Paul meant some alternate option for the church, he would have written this in another way. They knew from his teaching in person that they would be exempt from judgment.[301] Now they have a reminder of "when" it will take place--when the Lord comes in glory. Paul also uses the pronoun "us" which clarifies the larger issue of Paul's expectations regarding who will be present when the Lord comes to judge. His use of "us" is ample proof that Paul expected to see the Lord return in glory and not be raptured beforehand. Looking to the future, since this event has not yet occurred, it means the church will be present on the earth until the Lord is here in person (*parousia*). Dr. G. Campbell Morgan ably reckoned this event when he commented: "This is the Apocalypse or Unveiling aspect of the Parousia or Presence of the Lord, which is to consummate the age commenced

---

[300] 2 Thess 2:9-10; Rev 11:1ff
[301] 2 Thess 2:5; Rm 5:9; Ps 91:1-8

by His first Advent. It will be the Day of the Lord."[302] This is valuable insight, since it can be seen for what it is: the *parousia* (presence) will be occurring at the same time as the unveiling. Dr. Morgan brings these components together just as Paul intended.[303] This event begins at the seventh trumpet when the servants of the Lord are rewarded.[304] There is no seven year separation in any part of Paul's statement. Dr. Charles Erdman wrote: "It is evident that Paul mentions no interval between the time of deliverance and the time of retribution. No period of time elapses. The 'rest' and the 'destruction' follow in quick succession."[305] This is in total agreement with Matthew twenty-four. Note, also, how Paul echoes Zechariah who clearly stated that the Lord will do battle on that day, come to the Mount of Olives, "and all the holy ones with him."[306]

42. [2 Thess 2:1-12]. Paul continues his reminder to these believers about "the coming of our Lord Jesus Christ and our being gathered to him." He proceeds to portray this as a single event, combining His "coming" with "our gathering." The gathering is the rapture, and the coming is the Second Advent, both at the same time. The conjunction "and" links them together as a single subject. He goes on to warn about those who undermine, distort, or falsely teach that "the day of the Lord" has already occurred. This would be contrary to his earlier teaching (v.5) when he was with them. This, of course, would alarm the Thessalonians who had heard Paul teach and knew he was under the authority of the Lord.[307] The fact that Paul tells us that false letters and corrupt reports were circulated lends itself to the need for sound repetition of the genuine return of the Lord in the first chapter. He had been under attack from his own "countrymen"[308] and mentioned some enemies by name: Hymenaeus, Alexander, and Philetus. These foes of the Cross and the false reports being

---

[302] Morgan, G. Campbell. *Searchlights From the Word.* Westwood, NJ: Fleming H. Revell, n.d. p. 354
[303] See "G. Campbell Morgan" in the Appendix.
[304] Rev 11:15-18
[305] Erdman, Charles R. *The Epistles of Paul to the Thessalonians.* Philadelphia, PA: The Westminster Press, 1966. p. 83
[306] Zech 14:3-5
[307] 1 Cor 11:1; Heb 13:17; 1 Cor 15:11
[308] 2 Cor 11:26

circulated caused trouble for the early church.[309] Hence, Paul reinforced the Second Coming (some said the Lord's day was past, v.2) by asserting that two things must happen first: (1) the rebellion must occur; (2) the man of sin must be revealed. Since the last days will be filled with deception, just as the Lord warned,[310] Paul was emphatic that the church would see the Antichrist defile the temple, and he would proclaim "himself to be God." They would also see the rebellion which would be caused by this since the Antichrist will be empowered by Satan. The devil is thought to be a myth by many people. At this point, the veil is removed. The synopsis of the chapter is simple: first, Antichrist, then Christ (v.3). The "rebellion" and the revelation of the "man of sin" are closely related events. Paul had told them this. They needed a reminder. This letter accomplished that for them and serves the same purpose for us. John the Apostle, also, warned that the Antichrist was coming.[311] If the man of sin was not a threat to the church at that time--or yet to come--why did Jesus and the apostles warn us? We will see him. Paul said: "Don't let anyone deceive you in any way...." This is sound advice. Those who do not expect to see the Antichrist are under this deception. Remember Jesus' words![312] Paul reminded the church that the "man of sin" was being held back until "the proper time." They knew that lawlessness was "already at work."[313] Their trials, persecution, and deaths had already begun. At the proper time, "the one who holds it back will continue to do so until he is taken out of the way." This indicates an increase in lawlessness. There is much discussion as to who the "he" is. Many have offered the identity of the restrainer. However, no revelation of the man of sin can occur until the Lord permits. As Daniel noted, "it will still come at the appointed time."[314] The beginning and end of this final

---

[309] Mt 28:12-15; Titus 1:10-11; 1 Tim 1:3-4; Phil 3:18

[310] Mt 24:4, etc.

[311] 1 Jn 2:18

[312] Mt 24:15, 33

[313] Paul wrote the "secret power" or "mystery" of lawlessness was already at work, yet being restrained. G. Campbell Morgan noted: "The context shows that he was looking forward to the day of the Lord at the consummation of the present age, to the Parousia, or Presence of Christ, and especially to the Apocalypse aspect of it, in which the 'Man of sin' having also been revealed, should be slain." Morgan. *Searchlights*. p. 355

[314] Dan 11:35

period had a time set by God. We are called to watch for those events provided for us in scripture. A. J. Gordon remarked on the appearance of Antichrist: "He has his *Parousia* and his Apocalypse--his coming and revelation--as does the Christ."[315] The one who restrains is in control of that right now. Otherwise, all these events would be occurring in our sight, and the earth would be flooded with calamitous events. They are not, but they will come at the appointed time. The ultimate restrainer is God Himself. He holds the foundations of the earth together and its pillars firm.[316] When the Lord gives the approval, all the final events will come upon us with no human force able to prevent them or bring them to a halt. Some erroneous views on the restrainer have been: (1) the Church--not possible, it is lukewarm, tolerant, and has been warned in Revelation two and three; (2) government--not restraining now; has no record of success with famine or war; an unlikely choice based on some early interpretations which identified the Roman Empire as maintaining order, *Pax Romana*; (3) the Holy Spirit--cannot be removed or all mankind would perish. As stated in Job: "If it were his intention and he withdrew his spirit and breath, all mankind would perish together and man would return to the dust."[317] Other views see Michael as the restrainer or angels.[318] However, all of the choices come under the authority of the Creator which leaves men, the angels, and every earthly institution without power to initiate or alter any part of what is coming.[319] It can only commence when the seals in the Book of Revelation are opened. Nothing can proceed until the scroll begins to unfold--not a single portion of the final phase can begin. There is only one who is worthy: the Lord Jesus: "the Lion of the Tribe of Judah."[320] Once each of the seals is opened, the events described in the scroll will begin and proceed in order. This includes the hand of restraint against evil withdrawn so the man of sin can be revealed. No man can do any of this. The proof is in the multitude of false identifications of the Antichrist through the ages. Nevertheless, the church will see it all until the

---

[315] Gordon, A. J. *Ecce Venit. Behold He Cometh.* Chicago, IL: Fleming H. Revell Co., 1889. p. 115
[316] Ps 75:3
[317] Job 34:14-15
[318] Dan 12:1; Rev 7:1
[319] Is 46:10
[320] Rev 5:1-5

Lord's arrival. We are called to "stand firm and hold to the teachings" passed on to us from Paul and the other New Testament writers--not modern-day theories. Those who will not repent at the last hours will be facing "delusion" and be swept away.[321] They will have rejected the truth of the gospel preached at that time[322] and the testimony of the two witnesses.[323] They "will believe the lie." This portion of Paul's letter is often misunderstood. The lie is not explained, since pre-trib advocates think it is not for them. The lie will be large, just as it was in the Garden of Eden.[324] This is Satan's last chance at deception. His own love it.[325] This is his work and will be accompanied by "every sort of evil." At the proper time, God will send delusion on them to seal their fate. Then, they are condemned for all eternity. At this time, the Lord "will appear over them, his arrow will flash like lightning. The sovereign Lord will sound the trumpet."[326] Then, we will be changed and join the heavenly host coming to the earth.

43. [2 Thess 3:3]. Paul assures the Thessalonians that they will be protected when the man of sin appears. "The Lord...will strengthen and protect you from the evil one." When the Antichrist is revealed and comes on the scene, divine protection will be provided. Peter notes that we "are shielded by God's power" until the Lord is revealed.[327] Jesus previously prayed that we would be kept from the evil one.[328] Paul gave the same assurance to the Corinthians: "He will keep you strong to the end."[329]

44. [2 Thess 3:6]. Paul is not only warning about idleness. He is repeating his warning to stay away from those who do not hold to his teaching about the Second Coming. He already warned them about false letters, prophecies, and reports which were being circulated. Now, he stresses the danger of the false

---

[321] Pr 10:25
[322] Mt 24:14
[323] Rev 11:3ff
[324] Gen 3:4, "You will surely not die," the serpent said to the woman.
[325] Jn 8:44-47; Rm 1:25
[326] Zech 9:14
[327] 1 Pt 1:5
[328] Jn 17:15
[329] 1 Cor 1:8

teaching about this doctrine. The brothers must hold to and follow "the instruction in this letter."[330] This is why Paul outlined again the picture of the Lord's coming in chapter one. The church would have heard this letter read to them. They were now obligated to firmly hold to the Second Coming and the rapture occurring after the man of sin was revealed.

45. [1 Tim 4:1]. Paul warns Timothy of the demonic work to surface in the last days. He states some will "abandon the faith and follow deceiving spirits." This aligns with the Lord's ample warning in the Olivet Discourse regarding false Christs and false prophets who "will appear and perform great signs and miracles to deceive even the elect."[331] Truth will be abandoned.[332]

46. [2 Tim 1:10]. Here Timothy is reminded by his mentor and teacher that death has been abolished. Paul says this is "through the gospel" which culminated in the death of Christ who was victorious over the grave. The Gospel includes His return, then our resurrection, which Paul elaborated in 1 Corinthians fifteen. Death has lost its sting. Paul tells Timothy it has been "destroyed." This will be reality at the Second Coming and not before.

47. [2 Tim 3:1]. Paul warns of terrible times in the last days. It will increase and worsen. The imposters "will have a form of godliness," but they will be exposed by those who know Truth. The church will be here on earth to rebuke them and call them to account.

48. [2 Tim 4:1]. Paul now charges Timothy to preach whether convenient or not and fulfill all of his duties as God's servant (v.2-5). Notice that Paul issues this under the authority of "God and of Christ Jesus, who will judge the living and the dead." Paul states this "in view of his appearing and his kingdom." He is reminding Timothy of the nature of the Lord's return when the kingdom comes and He appears. The two events are one in Paul's mind.

49. [2 Tim 4:8]. Paul maintains the same thought, encouraging Timothy with regard to the "crown of righteousness" to be awarded to him and all others who

---

[330] 2 Thess 3:15
[331] Mt 24:24
[332] 2 Thess 2:9-12

have longed for His appearing. The rewards are to be given when the Lord comes in glory, as recorded by John: "Behold, I am coming soon! My reward is with me, and I will give to everyone according to what he has done."[333] The Lord's appearing will be visible, and His rewards will be passed out then.

50. [Titus 2:13]. Paul reminds Titus of what believers are waiting for: the glorious appearing of the Lord, "our great God and Savior, Jesus Christ." This brief epistle is from one apostle to another. Extra words are not needed. However, Paul is charging Titus to silence false teachers and to "teach what is in accord with sound doctrine."[334] This includes the Second Coming which Paul notes here. In context, the "blessed hope" is "the glorious appearing." The text supports this as does the propensity of other Biblical references.[335] Paul is also reminding Titus that we "wait" for this which sets aside the thought of an anytime, imminent rapture. Isaiah reminds us that "…the Lord is a God of justice. Blessed are all who wait for him!"[336] He will appear in glory!

51. [Heb 3:14]. The admonition, again, is to wait and be patient to the end. We must "hold firmly to the end." This agrees with the Lord's words: "he who stands firm to the end will be saved." [337] No hint is given of an early departure. We must "stand" in "the day of evil.[338]

52. [Heb 6:10-11]. The Lord will not forget the believer's good work. It will be rewarded when He comes. Meanwhile, we must stand firm and "show this same diligence to the very end."

53. [Heb 9:26-28]. As the writer of Hebrews states, He appeared *once* to "do away with sin." In the same way He will appear a "*second* time, not to bear sin, but to bring salvation to those who are waiting for him." The clarity is here: once to deal with sin, and once to bring salvation. This leaves no third option.

---

[333] Rev 22:12
[334] Titus 1:9, 11; 2;1
[335] See comments in "The Blessed Hope" in the chapter "Some Little Words."
[336] Is 30:18
[337] Mt 24:13
[338] Eph 6:11ff

There is only *one* "second time." He will appear, just as it states here. This will be the Second Coming with no intervening removal events.

54. [Heb 10:25]. You will "see the Day approaching." The "Day" is the day of the Lord when He comes to judge the wicked, rescue His saints, and be glorified in them. The approach will be seen and the outcome is sure.[339]

55. [Heb 10:32-38]. The admonition is clear: persevere. The Lord is coming. We must be patient, stand by faith, and not "shrink back." The Lord will not be pleased with those who do not stand firm to the end.[340] We, the faithful, are anticipating the completion of our salvation.[341]

56. [Heb 11:39-40]. The promise here is for all those who belong to God, both the saints under the Old Testament covenant and the saints under the New Testament covenant. This is an echo of the Apostle Paul writing to the Galatians: "If you belong to Christ, then you are Abraham's seed and heirs according to the promise."[342] He repeated this to the Ephesians: "This mystery is that through the gospel the Gentiles are heirs together with Israel, members together of one body, and sharers together in the promise in Christ Jesus."[343] This emphasis on the promise looks to its fulfillment, once, at the end of the age when Christ comes. It does not allow for two separate arrangements, one for Israel/Jews and another for Gentiles. There will be one body gathered and drawn together when the Lord returns. All are His saints. Thus, there is one Second Coming and one body of the faithful. All the faithful will be raised from the dead or changed immortal at the *parousia*. This is a sound refutation of the dispensational program which teaches one plan for Israel and another for the church. There is neither Jew or Gentile once "in Christ."[344]

---

[339] 1 Cor 15:22-13, 51-54; Lk 21:31
[340] Mt 24:13
[341] Heb 9:28
[342] Gal 3:29
[343] Eph 3:6
[344] Gal 3:28

57. [Heb 12:26-28]. The Lord is coming to shake the heavens and the earth. This is the judgment of the wicked and the elements will be destroyed by fire.[345] We will receive the kingdom, and fire will consume His enemies.[346]

58. [Jas 5:7-9]. "The Lord's coming is near." James here warns of the fact of judgment. That is his context. He does not intend to teach imminency with these words. He is reminding "the twelve tribes" who are scattered that they will not escape the Judge of all men. He is standing at the doorway, a pointed admonition to be sound in the faith and not be judged with the wicked.[347] Some of the brethren in the diaspora may not have remembered Ananias and Sapphira who were judged immediately for lying to the Holy Spirit[348] which spread fear through the church. The fear of the Lord is much needed today, since all will face the Judge. James says be patient until He comes.

59. [1 Pt 1:5]. Peter is writing plainly: we are "shielded by God's power until the coming of the salvation to be revealed in the last time." This occurs at the Second Coming and not before. It is a one-time event.[349] This apostle is looking to the day "when Jesus Christ is revealed" and not a prior event, *i.e.* a pre-trib rapture.[350] His wording agrees with Paul and Jesus. Peter acknowledges their suffering and trials while pointing to the time of relief when the Lord Jesus comes.[351] This will be a time of testing for God's people.[352] Yet, we will be preserved--safe in His hand.[353]

60. [1 Pt 1:7]. Peter points to the day "when Jesus Christ is revealed." This tells us that the Second Coming will be visible, a confirmation of the two witnesses in Acts who said the Lord will return in the same way he left--visibly.

---

[345] Mt 24:29; 2 Pt 3:10
[346] Mt 24:30-31; Heb 10:27; 12:28
[347] Jas 5:12
[348] Acts 5:1-11
[349] Heb 9:26-28
[350] 1 Pt 1:7
[351] 1 Pt 1:6; 2 Thess 2:3
[352] Dan 11:35; Is 48:10-11; Lk 8:13
[353] Jn 10:29-30; Pr 2:7-8; 2 Thess 3:3; Is 54:14; Ps 91:7-8

61. [1 Pt 1:13]. Peter directs believers to "prepare" their minds for action. This will be necessary at the time of Antichrist when Satan's powers are unleashed. This apostle again points to the time "when Jesus Christ is revealed" and not some previous event. He refers to the Second Advent when the Lord returns to fully establish His kingdom.

62. [1 Pt 2:12]. Peter echoes James calling for believers to live "good lives" and continue to do this until the Day of the Lord. This will be a time of glory "on the day he visits us." There is no hint from Peter that anyone leaves prior to the Day of the Lord.

63. [1 Pt 4:5]. Peter affirms that the Lord is "ready to judge the living and the dead." This is an agreement with James' admonition about the Judge standing at the door. Neither of these men alluded to an earlier removal. They are looking for Jesus' return to judge the wicked.

64. [1 Pt 4:7]. "The end of all things is near." Believers--"you"--will need a "clear mind" to deal with these events and to continue to pray. Believers will be there and will need "self-control."

65. [1 Pt 4:13]. Peter, like Paul, knew that the church was suffering great persecution.[354] This apostle related the church's trials and the death of believers to be akin to "the sufferings of Christ." He encouraged each of them as this was occurring so "you may be overjoyed when his glory is revealed." This is to raise their spirits until the appearing--the Second Advent. This affirms suffering first and then his glory to be revealed. This will be visible.

66. [1 Pt 4:17]. Peter affirms that judgment begins with us--the family of God. This lays out the two aspects of the Lord's return: He is coming to judge; it "begins with us" who will be here.[355]

67. [1 Pt 5:1]. His glory will be revealed. It will be visible--not a secret coming at all.

---

[354] This is noted by Paul throughout 1 and 2 Thessalonians.
[355] Ezek 9:6

68. [1 Pt 5:4]. Peter states: the "Chief Shepherd" will appear. It will be visible, and each believer will receive their "crown of glory" at that time--not some seven years prior.

69. [2 Pt 2:5]. Peter reminds these believers that the Lord protected Noah at the time of the flood. The "ungodly" were judged--taken away--and the righteous were spared and preserved thru it. They were not removed from the calamity-- just protected, like Lot, who was rescued and not raptured. The Lord surely knows how to protect His people.[356] This was the case as the nation of Israel was about to leave Egypt. Moses had unleashed multiple plagues, and Pharaoh hardened more and more. The last straw was the death of the firstborn of Egypt. The blood on the lintels and the doorposts protected the whole community of Israel, just as the Lord said. He assured them they would be protected. When He saw the blood, as He said: "I will pass over you. No destructive plague will touch you when I strike Egypt."[357] They were protected through this and not removed from it. The Lord has protected us by the blood of Christ.[358] The Holy Spirit indwelling is our assurance. We are sealed for the day of redemption and are safe forever.[359]

70. [2 Pt 3:4]. "Where is the 'coming' he promised?"[360] Even the last days' "scoffers" will be looking for the promise of His return--noticeable from their mockery. Peter used the word *parousia* here meaning presence, the same word Paul wrote to the Thessalonians when he described the Lord's return and the rapture.[361] These men agree: we will be here until the end.

71. [2 Pt 3:7]. Fire will destroy the heavens and the earth. They are to be judged at the same time as "ungodly men." This parallels David: "At the time of your appearing you will make them like a fiery furnace."[362] The ungodly

---

[356] Ps 91:7-8; Jn 17:15; 2 Pt 2:9
[357] Ex 12:1-13
[358] Rm 5:9
[359] Eph 2:13; 1:13-14
[360] cf. Ezek 12:21-28
[361] 1Thess 4:15-17; Mt 24:3
[362] Ps 21:8-10

will be consumed. They will be destroyed--and their posterity. None will be left. This takes place at His *parousia*--His physical presence--and not before.

72. [2 Pt 3:10-14]. The heavens and earth will be destroyed by fire on the Day of the Lord. Peter says: "you look forward" to this. Christians are to be "looking forward" to this, since the Lord will deliver us at this time, bringing salvation, rescue, and resurrection on that Day. Notice that Peter connected the Old Testament prophets' words regarding the end of the age well before John wrote the Apocalypse. Peter knew all these events coincided at the end. The evidence of this is found in his first message when he quoted the prophet Joel about the last days.[363]

73. [2 Pt 3:15-18]. Peter knew that Paul's teaching on the Second Coming was being distorted. Paul warned about this in his second letter to the Thessalonians.[364] This was a real danger for the apostles, since many enemies of the Cross worked to disqualify the Gospel message. Peter takes a moment to admonish the church to pay close attention to "these matters" and be patient while waiting for the Lord to return. He cautioned that "ignorant and unstable people" are the ones who distort this doctrine. The answer is to "grow in the grace and knowledge of our Lord and Savior Jesus Christ" and not embrace the false teaching from false teachers.[365]

74. [1 Jn 2:18]. John writes plainly: "...you have heard that the antichrist is coming." This apostle agrees with the others--and Jesus--first, the Antichrist will appear--then Jesus comes.

75. [1 Jn 2:26-28]. John cautions about "those who are trying to lead you astray." Peter did the same. John, then, reminds them about their anointing from the Holy Spirit and to rely on that. His encouragement is for all of them to hold to what they heard from the beginning[366] and not be yielding to false promises of avoiding Antichrist. He wants them to be "confident and

---

[363] Acts 2:16-21
[364] 2 Thess 2:1-2
[365] 1 Pt 1:23-25; 2 Pt 1:1-3
[366] 1 Jn 2:24

unashamed before him at his coming" (*parousia*/His presence) when He is revealed. Charles Spurgeon noted John's use of the terms "appears" and "at his coming" to be "the same thing," both referring to "the second advent." He affirmed this to be "the glorious manifestation of our Lord" when "the stars fall like autumn leaves," the sun and moon changed to "darkness" and "blood," when "the graves shall be opened, and the dead shall rise.," This is to be at the time "when the heavens being on fire, shall be dissolved, and the elements shall melt with fervent heat, the earth also, and the works that are therein shall be burned up."[367] These remarks leave no room for an early removal of the church and clearly place the Lord's judgment by fire at the same time He returns in glory at which time all sinners will be destroyed--none will be left.[368]

76. [1 Jn 3:2-3]. John reminds them that Jesus will appear, and we will be like Him. This is the change to immortal that Paul wrote of in 1 Corinthians fifteen. We "shall see him as he is" when He appears and "be like him." This short remark by John follows his warning about the Antichrist. Hence, John expresses simply that the Antichrist will come, and then the Lord Jesus will come. Both Antichrist and Christ will be seen. This agrees with Paul and Jesus.[369]

77. [1 Jn 4:3]. John reminds them again that Antichrist is coming. They saw his spirit already at work.[370] He is going to come in person being "revealed at the proper time."[371]

78. [Jude 14-15]. The Lord is coming with His "holy ones" to "judge everyone." This is the same event Paul mentioned to the Thessalonians when he noted the Lord coming with "all his holy ones."[372] Paul used the word

---

[367] Spurgeon, Charles H. Sermon: "Preparation for the Coming of the Lord." *The Metropolitan Tabernacle Pulpit*. V*ol. XXXV*. 1889. rpt. Pasadena, TX: Pilgrim Publications, 1975. p. 513-514

[368] See chapter "None Will Be Left."

[369] 2 Thess 2:3-4; Mt 24:15, 33

[370] 2 Thess 2:7

[371] 2 Thess 2:6

[372] 1 Thess 3:13: Is 13:3; Zech 14:5

parousia in this context (the Lord's physical presence). Jude also indicated this will be the time of judgment--not a pre-trib event.

79. [Jude 21]. Jude also encouraged believers to remain in God's love as they "wait for the mercy of the Lord Jesus Christ to bring you to eternal life." Jude details examples of God's judgment in this short letter and reminds the Christians we must "wait" for the Lord to be present with us. This is the Second Coming.

80. [Rev 1:7]. John commences this full account of the revelation of the Lord with an emphatic reminder that this will be visible. He is pointing out to these seven churches that Jesus Christ will come just as He said in the Olivet Discourse fully displayed in the heavens, in the same manner as He left. This apostle is privileged to not only confirm the Lord's promise to come again but to reinforce the guarantee that "every eye will see him." All those on the earth will be affected by this, even to mourn. John does not allude to any previous removal of the church here or anywhere else in the Book of Revelation. Those that teach the church being removed from this are mistaken and have taken great liberty reading into the text events which John never suggested.[373]

81. [Rev 3:3]. The fifth church warned has a significant issue to deal with. They are asleep. They are told: "If you do not wake up, I will come like a thief, and you will not know what time I will come to you." This is an important admonition. It is informing them that their sleep--willful and open deadness-- will prevent them from knowing when the Lord will come. Jesus was thorough in the Olivet Discourse to tell believers to watch, be ready, and be alert. These people had dozed off into lethargy. Yet, there were still "a few in Sardis" who were alert along with many who were past being drowsy.[374] They are charged to "wake up" and be the individual who "overcomes" what is coming. There would be no need to awaken and be prepared to face what the Apostle John describes soon to come if the church was going to be removed beforehand. All seven of these churches are being called to overcome. This clearly indicates

---

[373] See comments elsewhere in this book regarding particular false claims about a rapture in the Book of Revelation.

[374] Note Mt 25:5

they are being told they will face Antichrist and the tribulation days ahead. Those "who are wise will understand."[375]

82. [Rev 4:1]. This verse calls John to come up. The church is nowhere in the context.[376]

83. [Rev 6:17]. This is the time that the sixth seal of the scroll is opened. At this time, the sun is darkened, the moon is turned to blood, and the stars begin to fall.[377] The kings of the earth, the rich, the powerful, and men at large will seek shelter for fear of what is occurring.[378] This is the foretaste of the great wrath to come when the trumpets are sounded and the bowls are poured out. There is no verse from chapter one to this point which states the church has been removed.

84. [Rev 8:3]. At the time the angels receive their trumpets from God, another angel appears at the altar with a golden censer. He is "given much incense to offer, with the prayers of all the saints, on the golden altar before the throne." This indicates that the prayers of the saints who are still on the earth are to increase as the rampage of Antichrist escalates.[379] This golden altar is the heavenly prototype from which the earthly altar of incense was patterned.[380] From the time of Moses, the altar was to be maintained for generations. Prayers would be offered from the Tabernacle or Temple on earth and received in heaven. The golden altar is where the prayers and petitions are received in heaven from the Lord's people on the earth. The increase of incense at this point in the Book of Revelation indicates the church is yet on the earth. This is a continuance of "the prayers of the saints" which were being honored before the throne of God with the four living creatures and the twenty-four elders.[381] These prayers have been uninterrupted and must not be

---

[375] Dan 12:10; 1 Thess 5:4-6
[376] See our comments on this in the chapter "Some Little Words."
[377] Is 13:9-13; Mt 24:29-31
[378] Ps 1:5; 2:10-12
[379] Rev 13:1ff
[380] Ex 30:1ff
[381] Rev 5:8

confused with the petitions of the martyrs already in heaven. The martyrs' concern is for those who are still on the earth as they call out: "How long, Sovereign Lord, holy and true, until you judge the inhabitants of the earth and avenge our blood?"[382] Here we have the spoken words to reflect on. With the offering of the incense, we have clear evidence of a multitude of prayers of the saints rising to heaven. These two groups must not be mixed up. They are very different: saints/believers/the church on the earth and martyrs in heaven. The martyrs are given white robes and told to "wait a little longer" until the number of martyrs is complete. This confirms the body of Christ is on the earth facing the iron hand of Antichrist who will condemn many to death for their faith. Their prayers will rise to the golden altar until the end when Christ comes.

85. [Rev 10:7]. At this point, events are moving quickly. The "last trumpet" is about to sound. This will unleash the final seven bowls which will complete the judgment, the wrath of God. This angel is about to herald the culmination of all the retributive acts from heaven, at which time the "mystery of God will be accomplished." Believers on earth at this time--the church--will be removed. They will not face the wrath and final judgment of God. Up to this point, they have been protected on the earth by the Lord.[383] Now, those "who are alive and remain" will be taken out of harms' way.[384] This is the mystery that Paul wrote about to the Corinthians when he reminded them of the coming of the Lord. It is at this time the resurrection occurs, since the last of the judgments will destroy all the remaining wicked. The righteous believers will be transformed at the sound of this trumpet, "in a flash, in a twinkling of an eye, at the last trumpet."[385] This is the last trumpet. None follow this. The next judgments, the bowls, eliminate all that is corrupt on the earth. Unrepentant men will not survive. None will be left. They are condemned forever.[386] Death, then, will be swallowed up forever, and Christ will appear in glory.[387]

---

[382] Rev 6:9-11
[383] Jn 17:15
[384] 1 Thess 4:15-17
[385] 1 Cor 15:50-54
[386] 2 Thess 2:11-12
[387] 1 Cor 15:55-57; Mt 24:30-31

86. [Rev 11:15-19]. At the sound of this last trumpet, the announcement is made in heaven that the time for "the kingdom of our Lord and of his Christ" has come. He is about to begin His reign on the earth. The twenty-four elders (not the church) acknowledge this, and that the time has now come for "rewarding your servants the prophets and your saints and those who reverence your name." This tells us that the crowns and accolades have not yet been awarded. The Lord does this when He comes--at the very end--which again refutes the idea that He came earlier for the church.[388] Believers will remain earthbound until the very end of these days and are told to be patient, be alert, be ready, and stand firm. Then, those who belong to the Lord will hear the invitation to "the wedding supper of the Lamb" who is coming quickly to finish His work of eradicating the wicked foes of God.[389] The judging and rewarding of His servants will occur at the same time and not before.[390]

87. [Rev 13:10]. The saints are still on the earth. This is the church preparing for glory.

88. [Rev 18:4]. The Lord's people remain on earth and are about to be taken out: "Come out of her my people." The finality of judgment is impending. The Lord's people are mentioned by name: "saints and apostles and prophets" [Rev 18:20], since the system of "Babylon" has been responsible for "leading the nations astray" and "the blood of the prophets and saints" [Rev 18:24]. Believers continue to be encouraged throughout the tribulation and to the end.

89. [Rev 19:1, 6]. A great multitude is now in heaven joining the martyrs already present. These souls are the remnant of the martyrs and await the marriage supper of the Lamb. They are given the invitation: "Blessed are those who are invited to the wedding supper of the Lamb!"[391] The ones in heaven have now made themselves ready.[392] The Lord's "servants" are noted as now being present--and not before (v.2, 5) indicating they have been on the earth--

---

[388] Rev 22:12-13
[389] Rev 19:9, 11-16
[390] Ps 50:3-6; Is 35:4
[391] Rev 19:9
[392] Rev 19:7

not previously raptured. The marriage supper has not yet occurred since the entire Body of Christ is not yet complete. This will take place as the King of Kings comes to the earth to deliver "the fury of the wrath of God Almighty"[393] and rescue those who remain.[394] This is the Second Coming. This encompasses the resurrection and, then, the millennial reign of Christ.[395]

There are many other important verses in the Book of Revelation which, of course, relate to the eschatological significance of the Second Coming. However, these above, along with the texts which precede them, are sufficient as scriptural evidence to set aside a two-phase return of the Lord.

---

[393] Rev 19:11-16
[394] 1 Thess 4:15-18
[395] Rev 20:5

THE SECOND COMING

The promise for Jesus to return to earth has been established by the Word of God and held as a cardinal doctrine of the church for centuries. This teaching had its formal acceptance and its proclamation at the outset when the Apostles took up the work of preaching and teaching. We see the initial evidence of this in Acts chapter two when Peter even refers to the conditions "before the coming of the great and glorious day of the Lord."[1] The authority to undertake this major effort to preach and teach was given by the Lord Jesus Himself at the time the men were officially commissioned as recorded by Matthew at the end of his gospel.[2] At that time, Jesus included in His commission the promise to also be with them "to the very end of the age."[3] Subsequent to Peter's preaching, the eleven Apostles, and also Matthias, who completed the Twelve, began this work in earnest. They had heard, either together or separately, Jesus speak on a number of occasions of His return to be sometime in the future. Jesus made it clear that the Second Advent would not be like the first. His incarnation was by design a sacrifice, an offering of His body to atone for sin. His return is to be the final judgment of all mankind living or dead.[4] At that future time, the righteous dead will be resurrected[5] if they have passed on, and if alive when Jesus returns, they will be changed in the "twinkling of an eye."[6] Jesus affirmed what the Prophets had said, as He heralded the kingdom during His ministry. There would be no change between their earlier predictions and the statements of Jesus--or the many disciples, now empowered by the Holy Spirit. We can deduce clearly, thus far, that Jesus is going to return. He is going

---

[1] Acts 2:20

[2] Mt 28:18-20; Lk 24:45-49

[3] Mt 28:30

[4] Mt 16:21; 16:27 (Jesus predicts His betrayal, death, and His return in glory); Jn 5:24-25

[5] Jn 5:28-29

[6] 1 Cor 15:51-54

to judge. He will also gather His own at the same time.[7] This will occur at the very end of this age.[8] Jesus emphasized at the outset of His ministry that not one jot or tittle would disappear until "all be fulfilled."[9] All of the New Testament writings concur with and support the validity of the Second Coming in glory.[10] All believers look ahead to this.

As Jesus ministered to the multitudes that came to hear Him, there were a number of teachings which pointed ahead to another advent. Sometimes He would publicly state this, and at other times He would privately explain this event to His disciples. Never did His theme alter. He was doing His Father's work while with them, but later He would come back at the end of time as we know it. In dealing with the Pharisees on one occasion, He made it clear that there was this present age and "the age to come."[11] This idea was known to those under the old covenant, too. We see this summarized in the New Testament book of Hebrews where the Old Testament saints and those of us who have trusted and believed Jesus[12] will share together in the future all that has been promised.[13] As Abraham rejoiced to see Jesus' day,[14] so we also look forward, sharing this hope like all the departed saints whose faith anticipated a glorious day yet to come. Just as the Old Testament saints were given details in Scripture in order to be watchful for their Messiah, so we, too, have been given specifics within various sections of the Bible to watch for Him when He returns. In addition, we can draw from the same source of hope the Old Testament saints placed their faith in, since all of scripture is by inspiration and trustworthy.[15] Part of Jesus' ongoing, open, public testimony was deliberately

---

[7] Mt 24:30-31

[8] Mt 13:40-43; 13:49-50; 16:27; Jn 11:24

[9] Mt 5:17-18

[10] Tit 2:13; 1 Thess 2:19; 3:13; Jas 5:7-9; 1 Pt 1:7, 13

[11] Mt 12:32

[12] Jn 3:3, 5; 17:3; Rm 8:9

[13] Heb 11:39-40; Also, note Paul, Eph 3:6

[14] Jn 8:56

[15] 2 Pt 1:19-21; 2 Tim 3:14-17

set before Israel as a fulfillment of the Prophets. This was tested and affirmed many times as He spoke and performed miracles in order to cause men to believe that His Father had indeed sent Him.[16] The same test runs through the Bible for us, as we examine the New Testament along with the earlier writings in the Old Testament and look ahead to His return. All of Christ's disciples relied on the fullness of Scriptural truth. So must we.[17]

Looking again at Peter who preached openly in Jerusalem in Acts chapter two, we find that he outlined the Second Coming by quoting Joel the Prophet. While Peter was attempting to explain the new phenomena of the various languages, he made clear through Scripture that Jesus' return would not precede the signs in the heavens when the sun would be darkened and the moon turned to blood. Joel, along with many of the prophets, spoke openly about the final judgment of God.[18] Peter also briefly laid this before his audience, reflecting the specific conditions and the sequence of the Lord's return to be without question.[19] Peter said that the heavens would be greatly disturbed first, and then the Lord would return in glory. Later, he affirms this again when writing his epistles to some of the same people he preached to, now back in Asia in various churches. He said that the elements will melt. They will be destroyed by fire. The earth will be completely laid to waste.[20] He echoed the prophets and confirmed it all by his colorful warning that the church would have to anticipate this. He never stated that they would suffer under this catastrophic outpouring--just to be prepared for it in conjunction with the return of the Lord Jesus. Peter referred them back to Paul's letters, assuring them to expect salvation and not personal judgment. They, as Paul wrote, would never face God's wrath.[21] The promise was to be

---

[16] Jn 7:16-17

[17] Jn 17:17

[18] Joel 1:15; 2:1-2; 2:28-32; Is 13:9-13, etc. See Acts 2:16-21

[19] This does not exclude the natural questions we have as we seek to understand. Also, those who have hardened their belief in favor of another interpretation will not readily accept the position as expressed here.

[20] 2 Pt 3:10

[21] 1 Thess 1:10; 5:9-10

gathered and with Him--not separated for judgment. The church was always to be prepared for this time of upheaval, just as Jesus described it as a time of great distress like no other ever before or ever again.[22] Since no jots or tittles will be overlooked in the outworking of this final event, so must our personal Bible reading encompass all the details regarding this critical doctrine. When we examine eschatological views which disagree with Scripture, we often find that single verses are used out of context. The speaker or commentator will state the erroneous position and then explain it according to their personal theory. This will compare poorly to Scripture, thanks to their isolation of it from the original context. Jesus warned about deception.[23]

Peter's message was well received in Acts chapter two. Many souls were saved that day. He and the other Apostles continued to openly present the facts of Jesus' ministry, including the reason for His death and the Resurrection on the third day. The Apostles suffered for speaking publicly about this from the beginning. Previously, Jesus had warned them about opposition. Suffering and persecution would be part of their work.[24] Paul and others faced this, too.[25] They were able to face much hostility with the Holy Spirit's power and direction. Without the third person of the Trinity, they might have slacked off. All followers of Jesus are to expect persecution.[26] There is no assurance in Scripture that we are to expect some kind of escape from it. We are told that He will never leave us, no matter how our life ends. The Holy Spirit guarantees this,[27] and we have assurance that we will see His glory, even if we suffer as Stephen the first martyr did.[28] Trials, suffering, and persecution are part of Christian life. Jesus spoke of this from the very beginning of His ministry.[29]

---

[22] Mt 24:21

[23] Mt 24:4

[24] Mt 10:16-20; Note the initial arrest, Acts 4:1-3; remember Stephen, Acts 6:8-8:1

[25] Acts 9:15-16; 1 Thess 1:6; 3:4; 2 Thess 1:4, etc.

[26] Mt 5:11-12

[27] Eph 1:11-14

[28] Acts 7:55-56: Jn 17:24; 1 Thess 2:19

[29] Mt 5:11-12; note, also, Jn 15:20, spoken in the upper room.

The nature of the truth being heralded will bring a response and at times will be extremely hostile. Stephen was first to face this and give up his life. Many Christians have followed in his steps. None of the faithful witnesses, like the prophets who preceded the apostles and first believers, expected some kind of exemption from suffering. It was God's Spirit who enabled them to stand and not waver. Church history confirms this with numerous martyrs. It continues today in many locations throughout the world where the enemies of the Cross hold the reins of government. Persecution will increase as the end of the age approaches. There are multiple warnings in advance of this in God's word.[30]

Once again, as we look in the Book of Acts, Luke has included details which are important for discerning the return of the Lord. In Acts chapter one, notice that when Jesus was with the disciples prior to His ascension, He spent forty days ministering to their needs. He encouraged them and after the forty-day period, He ascended back to heaven. As the disciples were standing by watching this spectacle, two men dressed in white appeared and stood with them. They questioned the disciples as to why they were just standing and looking up at the sky. The two heavenly messengers emphasized that the very same Jesus would return in the very same way.[31] As a result, the disciples now possessed the affirmation that Jesus would return from heaven visibly in the same manner as He departed. Meanwhile, they had work to do. The disciples knew from previous teaching that He had promised to return. The Apostle John affirmed this when he wrote his gospel later. His mention of this truth firmly establishes the Lord's promise to come again.[32] Jesus had said that He would "come back."[33] With this in mind, there is no reason to assume that the Lord's return will vary in any significant way from His visible departure. Thus far, we can see that Jesus is set to return visibly after a cosmic disturbance at the end of the age.[34]

---

[30] Paul the Apostle gave full warning to the Thessalonians: see 1 Thess 3:4; also, Jesus, Mt 24:9

[31] Acts 1:9-11

[32] Jn 14:1-3

[33] Lk 18:8; Jn 14:3; Mt 26:29; Mk 14:25; Lk 18:9; 22:16, 18. See Mt 16:27

Let us continue to follow Peter with his early work in Jerusalem. In Acts chapter three we find him again preaching to a crowd, this time in the courts of the Temple at Solomon's Colonnade. Since a beggar had been healed, many in the area came running to investigate. Peter seized the opportunity to preach to them and hold them to account for the death of Christ.[35] He called them to repentance for this. He explained that times of refreshing may result and that God may send Christ--the very Jesus they had crucified. Next, Peter offered details and the conditions that would precede the Lord's return. This apostle was clear: Jesus "must remain in heaven until the time comes for God to restore everything as he promised long ago through his holy prophets."[36] Again, as Peter quoted Joel earlier, we find that he had a working knowledge of Scripture. He continued in this discourse to quote Deuteronomy, but in the process made a bold statement about the return of the Lord. Peter stated that Jesus must remain in heaven until the time of restoration. This is a reference to the time of Elijah who will participate directly with the act of restoring the people in advance of the Lord's return. What Peter is saying is that Elijah must come first. Darrell Bock, in an article, "Evidence from Acts," noted in his comments on verse twenty-one: "In other words, heaven holds Jesus until the time of Israel's restoration."[37] This is a candid admission that the Lord cannot return before the time Israel is being restored and Elijah is present again. This sets aside the idea that Jesus could come at an earlier time. It is worth noting that Peter was present on the occasion when a rich young man came to query Jesus about obtaining eternal life. After the man departed, Jesus spoke to His disciples about the difficulty of entering the kingdom. Peter asked the Lord: "What then will there be for us?" The Lord explained to Peter that "*at the renewal of all things*, when the Son of Man comes to sit on his glorious throne, you who have followed me will also sit on twelve thrones, judging the twelve

---

[34] Acts 2:19-20, as noted above with Peter's preaching at Pentecost.

[35] Acts 3:13

[36] Acts 3:21

[37] Located in: Campbell, Donald K., and Jeffrey L. Townsend. *The Coming Millennial Kingdom. A Case for Premllennial Interpretation.* Grand Rapids, MI: Kregel Pub., 1997. p. 189

tribes of Israel."[38] Clearly, the Lord placed His return at the time of judgment and renewal and not before. Peter heard this and would not have contradicted Jesus in Acts three. Everett Harrison connected the two statements as being in accord, with Jesus anticipating "the *palingenesia*, or regeneration, of the present order in connection with His return in glory."[39] Peter confirmed this as he addressed men of Israel in Jerusalem. He knew the Lord Jesus was going to come following Elijah and not before. First, Elijah, then, Jesus.

The validity of the prophet Elijah's return was previously established by another prophet named Malachi. This is clearly revealed in his short book at the close of the Old Testament.[40] Malachi describes the return of the Lord as a time of great destruction. He gives us a further reminder that the Lord will judge with fire, and all those who are arrogant, evil, and are God's enemies will be destroyed. This prophet says, "it will burn like a furnace."[41] Elsewhere, Scripture states He will send fire upon the earth and remove all of the wicked.[42] Malachi, though, helps us to see God's hand of mercy, as Elijah will be sent before the "great and dreadful day of the Lord" to turn the hearts of many back to the members of their own families. In other words, before Christ comes, Elijah will appear in public. Some Bible expositors consider him to be one of the two witnesses mentioned by John in the Book of Revelation. Wilbur Smith called attention to this in his comments on Malachi. He noted A. R. Fausset who is in agreement with Peter. Fausset stated that this "proves that Elijah will come at the time of the *second* coming."[43] Smith's affirmation tells us that Elijah is to precede Jesus at His second coming and not at some prior time, as if

---

[38] Mt 19:28 [emphasis added].

[39] Harrison, Everett F. *Acts: the Expanding Church.* Chicago, IL: Moody Press, 1975. p. 76

[40] Mal 4:5

[41] Mal 4:1-6

[42] Is 30:27-30; Hos 8:14; Mic 1:3-4; Nah 1:2-6; Mal 3:2; Ps 97:3-7; Prov 10:25; Rev 8:7. Many references are directed toward Israel, since they first are accountable, Ps 147:19-20; Am 3:2

[43] Smith, Wilbur M. *Peloubet's Select Notes…1959.* Boston, MA: W. A. Wilde Co., 1958. p. 310 [emphasis added].

he might come some seven years before. If this is indeed Elijah, he will have forty-two months to carry out his ministry prior to the return of Christ.[44] However, the understanding that Elijah was to return before the Day of the Lord was evident at the time Jesus was ministering, as many thought John the Baptist might be Elijah. He was not and said so.[45] Even the disciples with Jesus knew about the concept that Elijah was to appear first, and then the end would come. This is demonstrated at the time of the Transfiguration when Peter, James, and John saw Moses and Elijah together. The two great men of renown appeared on the mount with Jesus, as the Father spoke from a bright cloud. When this event concluded, only Jesus remained, and the disciples were confused. They were told not to speak of this until after the Son of Man was raised from the dead. Then, Jesus brought up the resurrection--since they had just seen Elijah. In their minds, they were thinking the end was upon them, since they knew that Elijah must come first, and the resurrection was to take place at the last day.[46] Jesus, then, affirmed the future ministry of Elijah. He said, "To be sure, Elijah must come first and will restore all things."[47] He went on to offer the thought that John the Baptist was like Elijah, though the leaders of the people did not accept him in that way, since they were hardened against John through his bold message of repentance. The confusion about the Baptist and Elijah continues to the present day. However, a careful reading of Matthew and his description of the Transfiguration will help to see the prophet, John the Baptist, as he was intended.[48] Nonetheless, the fact that Elijah is yet to come-- and must come first--still stands, exactly as the Lord Jesus stated it. Once Elijah is on the scene, then the world can expect a restoration of families and relationships to commence before it will be too late. In the process, there will be open resistance to his call to repent. There will be rejection of the idea that God will soon judge the world. The rebellious, especially world leaders, will

---

[44] Rev 11:3-12

[45] Jn 1:21

[46] Jn 6:40, 44, 54; 11:24

[47] Mt 17:11. In other words, those alive at the end of the age, will see Elijah before Jesus returns.

[48] Mt 17:1-13; also, Jn 1:19-27; Mk 9:9-13; Lk 1:76-80

begin a concentrated effort to squash the Truth. They will plot to retaliate against the Lord and His people.[49] As this unfolds, Elijah will have the honor of calling men to repent in preparation for the Lord and His appearance. This is why John the Baptist was thought to be Elijah. Both men are voices crying out; both being sent in advance as forerunners of the Lord.[50] All this is to take place *before* the Lord returns. This event will be visible to all. Isaiah states this.[51] So does the Apostle John as he begins to unfold the events in the Apocalypse. Revelation chapter one is clear: "Look, he is coming with the clouds, and every eye will see him, even those who pierced him; and all the peoples of the earth will mourn because of him. So shall it be! Amen."[52] This affirmation by the Apostle John agrees with the two men in white in Acts chapter one. From the beginning of the church to the end of the age, the emphasis of the visible return of the Lord has been the core of the doctrine of the Second Coming. In addition, nowhere does it state that anyone leaves before this glorious event. Consequently, Peter's short message in Acts three is a notable summary of the Lord's own statements. "So the apostle Peter was but repeating what he heard from the lips of his Lord and Master. Our Lord held out, as the only hope, something that He was yet to do."[53] This is the restoration occurring at the time of His glorious return.

Briefly, let us recap the simplicity of the return of Christ. First, He comes again just as the disciples saw Him leave--visibly. Second, He returns after the heavens are disturbed at the end of the age, just as Peter preached. Third, Elijah is to return prior to the great and dreadful Day of the Lord, as recorded in Malachi and clearly restated by Peter in Acts three. Thus, the Second Coming will be visible. It will be after the cosmos are displaced. It will be after Elijah

---

[49] Ps 2:1-12; Rev 13. Note: the Antichrist will be in view at this time.

[50] Is 40:3-5

[51] *Ibid.*

[52] Revelation 1:7. This agrees with Zechariah 12:10ff, as the Lord returns visibly and raises up David and the clans.

[53] Lloyd-Jones, Martyn. *Authentic Christianity .Studies in the Book of Acts. Volume One.* Wheaton, IL: Crossway Books, 2000. p. 256.

appears. This clear doctrinal overview is repeated in various other portions of Scripture. The prophets foresaw it this way. Jesus described it in this manner in the Olivet Discourse. The Apostles continued the same view as they preached and taught. What we have looked at thus far, just from the first three chapters of Acts, is the early doctrinal position of the church regarding the Second Coming which subsequent events and revelation do not alter. This would represent the position of the Apostles and others as they taught believers about the return of the Lord. In Acts two, many of the new converts devoted themselves to the teaching of the Apostles.[54] This position on the Second Coming would qualify as an important portion of that.[55] The later writings of Paul and the other New Testament writers only reinforce this view.[56] Those today who seek to remove the church before any of this occurs are tampering with the Word of God. This is dangerous, indeed.

Background

When Peter wrote his epistles, he affirmed for us the veracity of the Scriptures. He agreed with the Apostle Paul[57] that all Scripture is by inspiration, meaning that all of the books of the Bible are God-breathed. The Holy Spirit has made the words, not only true, but alive.[58] This is why the Bible is different from any other book. Peter assures us that the writings of the Prophets are true, exact, without flaw,[59] and valuable for understanding our faith and looking ahead to

---

[54] Acts 2:42

[55] Heb 6:1-3. Notice that "resurrection" and "eternal judgment" are part of the "elementary teachings"!

[56] See Paul and his detailed explanation of the Gospel covering the entire fifteenth chapter of First Corinthians. Note that he fully describes judgment, the second advent, and our changed bodies when Christ returns. Read carefully verses 22 through 24, as Paul outlines the return itself in simple terms. It is at that time we are "changed," v.50ff.

[57] 2 Tim 3:16

[58] Heb 4:12-13

the future. When he wrote, he said that we "have the word of the prophets made more certain,"[60] and we need to pay attention to what they wrote. These are the same prophets that Peter and the others read and learned. They had faith in the truth they expressed. But when Jesus arrived and fulfilled them, the Scriptures were made more certain. These are the same writings that Peter quoted as he preached. His understanding of the Second Coming which were bolstered by his knowledge of the Hebrew scriptures, our Old Testament. The Holy Spirit, then, indwelling this apostle empowered him to speak the truth and write the truth. The promise of this goes back to the upper room on the night before Jesus was crucified. It was there that Jesus introduced His men to the Holy Spirit, His place, and His functions. The Holy Spirit, of course, is the Spirit of Truth.[61] This would enable them to fulfill their commission and to write the New Testament. Together, these two portions, the Old Testament and the New Testament, make up our Bible. There is no difference between the older part or the new as far as truth is concerned. It is all true and useful for us to use to study and learn what has been prophesied about the future. The Holy Spirit was given also to inform these men what was yet to come--valuable insight into the future for them and for us.[62]

In Acts two, Peter quoted both the prophet Joel and, also, David who wrote many of the psalms. Since he did this, and was speaking directly to the men of Israel, if any corrupt variation of the scripture was used, then Peter would have been challenged on the spot. Instead, men were convicted by this powerful preaching and accepted the events associated with the death and resurrection of Christ. Both the prophets and the psalms spoke of the coming of Christ--the Anointed One. They also pointed to His coming again. Peter and the others would have looked to those writings for understanding about this future event when God would render judgment upon the earth, holding all mankind to account. In the book of Isaiah, the Day of the Lord is clearly stated. Just as

[59] Prov 30:5-6
[60] 2 Pt 1:19
[61] Jn 14:16-17
[62] Jn 16:12-15

305

Isaiah spoke of the suffering servant, describing Jesus and His suffering in chapter fifty-three, so he wrote of the end of the age. He was among the first to warn Israel about judgment unless they turned back to God. Then, he was given additional details about things in the distant future. These things regarding the end of the age and judgment are still ahead of us. At that time, the Lord will appear.

In Isaiah chapter two, we find Isaiah, like Joel, mentioning "the last days." He then proceeds to describe the time when the "mountain of the Lord's temple will be established,"[63] and then notes events which will precede this restoration. He speaks of the Lord's judgment at that time, when He brings down the arrogant, removes the idols, and then "shakes the earth."[64] This chapter introduces a broad set of events which will result in the Kingdom being established on the earth. The Apostles understood this and looked forward to this taking place at the end the age. This is why four of them asked Jesus about this in Matthew twenty-four.[65] There are many references to what Isaiah describes. In chapter sixty-one, a portion of which the Lord quoted in the synagogue in Nazareth, Isaiah points to "the day of vengeance."[66] In chapter thirty, he points to the Lord coming from afar to bring wrath upon the wicked. At the same time His tongue will be a "consuming fire."[67] Concurrently, when He comes down to judge the wicked, He will also shield Jerusalem--he "will shield it and deliver it."[68] This will be like a second Passover, when those who belong to Him will be preserved.[69] In chapter sixty-two, Isaiah speaks of the Lord coming, that "his reward is with him," and He will "recompense" those who deserve full judgment.[70] This is the time of the Lord's retribution for those

---

[63] Is 2:2

[64] Is 2:6-22

[65] See the Olivet Discourse in Mt 24:1ff. Note their question in verse 3. [Also: Mk 13 and Lk 21].

[66] Is 61:2

[67] Is 30:27

[68] Is 31:5. Note verses 27 through 30 and compare to Paul in 2 Thess 1:6-10.

[69] Ex 12:12

on the earth. The description of this event is repeated in varying forms by the other prophets. They all mention the final judgment. Many mention the Lord accomplishing this by fire. Peter described this in his second epistle, as well. The Lord will repay all of His enemies "in full."[71] At the same time He will preserve His own and put all the wicked to death.[72] It should be clear by reading Isaiah, we see the Lord's first advent with His suffering[73] and His return, the Second Coming, when He executes judgment upon mankind. This event will be visible--we will see it.[74] There is no reason to assume that Peter or any of the other New Testament writers had a different understanding than Isaiah. They write the same way and quote Him along with the other prophets in order to accurately portray the Lord's return in the New Testament. Reading all of the prophets will confirm this.

In the book of the Psalms, there are also direct references to Jesus' first[75] and second advents.[76] Since, Jesus fulfilled all of the various prophecies regarding His first advent, those remaining will be fulfilled at the time of His return. In Psalm one hundred two, it states that the Lord "will rebuild Zion and appear in his glory."[77] The Jews at the time of Jesus anticipated this. Likewise, the early Christians would have accepted this understanding from the Apostles and others later who qualified as teachers.[78] Because, Jesus came and was the final sacrifice for sin,[79] the church would have looked ahead to the many scriptural references regarding future Zion, Jerusalem, and Israel to be resolved and

---

[70] Is 62:11; compare to Rev 22:12

[71] Is 65:6-7

[72] Is 65:13-15

[73] Is 52:13-53:12

[74] Is 52:8; 66:14-16, note that His servants and His foes will be together on earth when He comes. There will be no removal, just as Jesus said in Lk 21:35. We who are alive will see this event, Mt 24:33

[75] Note Psalm 22 which describes His suffering on the Cross.

[76] Ps 21:9; Ps 50:3-6ff; Ps 75:1-10

[77] Ps 102:16

[78] Acts 2:42; 1 Tim 3:2; Tit 1:9; 2:1

[79] Heb 10:11-14

brought to completion when Jesus returns in glory. Again, as stated in Psalm one hundred two, these events are for a future generation[80] and will be shared by all of the saints when the kingdom comes to earth.[81] These people, the redeemed of the Lord, will be with Him and will minister to Him.[82] Immediately prior to the Lord's glorious return, He will be the judge of all men. This is described in Revelation by John the Apostle, but the Psalms call our attention to this also. In Psalm twenty-one, David describes the Lord appearing at a time when His wrath will consume His enemies with fire. He will consume them "like a fiery furnace" when their descendants and posterity will be destroyed.[83] David is clear in forecasting their demise and the failure of all their wicked schemes. This scene is described, also, in Psalm two where the nations and their kings plot, rail, and stand against God and His Son, the Anointed One.[84] The Lord's warning there is accompanied with an offer of grace, since the people and their rulers will still be able to repent up until the very end. They must "kiss the Son," having first been brought to their senses for fear of what is coming on the earth--the wrath of God.[85]

In Psalm fifty, written by Asaph, he describes the time when the Lord comes-- no longer silent--to judge the people on the earth. A devouring fire will precede Him. It will be like a raging storm to consume His foes. The "heavens above" are summoned to participate, which parallels the writings of the apostles.[86] This is not only judgment, but also a time when the Lord will gather His own and protect them. Asaph states the instructions of the Lord plainly as this event transpires: "Gather to me my consecrated ones, who made a covenant with me by sacrifice."[87]This gathering is the time when His angels are sent forth to

---

[80] Ps 102:18
[81] Heb 11:39-40
[82] Ps 101:6; 24:3-6
[83] Ps 21:9-11
[84] Ps 2:1-2, 7
[85] Ps 2:10-12
[86] Ps 50:3-4; Rev 19:11-14; 1 Thess 3:13; Jd 14-15
[87] Ps 50:5

gather the elect as found in the Olivet Discourse.[88] It will be the time of full redemption for the chosen of God and also retribution for the wicked.[89] This will all occur at the same time when He comes as the judge. The righteous will enter His kingdom, and the wicked will be rebuked with eternal consequences. There will be no one to rescue them. It is over.[90] This event will be observed by the righteous. All of God's people will be protected and preserved. It will not come near them.[91] His salvation, already assured to believers by the indwelling Holy Spirit, will guarantee this deliverance from judgment and a welcome into His eternal dwellings.[92] Those who trust Him now will find Him their refuge then.[93] We are not appointed to face His wrath.[94]

In Psalm ninety-six, we find assurance that the Lord will judge equitably. He will apply all of the righteous attributes of His character--love, mercy, truth, and grace.[95] He comes for us at this time. We will sing and rejoice, because we know His righteousness and understand His truth.[96] This has come to us through the Holy Spirit.[97] But for the wicked, it will be a different situation entirely. They will face eternal judgment with no recourse. In the next psalm, Psalm ninety-seven, this act by God to hold His enemies to account is graphic. The writer tells us that fire will precede Him, and His "foes on every side" will be consumed. His lightning will light up the world, and the mountains will melt.[98] This echoes Peter in his second epistle where he describes the elements melting. This will be proclaimed from the heavens, and "all the peoples will see his glory."[99] All of the wicked, the idolaters, and the corrupt rebels will be

---

[88] Mt 24:30-31; Mk 13:27; Lk 21:27-28
[89] Heb 9:28; Lk 17:26-37
[90] Ps 50:16-23
[91] Ps 91:7ff
[92] Ps 91:14-15; Eph 1:13-14
[93] Ps 91:1-8; 32:7; Eph 1:14-15; 2 Cor 110, 21-22
[94] 1 Thess 1:10; 5:9
[95] Ps 96:10
[96] Ps 96:13
[97] Jn 14:6-17
[98] Ps 97:1-5

shamed[100] and then taken away for the fullness of judgment.[101] This is the understanding that the Apostles held to. When Jesus spoke of coming again, they would have expected His protection at the time of His wrath, and that they would be preserved by Him through it all. Paul described it in these exact terms in Second Thessalonians.[102] Once Jesus returns in power and glory, the wicked will be removed and His glorious kingdom will begin with His chosen ones becoming the beneficiaries of God's complete restoration.[103]

This final act by the Lord to judge will initiate the Messianic age.[104] Only the righteous will survive. Only the righteous will be there.[105] All things will be made new.[106] This glorious age was noted by Solomon as he looked ahead. The kings and nations will bow to the Lord after this time of deliverance. They will have turned to Him, recognizing Him who has come in glory. These are the survivors of the earth's judgment who have been delivered and rescued, because their blood is precious in His sight.[107] They will praise God and "call him blessed."[108]

There are numerous references in the Old Testament to the coming kingdom. The early church, using the Old Testament scriptures while they spread the Gospel, would have followed this template for what was to come. The oral teaching and affirmation of truth would have echoed Peter and his preaching in Acts two. Paul reminds us in his first letter to the Corinthian church that this is what was preached and what was believed in all the churches.[109] We see

---

[99] Ps 97:6

[100] Ps 97:7

[101] Ps 5:4-6; 37:20; 75:8; 92:6-7; 104:35; 145:20; Prov 10:25

[102] 2 Thess 1:6-10

[103] Is 11:6-9; Eph 1:13-14

[104] Ps 110 from David anticipates the establishment of the Messianic kingdom.

[105] Is 35:8-10

[106] Is 65:17-19

[107] Ps 72:8-14

[108] Ps 72:17-19

[109] 1 Cor 15

evidence of Paul applying this approach when he was brought before Felix the governor who heard the case against this apostle and also spoke with him privately. Paul was deliberate in his focus on "righteousness, self-control and the judgment to come."[110] It can be seen from this discourse by Paul that future concerns were a normal part of the church's commission to make disciples by teaching truth about the end of the age. This has not changed. Those who alter this are taking a great risk.

Focus

Now that we have considered some of the background that was part of the disciples' mindset, it will be helpful to remember what these men heard directly from the Lord regarding His return. They were not merely observing a good teacher from Nazareth, they were eyewitnesses of the Redeemer who would one day return to finish all that was being set in motion as a result of the First Advent. With the help of the Holy Spirit who would come after Jesus' ascension, they would be able to resolve theological issues under the direction and counsel of the third person of the Trinity.[111] Prior to Pentecost, while they were with Jesus day and night, they observed and participated in numerous events which would in the future be transposed into real-time teaching, especially in relation to the return of Christ. All of the Apostles knew and understood the Gospel this way.[112] The key lessons these men learned came through observing Jesus as He dealt with many controversial matters. Those who encountered Jesus were either genuinely seeking an answer and a resolution to their dilemma, or they were the opposition--enemies who sought

---

[110] Acts 24:24-26

[111] See John 14 through 16. The Holy Spirit will be in them and empower the work, especially teaching the Truth.

[112] 1 Cor 15:11; 1 Cor 4:16-17; Jd 3

to entrap Him. All of this was a part of apostolic training. Peter and the others were going to benefit from their eyewitness participation and aid our understanding as well. What did Peter and the other disciples hear and learn along the way? These men heard about the Second Coming on at least six occasions.

First, with regard to Christ's return, think about the parables in Matthew chapter thirteen. It is here that Jesus taught openly about the end of the age, the issue of judgment, the participation of the angels, the finality of the intervention of heaven to put an end to all wickedness, and the eternal nature of man's state with regard to salvation. Jesus expounded about the kingdom of heaven, yet the picture is definite and points towards what will occur at the end of the age. With Jesus' preaching, the introduction of the kingdom was now among them, and the end of the age would bring about its completion and full presence.[113] The basic components of eschatology are here in the parable of the wheat and the tares as Jesus explained their significance. Notice that the tares--or the weeds--are first collected, then bundled, and burned in mass.[114] At this time, not before, the wheat is gathered and brought into the Lord's barn.[115] It is interesting to note that the "gathering" is the same term that Paul applies later when he writes about the rapture of the church.[116] The lesson is simple: the wicked are bundled and burned; the righteous are gathered and taken to be with the Lord. The disciples asked for an explanation of this parable,[117] so we have the benefit of the Lord's own word[118] to aid us today. He told them that this harvest is the end of the age, and that the angels will first weed out all and everything evil.[119] He is clear that the Son of Man is the one who will do the

---

[113] Mt 4:17; 6:10; 8:11; 25:34; Rev 12:10

[114] Mt 13:30

[115] *Ibid.*

[116] 2 Thess 2:1

[117] Mt 13:36

[118] 1 Thess 4:15. It is important to note that nothing Paul taught could conflict with the Lord's teaching.

[119] Mt 13:41

sending. This is the same Son of Man who is heralding the Gospel they are learning, the same Son of Man who is to be crucified, and the same Son of Man who is to return visibly at the end of the age.[120] Jesus is the Son of Man. Here, He says He will send angels forth to gather. It is the wicked who are taken.[121] Those who remain[122] are the righteous. According to the prophet Daniel, they will be shining in the kingdom.[123] As Paul tells us, it is at this point that the bodies of the righteous are changed--in the twinkling of an eye.[124] This will be quick. There will be no hindrance,[125] once the angels are sent forth. The Lord says this will happen without delay.[126] The individuals who have been taken for judgment will be weeping and gnashing their teeth. They are among those who railed against God, rejected His truth, and believed the lie.[127] Though Paul expounded on some of this later in his epistles, the disciples with Jesus heard Him explain this plainly at the time. It is for those who have ears to hear, both then and now.[128] At this same time, Jesus continued to teach using parables. He illustrated again the kingdom of heaven at the time of the end. He said it was like a net that fisherman use. He wished to make this lesson very clear, since at least four of them were fisherman. Jesus reminded them that the good fish were collected in baskets, while the bad fish were thrown away.[129] He explained that this is just the way it will be at the end of the present age: the bad will be cast out, and good will be gathered in. If they were not good fish, they did not get into the basket. For men who fished on the lake at Galilee, this would be a standing reminder of what is to come. Jesus reiterated this as being the end, when the angels separate the wicked and pitch them into the fiery furnace.[130]

---

[120] Jn 3:13; Mt 12:40; 20:28; 17:22-23; 19:28; 25:31; 24:27, 30; Lk 18:8; Acts 1:11

[121] Compare this to Lk 17:34-37

[122] See Paul in 1 Thess 4:15, 17, "alive and remain."

[123] Dan 12:3

[124] 1 Cor 15:52-54. Paul states this to occur at the last trumpet--not before!

[125] 2 Thess 2:6-8

[126] Heb 10:37; Rev 10:6; Rev 22:20 [KJV]

[127] 2 Thess 2:10-12; also, Ps 2

[128] Mt 13:43

[129] Mt 13:47-48

With these two stunning examples which include the sequence in its simple form, these men had a lesson for all time to pass on to us. Jesus, then, directly asked them if they understood this.[131] They said, yes, but they could not fully understand until the Holy Spirit came, which we see occurring in Acts chapter two. It is there that Peter preaches and confirms the lesson learned from years before.[132]

Second, it is helpful to recall another occasion during Jesus' ministry when the disciples heard the Lord speak of the end of the age. The teaching often referred to as the Olivet Discourse[133] is not the only mention of the Second Coming. Jesus brought up this subject at other times. Another discourse, recorded in Luke seventeen, which helps lay this out was given in response to the Pharisees who had challenged Jesus about the Kingdom of God.[134] Jesus' explanation to them was brief. He said the kingdom was not visible, but that it is within you. Since the Pharisees were blind,[135] Jesus, then, turned to the disciples and offered important insight into the future event when He would come back. The context tells us that Jesus wanted His men to understand that He would return at the end of the age. They would also have to teach the Second Coming within their own ministries as part of the Great Commission.[136] In this lesson, He referred to Himself a number of times as the Son of Man. This would reinforce the idea that it would be Him returning and not someone else. It would be the very same Jesus.[137] This short conversation tells us that the Son of Man would be leaving, and they would long to see Him. This suggests that it would be some time before Jesus' return.[138] It would not be an imminent

---

[130] Mt 13:48-49

[131] Mt 13:51

[132] Acts 2:16-21. As previously noted, the two men in white had dealt with this in Acts 1; Peter, also, in Acts 3.

[133] Mt 24; Mk 13; Lk 21

[134] Lk 17:20-21

[135] Jn 9:40-41

[136] Mt 28:19-20. Also, see Acts 5:20

[137] Acts 1:11

event. Jesus, then, issued a warning about those who tell believers that He is here, or He is there, as if His return would be secret, and they would have to run off somewhere to find Him. The opposite is true. Jesus will come boldly, gloriously in public view. They must not run after false promises which would be the deception of the elect that Jesus warned about in the Olivet Discourse.[139] He likened His return to lightning--the brilliant flashing of light from the east to the west. This would cover the heavens from one end to the other. This is not a description of a secret coming where only the church would be affected. If it were, then Jesus would have stated that here. He did not. The picture is one that portrays the same image as described later during His last week on the Mount of Olives when He expanded this lesson related here by Luke.[140] The "lightning" is also mentioned as a sign of this in Matthew.[141] Of course, lightning is not hidden too easily. In addition, this picture of lightning is referenced in the Psalms (and the prophets) to illustrate the Lord's judgment at the end of the age.[142] Jesus is confirming that the scripture already in place would not be altered with regard to His return. This would include His death and resurrection.[143] He then continued to illustrate the conditions on the earth at the time of His return. He compared it to the time of Noah and the time of Lot. In both cases people were not paying attention to the Lord, either through the preaching of Noah or the righteous influence of Lot in Sodom. People rebelled and continued in their wickedness, oblivious to impending judgment. This vile, corrupt offense proceeded without the least consideration of God "up to the day" that the Lord's judgment fell on them. In both of the cases that Jesus described, God "destroyed them all."[144] None escaped the flood or the sulfur. It was over. None survived. Jesus stated clearly that it will be "just like this" on

---

[138] Lk 17:22

[139] Mt 24:4, 11, 23-26; Mk 13:5, 9, 21-23; Lk 21:8

[140] Note the Olivet Discourse: Matthew 24, Mark 13, and Luke 21 for more description.

[141] Mt 24:27

[142] Ps 97:1-7; 18:12-14; 29:7; 144:5-7; 2 Sam 22:13-15; Hos 6:5; Zech 9:14; Ezek 21:8-10, etc.

[143] Lk 17:25

[144] Lk 17:27, 29

the day that He returns. The Son of Man will come, and His "sharp sword" will strike the wicked down for the last time.[145] There is no hint here or elsewhere that He will appear at some time prior to this judgment to retrieve believers. Again, the Bible is silent about this. Jesus would have used a very different illustration here, if the Second Coming was to be in two phases. It is not. He did not. Those who hold a pre-trib view normally use this section of Luke to infer that the ones "taken" are those raptured. Not so. Jesus speaks here of judgment--the one and final judgment at the end of the age when He returns. That is the context. Note that in His two illustrations, the ones taken were taken--by flood or sulfur--and destroyed. This section must be read fully--not just a verse or two to support a theory. Notice, too, that Jesus continues this lesson beyond Noah and Lot. He tells the disciples a parable to aid their understanding. The widow in Luke eighteen who persists in seeking justice from the judge relates directly to the judgment in Luke seventeen.[146] Jesus instructed His men to remember to always pray. They are not to give up. Why? Because His return will be in the distant future, and it will be at a time of great distress unequaled from the beginning.[147] Christ's disciples--those alive at the time of the Second Coming--will need to be persistent in their prayers in order to gain wisdom, strength, and direction, since deception will abound. Those at the end must stand.[148] In addition, in this parable Jesus makes it clear that God will bring justice at this time for His own. He mentions the "chosen ones."[149] These are the elect who have been redeemed by His blood and will be gathered at the end and not before.[150] Those who hold a pre-trib view often define the "elect" as Jews. This is not possible, since in Luke, Jesus tells elect believers who are His own that their redemption is near.[151] Since this period at the very end will be a time of great tribulation, those alive will face a severe testing of

---

[145] Lk 17:30; Revelation 19:11-15
[146] Lk 18:1-8
[147] Mt 24:21; Mk 13:19
[148] Lk 21:19; Heb 6:11
[149] Lk 18:6
[150] Mt 24:30-31; Mk 13:26-27; Lk 21:27-28. Note, also: Is 35:8-10; 59:15-20; 62:12
[151] Lk 21:28.

their faith.[152] Consequently, Jesus concludes this parable by asking if He will find faith on the earth when He returns.[153] If He was going to return earlier than "the end," then this parable and the preceding discourse would be meaningless. The full implication of His teaching here, to a question originally posed by the Pharisees, is revealing. He is stating that He will return, that this event will be like lightning in the heavens, that judgment for the wicked will occur, and those who belong to Him must hold to their faith without wavering. The lesson here is affirmed in the Olivet Discourse and later by the Apostle Paul, the Apostle Peter, and the Apostle John. Those with Him here knew what Jesus meant.

A third opportunity for the disciples to hear about the end of the age is found in the Gospel of Matthew. Jesus had just predicted His death at the hands of the authorities in Jerusalem. He firmly rebuked Peter for objecting to this saying, "Out of my sight, Satan!"[154] Jesus then went on to address the disciples as a group. Within His emphatic reminder to follow Him, He also alerted them to where all of this was going to lead: the fulfillment of all things at the end of the age. Jesus said: "For the Son of Man is going to come in His Father's glory with his angels, and then he will reward each person according to what he has done."[155] Jesus did not expound the subject here, but the disciples were privy once again to the reality of what was to occur in the future. This particular verse is important, since Jesus provides a condensed view of the Second Coming which confirms what we see elsewhere. Notice, there is no hint of any prior return. There is no mention of two phases. The connection is simple, that when He comes--in His Father's glory with the angels[156]--He will reward each believer for what they have done. This verse concisely brings all of this together into a single event at one time--not a series of events drawn out over

---

[152] Rev 13:10; note Paul's consistent concern about persecution, trial, and suffering in 1 & 2 Thessalonians.

[153] Lk 18:8

[154] Mt 16:23

[155] Mt 16:27

[156] Mt 24:30-31; 1 Thess 3:13; 2 Thess 1:6-7

seven or more years. Jesus spoke this way to His disciples, so we would benefit by understanding His timing at the end of the age.

A fourth occasion for this subject to come into focus has been mentioned earlier in this chapter. In Matthew 19, the disciples had just heard Jesus describe the difficulty of a rich man being able to enter heaven. The Lord said it would be easier for a camel to go through the eye of a needle than for a rich man to gain access to heaven. His disciples were astonished and asked, if this is so "who then can be saved."[157] Jesus explained this was all possible through God. Peter challenged Him and said they had left everything for Him, "What then will be left for us?" Jesus was clear in His reply that they would receive their rewards "at the renewal of all things, when the Son of Man sits on his glorious throne" when they sit with Him "judging the twelve tribes of Israel."[158] Once more Jesus elucidates the Second Coming being the time when He returns in glory to judge. There is no hint of an expectation of some mysterious arrival some years prior to this. Peter in particular understood this, since he wrote years later of the Lord's return, especially noting the judgment factor, and the earth to be destroyed by fire and "everything in it laid bare."[159] Consequently, the disciples heard a consistent message of judgment when the Lord returns with no "any moment" inference. This holds true all through the New Testament, unless someone contradicts Jesus' words. His men who carried forth the good news of the gospel always held to a firm grasp of the order of events.

We find a fifth opportunity again in the Gospel of Luke. In chapter 20, Jesus is dealing with the Sadducees who challenged Him about marriage in heaven.[160] It is significant that these men who did not believe in the resurrection of the dead brought a question about this to Jesus. However, since their main purpose was to entrap Him, and none of their schemes were successful up to this point, they attempted a last resort. Also, these opponents, along with Pharisees and

---

[157] Mt 19:25
[158] Mt 19:28
[159] 2 Pt 3:8-10. Note, also, Is 24:2, 19-23
[160] Lk 20:27-40. Also, in Mt 22:23-33

other leaders, were seeking evidence to bring against Jesus and soon would be giving approval for His death in the Sanhedrin.[161] However, this short discourse offers insight into the end when the resurrection takes place. This is the resurrection of the righteous who are worthy and will take part in the age to come.[162] The sly Sadducees did not get the answer they wanted. They hoped Jesus would contradict Moses. This did not happen. He silenced them quickly. They asked no more questions. Yet, the disciples were the ones to benefit, since they now had further insight into the day when Jesus would return and raise the righteous dead. The details help believers to see that those who are resurrected will not marry, will not die, and will be alive thanks to the God of Abraham, Isaac, and Jacob. This is the first resurrection of which John wrote in the Apocalypse.[163] Those who have died in faith will be part of this group. It is the same group that Jesus defined in John's gospel--those He would raise up at the last day and not before.[164] This, also, is the hope that Job had,[165] David had,[166] and other Old Testament saints.[167] We must remember that the encounter with the Sadducees took place soon after the event in Bethany when Jesus raised Lazarus. This astounding miracle caused repercussions within the Sanhedrin.[168] From this point on, the leadership of Israel was committed to ending Jesus' life, and Lazarus' as well.[169] However, when we follow this account of Jesus' return to Judea to attend to Lazarus in Bethany, we find affirmation from his sister, Martha, that the resurrection was a known truth. She knew her brother would be among those resurrected. Further, the statement by Martha to Jesus confirms the resurrection to be "at the last day."[170] Again, the understanding

---

[161] Note Jn 11:45-53; 12:10-11; Mt 26:3-5; Mk 14:1-2; Lk 19:47-38

[162] Lk 20:35

[163] Rev 20:5

[164] Jn 5:24-27; 6:39-40, 43-45, 54

[165] Job 19:25-27

[166] Ps 16:9-11

[167] Note the partial list and exploits in Heb 11:1-40

[168] Jn 11:45-53

[169] Jn 12:9-11

[170] Jn 11:24

about this subject at the time of Jesus was that at the last day of the present age, the righteous dead would be raised. The disciples would have learned this, too, and now had a faith-affirming, visual demonstration of the power behind the promise upon seeing Lazarus exit the tomb. Many other witnesses saw this, also. Since the "last day" and the resurrection were brought up earlier in Jesus' teaching,[171] this subsequent event in Bethany would only strengthen those who had faith in God who would truly honor them in the future. This late attempt by the Sadducees to challenge Jesus, so soon after Bethany, would become an additional opportunity for His disciples to learn facts surrounding the Lord's return and the truth about those who will be raised from the dead at that time. Just as the disciples were eyewitnesses at Jesus' transfiguration, now through Lazarus there were additional eyewitness testimonies of these powerful, amazing events.[172]

A sixth occasion when the disciples were exposed to this subject took place in the upper room. The church today continues the ordinance initiated here by Jesus. Often Communion is done as ritual, and the actual setting and words are masked over by tradition. In Luke's gospel in chapter twenty-two, he recorded the words of Jesus: "I have eagerly desired to eat this Passover with you before I suffer. For I tell you, I will not eat it again until it finds fulfillment in the kingdom of God."[173] This tells us that until the final fulfillment at the end of the age, there will be no celebration like this. The future gathering when He comes will make possible for the first time all of the saints to be joined together as one body. Up to this point, the saints only have met to honor Christ's death on occasions within their lifetime. This is done to "proclaim the Lord's death until he comes."[174] As Paul reminded the Corinthians, we are to continue this until He returns personally. The upper room statement by Jesus reminds us that all things must be fulfilled.[175] The heavens and earth will "disappear," and then

---

[171] Jn 6:39-40

[172] 2 Pt 1:16

[173] Lk 22:15-16

[174] 1 Cor 11:26

[175] Mt 5:18. Jesus says here [Lk 22:16], "until it finds fulfillment in the kingdom of

He will appear and remove us.[176] The context of these statements does not allow for the church to be removed prior to the fulfillment of His personal presence (*parousia*). It does not permit some kind of heavenly celebration until the entire Body of Christ is complete at the end of the seventieth week.[177] Jesus' words must be pondered with care. This practice of the Lord's Supper has been a continuing observance and a profession of the faithful through many generations. Once the resurrection takes place, the entire Body of Christ along with all the faithful of ages past, will rejoice as a multitude in glorious celebration. This is the marriage supper of the Lamb. It must be stressed that this does not happen until after the tribulation and at the end of this age when Jesus comes personally.[178] In the upper room, after taking the cup, He told them again, "...I will not drink of the fruit of the vine until the kingdom of God comes."[179] The church today remembers Him, but neglects to think clearly about these very simple words which inform us of the timing of His return. His words remind us that the Kingdom of God will come. He will come. He will bring in the Kingdom. He will judge.[180] This all occurs at the end and not prior. Any other suggestion is a distortion of the Lord's words and the sequence emphasized elsewhere in the Scripture. After the meal was concluded, Jesus interrupted the disciples' dispute regarding "the greatest" among them. He informed them that He would confer on them a kingdom and at that time they would "eat and drink at my table in my kingdom and sit on thrones, judging the twelve tribes of Israel."[181] The eating, drinking, sitting, and judging take place after the Kingdom comes. There is no participation in these divine privileges until Jesus returns personally--the Second Coming--visibly and then sets His feet down once more on the earth.[182]

God."

[176] *Ibid.* Also, Mt 24:29-30.

[177] Some prophecy teachers propose a "marriage supper" long before Revelation 19.

[178] Rev 19:6-9; also, Rev 19:11-16, when He comes; Heb 11:13-16, 39-40, all together.

[179] Lk 22:18

[180] Jude 14-15

[181] Lk 22:29-30; 1 Cor 6:3; 2 Pt 2:4, 9; Jd 6

[182] Zech 14:3-5

There is no evidence within the context of these six encounters or any of Jesus' statements that the end of the age or the resurrection at that time will be divided into phases, multiple comings, and separate resurrections. He is returning once. He will raise the righteous once.[183] This is the established understanding of this doctrine at the time Jesus was teaching. His disciples and the people who listened to Him face-to-face looked ahead to the promise of "the resurrection at the last day."[184] It would not change. The consistency of their mutual understanding is expressed by the New Testament writers who faithfully recorded these events and things that followed. If they held to a different understanding about the return of Christ, then we would see glaring points of conflict and blatant discrepancies.[185] We do not. A vast number of the forbears in the church understood it exactly this way. John Wesley's brother, Charles, born in 1707, wrote a classic hymn in which the opening words are very clear: "Lo, He comes with clouds descending, Once for favored sinners slain...." The simple truth is outstanding, since his hymn notes that Jesus is coming but once. He based these words on the gospel of Matthew chapter twenty-four verse thirty where we are told the Son of Man will come in the clouds--visibly. The hymn clearly speaks of the time when Jesus comes to the earth--to reign. This short work by Wesley affirms the doctrinal view of the church regarding the Second Coming--visibly, once, to reign.[186] Bishop J. C. Ryle, who consistently affirmed sound doctrine in the Church of England, warned about the troublesome errors which abound in the teaching of the Second Coming. His concern was for those inside the Body of Christ, not just scoffers on the outside. He said, "It is a sad truth, but a truth never to be forgotten, that none

---

[183] Heb 9:27-28

[184] Jn 11:24

[185] Discrepancies are created through textual mishandling and when personal views are promoted in conflict with Scripture. Through the years, a broad range of these have been rectified. See: Haley, John W. *Alleged Discrepancies of the Bible.* 1874. rpt. Nashville, TN: Gospel Advocate Co., 1974. *e.g.,* p. 132-136.

[186] Wesley, Charles. *Lo, He Comes with Clouds Descending.* [Commonly found in standard hymnals].

have injured the doctrine of the second advent so much as over-zealous friends."[187] The church must heed these words.

Affirmation

Since the Apostles and disciples of Christ heard directly about His return a number of times, it would be beneficial to identify a further indicator of the reality of judgment from the Psalms and some of the prophets. Those closest to Jesus would not have accepted distortion of the intent of scripture, the word of God they were already familiar with. This is important, since much of what is circulating in evangelical circles today is speculation having been based on the thoughts of those who have too often overlooked the Old Testament and its precepts regarding eschatology. Regrettably, this has assisted some prophecy teachers in their reinterpretation of New Testament verses that relate to the doctrine of Christ's return. Peter, when writing his second epistle, made note of the fact that the word of the prophets was made more certain, finding its fulfillment in Christ.[188] He wrote this within the context of what was yet to come, as he continued with more specific details in his letter. Further on, he warned about false teachers, heresies, standing firm, and the graphics of the second coming with the fullness of judgment. Both chapters two and three provide the specifics. He based his assurance on the future having been confirmed by voices from the past--the prophets. He emphasized the fact that the words from the past were not merely words from men, but were messages divinely inspired from God Himself. He was clear: no man did this. It was God working through them. The Holy Spirit worked in them, counseling much the way He does today.[189] He echoed Paul when the apostle wrote that all of

---

[187] Ryle, John Charles. "The Second Advent: The Ten Virgins." *The True Christian.*
Welwyn, England: Evangelical Press, 1978. p. 206
[188] 2 Pt 1:19

scripture has come by inspiration.[190] This is very similar to what we find in Hebrews where it states in the beginning verses of chapter one that in past times the message from God came through His prophets--that He did this in a variety of ways--again and again.[191] The writer continues pointing to the last, ultimate, final voice as being His Son. This, too, is the emphasis of John in his Gospel where he informs us that the Word became flesh and spoke to us in person.[192] These men all agree that the Truth which has been imparted to us has come from a long line of men sent by God, the last of which has been His Son, the second person of the Trinity. All of this is affirmation that the words transcribed under the old covenant are reliable, useful, and most of all represent the eternal line of communication from the throne of God to us. So, if we choose to consider the earlier writings, we will find much that relates to the second coming and judgment. Some who teach this subject today minimize the Old Testament in this regard. The Old Testament inclusion these teachers provide is selective and neglects the seriousness which should be applied when attempting to interpret the end of this age.

A few references will help us at this point. An exhaustive list is outside our purpose here. Obviously, a good thing to remember is that God is the supreme judge in all matters from the beginning to the end. He is sovereign. There is no one above Him. He is the final appeal. He is eternal. This means that whatever men do, whether it qualifies as being righteous or is outright wicked, the standard for evaluating all of it has been established by God alone. Since the fall of man, no individual's conscience by itself has been sufficient, especially in matters of redemption and salvation. For this reason we have God's word to define these things and set us straight. Also, He is the ultimate judge. David, the sweet singer of Israel, wrote in Psalm nine that the Lord's reign is forever, that His throne has been established for judgment, and that He will judge the world with the righteousness which is within Himself. Then, He will govern.[193]

---

[189] 2 Pt 1:21
[190] 2 Tim 3:16
[191] Heb 1:1-4; Jer 7:13, 25; 25:4; 29:19, etc.
[192] Jn 1:1-2, 14

In just two verses from David, we see the focus of God's omnipotence being directed toward producing a people who will obey Him within His kingdom. In the next two verses, we are called to trust in His name, to seek Him, and learn that He never forsakes those who do.[194] This is a call for us to consider this with care, turn to Him, and repent. Otherwise, judgment will come. Since He hates evil and those who are wicked and arrogant, they will be judged severely. They will never enter His kingdom.[195] The precept established here affirms the earlier psalm where we are told that those who reject God's Son will be destroyed when His wrath is unleashed--in a moment.[196] Judgment is unquestionably placed within these psalms to cause readers to fully consider a future event, when the Lord will call all men to account. These initial psalms aid us to see the burden that the Lord has for men to heed His warnings by listening to Him, repenting, and to become obedient. This precept regarding judgment does not change anywhere in scripture, even to the end of the age. This is another reason that the writings of the apostles are quite forceful when speaking of the judgment to come. They knew, as did the writers of the psalms and the prophets, that they will be held to account for their words.[197] It is not just the thought of elements melting that should cause us to shudder. It must be the thought of standing before the Creator and defending our rebellious nature.[198] He is the One who decides our fate. This is a sobering reality to consider and should nurture a sense of fear. He is the Judge who can cast our body into hell.[199] With this in mind, it is a foolhardy venture to tinker with the teaching surrounding the final judgment. Believers must think carefully as they deal with the entire area of eschatology and amend their views when necessary. Some will need to repent. The call for repentance with which Jesus opened His earthly ministry continues to the very end of this age.[200]

---

[193] Ps 9:7-8
[194] Ps 9:9-10
[195] Ps 5:4-7
[196] Ps 2:10-12
[197] Mt 12:37; Rm 2:21; Jas 3:1
[198] Rom 14:12; 2 Cor 5:10
[199] Lk 12:4-5

Elsewhere in Psalms there are warnings about careful consideration of what God has stated. As His concerns were translated into Law, the psalmist often had these precepts in mind. The writer expressed a purpose to cause the audience--in this case Israel--to rethink God's requirements for holy living and understand clearly the penalties involved with disobedience. Hence, in Psalm one there is a call to meditate on the Law both day and night. God's children are to turn to Him for instruction, knowledge, and understanding. The psalmist is very obvious in stating that the wicked are counseled by themselves--leaning on the earthly mindset of others who are wicked or adhering to the pattern of sinners or hardening themselves with the company of mockers. In this first psalm, the penalty is severe: they will be blown away "like chaff." They will fail to withstand the judgment and will be absent when the righteous are gathered.[201] However, the righteous will be accounted worthy, because they take God's word seriously and expect Him to do exactly what He says. Since they have honored Him, He will honor them. This principle holds throughout Scripture.[202] When we compare this to the words of the prophet Malachi, we see that those who fear God, honor His name, and follow His path will be among those redeemed "in the day" when He "makes up His treasured possession."[203] Further, this prophet assures us that at that time in the future, we will "see the distinction between the righteous and the wicked."[204] This conforms exactly to the picture revealed in Psalm one where the paths of the wicked and the righteous are on display. This final revelation as part of the judgment at the "last day" will let us see who serves God and who does not. The wicked, of course, will not be part of the group belonging to God. Only the righteous who serve Him will stand at the judgment and survive. This is why Jesus said the wheat and the tares will grow together until the end of the age. He affirmed that the wicked will be gathered together and taken in judgment.[205]

---

[200] Mt 4:17; Acts 3:19; Rev 3:3, etc.

[201] Ps 1:4-5

[202] Heb 11:6; Zech 7:13

[203] Mal 3:16-17

[204] Mal 3:18

[205] Mt 13:10. Note Jesus' clear explanation in verses 36 through 43.

Since the Mosaic Law has been available as a declaration of God's requirements since the time of Moses, people can read and learn their true condition as sinners and determine their fate accordingly. The Lord God of Israel made His requirements conditional. If His people were obedient, He would care for them and watch over them. If they disobeyed, He would hold them to account and punish accordingly. The words of Moses lay out these conditional aspects of God's relationship with the children of Abraham in various places within the Pentateuch. God did this with complete foreknowledge, so His people would be protected as they took possession of the lands of wicked people whom God Himself was going to displace. They were not to imitate the "neighbors." They did enter the promised land, but even Moses did not qualify. Hence, the imperative for obedience was considerable from the outset. When we arrive at the psalms, the writers there had this historical element in place and in mind.[206] This is part of the context of Psalm one and many of the others. Psalm one hundred nineteen is a lengthy broadside reaffirming the wisdom found in Psalm one. Israel then, and believers today, must reconsider this in God's terms or possibly come under a cloud of judgment for minimizing the importance of God's word. We sometimes forget that God's plan is an eternal one. We tend to think "today." The Lord is the eternal God. Jesus is in the center of this, and He will attend to the judgment of all.[207] It is He who is the judge in Psalm one who "watches over the way of the righteous" and guarantees that "the way of the wicked will perish."[208] He is the "Son" in Psalm two who will "rule them with an iron scepter."[209] It is His wrath that will destroy those who rebel against God.[210] All of these scripture portions are an affirmation that Jesus is Lord and will be the one returning to judge the reprobate and bring salvation to those who look forward to His coming to earth as King of Kings and Lord of Lords.[211]

---

[206] Note Psalm 8, Psalm 24, Psalm 46, Psalm 78, Psalm 95, Psalm 105, Psalm 107, Psalm 119, Psalm 147

[207] Acts 17:30-31; Heb 13:8

[208] Ps 1:6

[209] Ps 2:7-9

[210] Ps 2:1-3, 12

In Psalm twenty-one, David amplifies the concerns that are the overriding features within the Second Coming. God's enemies will pay for their violations of the standards which He prescribed for mankind. They will have no excuse. Paul the Apostle explains this in his epistle to the church in Rome.[212] Because the heavens, meaning creation, are a living testimony available for the wicked to consider, and the Law of Moses is a reliable resource to find out what God requires, their rejection of this will yield the harshest penalty.[213] David paints the picture. He says the Lord will "lay hold" of all His enemies. He will "seize" them when He appears, and they will become "like a fiery furnace." This description is a direct parallel to Jesus' parable in Matthew thirteen and Peter's description of the end in his second epistle.[214] This is no coincidence. The Lord is making sure that those who wish to stand with the righteous at the end will be able to do so. David continues stating that God's wrath will "swallow them up," and God's "fire will consume them."[215] As if this were not enough, the Lord will "destroy their descendants from the earth"--no posterity and no inheritance. Their evil plots and schemes will utterly fail.[216] This means that once judgment is concluded, none of the wicked will survive--none will be left. David writes again of this in Psalm thirty-seven. He says "all sinners will be destroyed," the "future of the wicked will be cut off," and the righteous will be delivered, "because they take refuge in him."[217] Again, we see the two options and the two outcomes. One for the wicked--cut off--and for the righteous: salvation. This conforms to many other portions of the psalms, the prophets, and Moses' writings. David, also, says that when this occurs--"when the wicked are cut off"--"you will see it."[218] The similitude found here in these two

---

[211] Rev 19:15-16; 17:14

[212] Rm 1:18ff. Paul states they know "about God" and are "without excuse."

[213] Note the progression in Psalm 19. The wicked have no righteous thoughts and are not "pleasing" to Him (v.14).

[214] Mt 13:40-43; 13:49-50; 2 Pt 3:10

[215] Ps 21:8-9

[216] Ps 21:10-11. Note, too, the similarity between Israel's prophets and the Apostles who warned of judgment.

[217] Ps 37:38-40

psalms is the model which affirms the pattern found later in the New Testament. Scripture is clear: judgment awaits the wicked, and God's own people will be delivered at that time--not removed prior to this. As David said, "you will see it." The Lord Jesus affirmed this in the Olivet Discourse, as He said "when you see all these things, you know that it is near, right at the door."[219]

The affirmation we need regarding Christ's return is found throughout Scripture. The revelation of this is part of His plan of redemption. This final act will center on mankind, those who have repented and honor Him. It will also bring forth "new heavens and a new earth."[220] This change will be drastic. All things will be new. In that context, even His own are at a loss as to what the exact design will look like. We only have His word to go by. This includes John's testimony: "Dear friends, now we are children of God, and what we will be has not yet been made known. But we know that when he appears, we shall be like him, for we shall see him as he is."[221] There is certain hope within John's statement, and, also, a caution to proceed with care as we look ahead to that glorious day. The Second Coming will bring forth the heavenly host and the glory of God. He will have His reward with Him.[222] Because of that, we must measure carefully much of what we have been told about His return. He will come. He will redeem us fully. We must be sure we understand what He has already told us and not speculate on portions left in doubt. Details abound in the Olivet Discourse about the Second Coming. Our great need is to understand what Christ said then, as He answered basic questions from His Apostles. We must go by His word.[223]

As we consider the return of Christ, there is His own promise to come back as recorded in John fourteen.[224] There is also Paul's explanation of what will

---

[218] Ps 37:34
[219] Mt 24:33
[220] Is 65:17
[221] 1 Jn 3:2
[222] Rev 22:12
[223] Rom 4:3; 1 Cor 4:6
[224] Jn 14:3

happen at this time. He stated clearly that each believer will be changed from a corrupt body into a new body. The transition will be instantaneous upon the return of the Lord Jesus.[225] He explained this to those in Corinth in the same way he taught the church in Thessalonica. For the Thessalonians, he reminded them that this will occur at the time "the Lord Himself will come down from heaven."[226] At that very moment, the dead who belong to Christ will be resurrected and those still alive will be changed from mortal to immortal. We will then be with the Lord forever. The Christian church knows this, yet the timing is still in dispute. It should not be a problem, if Scripture alone is the guide. As J. I. Packer commented:

> In 1 Thessalonians 4:16-17 Paul teaches that Christ's coming will take the form of a descent from the sky, heralded by a trumpet fanfare, a shout, and the voice of the archangel. Those who died in Christ will already have been raised and will be with him, and all Christians on earth will be "raptured" (i.e., caught up among the clouds to meet Christ in the air) so that they may at once return to earth with him as part of his triumphant escort. The idea that the rapture takes them out of this world for a second "second coming" has been widely held but lacks scriptural support.[227]

Packer is right. There is no Biblical support for an early departure. All those who are "in Christ" will be raised from the grave, first. Then, those who remain alive will be raptured. This will all occur in a moment as Christ descends to the earth. The very nature of this event and its finality demands that believers must lucidly understand what lies ahead, especially the order of events. Dr. Packer warned that this "will be a tragic disaster if the *parousia* finds anyone in an unprepared state...."[228] Those who do not know the order of the events at the

---

[225] 1 Cor 15:50-52

[226] 1 Thess 4:16

[227] Packer, J. I. *Concise Theology. A Guide to Historic Christian Beliefs.* Wheaton, IL: Tyndale House Pub., Inc., 1993. p. 251

[228] *Ibid.* p. 253

end of the age, that the church will be on the earth as this unfolds, are unprepared. They are totally at risk. They have already fallen into deceptive hands. There is but one Second Coming. The Body of Christ must anticipate the full specter of spiritual deception already in place, which will increase at the end of the age,[229] and respond with Scriptural orthodoxy and reject all other theories.

About one hundred years before Packer, Bishop J. C. Ryle affirmed the same view. He taught and wrote in plain terms that the wheat and tares will remain on the earth "until the end of the age." His words were related to the parable in Matthew chapter thirteen.[230] He explained that the church will be here as a mixed multitude with both professing Christians and confessing Christians together. He noted that there will be "a day of separation," and this will occur "at the end of the world."[231] As the parable states, when the Lord Jesus returns, He will send forth His angels. They will separate the wheat from the tares, and each congregation will then be winnowed with the righteous alone joining Christ eternally. This is another sound reason to review the beliefs in place today. Error in doctrine only compounds the difficulty in rectifying the challenge of facing the Second Coming as written. The Bible holds the orthodox position. Yet, the church often leans toward other ideas. The church will be accountable for promoting theories. The words of Packer, Ryle, and others must be heeded.

---

[229] 2 Thess 2:9-10

[230] Mt 13:24-50

[231] Ryle, John Charles. *Expository Thoughts on the Gospel of St. Matthew*. London: Hodder & Stoughton, 1900. p. 146-150.

Summary

The material herein has brought together a number of facts relating to the Second Coming of Christ which are in need of better understanding by believers. Many Christians are unaware of the importance of this doctrine or have been taught incorrectly about the timing and various, key Biblical details. The core truth of this was taught by the Apostles and disseminated in the early church. Today, an excess of distortions abound. The following points are a concise synopsis of the true nature of the return of Jesus Christ which has been discussed in this book.

1. Scripture states the Lord Jesus will return one time only. This is the core of the doctrinal   position taught by the Church Fathers, expressed in the creeds, and accepted by all major denominational groups. This is in accord with Jesus' own teaching as found in the Olivet Discourse and elsewhere. See Mt 16:27; 24:30; Lk 17:20-18:8; Jn 14:3; Heb 9:28

2. The arrival of Christ (the *parousia*/physical presence) commences the age to come which is called the Millennium: the thousand year reign of Christ. This is the basis for premillennialism which is the emphasis of the material herein. See Mt 24:30-31; 25:31; Rev 20:5; 21:1-5

3. The church alive at the time of the Second Coming will be comprised of individuals who face the Antichrist. This will cause great consternation and turmoil for all men, but it will bring severe persecution for Christians since Satan's power will be unleashed against all of God's people (Jews, also). The Lord warned of this as did Paul. Antichrist will be revealed, and the great rebellion will occur. See Mt 24:15, 21-22; 2 Thess 2:3-4; 2:9-10 1 Jn 2:18

3. All of the wicked will be judged at the time Jesus returns. None of the ungodly will survive the judgment which will be carried out by the Lord with fire. The justice of God requires that the unrepentant enemies of God receive

their due. The angels will assist in carrying this out. None of the wicked will enter the eternal kingdom. See Mt 13:40-43; 25:41; 2 Pt 3:10; Pr 10:25

4. All of God's people will be raised from their graves when Christ comes. Each will receive their incorruptible body and enter the eternal kingdom. They will be immortal, having obtained the gift of life forever. Those still alive when the Lord returns will have their bodies changed in an instant and be brought together will all other believers from all the ages to be with Christ forever. See. Mt 24:31; 1 Cor 15:50-54; 1 Thess 4:16-17; Heb 11:39-40

5. There will be no previous, secret return of Jesus to remove the church. No scripture denotes a two-phase second advent. No apostle or early church father taught or wrote of any other return by Jesus except the single return when He comes in glory with all the angels. See 2 Thess 1:6-10

6. The new heavens and the new earth will be set in place at this time, being renewed, since all will have been destroyed by the fire of judgment. See Is 24:1-6; 2 Pt 3:10; Is 65:17; Rev 21:1

These points need to be examined carefully. Scripture must be the guide when considering the basis for this or any other doctrine. The chapters in this book have expanded on various texts which support a single return of the Lord Jesus. Objections and false assertions have been dealt with as well.

Differences in doctrinal understanding have always been problematic for the church. Out of the discussion and debate, it is possible to come to agreement and conformity with the truth. Bible prophecy, end-times prognostications, and the subject of eschatology have had no shortage of conflict. Regarding the singular return of Christ presented here, there is a similarity to debates in the past on the particulars of the Lord's return, judgment, and the eternal state. Dr. George Harris noted the difficulties with this and wrote, "...we cannot refrain from expressing surprise that the adherents of a view which is manifestly open to grave objections and serious inconsistencies should be horrified at others who do not happen to agree with them in reference to a question which has always been perplexing, and to which no answer yet given is entirely free from objections."[232] His subject was eschatology and in another vein of the doctrine, but the concern about objections is valid, since many theologians simply bypass scripture or adjust it at will. This is why numerous scriptural footnotes abound in this book. The reader is then free to conclude a view based on the word of truth and not follow popular opinion.

Another important area of concern is history. Through the years, the record reflects a variety of thoughts integrated into the interpretation of the Second Coming. The most reliable statements are those which arose from the time of Jesus and the apostles. The only legitimate assertions are those which totally align with God's word. When men attempt to modify Biblical passages, merely as they see them in their day, distortion and error can result. This is the type of subjective reasoning which breeds confusion. All the views, whether they are amillennial, premillennial, or postmillennial, must be substantiated by clear Biblical passages. We have presented and contended for premillennialism here, and for that reason have included a section on history. It is a summary, yet covers sufficient, pertinent detail to show that the later additions to historical premillennialsm are not justified. This includes a secret rapture and the removal of the church some seven years prior to the Second Coming. This latter-day idea was manufactured at prophecy conferences, a product of discussion among men, and not scripture alone. Deviation from the word of God, once accepted and promoted, leads to unorthodox teaching and disputes in the church. This is not merely a conflict between views that oppose each other. It affects what will actually happen to people, especially innocent believers, who have placed their hope in false teaching and will then face the Antichrist. This is worthy of a healthy debate. The chapters herein have been for that purpose. Nevertheless, there is but one Second Coming and one time of judgment.

---

[232]Harris, George. "Eschatology." *Progressive Orthodoxy*. 1892. rpt. Hicksville, NY: The Regina Press, 1975. p. 92

---- 0 ----

We trust the reading of these chapters has been a helpful theological journey, one which has strengthened your understanding of the future day when Christ the Lord returns.

---- 0 ----

Recommended Reading List

Bass, Clarence. *Backgrounds to Dispensationalism.*

Cameron, Robert. *Scriptural Truth About The Lord's Return.*

Clouse, Robert G. *The Meaning of the Millennium: Four Views.*

Edwards, Wesley G. *The Rapture of the Church. Pre or Post Tribulation?*

Fraser, Alexander. *The "Any Moment" Return of Christ.*

Frost, Henry W. *The Second Coming of Christ. A Review of the teaching of Scripture concerning the return of Christ.*

Gundry, Bob. *First the Antichrist.*

Gundry, Robert H. *The Church and the Tribulation.*

Kennedy, H. A. A. *St. Paul's Conception of the Last Things.*

Kimball, William R. *The Rapture. A Question of Timing.*

La Sor, William Sanford. *The Truth About Armageddon.*

Ladd, George Eldon. *The Blessed Hope.*

McMillen, S. I. *Discern These Times.*

MacPherson, Dave. *The Rapture Plot.*

MacPherson, Norman Spurgeon. *Triumph Through Tribulation.*

Payne, J. Barton. *The Imminent Appearing of Christ.*

Reese, Alexander. *The Approaching Advent of Christ.*

Sandeen, Ernest R. *The Roots of Fundamentalism.*

Tregelles, Samuel P. *The Hope Of Christ's Second Coming.*

Van Kampen, Robert. *The Rapture Question Answered. Plain and Simple.*

West, Nathaniel. *The Thousand Years in Both Testaments. Studies in Eschatology.*

White, Frank H. *The Saints' Rest and Rapture.*

GLOSSARY

Amillennialism. The teaching that does not accept a literal thousand year reign by Christ. He will return at the time the world has been prepared for Him by the Church. This view is traced back to Origen and Augustine.

Antichrist. The man who will arise at the end of the age to deceive the world, dominate the global systems, and persecute God's people. He will be empowered by Satan in a final attempt to establish another kingdom. He will proclaim himself to be God, demand worship, and persecute the church. Jesus Christ will destroy Him at the Second Coming as described in Revelation 19. See Rev 13:1-10; 2 Thess 2:3-4, Mt 24:15.

Apokalypsis. The Greek term denoting the Second Coming of Christ as He is revealed at the time of the event. This will be the unveiling.

Apostasy. The event described by Paul the Apostle which must occur before the Antichrist is revealed [2 Thess 2:3-4]. Also, called "the rebellion," "the defection," "departure." Not to be confused with the ongoing degeneration of the church caused by false teachers and perennial backsliding [2 Tim 3:1-9; 1 Tim 4:1-3].

Chiliasm. The older name for the view that espouses a future millennium; a period of 1,000 years. See "Premillennialism."

Covenant Theology. A system that relates God's dealings with men according to the covenantal agreements He made with them.

Darby, John Nelson. A younger contemporary of Edward Irving who gleaned information from attending the Albury and the Powersourt Conferences in the early 1800s which led to his formulating Dispensationalism. The resulting views included the separation of Israel and the church, the pre-tribulation rapture, and a literal interpretation of Scripture.

Didache. One of the earliest documents which relates to the teaching, life, and practice of the Church; likely written in the late first century or the early second century; quoted from by the Fathers; thought by some to be Scripture.

Dispensationalism. A system of teaching that divides the ages according to the way God dealt with His people. Three prime components: (1) the Church and Israel are treated differently in God's plan of redemption; (2) the pre-trib rapture is mandatory to teaching this view; (3) the Bible is taken literally. This theological system was promoted by J. N. Darby in the 1800s. See "John Nelson Darby."

Dispensations. Periods of time since Genesis defining the way God deals with man. Lewis Sperry Chafer noted seven dispensations following the template of C. I. Scofield. Some systems have more, others less.

Dispensational premillennialism. The proper name for the popular idea that the rapture of the church precedes the final seven years. This is distinct from true Premillennialism. See "Pretribulationalism."

Doctrine of a Second Chance. The teaching that provides another opportunity for salvation after death. This view was held by Origen and is aligned with Roman Catholic teaching of purgatory. The Jehovah's Witnesses maintain this view. It is rejected by orthodox Protestantism. Also known as "future probation" or "second probation." This view contradicts the call for repentance now and the basic doctrine of final judgment when Christ returns. A heretical cousin of universalism.

Dragon. Another name for Satan who will empower the Antichrist and the false prophet. See Revelation 13:4

Dual Covenant. The teaching that God has a distinct plan for Israel (the Jews) which is separate from the New Covenant for the Church (Christians). This

338

idea has been refuted since it establishes two ways for salvation when the Lord stated there is only one [Jn 14:6].

Epiphineia. The Greek term denoting manifestation; the public display of His Second Coming as He appears when every eye shall see Him.

Eschatology. The study of the last things. This includes death, the afterlife, judgment, the Second Coming, and the age to come.

False prophet. This man will assist the Antichrist in subduing the world. He will enforce false worship of Antichrist under the threat of imprisonment or death. He, also, will use the global economic system to force the submission of those who are being led astray during the final seven years. See Rev 13:11-17.

Futurism. The school of thought that places prophetic events in the future.

Great Tribulation. A term usually associated with the second half of the final seven years. The outpouring of God's wrath is inferred here, which is to be confined to the final hours of this time period.

Hermeneutics. The science of interpreting Scripture.

Historicism. The school of thought that places events in prophecy in the broad course of human history.

Historic Premillennialism. The teaching that presents Christ's return at the end of the great tribulation when He judges the world and raises the righteous dead. See "Premillennialism."

Idealism. The school of thought that focuses on the moral and ethical message of prophecy and underwrites a higher level of Christian living.

Imminency. The idea that the Lord could return at any moment without prior notice, that no other prophesied events must occur beforehand. This is the primary emphasis found in all pre-trib teaching.

Irving, Edward. Scottish minister who founded the Catholic Apostolic Church. Through the 1800s' Albury Conferences, he initiated an increase in interest in Bible prophecy. He is noted for influencing John Nelson Darby. Margaret Macdonald and her family were associated with Irving and his church.

Judgment. The occasion when God judges men and creation. This will occur when Christ returns and every form of corruption is eliminated. The living wicked will be slain and taken away for a later time when their penalty will be administered [Rev 20:11-15]. The righteous will be transformed into their incorruptible state [1 Cor 15:51-54]. Creation will be renewed when Christ completes His retribution, having struck down the kings, rulers, and nations that served the Antichrist [Rev 19:15; Ps 2:1-12; Rev 21:1]. See "Retribution."

Man of sin. This person is the Antichrist. Paul notes him to be the "man of lawlessness" who proclaims himself to be God and demands worship [2 Thess 2:3-4]. Jesus mentioned him [Mt 24:15]. See "Antichrist."

Mid-tribulationism. The teaching that the church will be raptured at the mid-point of the final seven years.

Millennium. The thousand year period after the Second Coming as reflected in Revelation 20:3, 5 at which time Christ will reign over His redeemed believers who have come to God by faith.

Olivet Discourse. The response to the Apostles who inquired of Jesus as to the destruction of the Temple and His future return. See Mt 24 and 25; Mk 13; Lk 21

Parousia. The Greek term denoting the Second Coming of Christ when He will be physically present on the earth. Hence, "coming." Commonly used by the Apostles to describe the Lord's return. It is the basis for their question in the Olivet Discourse [Mt 24:3].

340

Partial Rapture. The theory that only those who are in good standing spiritually will be raptured. Other believers who are left will be purged by the tribulation and, later, taken up.

Postmillennialism. The teaching that the Lord will return to the earth after the thousand year period mentioned in Revelation 20. The church is now engaged in bettering the world prior to Christ's return at which time there will be a resurrection of the just and unjust..

Post-tribulationism. The teaching that places the Second Coming and the rapture of the church at the end of the tribulation period, prior to the beginning of the age to come, the Millennium.

Premillennialism. The teaching that presents the Lord returning at the end of the seven year tribulation just prior to His thousand year reign on the earth.

Preterist. Refers to a person who adheres to the teaching of Preterism.

Preterism. The teaching that claims all or a portion of the events described in the Book of Revelation occurred in 70 A.D.

Pretribulationalism. The theory that Jesus Christ will return for His church before the seven year tribulation period and take those who belong to Him back to heaven for seven years, who will then return with Him at the time of judgment at the end of the seven years.

Pre-wrath rapture. The teaching that the church is to be removed from the earth shortly before the close of the final seven years. This view has been promoted by Robert Van Kampen and Marvin Rosenthal, both formerly pre-trib advocates.

Prophecy. The predictive element in God's word.

Rapture. The event described by the Apostle Paul in 1 Corinthians 15 and 1 Thessalonians 4 when those who belong to the Lord are raised from their graves or, if still alive when Christ returns, are changed into their immortal, imperishable bodies.

Replacement Theology. The teaching that claims the Church has replaced Israel and is the beneficiary of God's promises. This view contradicts scripture [See Rm 11:29].

Resurrection. Rising from the dead, as described by Paul [1 Cor 15] and Jesus [John 5 & 6] to receive an incorruptible body. This is not to be confused with being raised to life as with Lazarus who later died [Jn 11].

Retribution. The act of justice when God brings His judgment upon all of His foes. This will result in eternal punishment. See "Judgment."

Saints. A synonymous term for "believer," "elect," "body of Christ," or any of God's faithful through the ages.

Scofield, C. I. Editor of the *Scofield Reference Bible* which bears his name. He is the popularizer of dispensational teaching in its current form.

Secret rapture. The teaching that claims the removal of the church will be unseen by the world and only affect the believers who are taken to heaven. This is in contradiction to 1 Thessalonians 4:16 which states there will be "a loud command," "the voice of the archangel and the trumpet call of God." It also in no way conforms to Paul's assurance in 2 Thessalonians 1:6-10 where he states the Lord will return in "blazing fire with his powerful angels."

Second Coming. This is a cardinal doctrine of Christianity affirming that Jesus Christ will return to the earth a second time to rule and reign; also, called the Second Advent.

Seventieth week of Daniel. This is a synonymous term for the tribulation period as mentioned by the prophet Daniel in Daniel 9:27.

Translation Another term for rapture; the time when mortal believers' bodies are changed to immortal at the time Christ comes. See "Rapture."

Tribulation. A general term applied to the final seven years or Daniel's seventieth week as noted in Daniel 9:27. Wickedness will increase immensely during the final three and one-half years when the Antichrist assumes world control and receives power from Satan. The second half of the seven years is the Great Tribulation [Mt 24:21-25].

Two witnesses. Two witnesses are mentioned in Revelation 11 who will do God's bidding during the second half of the tribulation period. Their ministry will last 1,242 days commencing after Antichrist proclaims himself to be God [Mt 24:15; 2 Thess 2:3-4]. These two prophets will stand against the Antichrist's false claims and later perish.

Ultra-dispensationalism. A more extreme form of Dispensationalism which contends that the church began, not in Acts 2, but later with Paul.

Universalism. The view that all men will at some future point become restored to God. This negates the purpose for the Cross and stands in opposition to the orthodox doctrine of eternal punishment for those who have rejected God and never repented of their sin.

Wrath. A term denoting the retribution that God has prepared for those who have rejected Him. All believers are exempt from this.

Appendix

Teaching of the Twelve Apostles, or The Didache

[Chapter 16]

Watch for your life's sake; let your lamps not go out, and your loins not be relaxed, but be ready; for ye know not the hour in which our Lord cometh. But ye shall come together often, and seek the things which befit your souls; for the whole time of your faith *thus far* will not profit you, if ye do not become perfect in the last time. For in the last days the false prophets and the corruptors shall be multiplied, and the sheep turned into wolves, and love shall be turned into hate; for when lawlessness increases they shall hate one another, and shall persecute and shall deliver up, and then shall appear the world-deceiver as the Son of God, and shall do signs and wonders, and the earth shall be given into his hands, and he shall commit iniquities which have never yet been done since the beginning. Then all created men shall come into the fire of trial, and many shall be made to stumble and put to death. But they that endure in their faith shall be saved from this curse. And then shall appear the signs of the truth; first the sign of an opening in heaven, then the sign of the trumpet's sound, and thirdly, the resurrection of the dead; yet not of all, but as it has been said: The Lord will come and all the saints with him. Then shall the world see the Lord coming upon the clouds of heaven.[1]

---

[1] Hitchcock, Roswell D., and Francis Brown. *Teaching of the Twelve Apostles.* New York, NY: Charles Scriber's Sons, 1884. p. 37, 39

George Muller

Remarks preserved by his wife from a Christian Conference in Toronto, Ontario, Canada:

Question: "Are we to expect our Lord's return at *any moment*, or that certain events must be fulfilled before He comes again?"

Answer: "I know that on this subject there is great diversity of judgment, and I do not wish to force on other persons the light I have myself. The subject, however, is not new to me; for, having been a careful, diligent student of the Bible for nearly fifty years, my mind has long been settled on this point, and I have not the shadow of doubt about it. The Scripture declares plainly that the Lord Jesus will *not* come until the Apostasy shall have taken place, and the man of sin, the 'son of perdition' (or personal Antichrist) shall have been revealed, as seen in 2 Thess. 2:1-5. Many other portions also of the word of God distinctively teach that certain events are to be fulfilled before the Return of our Lord Jesus Christ. This does not, however, alter the fact, that the *Coming of Christ*, and not death, is the great Hope of the Church, and, if in the right state of heart, *we* (as the Thessalonian believers did) shall 'serve the living and true God; and wait for His Son from heaven'" (1 Thess. 1:10).[2]

From "The Second Coming of Christ." [A Leaflet]. Bristol Bible and Tract Depot, 1881:

---

[2] Harding, William Henry. *The Life of George Muller: A Record of Faith Triumphant.* London: Morgan & Scott, 1914. p. 331-332

From 2 Thessalonians 2:1-8 we learn that the Lord Jesus will not come until after the manifestation of the 'apostasy'. Has the apostasy here spoken of taken place, and has the man of lawlessness (or, the Antichrist) been revealed? The reply from Scripture is, the apostasy has *not* yet taken place, and the man of lawlessness has not *yet* been revealed.

This passage has not yet found its fulfillment either in popery or in the popes. Fearful as the delusions of popery are, and awful as is the picture of what the popes have been, the apostasy referred to will be far *more dreadful still*; for it will be no less than an entire renunciation of all that is divine, and the setting up as God of the man of lawlessness himself. For he 'even sets himself up in God's temple, proclaiming himself to be God' (v.4).

He will be a king, a mighty monarch, whose might is obtained through the energy given to him by Satan, for 'the dragon gave the beast his power and his throne and great authority' (Rev 13:2). This king, the Antichrist, will be at the head of the *ten kingdoms* of the Roman earth (that is, the ten kingdoms into which the countries which formerly constituted the Roman Empire will be finally divided), and the ten kings will agree to give him their power.

During the period of his especial glory, which will be only forty-two months, he will blaspheme God, His tabernacle, and those who dwell in Heaven. It will also be given him to make war with the saints and to overcome them; and he will be given authority over every tribe, people, language and nation. And all inhabitants of the earth shall worship him, 'all whose names have not been written in the book of life belonging to the Lamb that was slain from the creation of the world' (Rev 13:5-8).[3]

From *Scriptural Truth About The Lord's Return*:

> The late George Muller, of holy memory, when asked if the Lord's Coming was any less precious to him after he had given up the "any moment" expectation, replied: "Oh, no, the Coming of the Lord is infinitely more precious to me now. I used to be looking up to see the heavens part and the Lord to return, and I looked in vain. But now, when I see predicted events coming to pass, I say, 'Praise the Lord, He will soon be here--only a few more things to come to pass, and then I shall lift up my head and rejoice because I know He is coming soon.'"[4]

G. Campbell Morgan

Response to a question posed to him at Gordon College as published in "Christianity Today" in 1959:

> Dr. Loraine Boettner's review of Hughes' book, *A New Heaven and a NewEarth* (May 25 issue) gives a little known quotation from Dr. G. Campbell Morgan--a statement he made in 1943 indicating his change of views relating to "the promises made to Israel."

---

[3] Steer, Roger. *The George Muller Treasury*. Westchester, IL: Crossway Books, 1987. p. 178. [emphasis in the original].

[4] Cameron, Robert. *Scriptural Truth About The Lord's Return*. Chicago, IL: Fleming H. Revell, 1922. p. 102

A dozen or more years before that, during a Boston pastorate, I was privileged to attend a course of lectures given by Dr. Morgan at Gordon College. He was always most gracious in answering questions. At the end of one session I ventured to ask: "After your long study and extensive exposition of the Bible, Dr. Morgan, do you find any scriptural warrant for the distinction which many Bible teachers draw between the second coming of the Lord *for* his own (the rapture), and the coming of the Lord *with* his own (the revelation) with a time period of 3 ½ or 7 years between these two events?"

"Emphatically not!" Dr. Morgan replied. "I know that view well, for in the earlier years of my ministry I taught it, and incorporated it into one of my books entitled *God's Methods with Man*. But further study so convinced me of the error of this teaching that I actually went to the personal expense of buying the plates from the publisher and destroying them. The idea of a separate and secret coming of Christ to remove the church prior to his coming in power and glory is a vagary of prophetic interpretation without any Biblical basis whatsoever."

As I travel about the country in an itinerant ministry which takes me into a great variety of churches, I am impressed with the way which pastors are expressing their appreciation of CHRISTIANITY TODAY. Many of them say, "It's the most helpful and spiritually stimulating magazine that I receive."

Oak Park, Ill. Paul G. Jackson[5]

---

[5] "Christianity Today." August 31, 1959. 3:23. p. 16-17

The following letter from Dr. Morgan is addressed to Rowland Bingham, noted author, who also abandoned the pre-tribulation theory and the secret rapture:

> Westminster Chapel Congregational
> Buckingham Gate
> London, S.W. 1

Rev. Rowland V. Bingham, D.D.
Toronto, Ontario
My dear Dr. Bingham:

"Now about your book on *Matthew*.... I suppose I may say that across the years I have passed through very much of your own experience with regard to these prophetic matters. At any rate, at the moment I accept without any qualification the philosophy of your interpretation.... I think the view the view that makes *Matthew* Jewish is utterly false. The phrase "secret rapture" has to me for a long time been a very objectionable one, and utterly unwarranted in its wording, and in what it is made to stand for by the teaching of Scripture.

"There are, I think, certainly minor points of difference in your interpretation and my own.... I think you will know, without my entering into the matter, that your interpretation of the parables of the Great Tree and the Leaven are not mine. Whereas these are the points of difference, I do not think them to be vital; and I should like you to know how I agree with your general interpretation."

Fraternally yours,

G. Campbell Morgan[6]

From a letter [1934]:

With regard to the so-called Rapture, I would first like to say that the word has no warrant in Scripture. It is one that has been made use of in certain applications, and stands for that around which there has been very much difference of interpretation and, indeed, controversy. I am familiar with the view that you evidently hold, that there is to be a Rapture, or gathering to our Lord of a certain company within the church. I may say that at one time I held that view, and I cannot accept it now.[7]

He continued:

I realize the difficulty of interpretation in many of the passages; but

---

[6] Letter from Dr. G. Campbell Morgan: as published in *The "Any Moment" Return of Christ* by Alexander Fraser. Pittsburgh, PA: The Evangelical Fellowship, Inc., 1947. Letter follows title page.

[7] Morgan, Jill, ed. *This Was His Faith. The Expository Letters of G. Campbell Morgan.* Westwood, NJ: Fleming H. Revell Co., 1952. p. 276-277

I believe that at the Second Advent the whole Church will be gathered to our Lord, irrespective of varying degrees of realization.[8]

Robert Cameron

From his reflections published in 1902.

Now, amongst the many good things accepted from "Brethren teaching" were some I have been compelled to reject because, to my mind, they do not harmonize with the teachings of the Scriptures. "To the law and the testimony," "What saith the Scripture?" These are our final sources of authority and of truth. *The Teaching*, which is distinctively a doctrine of the "Brethren" is, what is sometimes called, the secret rapture of the church, or, what will be better understood as the belief, that the Lord will come, and change the living and raise the sleeping saints, and take them to himself, *before the great tribulation.* This I accepted with great enthusiasm, and taught with fervor, just as many godly men, the latchet of whose shoes I am unworthy to loose, are doing today. I, too, used to say that there must not be so much as a thickness of a sheet of tissue paper between my heart and the coming of the Lord. Often, oh, so often in my zeal, but not according to knowledge, have I appealed to the unsaved to trust Jesus now for the Lord might come before I had finished my sermon. In like manner I have often said that the hope is no hope, if there is a single event that *must* transpire before the Lord comes back for his own. I used to think that it gave me great comfort to believe and teach these things, although I confess that very often when teaching them, there would be a *twitch* at my heart, because some Scripture would flash across my

---

[8] Morgan, Jill. *Ibid.* p. 277

mind that did not harmonize with what I was saying respecting the Lord's return.

Cameron continued:

> It took only a few weeks of Scripture study to upset all that I believed and taught, and, of course, to give me great sorrow at heart that I had been emphasizing in my ministry, what now seemed to have no basis in the Scriptures.[9]

James H. Brookes

Brookes [1830-1897] was pastor of Walnut Street Baptist Church in St. Louis, Missouri. He wrote extensively focusing on the premillennial view and was one of the principal leaders at the Niagara Bible Conferences which began in 1875. Dr. Brookes was a staunch dispensationalist holding to imminency and the pre-trib rapture.[10] He, also, mentored C. I. Scofield.

Shortly before his death, he was interviewed by Robert Cameron who wrote regularly on the fallacy of the "any moment" return of the Lord.[11] From Cameron's record:

---

[9] From the *Watchword and Truth, 24 [1902]*. Quoted in Sandeen. *The Roots of Fundamentalism.* p. 278-281 [emphasis in the original].
[10] Note his work: *Maranatha.* Chicago, IL: Fleming H. Revell, 1889.
[11] Cameron was the editor of the *Watchword and Truth* and the author of books including *Scriptural Truth About The Lord's Return.* Chicago, IL: Fleming H. Revell, 1922.

During a heart-to-heart conversation that afternoon the Doctor said: "I have read that article of yours twice this morning, and I confess it is unanswerable. It is plain that the apostles and the early Christians *did not expect, and could not have expected, the Lord to return in their day*."[12]

The "article" referred to by Dr. Brookes was primarily the contents of Dr. Cameron's refutation of the "any moment" return which had been published previously in *The Truth* which was Brooke's own newsletter. This also represents the second chapter of Robert Cameron's book, *Scriptural Truth About The Lord's Return*, pages 21 through 58.

T. T. Shields ["The Canadian Spurgeon"]

From his sermon, "The Second Coming of Christ" [1931]:

I have repeatedly told you that I find myself compelled to dissent from the position which would imply that Christ is to come for his saints and with his saints. I believe there lurks in that doctrine a grievous error. I do not think it is a fundamental of the faith, and I have always said to you that I shall not quarrel with you on that issue; but I think it is a matter of historic truth that in all the history of doctrine you will find no suggestion anywhere of three comings of Christ,--of His having come once, and is yet to come for His saints and with His saints.

---

[12] Cameron, Robert. *Scriptural Truth About The Lord's Return.* p. 58-59 [emphasis in the original].

That doctrine was first set forth by Edward Irving, the founder of the Irvingites, or of the Catholic Apostolic Church as it is usually called. Mr. Irving did not propound that view as having any scriptural warrant at all: he gave it forth as a special revelation communicated to him. On that ground I have nothing to say except that I do not believe in special revelations. But if it is to be defended on that ground, it must not be defended on that ground alone. I am positive it cannot be defended from Scripture.

Let me remind you at this point that it is very easy for us to read into the Bible our own preconceptions.[13]

From published comments:

I cannot find, then, in this specific scripture (1 Thess. 4:13-18) any authority for the secret Rapture of the saints. I am myself persuaded that there is not one shred of scripture anywhere to support this theory. I am sure that it is a figment of human imagination.[14]

Corrie ten Boom

From "Getting Ready for the End":

I see over the whole world that there are two huge armies marching—

---

[13] Shields, T. T. *The Doctrines of Grace.* Toronto: The Gospel Witness, n.d. p. 197
[14] Shields, T. T. *The Gospel Witness.* Sept. 21, 1935. Quoted in: Kimball, Wm. R. *The Rapture--A Question of Timing.* Grand Rapids, MI: Baker Book House, 1985. p. 59

the army of the Antichrist and the army of Jesus Christ. We know from the Bible that Jesus Christ will have the victory, but now the Antichrist is preparing for the time that will come before Jesus returns.[15]

Letter from her written in 1974:

The world is deathly ill. It is dying. The Great Physician has already signed the death certificate. Yet there is still a great work for Christians to do. They are to be streams of living water, channels of mercy to those who are still in the world. It is possible for them to do this because they are overcomers.

Christians are ambassadors for Christ. They are representatives from Heaven to this dying world. And because of our presence here, things will change.

My sister, Betsy, and I were in the Nazi concentration camp at Ravensbruck because we committed the crime of loving Jews. Seven hundred of us from Holland, France, Russia, Poland and Belgium were herded into a room built for two hundred. As far as I knew, Betsy and I were the only two representatives of Heaven in that room.

We may have been the Lord's only representatives in that place of hatred, yet because of our presence there, things changed. Jesus said, "In the world you shall have tribulation; but be of good cheer, I have overcome the world." We too, are to be overcomers--bringing the light of Jesus into a world filled with darkness and hate.

---

[15] ten Boom, Corrie. *Tramp for the Lord.* Ft. Washington, PA: Christian Literature Crusade; Old Tappan, NJ: Fleming H. Revell Co., 1974. p. 186

Sometimes I get frightened as I read the Bible, and as I look in this world and see all of the tribulation and persecution promised by the Bible coming true. Now I can tell you, though, if you too are afraid, that I have just read the last pages. I can now come to shouting "Hallelujah! Hallelujah" for I have found where it is written that Jesus said, "He that overcometh shall inherit all things: and I will be His God, and he shall be my Son." This is the future and hope of this world. Not that the world will survive--but that we shall be overcomers in the midst of a dying world.

Betsy and I, in the concentration camp, prayed that God would heal Betsy who was so weak and sick. "Yes, the Lord will heal me," Betsy said with confidence. She died the next day and I could not understand it. They laid her thin body on the concrete floor along with all the other corpses of the women who died that day.

It was hard for me to understand, to believe that God had a purpose for all that. Yet because of Betsy's death, today I am traveling all over the world telling people about Jesus.

There are some among us teaching there will be no tribulation, that the Christians will be able to escape all this. These are the false teachers that Jesus was warning us to expect in the latter days. Most of them have little knowledge of what is already going on across the world. I have been in countries where the saints are already suffering terrible persecution. In China, the Christians were told, "Don't worry, before the tribulation comes you will be translated--raptured." Then came a terrible persecution. Millions of Christians were tortured to death. Later I heard a Bishop from China say, sadly, "We have failed. We should have made the people strong for persecution rather than telling them Jesus would come first. Tell the people how to be strong in times of persecution, how to stand when the tribulation comes--to stand and not faint."

I feel I have a divine mandate to go and tell people of this world that it is possible to be strong in the Lord Jesus Christ. We are in training for the tribulation, but more than sixty percent of the Body of Christ across the world has already entered into the tribulation. There is no way to escape it. We are next.

Since I have already gone through prison for Jesus' sake, and since I met the Bishop in China, now every time I read a good Bible text I think, "Hey, I can use that in the time of tribulation." Then I write it down and learn it by heart. When I was in the concentration camp, a camp where only twenty percent of the women came out alive, we tried to cheer each other up by saying, "Nothing could be any worse than today." But we would find the next day was even worse. During this time a Bible verse that I had committed to memory gave me great hope and joy. "If ye be reproached for the name of Christ, happy are ye; for the spirit of glory and of God resteth upon you; on their part evil is spoken of, but on your part He is glorified." (I Peter 3:14) I found myself saying, "Hallelujah! Because I am suffering, Jesus is glorified!"

In America, the churches sing, "Let the congregation escape tribulation," but in China and Africa the tribulation has already arrived. This last year alone more than two hundred thousand Christians were martyred in Africa. Now things like that never get into the newspapers because they cause bad political relations. But I know. I have been there. We need to think about that when we sit down in our nice houses with our nice clothes to eat our steak dinners. Many, many members of the Body of Christ are being tortured to death at this very moment, yet we continue on as though we are all going to escape the tribulation.

Several years ago I was in Africa in a nation where a new government had come into power. The first night I was there some of the Christians were commanded to come to the police station to register. When they arrived they were arrested and that same night they were executed. The next day the same thing happened with other Christians. The third day it was the same. All the Christians in the district were being systematically murdered.

The fourth day I was to speak in a little church. The people came, but they were filled with fear and tension. All during the service they were looking at each other, their eyes asking, "Will this one I am sitting beside be the next one killed? Will I be the next one?"

The room was hot and stuffy with insects that came through the screenless windows and swirled around the naked bulbs over the bare wooden benches. I told them a story out of my childhood.

"When I was a little girl," I said, "I went to my father and said, "Daddy, I am afraid that I will never be strong enough to be a martyr for Jesus Christ." "Tell me," said Father, "When you take a train trip to Amsterdam, when do I give you the money for the ticket? Three weeks before?" "No, Daddy, you give me the money for the ticket just before we get on the train." "That is right," my father said, "and so it is with God's strength. Our Father in Heaven knows when you will need the strength to be a martyr for Jesus Christ. He will supply all you need—

358

just in time...."

My African friends were nodding and smiling. Suddenly a spirit of joy descended upon that church and the people began singing, "In the sweet, by and by, we shall meet on that beautiful shore." Later that week, half the congregation of that church was executed. I heard later that the other half was killed some months ago.

But I must tell you something. I was so happy that the Lord used me to encourage these people, for unlike many of their leaders, I had the word of God. I had been to the Bible and discovered that Jesus said He not only had overcome the world, but to all those who remained faithful to the end, He would give a crown of life.

How can we get ready for the persecution? First we need to feed on the word of God, digest it, make it a part of our being. This will mean disciplined Bible study each day as we not only memorize long passages of scripture, but put the principles to work in our lives. Next we need to develop a personal relationship with Jesus Christ. Not just the Jesus of yesterday, the Jesus of History, but the life-changing Jesus of today who is alive and sitting at the right hand of God.

We must be filled with the Holy Spirit. This is no optional command of the Bible, it is absolutely necessary. Those earthly disciples could never have stood up under persecution of the Jews and Romans had they not waited for Pentecost. Each of us needs our own personal Pentecost, the baptism of the Holy Spirit. We will never be able to stand in the tribulation without it.

In the coming persecution we must be ready to help each other and encourage each other. But we must not wait until the tribulation comes before starting. The fruit of the Spirit should be the dominant force of every Christian's life.

Many are fearful of the coming tribulation, they want to run. I, too, am a little bit afraid when I think that after all my eighty years, including the horrible Nazi concentration camp, that I might have to go through the tribulation also. But then I read the Bible and I am glad.

When I am weak, then I shall be strong, the Bible says. Betsy and I were prisoners for the Lord, we were so weak, but we got power because the Holy Spirit was on us. That mighty inner strengthening of the Holy Spirit helped us through. No, you will not be strong yourself when the tribulation comes. Rather, you will be strong in the power of Him who will not forsake you. For seventy-six years I have known the Lord Jesus and not once has He ever left me, or let me down. Though He slay me, yet I will trust Him, for I know that to all who overcome, He shall give the crown of life. Hallelujah!

--Corrie ten Boom, 1974[16]

Oswald J. Smith

Now, after years of study and prayer, I am absolutely convinced that there will be no rapture *before* the Tribulation, but that the church will

---

[16] ten Boom, Corrie. Her letter, 1974. Accessed 03-05-02 at http://www.jesus-is-lord.com/corrie.htm

undoubtedly be called upon to face the Antichrist, and that Christ will come at the close and not at the beginning of that awful period. I believed the other theory simply because I was taught it by W. E. Blackstone in his book "Jesus is Coming", the Scofield Reference Bible and Prophetic Conferences and Bible Schools; but when I began to search the Scriptures myself I discovered that there is not a single verse in the Bible that upholds the pre-tribulation theory, but that the uniform teaching of the Word of God is of a post-tribulation Rapture: pre-millennial always, everywhere pre-millennial, but post-tribulation.[17]

I discovered that no time element is ever mentioned so far as the rapture is concerned, except as it is related to the Resurrection. And that the Resurrection is always placed at the time of the sounding of the Last Trump (1 Cor. 15:51-54). This Trump, without doubt, closes the Tribulation. There is no eighth. The saints are rewarded (Rev 11:18). The "mystery of God", is then finished, there is time (delay) no longer (Rev 10:6 and 7), and the Resurrection, of course, immediately precedes the Rapture (1 Thess 4:16).[18] [Re: 1 Thess 4:17]. There is no Secret Rapture. That theory must be deliberately read into the passage. There is no Rapture in Revelation until chapter nineteen is reached.[19]

While it is clear that the Church must endure the wrath of the Antichrist, it is certain that the Church will not have to endure the wrath of God. When His judgments are poured out on the Antichrist and his followers, the Church will be divinely protected by God even as the Israelites were protected when His wrath was poured upon the

---

[17] Smith, Oswald J. *Translation or Rapture--Which?* Chelmsford, UK: Sovereign Grace Advent Testimony, n.d. p. 2-3

[18] *Ibid.* p. 8

[19] *Ibid.* p. 10

Egyptians--not by being raptured, but by being kept.[20]

Robert Chapman

From his biography:

> Chapman, together with George Muller and a small number of other
> leadersamong the Brethren, did not believe that the Scriptures told of a
> secret rapture of all believers before a period of great tribulation on the
> earth. They believed that the church as a whole must go through the
> period of tribulation. William Hake did not agree with Chapman's
> views and once told Chapman of a conversation he had with someone
> who was assured that the Lord might come (initiating the rapture) at
> any moment. Chapman replied, "Well, brother Hake, I am ready, but
> it's not in the Bible."[21]

Charles H. Spurgeon

Everyone has great admiration for Charles Haddon Spurgeon who was the
foremost of British preachers during the last half of the nineteenth century. His
messages consistently called his hearers to examine themselves, to admit their
true sinful state, and to turn to Christ for forgiveness. He was in the line of
great Puritan preachers who sought the Scripture for their texts and expounded

---

[20] *Ibid.* p. 10

[21] Peterson, Robert L. *Robert Chapman. A Biography.* Neptune, NJ: Loizeaux Bros.,
1995. p. 171

the need for repentance without which salvation was not possible. His mastery of the English language and his use of illustrations were unmatched. Many thousands entered the kingdom through his pulpit ministry and his published writings. He and his church sponsored an orphanage. Many entered the ministry through the Pastors' College. Since most of his preaching was textual, he did not deliberate extensively on eschatology. Some of his sermons, though, covered the subject broadly. Because of this, many prophecy teachers would like him to be in their camp. However, in simple terms, he was a sound pre-millennialist.

Note the following regarding Spurgeon:

> I do look for His pre-millennial advent, and expect He will come here again. Jesus our Lord is to be King of all the earth, and rule all nations in a glorious personal reign.[22]

He was firmly opposed to date-setting and those who promoted imminence. In the following remarks, he set aside the notion of a secret, any-moment coming:

> The Lord may come in 1866, and I shall be glad to see Him; but I do not believe He will, and the reason I do not believe He will is, because all these twopenny-halfpenny false prophets say He will. If they say He would not come, I should begin to think He would; but, inasmuch as they are all crying out as one man that He will come in 1866 or 1867, I am inclined to think He will not arrive at any such time. It seems to me that there are a great many prophecies which must be fulfilled before

---

[22] Quoted by: Silver, Jesse Forest. *The Lord's Return. Seen in History and In Scripture As Pre-Millennial and Imminent.* Chicago, IL: Fleming H. Revell, 1914. p. 169

the coming of Christ....[23]

He looked to Christ coming in Glory:

> We believe in a personal reign and coming of our Lord Jesus Christ.
> But how will he come? He will doubtless come with great splendor;
> the angels of God shall be his attendants. We gather from Scripture,
> that he will come to reign in the midst of his people, that the house of
> Israel will acknowledge him as King, yea, all nations shall bow down
> before him, and kings shall pay him homage.[24]

He anticipated that every eye would see him. Spurgeon preached on
Revelation1:7 in 1887:

> Our Lord's coming will be seen of all. 'Behold, he cometh with
> clouds, *and every eye shall see him, and they also which pierced him.'*
> I gather from this expression, first, that *it will be a literal appearing,
> and an actual sight.*[25]

He placed this at the time of judgment:

---

[23] Pike, G. Holden. *The Life and Work of Charles Haddon Spurgeon.* 1894. rpt. Banner
of Truth, 1991. Vol. 1, Part III, p. 141-142

[24] Spurgeon, Charles H. "Christ Our Life—Soon To Appear." *Sermons on the Second
Coming and the Last Things.* Grand Rapids, MI: Zondervan Pub., 1962. p. 70-71

[25] Spurgeon, Charles H. "He Cometh With Clouds." 1887. rpt. Pasadena TX: Pilgrim
Pub., n.d. p. 595 [emphasis in the original].

With clouds of angels, cherubim and seraphim, and all the armies of
heaven he comes. With all the forces of nature, thundercloud and
blackness of tempest, the Lord of all makes his triumphant entrance to
judge the world.[26]

He opposed post-millennialism and affirmed pre-millennialism:

Some think that this descent of the Lord will be postmillennial--that is,
after the thousand years of his reign. I cannot think so. I conceive that
the advent will be premillennial--that he will come first, and then will
come the millennium as the result of his personal reign on the earth.[27]

There is no hint here in these brief excerpts that Charles Spurgeon held any
affinity to a pre-tribulational event. He was pre-millennial without any
dispensational additions. The compiler of the above quote, Tom Carter, simply
concluded that Spurgeon "believed the church would pass through the
tribulation before the second coming. This would make him a premillennial
posttribulationist."[28] In his work, *The Imminent Appearing of Christ*, J. Barton
Payne noted Spurgeon to have reconciled himself, along with others, to "a
post-tribulational view that could not be imminent."[29] Biographer, G. Holden
Pike, noted that Spurgeon did not often preach on prophetical themes as did
some others,[30] but one of his acclaimed graduates from Spurgeon's Pastors'
College did. Spurgeon commended Frank H. White as "My dear friend...who
has worked hard."[31] White was one of the graduates who had achieved great

---

[26] *Ibid.* p. 594-595
[27] Quoted in: Carter, Tom. *2,200 Quotations from the Writings of Charles H.
Spurgeon.* Grand Rapids, MI: BakerBooks, 1996. p. 183
[28] *Ibid.* p. 183-184
[29] Payne, J. Barton. *The Imminent Appearing of Christ.* p. 56-57
[30] Pike. *Ibid.* Vol. 2, Part V, p. 133
[31] Pike. *Ibid.* Vol. 1. Part III, p. 79

success in the early days of Spurgeon's ministry. His short work, *The Saints' Rest and Rapture*, is a succinct presentation of the orthodox views which agree completely with the word of God. White's work is highly recommended.[32]

In an article by Dennis Swanson, librarian at John MacArthur's The Master's Seminary, he devoted much thought to Spurgeon's treatment of the millennial views. Swanson identified two components of Historic Premillennialism: (1) the kingdom to commence at "the culmination of the church age;" (2) "the Rapture will follow the Tribulation, with the church going through the Tribulation under the protection of God."[33] In quoting portions of Spurgeon's own words, Swanson confirmed that "Spurgeon believed that the church would go through the totality of the Tribulation but be protected."[34] Obviously Spurgeon was sound as a Biblical preacher. He was a contemporary of J. N. Darby and was well acquainted with Darbyist teaching. Spurgeon held the orthodox position that Jesus comes once at the end of the age. He was a firm post-tribulationist.

Conclusion

The Godly men noted above all came to the same conclusion. They realized from Scripture that the Lord's return is a single event. This is the common thread in the testimony of others through the years that have rejected the weak assertions of the "any moment" coming of Christ. Conclusions with

---

[32] White, Frank H. *The Saints' Rest and Rapture*. Chelmsford, Essex: The Sovereign Grace Advent Testimony, n.d.

[33] Swanson, Dennis M. "The Millennial Position of Spurgeon." *The Master's Perspective on Biblical Prophecy*. Richard L. Mayhue & Robert L. Thomas, eds. Grand Rapids, MI: Kregel Pub., 2002. p. 249

[34] Swanson. *Ibid.*

eschatology must be based on the truth in the Word of God. Those who seek truth will find that pre-millennialism conforms to the teaching of the Apostles, the Church Fathers, and to the Lord's own word. Believers must consider this with care and look to the Scripture alone for clear understanding of the singular event known as the Second Coming.

---- 0 ----

Many thanks to those who assisted in the research, preparation and publishing of this effort to bring to light much needed focus on the Second Coming of Christ. Your suggestions and contributions have been invaluable.

---- 0 ----

BIBLIOGRAPHY

Africa, Thomas W. *Rome of the Caesars*. New York, NY: John Wiley & Sons, 1965.

Alford, Henry. *The Greek Testament*. 2 Volumes. Chicago, IL: Moody Press, 1958.

Alford, Henry. *The New Testament for English Readers*. rpt. Chicago, IL: Moody Press, n.d.

Allis, Oswald T. *Prophecy and the Church*. Philadelphia, PA: The Presbyterian and Reformed Pub. Co., 1947.

Angus, S. *The Environment of Early Christian.[Studies in Theology]*. New York, NY: Charles Scribner's Sons, 1917.

Armerding, Carl E., and W. Ward Gasque. *Handbook of Biblical Prophecy*. Grand Rapids, MI: Baker Book House, 1978.

Ayer, Joseph Cullen. *A Source Book for Ancient Church History. From the Apostolic Age to the Close of the Conciliar Period*. New York, NY: Charles Scribner's Sons, 1926.

Bakker, Jim. *Prosperity and the Coming Apocalypse: Avoiding the Dangers of Materialistic Christianity in the End Times*. Nashville, TN: Thomas Nelson, Inc., 1998.

Barber, Cyril J. *Job. The Sovereignty of God and the Suffering of Man*. Eugene, OR: Wipf & Stock, 2013.

Barnhouse, Donald Grey. *The Invisible War*. Grand Rapids, MI: Zondervan Pub. House, 1965.

Barnhouse, Donald Grey. *Thessalonians. An Expositional Commentary*. Grand Rapids, MI: Zondervan, 1988.

Bass. Clarence B. *Backgrounds to Dispensationalism*. Grand Rapids, MI: Wm. B. Eerdmans, 1960.

Baxter, J. Sidlow. *Explore the Book*. Grand Rapids, MI: Zondervan Pub. House, 1975.

Bebbington, David. *Evangelicalism in Modern Britain. A History from the 1730s to the 1980s*. Grand Rapids, MI: Baker Book House, 1992.

Beegle, Dewey M. *Prophecy and Prediction*. Ann Arbor, MI: Pryor Pettingill Pub., 1978.

Belcher, Richard P. *Arthur W. Pink. Born to Write. A Biography*. Columbia, SC: Richbarry Press, 1980.

Benko, Stephen. *Pagan Rome and the Early Christians*. Bloomington, IN:

Indiana University Press, 1996.

Benware, Paul N. *Understanding End Times. A Comprehensive Approach.* Chicago, IL: Moody Pres, 1995.

Berkouwer, Louis. *The History of Christian Doctrines.* Grand Rapids, MI: Wm. B. Eerdmans Pub., 1949.

Bock, Darrell L; Craig A. Blaising; Kenneth L. Gentry; Robert B. Strimple. *Three Views on the Millennium and Beyond.* Grand Rapids, MI: Zondervan, 2002.

Bock, Darrell L. *Luke. [Baker Exegetical Commentary on the N. T.].* 2 Volumes. Grand Rapids, MI: Baker Academic, 2002.

Breese, David. *What to Do If You Miss the Rapture.* Colton, CA: World Prophetic Ministry, Inc., 1995.

Broadus, John A. *Commentary on the Gospel of Matthew. [An American Commentary on the N.T.].* 1886. rpt. Valley Forge, PA: The Judson Press, n.d.

Brooks, Keith L. *Prophecies of Daniel and Revelation. Verse by Verse.* Los Angeles, CA: Brooks, 1925.

Brown, Colin. *The New International Dictionary of New Testament Theology.* 4 Volumes. Grand Rapids, MI: Zondervan Pub., 1993.

Bruce, F. F. *The Letters of Paul. An Expanded Paraphrase.* Grand Rapids, MI: Wm. B. Eerdmans Pub. Co., 1965.

Cadoux, Cecil John. *The Early Church and the World.* Edinburgh: T. & T. Clark, 1955.

Caird, G.B. *The Apostolic Age. [Studies in Theology].* London: Gerald Duckworth & Co., Ltd., 1955.

Cambron, Mark G. *Bible Doctrines. Beliefs That Matter.* Grand Rapids, MI: Zondervan, 1981.

Cameron, Robert. *Scriptural Truth About The Lord's Return.* Chicago, IL: Fleming H. Revell, 1922.

Campbell, Donald K, and Jeffrey L. Townsend. *The Coming Millennial Kingdom. A Case for Premillennial Interpretation.* Grand Rapids, MI: Kregel Pub., 1997.

Capps, Charles. *End Times Events—Journey to the End of the Age.* Tulsa, OK: Harrison House, Inc., 1997.

Carlyle, Gavin. *The Prophetical Works of Edward Irving*. 2 Volumes. London: Alexander Strahan, Pub., 1867.

Carson, D. A. *Exegetical Fallacies. Second Edition*. Grand Rapids, MI: Baker Books/Paternoster, 1998.

Carson, D.A. *The Gagging of God: Christianity Confronts Pluralism*. Grand Rapids, MI: ZondervanPublishingHouse, 1996.

Carter, Tom. *2,200 Quotations from the Writings of Charles H. Spurgeon*. Grand Rapids, MI: Baker Books, 1995.

Chafer, Lewis Sperry. Revised by John F. Walvoord. *Major Bible Themes. 52 Vital Doctrines of the Scripture Simplified and Explained*. Grand Rapids, MI: Zondervan Pub., 1980.

Chafer, Lewis Sperry. *Systematic Theology*. 8 Volumes. Dallas, TX: Dallas Seminary Press, 1962.

Chrysostom, John. *The Homilies of S. John Chrysostom, Archbishop of Constantinople, on the Epistles of St. Paul the Apostle to the Philippians, Colossians, and Thessalonians*. Oxford: John Henry Parker, 1843.

Cleveland, Grover. *Good Citizenship*. Philadelphia, PA: Henry Altemus Co., 1908.

Clouse, Robert G. *The Meaning of the Millennium: Four Views*. Downers Grove, IL: InterVarsity Press, 1984.

Cohn, Norman. *The Pursuit of the Millennium*. New York, NY: Harper & Bros., 1961.

Colwell, Ernest Cadman. *The Study of the Bible. Revised Edition*. Chicago, IL: The University of Chicago Press, 1976.

Conybeare, W. J., and J. S. Howson. *The Life and Epistles of St. Paul*. rpt. Grand Rapids, MI: Wm. B. Eerdmans, 1951.

Cooper, David L. *Future Events Revealed. An Exposition of the Olivet Discourse*. Los Angeles, CA: Biblical Research Society [1935], 1983.

Cooper, David L. *What Men Must Believe*. Los Angeles, CA: Biblical Research Society, 1953.

Couch, Mal. *Dictionary of Premillennial Theology*. Grand Rapids, MI: Kregel Pub., 2006.

Crouch, Paul. *The Shadow of the Apocalypse. When All Hell Breaks Loose*. New York, NY: G. Putnam's Sons, 2004.

Culbertson, William, and Herman B. Centz, eds. *Understanding the Times*.

Prophetic Messages Delivered at the 2nd International Congress on Prophecy, New York City. Grand Rapids, MI: Zondervan Pub., 1956.

Culver, Robert. *Daniel and the Latter Days*. Westwood, NJ: Fleming H. Revell, 1954.

Dallimore, Arnold. *The Life of Edward Irving: Fore-runner of the Charismatic Movement*. Edinburgh: The Banner of Truth Trust, 1983.

Damer, T. Edward. *Attacking Faulty Reasoning*. Belmont, CA: Wadsworth Pub., 1987.

Darby, J. N. [John Nelson]. *The Holy Scriptures. A New Translation from the Original Languages*. Lancing, Sussex: Kensington Bible Trust, 1984.

DeHaan, M. R. *Daniel the Prophet: 35 Simple Studies in the Book of Daniel*. Grand Rapids, MI: Zondervan, 1975.

DeHaan, M. R. *35 Simple Studies in the Book of Revelation*. Grand Rapids, MI: Zondervan, 1988.

Deissmann, Adolph. *Light from the Ancient East*. 1927. rpt. Grand Rapids, MI: Baker Book House, 1980.

Dixon, Michael E. *Where Did the Pretribulation Rapture Go?* Cypress, CA: Sheva Foundation, 1981.

Douglas, J. D. *The New International Dictionary of the Christian Church*. Grand Rapids, MI: Zondervan Pub., 1983.

Douty, Norman. *The Great Tribulation Debate—Has Christ's Return Two Stages?* Harrison, AR: Gibbs Pub., 1976.

Eadie, John. *Commentary on the Greek Text of the Epistles of St. Paul to the Thessalonians*. 1887. rpt. Grand Rapids, MI: Baker Book House, 1979.

Earle, Ralph. *Word Meanings in the New Testament*. Peabody, MA: Hendrickson Pub., 2002.

Edersheim, Alfred. *Prophecy and History in Relation to the Messiah. The Warburton Lectures for 1880-1884*. New York: Anson D. F. Randolph & Company, 1885.

Ellis, E. Earle. *Paul's Use of the Old Testament*. Grand Rapids, MI: Baker Book House, 1981.

Erdman, Charles R. *The Epistles of Paul to the Thessalonians*.

Philadelphia, PA: The Westminster Press, 1966.

Erdman, Charles R. *The Return of Christ*. New York, NY: George H. Doran Co., 1922.

Erickson, Millard. *Christian Theology*. Grand Rapids, MI: Baker Book House, 1986.

[Eusebius]. *The Ecclesiastical History of Eusebius Pamphilus*. Christian Frederick Cruse, trans. 1850. rpt. Grand Rapids, MI: Baker Book House, 1988.

Evans, William. *The Great Doctrines of the Bible*. Chicago, IL: Moody Press, 1949.

Dixon, A. C.; Louis Meyer, R. A. Torrey, eds. *The Fundamentals*. 4 Volumes. Los Angeles, CA: The Bible Institute of Los Angeles, 1917.

Farrar, Frederic W. *Eternal Hope. Five Sermons*. London: Macmillan & Co., 1901.

Ferguson, Everett. *Backgrounds of Early Christianity. Second Edition*. Grand Rapids, MI: William B. Eerdmans Pub. Co., 2003.

Fisher, George Park. *History of Christian Doctrines. [Int'l. Theological Library]*. New York, NY: Charles Scribner's Sons, 1896.

Fraser, Alexander. *The "Any Moment" Return of Christ*. Pittsburgh, PA: The Evangelical Fellowship, Inc., 1947.

Fraser, Donald. *Metaphors in the Gospels. A Series of Short Studies*. New York, NY: Robert Carter & Bros., 1885.

Froese, Arno. *The Great Mystery of the Rapture*. West Columbia, SC: The Olive Press, 1999.

Froese, Arno. *119 Most Frequently Asked Questions About Prophecy*. Columbia, SC: The Olive Press, 2003.

Fromow, George H. *B. W. Newton and Dr. S. P. Tregelles. Teachers of the Faith and the Future*. London: The Sovereign Grace Advent Testimony, 1969.

Froom, Leroy. *The Prophetic Faith of Our Fathers*. 4 Volumes. Washington, DC: Review & Herald, 1950-1954.

Frost, Henry W. *The Second Coming of Christ. A review of the teaching of Scripture concerning the return of Christ*. Grand Rapids, MI: Wm. B. Eerdmans Pub., 1934.

Fruchtenbaum, Arnold. *The Footsteps of the Messiah. A Study of the*

Sequence of Prophetic Events. Tustin, CA: Ariel Press, 1984.

Fruchtenbaum, Arnold. "Ariel Ministries Newsletter." Tustin, CA: Winter, 2003.

Fuller, Robert. *Naming the Antichrist: the History of an American Obsession.* New York, NY: Oxford University Press, 1995.

Gaebelein, Arno C. *Meat in Due Season.* New York, NY: Arno C. Gaebelein, Inc. n.d.

Geisler, Norman L., and William E. Nix. *A General Introduction to the Bible.* Chicago, IL: Moody Press, 1986.

Gerstner, John. *A Primer on Dispensationalism.* Phillipsburg, NJ: P & R Pub., 1982.

Gerstner, John H. *Wrongly Dividing the Truth. A Critique of Dispensationalism.* Brentwood, TN: Wolgemuth & Hyatt, 1991.

Gill, John. *A Body of Divinity.* One Volume Edition. rpt. Grand Rapids, MI: Sovereign Grace Publishers, 1971.

Glover, T.R. *The Conflict of Religions in the Early Roman Empire.* Boston, MA: Beacon Press, 1960.

Godet, Frederic Louis. *Commentary on First Corinthians.* 1889. rpt. Grand Rapids, MI: Kregel Pub., 1979.

Godet, Frederic L. *Studies in Paul's Epistles.* 1889. rpt. Grand Rapids, MI: Kregel Pub., 1984.

Goodwin, Frank J. *A Harmony of the Life of St. Paul.* rpt. Grand Rapids, MI: Baker Book House, 1977.

Gordon, A. J. *Ecce Venit. Behold He Cometh.* Chicago, IL: Fleming H. Revell, 1889.

Gray, James M. *My Faith in Jesus Christ. A Personal Testimony.* Chicago IL: Fleming H. Revell, 1927.

Grudem, Wayne. *Systematic Theology. An Introduction to Biblical Doctrine.* Grand Rapids, MI: Zondervan, 2006.

Gundry, Bob. *First the Antichrist.* Grand Rapids, MI: BakerBooks, 1997.

Gundry, Robert H. *The Church and the Tribulation.* Grand Rapids, MI: Zondervan, 1973.

Guthrie, Donald. *The Relevance of John's Apocalypse.* Grand Rapids, MI: William B. Eerdmans Pub. Co., 1987.

Hagglund, Bengt. *History of Theology.* St. Louis, MO: Concordia Pub. House, 1968.

Haldeman, I. M. *Bible Messages.* Greenville, SC: The Gospel Hour, n.d.

Haley, John W. *Alleged Discrepancies of the Bible.* 1874. rpt. Nashville, TN: Gospel Advocate Co., 1974.

Harding, William Henry. *The Life of George Muller: A Record of Faith Triumphant.* London: Morgan & Scott, 1914.

Harris, George. "Eschatology." *Progressive Orthodoxy.* 1892. rpt. Hicksville, NY: The Regina Press, 1975

Harrison, Everett F. *Acts: the Expanding Church.* Chicago, IL: Moody Press, 1975.

Hawthorne, Gerald F.; Ralph P. Martin; Daniel G. Reid. *Dictionary of Paul and His Letters.* Downers Grove, IL: InterVarsity Press, 2004.

Helm, Paul. *The Last Things. Death, Judgment, Heaven and Hell.* Carlisle, PA: The Banner of Truth Trust, 1989.

Hendriksen, William. *Exposition on the Gospel According to Matthew. [New Testament Commentary].* Grand Rapids, MI: Baker Book House, 1981.

Hendriksen, William. *The Bible on the Life Hereafter.* Grand Rapids, MI: Baker Book House, 1972.

Hiebert, D. Edmond. *The Thessalonian Epistles. A Call to Readiness.* Chicago, IL: Moody Press, 1977.

Hindson, Ed. *Earth's Final Hours.* Eugene, OR: Harvest House, 1999.

Hindson, Ed. *Is the Antichrist Alive and Well?* Eugene, OR: Harvest House, 1998.

Hitchcock, Mark. *The Complete Book of Bible Prophecy.* Wheaton, IL: Tyndale House Pub., 1999.

Hitchcock, Mark. *101 Answers to the Most Asked Questions About the End Times.* Sisters, OR: Multnomah Publishers, 2002.

Hitchcock, Roswell D., and Francis Brown. *Teaching of the Twelve Apostles.* New York, NY: Charles Scribner's Sons, 1884.

Hocking, David. *What Christians Believe.* Tustin, CA: Hope For Today Pub., 1998.

Hodge, Charles. *Commentary on the First Epistle to the Corinthians.* 1857.

rpt. Grand Rapids, MI: Wm. B. Eerdmans, 1994.

Hoekema, Anthony A. *The Bible and the Future.* Grand Rapids, MI: Wm. B. Eerdmans Pub. Co., 1982.

Hogg, C. F. and W. E. Vine. *The Epistles to the Thessalonians. With Notes Exegetical and Expository.* 1914. rpt. Grand Rapids, MI: Kregel Publications, 1959.

Hunt, Dave. *Global Peace and the Rise of Antichrist.* Eugene, OR: Harvest House, 1990.

Hunt, Dave. *How Close Are We?* Eugene, OR: Harvest House, 1993.

Hunt, Dave. *When Will Jesus Come?* Eugene, OR: Harvest House, 2003.

Hunt, Dave. "The Berean Call." Vol. XXIII, No. 3, March 2008.

Hutchinson, John. *Lectures Chiefly Expository on St. Paul's First and Second Epistles to the Thessalonians. With Notes and Illustrations.* Edinburgh: T. & T. Clark, 1884.

Hutson, Curtis. *Great Preaching on the Second Coming.* Murfreesboro, TN: Sword of the Lord, 1989.

Ice, Thomas, & Timothy Demy. *Fast Facts on Bible Prophecy.* Eugene, OR: Harvest House, 1999.

Ice, Thomas, & Timothy Demy. *When the Trumpet Sounds.* Eugene, OR: Harvest House Pub., 1996.

Ice, Thomas, & Tim LaHaye. "Pre-Trib Perspectives." El Cajon, CA: various issues.

Ironside, H. A. *Expository Notes on the Gospel of Matthew.* Neptune, NJ: Loizeaux Bros., 1974.

Ironside, H. A. *Lectures on the Book of Revelation.* Neptune, NJ: Loizeaux Bros., 1973.

Ironside, H. A. *The Mysteries of God.* New York, NY: Loizeaux Bros., n.d. [c1931].

Ironside, H. A. *Wrongly Dividing the Word of Truth. Ultra-Dispensationalism Examined in the Light of Holy Scripture.* Philadelphia, PA: Approved-Books Store, n.d.

Jackson, George Anson. *The Apostolic Fathers and the Apologists of the Second Century/The Fathers of the Third Century. [Early Christian Literature Primers].* 2 Volumes. New York, NY: D. Appleton & Co.,

1879, 1880.

Jeffress, Robert. *As Time Runs Out: A Simple Guide to Bible Prophecy.* Nashville, TN: Broadman & Holman Pub., 1999.

Jeffrey, Grant R. *Final Warning.* Eugene, OR: Harvest House, 1996.

Jeffrey, Grant R. *Heaven—the Mystery of Angels.* Toronto, ON: Frontier Research, 1996.

Jennings, F.C. *The Seven Letters or, a Divine Church History (Revelation II, III).* London: Pickering & Inglis, n.d.

Jeremiah, David. *Jesus' Final Warning.* Nashville, TN: Word Pub., 1999.

Johnson, Phillip E. *The Wedge of Truth. Splitting the Foundations of Naturalism.* Downers Grove, IL: InterVarsity Press, 2000.

Kaiser, Walter C., Jr. *Toward An Old Testament Theology.* Grand Rapids, MI: Zondervan, 1978.

Keener, Craig S. *The IVP Bible Background Commentary: New Testament.* Downers Grove, IL: InterVarsity Press, 1999.

Kelly, W. *Lectures on the Second Coming and the Kingdom of the Lord and Saviour Jesus Christ.* London: W. H. Broom, 1876.

Kelly, W. *The Heavenly Hope; The So-called Apostolical Fathers on the Lord's Second Coming.* London: T. Weston, 1910.

Kennedy, H. A. A. *St. Paul's Conception of the Last Things.* London: Hodder & Stoughton, 1904.

Kennedy, John W. *The Torch of the Testimony.* 1963. rpt. Goleta, CA: Christian Books, 1987.

Kimball, William R. *The Rapture—A Question of Timing.* Grand Rapids, MI: Baker Book House, 1985.

Kurtz, Johann Heinrich. *Church History.* 3 Volumes. New York, NY: Funk & Wagnalls, 1889.

Ladd, George Eldon. *The Blessed Hope.* Grand Rapids, MI: Wm. B. Eerdmans, 1973.

Ladd, George Eldon. *The Young Church. Acts of the Apostles. [Bible Guides, no. 15].* London: Lutterworth Press, 1964.

Ladd, George Eldon. *A Commentary on the Revelation of John.* Grand Rapids, MI: William. B. Eerdmans Pub. Co., 1987.

LaHaye, Tim F. *Christ and the Tribulation. Revelation. Volume II.* La

Mesa, CA: Post, Inc., 1966.

LaHaye. Tim. *The Beginning of the End*. Wheaton, IL: Tyndale House Pub., 1972.

LaHaye, Tim. *No Fear of the Storm. Why Christians Will Escape All the Tribulation*. Sisters, OR: Multnomah Press Books, 1993.

LaHaye, Tim, and Ed Hindson. *The Popular Encyclopedia of Bible Prophecy*. Eugene, OR: Harvest House, 2004.

LaHaye, Tim. *Revelation—Illustrated and Made Plain*. Grand Rapids, MI: Zondervan Corp., 1975.

LaHaye, Tim, and Jerry B. Jenkins. *Are We Living in the End Times?* Wheaton, IL: Tyndale House Pub., 1999.

LaHaye, Tim, and Jerry B. Jenkins. *Perhaps Today. Living Every Day in the Light of Christ's Return*. Wheaton, IL: Tyndale House, 2001.

Lang, G. H. *Anthony Norris Groves: Saint and Pioneer. A Combined Study of a Man of God and the Original Principles and Practices of The Brethren with Applications to Present Conditions*. 1949. rpt. Miami Springs, FL: Schoettle Pub. Co., 1988.

Lang, G. H. *The Disciple*. 1954. rpt. Miami Springs, FL; Conley & Schoettle, 1984.

Larkin, Clarence. *The Book of Revelation*. Philadelphia, PA: Clarence Larkin Estate, 1919.

LaSor, William Sanford. *The Truth About Armageddon*. NY: Harper & Row, 1982.

Law, John. *The Tests of Life. A Study in the First Epistle of St. John*. Edinbrgh: T & T Clark, 1914.

Lawlor, Hugh Jackson, and John Ernest Leonard Oulton. *Eusebius, Bishop of Caesarea. The Ecclesiastical History and the Martyrs of Palestine*. London: S.P.C.K., 1954.

Lewis, Arthur H. *The Dark Side of the Millennium*. Grand Rapids, MI: Baker Book House, 1980

Lewis, C. S. *The World's Last Night and Other Essays*. New York, NY: Harcourt Brace Jovanovich, 1973.

Lietzmann, Hans. *A History of the Early Church*. 2 Volumes. London, UK: Lutterworth Press, 1961.

Lightfoot, J. B. *Biblical Essays*. 1893. rpt. Grand Rapids, MI: Baker Book House, 1979.

Lightfoot, J. B. *Notes on the Epistles of St. Paul*. Peabody, MA: Hendrickson, 1999.

Lightfoot, J. B., and J. R. Harmer. *The Apostolic Fathers*. Grand Rapids, MI: Baker Book House, 1987.

Lindsay, Thomas M. *The Church and the Ministry in the Early Centuries*. London: Hodder & Stoughton, 1907.

Lindsey, Hal. *Planet Earth: The Final Chapter*. Beverly Hills, CA: Western Front, Ltd., 1998.

Lloyd-Jones, Martyn. *Authentic Christianity. Studies in the Book of Acts. Volume One*. Wheaton, IL: Crossway Books, 2000.

Lloyd-Jones, D. Martyn. *Studies in the Sermon on the Mount*. One Volume Edition. Grand Rapids, MI: Wm. B. Eerdmans Pub. Co., 1979.

Lloyd-Jones, D. Martyn. *The Church and the Last Things*. Wheaton, IL: Crossway Books, 2003.

Lloyd-Jones, D. Martyn. *The Heart of the Gospel*. Wheaton, IL: Crossway Books, 1991.

Longenecker, Richard. *The Ministry and Message of Paul*. Grand Rapids, MI: Zondervan Pub., 1973.

Ludwigson, Ludwig. *A Survey of Bible Prophecy*. Grand Rapids, MI: Zondervan Pub., 1975.

MacArthur, John. *The MacArthur New Testament Commentary*. Nashville, TN: Thomas Nelson Pub., 2007.

MacArthur, John, Jr. *The Second Coming of the Lord Jesus Christ. Study Notes. Select Scriptures*. Panorama City, CA: Word of Grace Communications, 1981.

MacArthur, John. *The Second Coming of Christ. Signs of Christ's Return and the End of the Age*. Wheaton, IL: Crossway Books, 1999.

MacArthur, John F., Jr. *Titus. [The MacArthur New Testament Commentary]*. Chicago, IL: Moody Press, 1996.

MacArthur, John. *Truth Endures. Commemorating Forty Years of Unleashing God's Truth One Verse at a Time, 1969-2009*. Panorama City, CA: Grace to You, 2009.

MacLaren, Alexander. *The Epistles of John, Jude and the Book of Revelation. [Expositions of Holy Scripture].* New York, NY: A. C. Armstrong, 1910.

MacMullen, Ramsay. *Christianizing the Roman Empire (A.D. 100-400).* New Haven, CT: Yale University Press, 1984.

MacMullen, Ramsay. *Paganism in the Roman Empire.* New Haven, CT: Yale University Press, 1981.

MacPherson, Dave. *The Great Rapture Hoax.* Fletcher, NC: New Puritan Library, 1983.

MacPherson, Dave. *The Incredible Cover-Up. The True Story of the Pre-Trib Rapture.* Plainfield, NJ: Logos Int'l., 1975.

MacPherson, Norman Spurgeon. *Triumph Through Tribulation.* Otego, NY: By the Author, 1944

Malgo, Wim. *1000 Years Peace.* West Columbia, SC: The Midnight Call, Inc., 1984.

Malgo, Wim. *A New Heaven and a New Earth. An Exposition of Revelation Chapters 18 through 22.* West Columbia, SC: The Midnight Call, 1985.

Marsden, George M. *Fundamentalism and American Culture. The Shaping of Twentieth-Century Evangelicalism: 1870-1925.* New York, NY: Oxford University Press, 1982.

Marshall, Alfred. *Zondervan Parallel New Testament in Greek and English. [NIV/KJV].* Grand Rapids, MI: Zondervan Bible Pub., 1977.

Martin, Walter. *Essential Christianity. A Handbook of Basic Christian Doctrines.* Ventura, CA: Vision House, 1990.

Mattingly, Harold. *Christianity in the Roman Empire.* New York, NY: W. W. Norton & Co., Inc., 1967.

McClain, Alva J. *Daniel's Prophecy of the Seventy Weeks.* Grand Rapids, MI: Zondervan Pub., 1964.

McGee, J. Vernon. *Thru the Bible with J. Vernon McGee.* 5 Volumes. Nashville, TN: Thomas Nelson Pub., 1988.

McGee, J. Vernon. *On Prophecy: Man's Fascination with the Future.* Nashville, TN: Nelson Books, 2004.

McGinn, Bernard. *Antichrist: Two Thousand Years of the Human Fascination with Evil.* New York, NY: HarperSanFrancisco, 1995.

McQuilken, J. Robertson. *Understanding and Applying the Bible.* Chicago,

IL: Moody Press, 1985.

McReynolds, Paul R. *Word Study Greek-English New Testament.* Wheaton, IL: Tyndale Pub., 2003.

Miller, Andrew. *Miller's Church History. From First to Twentieth Century.* Fincastle, VA: Scripture Truth Book co., n.d.

Milligan, George. *St. Paul's Epistles to the Thessalonians. The Greek Text with Introduction and Notes.* London: Macmillan and Co., Ltd., 1908.

Missler, Chuck, & Mark Eastman. *Alien Encounters. The Secret Behind the UFO Phenomenon.* Coeur d'Alene, ID: Koinonia House, 1997.

Missler, Chuck. *Prophecy 20/20.* Nashville, TN: Thomas Nelson Pub., 2006.

Missler, Chuck. *Personal Update. The News Journal of Koinonia House.* Loeffler, John. "The Rapture Myth." Vol. 12. No. 3, March 2000.

Morgan, G. Campbell. *A First Century Message to Twentieth Century Christians.* Chicago, IL: Fleming H. Revell Co., 1902.

Morgan, G. Campbell. *The Parables and Metaphors of Our Lord.* Old Tappan, NJ: Fleming H. Revell Co., 1943.

Morgan, G. Campbell. *The Study and Teaching of the English Bible.* London: James Clarke, n.d.

Morgan, Jill, ed. *This Was His Faith. The Expository Letters of G. Campbell Morgan.* Westwood, NJ: Fleming H. Revell Co., 1952.

Morris, Leon. *The Book of Revelation. [Tyndale N. T. Commentaries].* Leicester, UK: IVP/Grand Rapids, MI: Eerdmans, 1989.

Mosheim, John Lawrence. *Ecclesiastical History. Ancient and Modern, from the Birth of Christ to the Beginning of the Eighteenth Century.* 2 Volumes.. 1826. rpt. Rosemead, CA: Old Paths Book Club, 1959.

Mounce, Robert H. *What Are We Waiting For? A Commentary on Revelation.* Grand Rapids, MI: Wm. B. Eerdmans Pub., 1992.

Murdock, James. *The New Testament or, the Book of the Holy Gospel of our Lord and Our God, Jesus the Messiah. A Literal translation from the Syriac Peshita Version.* New York, NY: Stanford and Swords, 1852.

Murray, John. *Collected Writings of John Murray.* 4 Volumes. Edinburgh: The Banner of Truth Trust, 1984.

Newell, William R. *The Book of Revelation.* Chicago, IL: Moody Press, 1935.

Newton, John. *The Works of the Rev. John Newton*. 4 Volumes. New Haven, CT: Nathan Whiting, 1826.

Newton, Thomas. *Dissertations on the Prophecies*. Philadelphia, PA: J. J. Woodward, 1838.

NIV Archaeological Study Bible. Grand Rapids, MI: Zondervan, 2005.

Oetting, Walter. *The Church of the Catacombs*. St. Louis, MO: Concordia Pub., 1970.

Olson, Carl E. *Will Catholics Be "Left Behind"? A Catholic Critique of the Rapture and Today's Prophecy Teachers*. San Francisco, CA: Ignatius Press, 2003.

Orr, James. *Neglected Factors in the Study of the Early Progress of Christianity*. London: Hodder & Stoughton, 1899.

Orr, James. *The International Standard Bible Encyclopedia*. 4 Volumes. Grand Rapids, MI: Wm. B. Eerdmans, 1939.

Osborne, Grant R. *Revelation. [Baker Exegetical Commentary on the N. T.]*. Grand Rapids, MI: Baker Academic, 2002.

Packer, J. I. *Concise Theology: A Guide to Historic Christian Beliefs*. Wheaton, IL: Tyndale House, Pub., Inc., 1973.

Payne, J. Barton. *The Imminent Appearing of Christ*. Grand Rapids, MI: Wm. B. Eerdmans Pub. Co., 1962.

Pentecost, J. Dwight. *Things to Come*. Grand Rapids, MI: Zondervan Pub., 1977.

Peters, George N.H. *The Theocratic Kingdom*. 3 Volumes. 1884. rpt. Kregel Pub., 1988.

Peterson, Robert L. *Robert Chapman. A Biography*. Neptune, NJ: Loizeaux Bros., 1995.

Pettingill, William L. *God's Prophecies for Plain People*. Wheaton, IL: Van Kampen Press, 1923.

Pettingill, William I.; J. R. Schaffer; J. D. Adams. *Light On Prophecy. A Coordinated, Constructive Teaching Being the Proceedings and Addresses at the Philadelphia Prophetic Conference .May 28-30, 1918*. New York, NY: The Christian Herald, 1918.

Pickering, Hy. *Chief Men Among the Bretheren*. London: Pickering & Inglis, n.d.

Pickering, Hy. *One Thousand Wonderful Things About the Bible*. London: Pickering & Inglis, 1946.

Pike, G. Holden. *The Life and Work of Charles Haddon Spurgeon*. 2 Volumes. 1894. rpt. Banner of Truth, 1991.

Plummer, Alfred. *An Exegetical Commentary on the Gospel of S. Matthew*. London: Elliot Stock, 1910.

Purves, George T. *Christianity in the Apostolic Age*. 1900. rpt. Grand Rapids, MI: Baker Book House, 1955.

Ramsay, Sir William M. *The Church in the Roman Empire. Before A.D. 170*. 1897. rpt. Grand Rapids, MI: Baker Book House, 1954.

Ramsay, Sir William M. *The Cities of St. Paul. Their Influence on His Life and Thought*. 1908. rpt. James Family Christian Pub., n.d.

Ray, Charles. *The Life of Charles Haddon Spurgeon*. London: Passmore and Alabaster, 1903.

Reese, Alexander. *The Approaching Advent of Christ*. 1937. rpt. Grand Rapids, MI: Grand Rapids International Pub., 1975.

Reid, Daniel G.; Robert D. Linder; Bruce L. Shelley; Harry S. Stout. *Dictionary of Christianity in America*. Downers Grove, IL: InterVarsity Press, 1991.

Richard, Ramesh P. "Levels of Biblical Meaning." *Bibliotheca Sacra*. Volume 143: April – June 1986, Number 570.

Roberts, Alexander, and James Donaldson. *The Ante-Nicene Fathers*. 10 Volumes. 1885. rpt. Grand Rapids, MI: Wm. B. Eerdmans, 1977.

Robertson, A.T. *Luke the Historian in the Light of Research*. NY: Charles Scribner's Sons, 1936.

Robertson, A.T. *Paul the Interpreter of Christ*. NY: George H. Doran, 1921.

Rogers, Adrian. *Unveiling the End Times in Our Time*. Nashville, TN: Broadman & Holman Pub., 2004.

Ross, Randall. *The Next 7 Great Events of the Future*. Orlando, FL: Creation House, 1997.

Rotherham, Joseph Bryant. *Rotherham's Emphasized Bible*. Grand Rapids, MI: Kregel Pub., 1994.

Rowdon, Harold H. *The Origins of the Brethren. 1825-1850*. London: Pickering & Inglis, 1967.

Ruffin, C. Bernard. *The Days of the Martyrs*. Huntington, IN: Our Sunday Visitor, 1985.

Ryle, John Charles. *Expository Thoughts on the Gospel of St. Matthew*. London: Hodder & Stoughton, 1900.

Ryle, John Charles. *Expository Thoughts on the Gospels. Mark*. rpt. Grand Rapids, MI: Zondervan Pub. House, n.d.

Ryle, John Charles. *The True Christian*. Welwyn, England: Evangelical Press, 1978.

Ryrie, Charles C. *Dispensationalism. Revised and Expanded*. Chicago, IL: Moody Press, 1995.

Ryrie, Charles C. *Revelation. [Everyman's Bible Commentary]*. Chicago, IL: Moody Press, 1982.

Ryrie, Charles Caldwell. *Ryrie Study Bible. Expanded Edition*. [NIV]. Chicago, IL: Moody Press, 1994.

Sale-Harrison, L. *The Wonders of the Great Unveiling. The Remarkable Book of Revelation*. London: Pickering & Inglis, n.d.

Sandeen, Ernest. *The Roots of Fundamentalism. British and American Millenarianism 1800-1930*. Chicago, IL: The University of Chicago Press, 1970.

Sargent, Tony. *The Sacred Anointing. The Preaching of Dr. Martyn Lloyd-Jones*. Wheaton, IL: Crossway Books, 1994.

Schaff, Philip. *History of the Christian Church*. 8 Volumes. 1910. rpt. Wm. B. Eerdmans Pub., 1979.

Scofield, C. I. *The Scofield Reference Bible*. New York, NY: Oxford University Press, 1945.

Scofield, C. I. *The Scofield Bible Correspondence Course*. 3 Volumes. Chicago, IL: Moody Bible Institute of Chicago, 1934.

Scofield, C. I. *Things Old and New. Old and New Testament Studies*. New York, NY: "Our Hope," 1920.

Selwyn, Edward Gordon. *The First Epistle of St. Peter. The Greek Text with Introduction, Notes and Essays*. New York, NY: Macmillan, 1969.

Sheldon, Henry C. *History of the Christian Church*. 4 Volumes. 1895. rpt. Peabody, MA: Hendrickson Pub., 1988.

Shields, T. T. *The Doctrines of Grace*. Toronto: The Gospel Witness, n.d.

Silver, Jesse Forest. *The Lord's Return. Seen In History and In Scripture As*

Pre-Millennial and Imminent. Chicago, IL: Fleming H. Revell, 1914.

Smith, Chuck. *End Times.* Costa Mesa, CA: Maranatha House Pub., 1978.

Smith, Chuck. *Dateline Earth. Countdown to Eternity.* Old Tappan, NJ: Fleming H. Revell, 1989.

Smith, Chuck. *The Tribulation and the Church.* Costa Mesa, CA: The Word for Today, 1980.

Smith, Chuck. *The Word For Today Bible. New Testament.* Nashville, TN: Thomas Nelson Pub., 2005.

Smith, Chuck. *The Final Act.* Costa Mesa, CA: The Word For Today, 2007.

Smith, Oswald J. *Tribulation or Rapture--Which?* Chelmsford, UK: The Sovereign Grace Advent Testimony, n.d.

Smith, Wilbur M. *Egypt in Biblical Prophecy.* Boston, MA: W. A. Wilde & Co., 1957.

Smith, Wilbur M. *Peloubet's Select Notes on the International Bible Lessons for Christian Teaching. Uniform Series 1959.* Boston, MA: W. A. Wilde Co., 1958.

Spence, H. D. M. *The Teaching of the Twelve Apostles. A Translation with Notes.* London: James Nisbet & Co., 1885.

Spurgeon, Charles H. *Sermons on the Second Coming and the Last Things.* Grand Rapids, MI: Zondervan Pub., 1962.

Spurgeon, C. H. *Spurgeon's Popular Exposition of Matthew.* Grand Rapids, MI: Zondervan Pub., n.d.

Spurgeon, Charles H. *The Metropolitan Tabernacle Pulpit. Vol. XII.* 1866. rpt. Pasadena, TX: Pilgrim Publications, 1973.

Spurgeon, Charles H. *The Metropolitan Tabernacle Pulpit. Vol. XIX.* 1873. rpt. Pasadena, TX: Pilgrim Publications, 1971.

Spurgeon, Charles H. *The Metropolitan Tabernacle Pulpit. Vol. XXXV.* 1889. rpt. Pasadena, TX: Pilgrim Publications, 1975.

Stalker, James. *The Life of St. Paul.* Chicago, IL: Fleming H. Revell, n.d.

Stanton, Gerald B. *Kept From The Hour. Biblical Evidence for the Pretribulational Return of Christ.* Miami Springs, FL: Schoettle Pub. Co., 1991.

Stanton, Gerald B. *Kept From The Hour. A Systematic Study of the Rapture in Bible Prophecy*. Grand Rapids, MI: Zondervan Pub., 1956.

Stanton, Gerald B. "Will the Church Enter the Tribulation?" *The Church and the End Times*. Los Angeles, CA: The Bible Institute Hour, n.d.

Steer, Roger. *The George Muller Treasury*. Westchester, IL: Crossway Books, 1978.

Stein, Robert H. *A Basic Guide to Interpreting the Bible: Playing by the Rules*. Grand Rapids, MI: Baker Books, 2001.

Stern, David H. *Jewish New Testament. A translation of the New Testament that expresses its Jewishness*. Clarksville, MD: Jewish New Testament Pub., Inc., 1989.

Stott, John R. W. *What Christ Thinks of the Church. Insights from Revelation 2 – 3*. Grand Rapids, MI: Wm. B. Eerdmans Pub. Co., 1972.

Strachan, Gordon. *The Pentecostal Theology of Edward Irving*. 1973. rpt. Peabody, MA: Hendrickson Pub., 1988.

Swanson, Dennis M. "The Millennial Position of Spurgeon." *The Master's Perspective on Biblical Prophecy*. Richard L. Mayhue & Robert L. Thomas, eds. Grand Rapids, MI: Kregel Pub., 2002

ten Boom, Corrie. *Tramp for the Lord*. Ft. Washington, PA: Christian Literature Crusade; and Old Tappan, NJ: Fleming H. Revell Co., 1974.

Tenney. Merrill C. *New Testament Times*. Grand Rapids, MI: Baker Book, 2004.

Thayer, Joseph Henry. *The New Thayer's Greek-English Lexicon to the New Testament*. Peabody, MA: Hendrickson Pub., 1981.

Thiessen, Henry C. *Lectures in Systematic Theology*. Grand Rapids, MI: Wm. B. Eerdmans Pub., 1974.

Thigpen, Paul. *The Rapture Trap. A Catholic Response to "End Times" Fever*. West Chester, PA: Ascension Press, 2001.

Torrey, R. A. *The Importance and Value of Proper Bible Study*. New York, NY: George H. Doran, 1921.

Torrey, R. A.; A. C. Dixon, and others. *The Fundamentals. A Testimony to the Truth*. 4 Volumes. Los Angeles, CA: The Bible Institute of Los Angeles, 1917.

Toussaint, Stanley D. *Behold The King. A Study of Matthew*. Portland, OR: Multnomah Press, 1980.

Tregelles, S. P. *The Hope of Christ's Second Coming*. 1886. rpt.

Chelmsford, UK: The Sovereign Grace Advent Testimony, n.d. [c1978].

Trench, Richard Chenevix. *Commentary on the Epistles to the Seven Churches in Asia. Revelation II. III.* New York, NY: Charles Scribner, 1861.

Unger, Merril F.; Harrison, R. K.; Howard F. Vos; Cyril J. Barber, eds. *The New Unger's Bible Dictionary.* Chicago, IL: Moody Press, 1990.

Van Impe, Jack. *The Great Escape. Preparing for the Rapture: the Next Event on God's Calendar.* Nashville, TN: Word Pub., 1998.

Van Kampen, Robert. *The Rapture Question Answered. Plain and Simple.* Grand Rapids, MI: Fleming H. Revell, 1997.

Van Kampen, Robert. *The Sign.* Wheaton, IL: Crossway Books, 1992.

Vincent, Marvin R. *Word Studies in the New Testament.* 4 Volumes. rpt. Hendrickson Pub., n.d.

Vine, W.E.; Merrill F. Unger; William White, Jr. *Vine's Complete Expository Dictionary of Old and New Testament Words.* Nashville, TN: Thomas Nelson, 1996.

Wake, William. *The Genuine Epistles of the Apostolic Fathers, St. Barnabas, St. Clement, St. Ignatius, St. Polycarp, the Shepherd of Hermas, and the Martyrdoms of St. Ignatius and St. Polycarp.* Manchester: W. Shelmerdine & Co., 1799.

Walters, Brent S. *Didache. The Unknown Teaching of the Twelve Apostles.* San Jose, CA: The Ante-Nicene Archive, 1991.

Walvoord, John F. *End Times. Understanding Today's World Events in Biblical Prophecy.* Nashville, TN: Word Pub., 1998.

Walvoord, John F. *The Return of the Lord.* Findlay, OH: Dunham Pub., 1955.

Walvoord, John F. *The Rapture Question.* Findlay, OH: Dunham Pub., 1957.

Walvoord, John F. *The Rapture Question.* Revised and Enlarged Edition. Grand Rapids, MI: Zondervan, 1979.

Walvoord, John F. *The Church in Prophecy.* Grand Rapids, MI: Zondervan, 1964.

Walvoord, John F. *The Millennial Kingdom.* Grand Rapids, MI: Zondervan, 1979.

Walvoord, John F. *The Blessed Hope and the Tribulation.* Grand Rapids,

MI: Zondervan, 1980.

Walvoord, John F. *The Prophecy Knowledge Handbook*. Wheaton, IL: Victor Books, 1990.

Walvoord, John F. *The Thessalonian Epistles. Bible Study Commentary*. Grand Rapids, MI: Zondervan, 1991.

Walvoord, John F. *Matthew: Thy Kingdom Come*. Chicago, IL: Moody Press, 1974.

Walvoord, John F. *The Revelation of Jesus Christ. A Commentary*. Chicago, IL: Moody Press, 1989.

Warfield, Benjamin B. *Biblical Doctrines*. 1929. rpt. Edinburgh: The Banner of Truth Trust, 1988.

Weremchuk, Max S. *John Nelson Darby. A Biography*. Neptune, NJ: Loizeaux Bros., 1992.

West, G. W. [George W.]. *Daniel. The Greatly Beloved*. London: Marshall, Morgan & Scott, n.d. [c1930].

Weston, Henry G. *Matthew. The Genesis of the New Testament. Its Purpose, Character and Method*. Philadelphia, PA: American Baptist Publication Society, n.d.

White, Frank H. *The Saints' Rest and Rapture*. Chemlsford, Essex: The Sovereign Grace Advent Testimony, n.d.

Wilken, Robert L. *The Christians As the Romans Saw Them*. New Haven, CT: Yale University Press, 1984

Williams, David J. *1 and 2 Thessalonians. [New International Bible Commentary]*. Peabody, MA: Hendrickson Pub, 1992.

Witherington, Ben, III. *Paul's Narrative Thought World*. Louisville, KY: Westminster/John Knox, 1994.

Workman, Herbert B. *Persecution in the Early Church*. Cincinnati, OH: Jennings & Graham, 1906.

Wuest, Kenneth S. *Bypaths in the Greek New Testament for the English Reader*. Grand Rapids, MI: Wm. B. Eerdmans Pub. Co., 1954.

Wuest, Kenneth S. *Great Truths To Live By*. [Wuest's Word Studies]. Grand Rapids, MI: Eerdmans, 1977.

Wuest, Kenneth S. *Wuest's Word Studies from the Greek New Testament*. 4 Volumes. Grand Rapids, MI: Wm B, Eerdmans, 1966.

Yohannan, Abraham. *The Death of a Nation or The Ever Persecuted Nestorians or Assyrian Christians.* New York, NY: G. P. Putnam & Sons, 1916.

Zahn, Theodor. *Introduction to the New Testament.* 3 Volumes. 1909. rpt. Minneapolis, MN: Klock & Klock, 1977.

Zodhiates, Spiros. *Conquering the Fear of Death. An exposition of I Corinthians 15, based on the original Greek text.* Grand Rapids, MI: Wm. B. Eerdmans Pub., 1970.

Zodhiates, Spiros. *The Hebrew-Greek Key Study Bible. [NAS].* Chattanooga, TN: AMG Pub., 1994.

Printed in Great Britain
by Amazon